War, Peace and World in European History

'*War, Peace and World Orders* is very readable and consistently interesting. This fascinating volume offers a stimulating demonstration of how war has varied through the history of the West.'

Patrick Morgan, *University of California, Irvine*

'What John Keegan set out to do in "A History of Warfare" this book completes: a scintillating collection of essays on how people at various times and places went to war, why they went to war, and what they went to war for.'

Martin Van Creveld, *The Hebrew University, Jerusalem*

'A major contribution: stimulating to historians, challenging to theorists, and fascinating to all who care about the eternal issues of war and peace.'

H. W. Brands, *Distinguished Professor of History and Ralph R. Thomas 21 Professor in Liberal Arts, Texas A&M University*

This book provides an innovative new way for students of International Relations to look at war, peace and world orders throughout European history. Rather than using the conventional 'Realist' paradigm that focuses on states and their self-interest – which in fact does not apply to the largest period of European history because states did not exist, or were only in the making – this book shows that we need to look through the eyes of historical entities to see how they understood the world in which they lived.

The book consists of separate case studies and theoretical contributions which challenge the ahistorical focus of much International Relations theory. Through these case studies, the authors put ideas back centre stage in this fascinating analysis of war and peace in history. People in different periods in different parts of the globe perceived the world differently, and cannot be said to have acted according to immutable principles shared by all societies through the ages. *War, Peace and World Order in European History* shows there are no constants in International Relations when it comes to waging wars, or making peace: we have to consider each age, and each society, in its own right. It will be a valuable, original resource for students of politics and International Relations.

Anja V. Hartmann is Research Fellow at the Institute for European History, and Lecturer in Early Modern History at the Johannes Gutenberg University, both in Mainz, Germany.

Beatrice Heuser is Professor of International and Strategic Studies at the Department of War Studies, King's College London. Her many publications include *Nuclear Strategies and Forces for Europe, 1949–2000*; *Nuclear Mentalities*; *The Bomb*; and *Western Containment Policies in the Cold War*.

The New International Relations
Edited by Barry Buzan, *University of Westminster* and
Richard Little, *University of Bristol*

The field of International Relations has changed dramatically in recent years. This new series will cover the major issues that have emerged and reflect the latest academic thinking in this particular dynamic area.

International Law, Rights and Politics
Developments in Eastern Europe and the CIS
Rein Mullerson

The Logic of Internationalism
Coercion and accommodation
Kjell Goldmann

Russia and the Idea of Europe
A study in identity and International Relations
Iver B. Neumann

The Future of International Relations
Masters in the making?
Edited by Iver B. Neumann and Ole Wæver

Constructing the World Polity
Essays on international institutionalization
John Gerard Ruggie

Realism in International Relations and International Political Economy
The continuing story of a death foretold
Stefano Guzzini

International Relations, Political Theory and the Problem of Order
Beyond International Relations theory?
N. J. Rengger

War, Peace and World Orders in European History
Edited by Anja V. Hartmann and Beatrice Heuser

European Integration and National Identity
The challenge of the Nordic states
Edited by Lene Hansen and Ole Wæver

War, Peace and World Orders in European History

Edited by
Anja V. Hartmann and Beatrice Heuser

London and New York

First published 2001
by Routledge
2 Park Square, Milton Park, Abingdon, Oxon, OX14 4RN

Simultaneously published in the USA and Canada
by Routledge
711 Third Avenue, New York NY 10017

Routledge is an imprint of the Taylor & Francis Group

Transferred to Digital Printing 2005

Typeset in Baskerville by
Florence Production Ltd, Stoodleigh, Devon

British Library Cataloguing in Publication Data
A catalogue record for this book is available
from the British Library

Library of Congress Cataloging in Publication Data
War, peace, and world orders in European history /
edited by Anja V. Hartmann and Beatrice Heuser.
   p. cm. – (The new international relations)
Includes bibliographical references and index.
ISBN 0–415–24440–4 (alk. paper) – ISBN 0–415–24441–2
(pbk. : alk. paper)
1. International relations – History. 2. Europe – Intellectual
life. I. Hartmann, Anja. II. Heuser, Beatrice, 1961–III. Series.
JZ1305 .W37 2001
327.1'6'094–dc21
                                              2001019130

ISBN 0–415–24440–4 (hbk)
ISBN 0–415–24441–2 (pbk)

Contents

Notes on contributors   viii
Series editors' preface   xii
Preface   xiv
Acknowledgements   xv

1 Introduction: methodology of this project   1
BEATRICE HEUSER AND ANJA V. HARTMANN

2 History and International Relations theory   14
ANDREAS OSIANDER

Part I
War and peace in classical antiquity
Introduction   25
HANS VAN WEES AND JOHN RICH

3 War and peace in ancient Greece   33
HANS VAN WEES

4 Greeks and Persians: West against East   48
SIMON HORNBLOWER

**5 Warfare and external relations in the middle
Roman Republic**   62
JOHN RICH

**6 Roman–Carthaginian relations: from co-operation
to annihilation**   72
RUTH STEPPER

Part II

War, peace and faith in the Middle Ages

Introduction   85
JULIAN CHRYSOSTOMIDES AND BEATRICE HEUSER

7   Byzantine concepts of war and peace   91
JULIAN CHRYSOSTOMIDES

8   Collective identities, war and integration in the
Early Middle Ages   102
BERNHARD ZELLER

9   Warfare in the Middle Ages   113
JAN WILLEM HONIG

10 The crusading movement   127
JONATHAN RILEY-SMITH

11 War, peace and national identity in the
Hundred Years' War   141
ANNE CURRY

Part III

War and peace in Early Modern Europe

Introduction   155
ANJA V. HARTMANN

12 Wars of religion: the examples of France, Spain
and the Low Countries in the sixteenth century   160
ALINE GOOSENS

13 Identities and mentalities in the Thirty Years' War   174
ANJA V. HARTMANN

14 Interstate war and peace in Early Modern Europe   185
HEINZ DUCHHARDT

Part IV

The era of ideological wars

Introduction   197
BEATRICE HEUSER

15 The revolutionary period, 1789–1802 203
MARC BELISSA AND PATRICE LECLERCQ

**16 From *Volkskrieg* to *Vernichtungskrieg*: German
concepts of warfare, 1871–1935** 214
ROBERT T. FOLEY

17 Enemy image and identity in the Warsaw Pact 226
MICHAEL PLOETZ

18 Conclusions 237
BEATRICE HEUSER AND ANJA V. HARTMANN

Select bibliography 252
Index 259

Contributors

Marc Belissa is a lecturer in modern history at the University of Nantes. His area of research is the political history between the European peoples in the eighteenth century. He has published *Fraternité Universelle et Intérêt National (1713–1795). Les cosmopolitiques du droit des gens* (Paris, 1998) and he has contributed to several multi-authored volumes including *La République, l'exception française, Actes du colloque pour le bicentenaire de la République* (Paris, 1994); *Robespierre: de la Nation artésienne à la République et aux Nations* (Lille, 1994); *l'An I et l'apprentissage de la démocratie* (Paris-Saint-Denis, 1995); *Aux armes citoyens! Conscription et armée de métier des Grecs à nos jours* (Paris, 1998).

Julian Chrysostomides is Director of the Hellenic Institute of Royal Holloway College, University of London, and Emeritus Reader in Byzantine history. Among her major works is the critical edition of Emperor Manuel II Palaeologus' *Funeral Oration on his Brother Theodore, of Thessalonike* (Camberley 1985); *Monumenta Peloponnesiaca* (1995) which is considered to be the most important contribution in the last decade in the field of sources related to the history of the Peloponnese; and joint editorship of *The Letters of the Three Patriarchs to Emperor Theophilos and Related Texts* (Camberley 1997).

Anne Curry is senior lecturer in history at the University of Reading and currently Head of Department. Her principal research interest is English military organization in the first half of the fifteenth century. She has written two books, *The Hundred Years War* (1993) and *The Battle of Agincourt: Sources and Interpretations* (2000), and edited three collections of essays in the area of her research, *Arms, Armies and Fortifications in the Hundred Years War, England and Normandy in the Middle Ages*, and *Agincourt 1415*, as well as contributing to several works in England and France.

Heinz Duchhardt studied at the universities of Mainz, Bonn and Vienna. He received his doctorate and his *Habilitation* from Mainz in 1968 and 1974 respectively, was full professor at the universities of Bayreuth (1984–88) and Münster (1988–95) before becoming Director of the

Institute of European History in 1994. His main fields of research are International Relations in pre-modern times and constitutional and social history of the German *ancien régime*. His main publications are *Balance of Power und Pentarchie. Internationale Beziehungen 1700–1785* (1997); *Deutsche Verfassungsgeschichte 1495–1806* (1991); *Das Zeitalter des Absolutismus* (3rd edn, 1998).

Robert T. Foley is a lecturer in the Department of Defence Studies, King's College London, from where he holds his doctorate, but is assigned to the Joint Services Command and Staff College. He has recently completed his Ph.D. on German strategic thought before and during the First World War and is editor and translator of *Schlieffen's Military Writings* (London, 2001).

Aline Goosens holds a doctorate in Modern History from the Free University of Brussels, where she has worked as assistant lecturer since 1991. She is Intelligence and Research Assistant to the Belgian Parliamentary Committee. Her publications include *Les Inquisitions modernes dans les anciens Pays-Bas méridionaux à la Renaissance, 1520–1633. Première partie, la législation. Deuxième partie, les victimes* (Brussels, 1997–98). Her research also focuses on the Revolt in the Netherlands, the symbolism of power, royal propaganda, the construction of the Modern State, cultural mentalities and habits in the old Netherlands and in Spain. She is currently completing a biography on Count Lamoral d'Egmont.

Anja V. Hartmann is postdoctoral Research Fellow at the Institute of European History in Mainz (Germany) and lecturer in Early Modern history at the Johannes Gutenberg University in Mainz. She is a specialist on International Relations in Early Modern Europe and has published two volumes of Richelieu's political correspondence (*Les Papiers de Richelieu*, Paris, 1997/2000) as well as a study on diplomatic relations in the Thirty Years' War (*Von Regensburg nach Hamburg*, Münster, 1998).

Beatrice Heuser is Professor of International and Strategic Studies at the Department of War Studies, King's College London. She has taught briefly at the University of Reims and has been a consultant/intern at NATO. Her publications include *NATO, Britain, France and the FRG: Nuclear Strategies and Forces in Europe, 1949–2000* (London, 1997 and pbk 1999); *Nuclear Mentalities?* (London, 1998); *Western 'Containment' Policies in the Cold War* (London, 1989); *The Bomb* (London, 1999). Her most recent work is on Clausewitz.

Jan Willem Honig is senior lecturer in war studies, King's College London. He holds degrees in medieval history from the University of Amsterdam and in war studies from the University of London. His most recent book was *Srebrenica: Record of a War Crime* (with Norbert Both).

The contribution to this volume was completed when he was a Visiting Fellow at the Remarque Institute at New York University.

Simon Hornblower is Professor of Classics and Ancient History at University College London. He was co-editor of the third edition of the *Oxford Classical Dictionary* (1996) and of the fourth-century BC volume (vol. 6) of the new *Cambridge Ancient History*. He has published two volumes (1991, 1996) of a large-scale commentary on Thucydides, also for Oxford University Press, and is now working on the third and final volume. His most recent book is *Greek Personal Names; their Value as Evidence* (2000, co-edited with Elaine Matthews and published by OUP for the British Academy). He is now writing a book for OUP on Thucydides and Pindar.

Patrice Leclercq has done his doctorate on the levée en masse of 1793 during the French Revolution at the University of Paris I (Sorbonne). He teaches at the Military School at St Cyr, and has published several articles in periodicals such as *Hypothèse*, *Revue d'Histoire* and in the Proceedings of the Conference of Cholet (1993).

Andreas Osiander studied political science, history and economics at Tübingen University and the Institut d'Etudes Politiques de Paris before going on to do a doctorate in International Relations at the University of Oxford. He has held a junior research fellowship at Balliol College Oxford and a similar position at Humboldt University Berlin. Still attached to that university, he is currently working on a research project on the relationship between social structures, political thought and systemic change in the evolution of western civilization. He is author of *The States System of Europe 1640–1990: Peacemaking and the Conditions of International Stability* (Oxford, 1994).

Michael Ploetz studied English literature at the University of Tübingen from 1989 to 1993. He received an MA in war studies from King's College London in 1995, where he also received his doctorate in 1998. Since 1999, he has been working for the Research Federation on the SED State at the Free University of Berlin. He has published *Wie die Sowjetunion den Kalten Krieg verlor: von der Nachrüstung zum Mauerfall* (Berlin, 2000).

John Rich is Reader in Roman History, University of Nottingham. His publications include *Declaring War in the Roman Republic in the Period of Transmarine Expansion* (1976); *Cassius Dio: The Augustan Settlement* (1991) and numerous articles. He has also edited four volumes in the Routledge series *Leicester-Nottingham Studies in Ancient Society*, including *War and Society in the Greek World* and *War and Society in the Roman World* (both with G. Shipley, 1993). His current projects include a study of war, expansion and society in early Rome.

Jonathan Riley-Smith is Dixie Professor of ecclesiastical history at the University of Cambridge, and a Fellow of Emmanuel College. He has previously held a Chair of history at Royal Holloway and Bedford College. His major publications include *The Knights of St John in Jerusalem and Cyprus* (London, 1967); *The Feudal Nobility and the Kingdom of Jerusalem* (London, 1973); *The First Crusade and the Idea of Crusading* (London, 1986); *The First Crusaders* (Cambridge, 1997).

Ruth Stepper is lecturer in ancient history at the Universitaet Potsdam/Germany. In her study *Leiden an der Geschichte* (1997) she has discussed the perception of Ancient Greek history and the well-known Swiss historian Jacob Burckhardt. Her current main research interest is in religion of imperial Rome, especially the priestly functions of the Roman emperors.

Hans van Wees is Reader in ancient history at University College London. His first degree (Drs/Doctorandus) was in History, from the University of Amsterdam; his Ph.D. from the University of Leiden. He is the author of *Status Warriors: War, Violence and Society in Homer and History* (1992) and *Greek Warfare: Myths and Realities* (2001), and editor of *Archaic Greece: New Approaches and New Evidence* (with Nick Fisher, 1998) and *War and Violence in Ancient Greece* (2000).

Bernhard Zeller has been studying history and German at the University of Vienna since 1995 and in 1999 to 2001 attended a postgraduate course at the Institute for Austrian Historical Research in Vienna. After its completion, he began work on his dissertation.

Series editors' preface

Throughout the twentieth century, the study of war and peace constituted the central core of the evolving field of international relations (IR). Although there were other dimensions to this field, none seemed as important as understanding why war has proved to be such a pervasive feature of human activity and why peace has always proved to be so impermanent. As we moved into the nuclear era, and the possibility of war precipitating human extinction became more than just theoretical, these issues acquired an added urgency. In his classic survey, *Man, the State and War*, Kenneth Waltz argues that three competing explanations of war have been identified by those who have given this matter their serious attention. Some thinkers have attributed war to human aggression, while others have argued that only certain types of state are prone to war. But Waltz argues that it is the anarchic structure of the international system that provides the most convincing explanation for why war has proved to be such a ubiquitous and perennial scourge. During the Cold War, a huge volume of research examined the features of the anarchic international system that purportedly promote or inhibit war. In the aftermath of the Cold War, however, the significance of the anarchic system has been downgraded and increasing attention has been paid to the political units that make up the system. Picking up on Kantian ideas, growing credence is now being given to the democratic peace theory that explains why a world of liberal democracies can expect to live together in peace and harmony.

The study of IR, however, has certainly not had a monopoly on the analysis of war and peace. Contemporary disciplines as diverse as anthropology and psychology have also periodically registered an interest in this area, but the most significant competitors to IR specialists in this field are diplomatic and military historians whose work centres on the study of war and peace. Although specialists in IR regularly use the work of these historians as a storehouse of information, all too often, an undesirable and unhelpful tension has formed between these two groups of scholars. From the perspective of IR, historians tend to be so bogged down in detail that they are unable to say anything of general interest about the phenomena of war and peace. On the other side of the coin, however, when historians appraise the work of IR specialists, they observe dubious generalizations that very frequently rest on highly distorted assessments of the past.

One aim of this ambitious book is to help bridge the gap that exists between historians and IR specialists. It draws together a group of distinguished historians who present the latest findings on how the nature of war and peace can be characterized over a period of more than two millennia. Historians are regularly required to reassess their frames of reference as new evidence and fresh insights become available. The image of the Roman Empire coming under endless attack from the barbarian hordes, for example, is shown here to misrepresent what actually happened during this period. Instead, the encounter requires us to identify a complex process which transformed the identities both of the invading tribes and the Roman Empire. By the same token, to understand the Crusades, we need to move away from the image of medieval European knights fighting the Saracen infidels, and think instead of a conflict taking place all round the periphery of Europe for an era that lasted seven centuries.

Ideas of this kind are almost impossible to fit into conventional models of the international system. Moreover, contrary to the preconceptions of many IR scholars, the historians in this book demonstrate, unequivocally, that war simply cannot be depicted as an unchanging feature of the international system. As a consequence, they seriously undermine the essentially ahistorical view of war and peace that dominates most IR theory. Here, war and peace are revealed to be essentially cultural phenomena that take radically different forms in different periods and in different world orders. Of course, it is not at all easy for IR scholars, locked into a Westphalian view of the international system, to take this approach on board. But what is exciting about this book is not just that it challenges conventional IR thinking about war and peace, but, implicitly, it invites specialists in IR to rethink what is meant by war and peace and to reassess how these phenomena can be embraced by the study of IR. Failure to accept this challenge to adopt a more historically sensitive approach threatens to push the contemporary study of IR along an arid and unproductive theoretical cul-de-sac. By contrast, accepting the challenge could open up a fruitful new route to theorizing about international relations.

Preface

The project, whose outlines Beatrice Heuser revealed to me in the autumn of 1997, was an exciting one and appeared to me from the very beginning as an extraordinarily stimulating venture. Therefore I did not hesitate to join in its organization together with her and Anja V. Hartmann and help with the securing of funds. I was pleased to receive a favourable response from the Volkswagen Foundation and the head of its programme 'Global structures and their management'. It was a wonderful experience to initiate a very international and very interdisciplinary dialogue, which moved at a high intellectual level and became a real challenge to all participants. As the person responsible for the project I can only join the editors and the authors of this volume in the expectation that the fruit of our efforts will find an interested public. Let yourself be taken for a walk through centuries of war and peace and the shaping of world orders.

Heinz Duchhardt

Acknowledgements

This book contains the results of a research project organized by the editors in collaboration with the Institute of European History in Mainz (Germany) and the Department of War Studies at King's College London. The project was financed by the Volkswagen Foundation in Hanover (Germany) whose representative, Dr Alfred Schmidt, not only helped us through many intricate administrative issues but also joined the second of our two successive workshops and took a vivid interest in the project's evolution. It would have been impossible to realize the project without the valuable support from the Institute of European History and its director, Professor Heinz Duchhardt, who has always been a generous patron and a critical adviser. All financial matters were competently dealt with by the Institute's bursar, Edith Kreis. The first workshop took place in Rothenburg ob der Tauber (Germany) in December 1998. Our assistants Anja Friedl, MA and Dr Natalie Klein managed all practical problems so as to give our participants the utmost liberty for inspiring discussions. At the second workshop in Mainz in September 1999, the Institute's secretaries Elisabeth Kuß and Gisela Schmitt as well as our assistant Stephan Schüller did equally well in supporting all participants and thus helped to promote the project's success. Our profound gratitude also goes to the editors of the series, Richard Little and Barry Buzan, who agreed to publish the book. In preparing the manuscripts for publication, we owe a great debt of gratitude to the accurate and exhaustive detailed work, including the translations from French, of our assistant Maria Vlahou in London. The bibliography was compiled by our assistant Christoph Krauß in Mainz. Finally, we would like to thank our families and friends who had to endure our crises, our involvement and our enthusiasm.

1 Introduction

Methodology of this project

Beatrice Heuser and Anja V. Hartmann

Specialists from a multitude of disciplines over the past two and a half centuries have shown interest in the causes of war, and in the question as to whether war is inevitably part of the human condition. From Kant's political philosophy and Freud's psychological insights to the studies of zoologists like Darwin and anthropologists like Dawkins, we have a wide variety of angles from which to approach the question of war. These specialists, however, have reached very different conclusions, from the highly pessimistic one that humans are inherently aggressive and that there is no way that organized aggression – war – can be contained or prevented, to the much more optimistic one that aggressive behaviour is learned, and that there are means of preventing both individual aggression and war.

The disciplines traditionally devoted to the study of war and peace – namely international relations (IR) and history, both military and diplomatic – have been constantly challenged by results presented in other fields of research. Yet they have paid surprisingly little attention to such research, in part, because of an almost exclusive focus on the behaviour of states. This long-standing state-centric bias in IR (as well as military and diplomatic history) has, if anything, been reinforced since the end of the Cold War when, initially, it was assumed that liberal democracy, encapsulated in the post-modern democratic state, had finally triumphed and that, in the future, we could expect general peace to prevail.[1] Almost immediately, however, with the outbreak of ethnic civil wars in places like the former Yugoslavia and the former USSR, the legitimacy of the sovereign state was challenged from within many established states. At the same time, the struggle to strengthen international organizations, like the United Nations, and entities with a potential for supra-state development, such as the European Union, also raised fundamental questions about both the legitimacy and the autonomy of the state. These conflicting developments encouraged the German foreign minister, Joschka Fischer, to identify a metamorphosis of the contemporary nation-state into a 'post-national nation-state'.[2] This paradoxical denomination reflects the uncertainty of politicians and theorists alike as to the future role of the state.

To conceptualize a world order that transcends the sovereign state, it is essential to move beyond the prevailing emphasis on the contemporary state. Such a move has important implications for the study of international relations, but it also affects the orientation of historical research on war and peace. The research orientation of historians, however, has not just been affected by the escalation of non-state violence. In recent decades, new research questions that originated from the study of violence and aggression in the social and biological sciences have been successfully imported into various branches of history, such as cultural history and historical anthropology. Although military and diplomatic history at first proved resistant to this development, they are also beginning to absorb these influences and are undergoing a profound change as a consequence. It is now widely acknowledged that in both war and peace individuals and groups act according to principles alien or even contrary to the demands of 'national interest' and 'reason of state'. By circumventing the traditional state-centric bias, through an accommodation of individual, group and supra-state levels of analysis, in conjunction with more traditional analyses of the state, a completely new research agenda has opened up for military and diplomatic historians. The main aim of this book is to explore this extended research agenda which we think has important consequences for the study of international relations, in general, and the study of international relations theory, in particular.

International Relations (IR) theory

International Relations is very much a hybrid discipline, containing a variety of theoretical schools that have little in common with each other. This fragmentation is encouraged by the tendency of IR theorists to explain international relations monocausally, or to work on a single level of analysis. To bolster their theoretical position, these theorists frequently quarry history for examples to illustrate their position. In doing so, however, they often fail to observe that the historical settings from which the examples are drawn can be radically different, rendering them inappropriate for the theory under investigation. A central objective of this book is to reveal the importance of historicizing the study of war and peace and to reveal the very different nature of these phenomena as the researcher moves from one historical era to another.

The dominance of what is sometimes called a 'system level' of analysis in IR has played a major role in the failure to adopt a more historically sensitive approach to the study of international relations. The systems level approach usually focuses on the structures, and rules (codified or unspoken) governing the behaviour between states and it occupies the centre of much IR analysis. Many theorists, writing in the Cold War, for example, devoted much of their energy to examining how the supposed 'bipolarity' between the USA and the USSR influenced international relations and what the effects of 'multipolarity' were during the nineteenth and early twentieth centuries. In developing a theory of bipolarity in the nuclear era, IR theorists repeatedly established inappropriate historical analogies with the Peloponnesian War and the long-standing hostilities between Hellenes and Persians. One aim of this book is to reveal the difficulties of making analogies of this kind.

Our first move is to replace a state-based level of analysis with a multi-level approach that draws on the idea of 'world order', but our use of this term needs to be distinguished from contemporary usage that equates world order with global order. By contrast, we draw on a much more geographically limited conception of world order. Our terminology is much closer to the Greek *kosmos* and the Latin *mundus*, concepts that mean both world and order, but which only extended to the geographical area that was familiar to the Greeks and the Romans. Drawing on the idea of world order (discussed in more detail below) helps us to escape from state-centrism and also to develop a much more historically sensitive approach to the study of war and peace.

However, not all system analysts have been constrained by state-centrism. Two other schools have emerged that, like ourselves, have aimed to break out from the confines of the state. On the one hand, there is a global interdependence school. This focuses on interstate economic links, but it also embraces important non-state actors from international organizations (such as the UN and NATO) to non-governmental organizations (from the Red Cross to Oxfam) and multinational corporations (from Shell to Cathay Pacific Airlines). On the other hand, there is a world systems school that posits a capitalist system, with lines of conflict that are defined along class as well as state boundaries. Although we share the desire of these two schools to escape state-centrism, our approach is very different, and endeavours, among other things, to take advantage of some of the features found in other schools of theory that can be found in IR.

These other schools of thought have all focused on the state level of policy-making. Ole Holsti distinguishes between schools that have conducted research on bureaucratic politics, on group dynamics, and on the decision-making of individual leaders.[3] The oldest school, following directly in the steps of classic diplomatic history, concentrates on the key decision-makers, the Napoleons and Hitlers, as well as the Wilsons and Kennedys of this world. It focuses on the policy options open to them, and their reasons as individuals to opt for one path rather than another. In the second half of the twentieth century, scholars with an interest in such individuals have often tried to draw on psychology to explain their decisions,[4] or to look at the perceptions and misperceptions of individual decision-makers.[5] This approach is more difficult for large groups, but there, the notion of 'generations' of decision-makers, influenced by common experiences such as wars, economic crises and large-scale unemployment, social unrest or even common schooling, has been introduced.[6]

The second of these schools, the bureaucratic politics school, has shown that, particularly within governments and among governments, 'decision making is . . . dominated by bargaining for resources, roles and missions, and by compromise rather than analysis'.[7] With some adaptation, this model could be applied throughout European history, except that, for many periods, there simply is not the source evidence that would allow a detailed study of decision-making processes, and in some periods it was unequivocally the monarch's privilege to form foreign policy. Most actual research done by members of this school consequently focuses on the twentieth century.

The third school analyses the dynamics within decision-making groups, showing how we reach different decisions when operating collectively as opposed to individually so that group decision-making is seen to be radically different from individual decision-making. The social psychologist Irving L. Janis has identified a phenomenon which he calls 'group think', meaning that the dynamics within a group can engender collective views, decisions and policies, persuading individuals to back these, even if these same individuals, in other differently composed groups, would have backed different decisions and policies.[8]

While the schools based on a system-level approach focus on states and inter- or supra-state entities as actors in the inter-'national' system and thus discard the individual completely from their analysis, the schools using a state level approach include the individual only as a member of governing institutions or as a statesman. We wish to accommodate aspects of both these levels, but, in addition, we want to take account of individuals and communities that operate on a level below or within the state and to explore the interaction between states and sub-state actors in the international arena. Our concept of world order is designed to capture these multiple and interconnected levels that tend to be bypassed in conventional IR theories. Before exploring our approach in more detail, however, we need some further reflection on the conventional approach to war and peace in IR.

'Realist' theory and its shortcomings

The dominant current in IR theory (espoused not only by many academics but also by many government officials) is identified as 'Realist', implying that it (alone) corresponds to reality. Realism is based on a very particular set of answers to questions about the causes of war. The fathers of this school were deeply influenced by the experience of the particularly belligerent period of Central European history, from the 1860s until the Second World War. They thought in terms of social Darwinism and fierce competition between states and indeed nations both in economics and wars.[9] 'Realists' posit the universality of states and identify persistent and repeated patterns of conflict in international history. Both men and states are seen to be narrowly selfish, acting according to a 'beggar thy neighbour' approach. 'Realists' assume, therefore, that states will do anything to increase their own power, wealth, influence and possessions; only weakness or fear will stop them. The currency is power, and the interstate order is stable only if there is a 'balance of power' between states. Without a balance of power a violent Hobbesian anarchy will prevail. The vocabulary of 'realism' is thus power, national (meaning state) interest, and national (meaning state) security.

'Realists' working in the tradition of Hedley Bull assume, however, that unlimited expansion can often only be achieved at a cost that can outweigh any potential gain, especially in the nuclear age. Bull therefore identified self-regulating mechanisms within any interstate anarchy, promoting peaceful co-existence rather than war, even in the absence of a world organization or central authority to impose order.[10] But states are still considered to be fundamentally self-interested. It is assumed that a state will only promote the well-being of others if a failure to assist would ultimately undermine its own security.

Unrealistically, Realists also assume that the world is (and always has been) neatly divided into geographical sectors identified as states, each with a government and a body of citizens (a nation in the political sense defined by the French Revolution). These citizens are seen to identify unequivocally with the fate of the state. No account is taken of the way that a state can itself be significantly divided by religion, language, class or ideology (thereby creating primary allegiance to entities beyond or below the state). It is important, therefore, to explain what Realists mean by 'nation', in contrast to the other confusingly large number of meanings attached to the term. In principle, Realists agree with the first definition, taken from the *Oxford English Dictionary*: a nation is 'an extensive aggregate of persons, so closely associated with each other by common descent, language, or history, as to form a distinct race or people, *usually organized as a separate political state and occupying a definite territory*'. However, the dictionary goes on to give fifteen other – mainly historical – definitions based on usage of the word in English since the fourteenth century. These include 'man's nation', meaning humankind, or 'the peoples of the earth'; 'a family, kindred'; 'the native population of a town or city'; and 'a particular class, kind, or race of persons'! These older usages specifically do not relate nation to state;[11] a correlation which was first made hard and fast with the French Revolution. The general correlation between nation, state and sovereignty is crucial to Realist IR theories, which, even at the more moderate end of the spectrum, tend to use 'nation' and 'state' as synonyms. This usage is inapplicable to earlier periods of European history. Realist theorists not only assume that every state is sovereign, but also that it has a politically defined nation living within its territorial borders.[12] Thus they ignore the great bulk of research into nationalism, which has shown that 'nations' are artificial constructs, and that most have come into existence within only the past 200 years. Moreover, even today, nations are more frequently defined in ethnic terms (particularly in the German and Russian traditions that influenced Central and Eastern Europe, and, beyond that, many other parts of the world), rather than in political terms.[13] Because of the extensive influence of Realists, however, the term 'nation-state' is widely used as a synonym for 'state', whether attention is being drawn to a monarchy, a multi-ethnic state or, indeed, any other kind of state. The Realists uncritically project an image of the world composed of homogeneous nation-states.

Crucial consequences flow from this assumption about the perfect correlation between nation and state. One is that 'nation-states' (applying the political, not the ethnic definition of 'nation') are viewed as the most highly developed form of political structure. Supra-state structures are not considered viable. Thus, decision-making in international organizations such as the United Nations, NATO, the Organization of Petrol-Exporting Countries, and even the European Union (EU) can ultimately be traced back to the state. Realist theory presupposes that no sovereign state would ever voluntarily relinquish its sovereign decision-making powers. From this perspective, majority decision-making in the EU represents an aberration, and the Realist perspective simply cannot accommodate the possibility of the EU or NATO or the Western European Union or the UN arriving at decisions through majority voting in the areas of war and peace (or indeed on a host of other matters of 'national interest'). War and peace are assumed to be indisputable matters of narrow state interest, to be decided at 'nation-state' level and nowhere else. Andreas Osiander's contribution to this book spells out this nexus.

In this book, we wish to escape from the Realist strait-jacket and reintroduce the individual and sub-state groups into the history of inter-'national' relations. The unchanging nature of states and thus of the inter-'national' system – understood as an interstate system – that is so central to Realist theory is fundamentally challenged. In preference to the systemic approach implied by the concept of an inter-'national' system, we prefer the notion of 'world order', conceived, on the one hand, as a structure of relations between communities and, on the other, as a construct of mental images supplied by the actors of those communities regarding themselves and others. We use 'world order' not in the nineteenth, twentieth or twenty-first centuries sense of 'global order', but in the sense of *kosmos*, the ordered world as it was known to Ancient Greeks, Romans, medieval men, etc. – an order that was originally largely confined to modern Europe and its adjacent areas. While ours is now an obsolescent use of the term, it fits earlier concepts which we are trying to grapple with in this book. For this reason we beg the indulgence of those who may have been misled by the title of this book. We are not equating world order with global order; our focus is essentially on Europe, although we acknowledge that other civilizations such as the Chinese have also adhered to an evolving conception of world order.

Beliefs and cultural peculiarities

Our research approach differs crucially from the principles of most schools of IR theory, and above all from Realist interpretations of international relations. We put the individual and the group back into the picture. Instead of treating the state as a reified abstraction that can act in the international system, we focus on individuals (as well as other groupings and entities many of which pre-date the modern state). Following Ranke, the nineteenth-century German historian, we emphasize the distinctness of different historical eras and cultures.[14] We show how far the collective identities, collective beliefs, collective memories and collective mythologies of different cultures and eras can diverge. Again we have to introduce definitions here for the sake of clarity, as, in particular, the term 'culture' has been used in almost as many different senses as 'nation'. For the historian Akira Iriye, 'Culture in international relations' is 'the sharing and transmitting of consciousness within and across national boundaries, and the cultural approach is a perspective that pays particular attention to this phenomenon'. For Iriye, culture is thus distinct from but complementary to power and economy. He defines culture as 'the creation and communication of memory, ideology, emotions, life styles, scholarly and artistic works, and other symbols'.[15] Etymologically, the word 'culture' refers to the raising of crops or animals, but also to a religious cult ('worship, referential homage' – *Oxford English Dictionary*). Today, the word is used generally more in the sense it has acquired in German, namely the collective spiritual and artistic output of a community or a people, its social order, its ideals and values.[16]

In current usage, the terms 'culture' and 'civilization'[17] are often incorrectly used as synonyms. In the following, we shall use culture to refer to the traditions, ideals, values, norms, patterns of behaviour, frameworks for discourse, myths,[18] beliefs[19] and aspirations, that are shared by a particular group, whether that be a tribe, a clan, a people, the citizens of a particular *polis*, *civitas*, *imperium* or state. We will thus distinguish between peoples by grouping them according to cultures they share, aware that the lines of division between such peoples are vague, and that any culture comprises subcultures, and that Europe as a whole forms a macro-culture with its common heritage of Judaism, ancient Greece, Rome, Christianity, and French and British state philosophy (our key reason for being so Euro-centric and for not bringing in the very different traditions of Asia and Africa). Using these definitions, the chapters in the book home in on how war and peace is conceived and practised within a particular culture and they highlight the nature of the 'world order' associated with this culture.

While 'culture' concerns a group, 'beliefs' and 'identity' are basically features of the individual. Of course, 'collective memories' (Maurice Halbwachs[20]), 'collective beliefs' or 'collective identities' can be constructed or deconstructed,[21] but generally speaking, 'mentality' and 'identity' are the results of reflection and appropriation of different aspects of culture in one individual. Speaking in Pierre Bourdieu's terms, 'culture' constitutes the habitude (*habitus*) of a given community, and 'mentality' and 'identity' form the life-style (*style de vie*) of the single individual as a part of the community.[22] The analysis of 'culture' as well as of 'mentality' and 'identity' thus cuts two ways in considering the dispositions both of a community and the individual. On the basis of these definitions broadly discussed in the first of our two successive workshops, we have tried to steer clear of terminology that in present circumstances has a very specific politically loaded meaning, using contemporary terms where at all possible.

Our study is limited to European history, because the evolution of states is a specifically European phenomenon: Europe, as Wolfgang Reinhard recently put it, invented the state.[23] This invention had serious consequences for the history of practice and theory of interstate relations. In political practice, the concept of state sovereignty and its intrinsic connection with the monopoly of the use of force (internally and externally), spreading from early modern France to the rest of the world, is fundamental to the world order spanning the entire globe as we enter the twenty-first century. The French Revolution's definition of the sovereign nation, linked with the sovereign state, underpins most of the states existing today,[24] albeit often in an ethnically perverted form. The idea of a national war, mobilizing the entire population, was born from it, engendering in turn the conscious aim of the total mobilization of society, economy and state in 'national', not to mention 'total', war.[25] In political theory, the succession of European cultures produced a chain of concepts, each period enjoying a growing heirloom of ideas conceived in previous periods of European history. Thucydides influenced many subsequent generations and indeed cultures, and is extensively quoted even now by international relations theorists, not always with great understanding, as three of our contributions show. Homer's heroes inspired Alexander the Great, Hannibal, medieval and Renaissance princes, many of whom in turn inspired future generations. The Christian concern about the need to limit the harm created by war, leading to restrictions both on the right to declare war and the way to conduct it – *ius ad bellum* and *ius in bello* – continue to leave their imprint on European attitudes to war and peace, generating a contemporary dynamic dialectic with the increased lethality of weapons. Thus, although we are examining a range of different periods and cultures, we find that they are often intrinsically related to each other. As a consequence, we can observe the evolution of a common set of ideas, concepts and practices, albeit with regional variations. Differences in the nature of war and peace that emerge are thus more obviously the result of a change in beliefs than would be the case if we compared divergent conceptions of war and peace in societies of Amazon Indians, Australian aborigines and China during the Ming dynasty. In Europe, certain points of reference about war and peace have endured across both time and space, so that where we can identify changes in different cultures and historical eras, we can look for the explanation in the evolving European mindset on war and peace.

One methodological problem of our project is the great diversity of the documentation for the different periods we are seeking to compare. For Greek antiquity we have to rely on the writings of two or three exceptional intellectuals and a handful of inscriptions, whereas for the East European worldviews of the Cold War period we find a surfeit of source material. The former leaves us to speculate extensively about how representative such individual historiographers were of their society. The difficult relations between 'culture', 'identity' and 'belief' are particularly obvious in this case, as the generalizations necessarily involved will inevitably create vulnerability to criticism that the key decision-makers may not have shared this or that aspect of a general set of beliefs. Nor can it ever be said that all individuals living in an area dominated by a particular culture and its concomitant beliefs necessarily share all those crucial transcendental tenets which urge upon them some action for this world justified by ideas of another world. As Simon Hornblower and Hans van Wees show in their chapters, Thucydides and Polybius were particularly sceptical of many beliefs (or 'superstitions', in the language of eighteenth- to twentieth-century historians) held by their contemporaries, or of miracles and popular credulity. But how can we extrapolate from this to demonstrate that key decision-makers such as Pericles shared their scepticism, or were entirely uninfluenced by religious considerations?

The surfeit of source material, as we approach our own age, presents us with the difficulty of selecting representative documents from the overwhelming mass of evidence. Yet even in twentieth-century historiography, most of the existing documentation leaves us with the question of whether views expressed here are élite views or represent the views of the proverbial man in the street. Usually, only opinion polls can aspire to do the latter, but experts have amply demonstrated the pitfalls of the wording of questions, the dangers of extrapolating from changes over time in answers, when the wording has been modified or the sample group has changed. Cynics argue, moreover, that there are issues – particularly complex political issues – on which the 'man on the Clapham omnibus' simply does not have an informed opinion, but at best a gut reaction.[26] Being fully conscious of these difficulties, we have attempted throughout to address three sets of questions.

The first set of questions is concerned with the main actors in Inter-'national' Relations. For these actors, we have adopted the term 'community' in order to avoid the dangers of any concept that is too closely related to any school of IR theory. In introducing the main actors/communities examined in each contribution, we try to establish the images they had of themselves and of each other, as reflected in mutual naming, nicknaming or 'bad-mouthing'. In addition, the inner structure of the communities, especially the means and effectiveness of communication between the leaders and their followers, is an important indicator for the diffusion and persuasiveness of the leaders' culture in relation to war and peace. Were the leaders able to transmit their views to their followers and thereby frame collective identities that in turn could be activated in wartime (or in peace)? And if communication failed, how did leaders manage to mobilize or prevent the collective actions of their followers? Was there, in short, a prevailing collective belief system pervading the whole population, or did beliefs differ or change, and if so, according to which principles? The analysis of the ideas, ideologies, attitudes and perceptions circulating within the communities can give us clues about a community's proclivity towards war or peace. Each contribution thus examines the interdependence between the contemporaries' schemes of justification or even glorification of war (or peace) invoking concepts like honour, glory, prestige, religion or justice, and the communities' friendly or hostile dispositions towards other communities.

The second set of questions focuses more closely on the conditions of war and peace in different eras. We try to determine the frequency and duration of wars in the respective periods, as well as the extent to which killing occurred in the wars. We rely primarily on qualitative data because quantitative figures are unreliable or difficult to identify for pre-modern history. So we look, for example, at who was killed – only combatants, or were those non-combatants not taken into slavery also killed? By this means we can distinguish different types of war. In 'limited' wars, destruction was confined to the battlefield, resulting at most in the depletion of the prince's purse and taxation, with the population by and large being left unscathed. Further along the scale are wars seeking the destruction of the entire enemy army – what Clausewitz referred to as an annihilation battle; such wars provided the model for his concept of absolute war. Finally, the war could – and did in the twentieth century – affect the entire population, resulting perhaps in the deliberate slaughter or enslavement of non-combatants – what Ludendorff would have called 'total war'.[27] A distinction can also be made between 'high' and 'low' intensity conflicts. In the former case there were proper 'battles', encounters between professional armed forces, large numbers of casualties on the battlefield but not among civilians. In the latter case, we find only a trickle of casualties, perhaps guerrilla, 'irregular' forms of fighting, perhaps with targeting of civilian populations, etc. Finally, the technical means available to those waging war have to be taken into account, as they could equally influence war and possibly the conclusion of peace. As to peace settlements, each contribution examines their duration, their effectiveness, and the possible correlations between the length and intensity of the preceding war and their seriousness or longevity.

The third set of questions investigates the relations between cultures and collective beliefs, war and peace, and world order. The analysis of contacts between different communities prior to and after the war raises the question of whether wars or peace settlements were seen as intercultural or intracultural (i.e. within one culture and interrelated state system or macrostructure, for instance, between different Greek cities, whose inhabitants thought of themselves and their adversaries collectively as Hellenes). Did the mental images that the respective actors or communities had of a wider order or macrostructure influence not only the way in which they conducted war but also their observations of norms and their forms of behaviour? The occurrence of formal declarations of war or peace, the acceptance of previously agreed limitations, and other codes of conduct in war and peace thus imply certain conclusions about the similarities and differences of the cultures, collective beliefs and world orders constructed in and between the respective communities.

When addressing these questions, we have sought to be critical at all times of our own angle of analysis, by bearing in mind the relative importance of factors other than culture and beliefs. In a short overview, our contributions assess what research on each period holds to be the relative importance of different factors and different levels of analysis, such as economic, geostrategic or demographic, and their influence on structures, norms and conventions of inter-entity relations, and finally, ideas. We thus depart from the practice of most theorists of international relations who focus excessively on one type of interpretation – economic, system-related, power-related, and so forth – and we try to take proper account of factors other than culture and beliefs when seeking an explanation for war and peace in any given era or among any particular cultures. Above all, we have sought to bring people with their specific mindsets and beliefs, with their different worldviews and self-perceptions, back into the analysis.

Notes

1 Francis Fukuyama, *The End of History and the Last Man*, New York, Avon, 1992. Boutros Boutros-Ghali, *An Agenda for Peace*, 1991.
2 Gunter Hofmann, 'Das Neue kommt. Vorhang auf!', in *Die Zeit* No. 24 (8 June 2000).
3 For a useful overview, see Ole R. Holsti, 'International Relations Models', in Michael J. Hogan and Thomas G. Paterson (eds), *Explaining the History of American Foreign Relations*, Cambridge, Cambridge University Press, 1991, pp. 57–88.
4 Examples include: Bruce Maylish, *In Search of Nixon: A Psychohistorical Inquiry*, New York, Basic Books, 1972; Ian Kershaw, *Hitler*, 2 vols, London, Allen Lane, 1998.
5 For example, Robert Jervis, *Perception and Misperception in International Politics*, Princeton, NJ, Princeton University Press, 1976.
6 For example, Donald Cameron Watt, *Personalities and Policies: Studies in the Formulation of British Foreign Policy in the 20th Century*, London, Longmans, 1965.
7 Holsti, 'International Relations Models', p. 75; see also Graham T. Allison, *Essence of Decision: Explaining the Cuban Missile Crisis*, Boston, MA, Little, Brown, 1971; Graham Allison and Morton Halperin, 'Bureaucratic Politics: A Paradigm and some Policy Implications', *World Politics* vol. 24 (Supplement of 1972), pp. 40–79; Morton Halperin, *Bureaucratic Politics and Foreign Policy*, Washington, DC, Brookings Institution, 1974.

8 Irving L. Janis, *Victims of Groupthink: A Psychological Study of Foreign Policy Decisions and Fiascos*, Boston, MA, Houghton, 1972; a new edition published as *Groupthink: Psychological Studies of Policy Decisions and Fiascos*, Boston, MA, Houghton Mifflin, 1982.

9 See esp. Hans J. Morgenthau, *Politics Among Nations: The Struggle for Power and Peace*, New York, Knopf, 1953; Norman A. Graebner, *Foundations of American Foreign Policy: A Realist Appraisal from Franklin to McKinley*, Wilmington, DE, Scholarly Resources, 1985, and *America as a World Power: A Realist Appraisal from Wilson to Reagan*, Wilmington, DE, Scholarly Resources, 1984; for the intellectual genesis of this school, see Jan Willem Honig, 'Totalitarianism and Realism: Hans Morgenthau's German Years', Security Studies Vol. 5, No. 2 (Winter 1995), pp. 283–313.

10 Hedley Bull, *The Anarchical Society: A Study of Order in World Politics*, London, Macmillan, 1977.

11 Which is why historians and nationalism specialists who project the existence of nationalism into the pre-eighteenth-century past merely because the term 'nation' existed, and at times, in some cultures, had connotations of group pride, are barking up the wrong tree.

12 See e.g. the 'nation-state'-centric interpretations of international history in the great classics by Raymond Aron, *Peace and War: A Theory of International Relations*, London, Weidenfeld & Nicolson, 1966; Henry Kissinger, *Diplomacy*, New York, Simon & Schuster, 1994, and Martin Wight, *Systems of State*, ed. Hedley Bull, Leicester, Leicester University Press, 1977, and *Power Politics*, ed. Hedley Bull and Carsten Holbraad, revised and expanded edition, Leicester, Leicester University Press, 1978.

13 See e.g. Eric Hobsbawm and Terence Ranger (eds), *The Invention of Tradition*, Cambridge, Cambridge University Press, 1993; Benedict Anderson, *Imagined Communities*, London, Verso, 1983.

14 Leopold von Ranke, *Über die Epochen der neueren Geschichte* (1854), ed. Walter Peter Fuchs (*Aus Werk und Nachlaß* 2), Munich, Oldenbourg, 1971.

15 Akira Iriye, 'Culture and International History', in Michael Hogan and Thomas Paterson (eds), *Explaining the History of American Foreign Relations*, Cambridge, Cambridge University Press, 1991, p. 215.

16 Paul Grebe (ed.), *Duden Etymologie: Herkunftswörterbuch der deutschen Sprache*, Mannheim, Dudenverlag, 1963, p. 376; Elmar Seebold (ed.), *Kluge. Etymologisches Wörterbuch der deutschen Sprache*, Berlin and New York, Walter de Gruyter, 1995, p. 492.

17 Following, again, the *Oxford English Dictionary*, a 'civilization' is a 'civilized condition or state; a developed or advanced state of human society; a particular stage or a particular type of this', 'civilized' meaning the state of having been brought out of barbarism, to have been instructed in the 'arts of life, and thus' to be elevated 'in the scale of humanity'. Conscious of the horror which this definition would provoke in the Levi Strauss school of social anthropology and its insistence on the equivalence of different 'civilizations', we understand the term here in a broader sense of sets of laws, rules and regulations and patterns of living which are common to a group of people.

18 In the sense of political programmes supported by reference to past events or timeless legends; for definitions of myth, see Cyril Buffet and Beatrice Heuser, 'Of Myths and Men', in Buffet and Heuser (eds), *Haunted by History: Myths in International Relations*, Oxford, Berghahn, 1998.

19 Unless we are speaking of well-thought-out philosophies or religions, we will shun the expression 'belief system', as a study of the beliefs held by different cultures suggest these are clusters of often quite contradictory views, which have been accumulated by these cultures over a long time. Belief system suggests too much logical coherence. This point will be discussed further in our conclusions.

20 Maurice Halbwachs, *La mémoire collective*, Paris, Presses universitaires de France, 1950.
21 For a discussion of mental maps, see Alan K. Henrikson, 'Mental Maps', in Hogan and Paterson (eds), *Explaining the History of American Foreign Relations*, pp. 177–92.
22 Pierre Bourdieu, *La distinction. Critique sociale du jugement*, Paris, Minuit, 1979.
23 Wolfgang Reinhard, *Die Geschichte der Staatsgewalt*, Munich, Beck, 1999. We have ignored prehistory, as by its very definition it lacks the documentation which could give us an idea of the mentality of the human groups of the time.
24 Indeed, when states implode or break up, the international community more often than not attempts to reconstruct them; see Gregory Fox, 'New Approaches to International Human Rights: The Sovereign State Revisited', in Sohail Hashmi (ed.), *State Sovereignty: Change and Persistence in International Relations*, University Park, PA, Pennsylvania State University Press, 1997.
25 See below for a definition of 'total' war.
26 In the 1990s, the quarrels between Britain and her major European neighbours about British beef exports, overshadowed by the problem of BSE contamination of British beef, were a famous example of the irrationality of popular attitudes towards these neighbours, and the trade dispute involved.
27 General Erich von Ludendorff, *Der Totale Krieg*, Munich, Ludendorff, 1935; translated by Rapoport as *The Nation in Arms*.

2 History and International Relations theory

Andreas Osiander

The historical origins of International Relations theory

International Relations as a discipline (hereafter referred to as IR) bears the imprint of the historical circumstances in which it was created. It is frequently claimed that the discipline came into being as a result of the shock caused by the First World War. It is true that the first research institutes and dedicated chairs were only established in the years immediately following the war. However, systematic thinking on interstate relations, on a scale unknown in previous history of thought, had already developed during the last third of the nineteenth century.[1]

Specialist IR thinking is a by-product of industrialization. Pre-First World War IR authors – such as Angell, Bloch, Riezler – concur that, as a result of industrialization, an ongoing, cumulative change in the character of interstate politics had become noticeable from about 1860–70.[2] The main feature of this process was (and, of course, still is) division of labour on an ever greater scale resulting in growing interdependence. In the early decades of industrialization, this phenomenon had in the main been observable within the boundaries of the sovereign territorial state, creating for the first time what could now be called national economies. But in the last third of the nineteenth century it began to outgrow the geographical and political area defined by the individual state.

Industrial-scale dependencies on raw materials and markets outside one's own boundaries and thus political control inexorably diminished the autonomy of the individual state. As authors like Angell and Riezler insisted even before the First World War, growing economic interdependence meant that, without necessarily being less intense than in the pre-industrial age, interstate competition had to take increasing account of the economic sphere. The crucial point that underlies virtually all reformist early twentieth-century IR theory (but which the authors in question found very difficult to put across to the public) was that, as a consequence, interstate competition could no longer be treated as a zero-sum game. While, in pre-industrial conditions, one could go to war over territories, populations and material riches, and gain for oneself what one managed to take away from one's adversary, in the industrial age harming one's adversary meant harming oneself. Much more than in any previous era, war now became a problem for society and this in turn became a problem for the state.

The ultimate cause of the appearance of systematic IR thought from the late nineteenth century onwards is the crisis of the state brought about by the process of industrialization. On the one hand, industrialization gave the sovereign territorial state greater relevance for the functioning of society than any system of supra-local rule had had before. Much more than in the pre-industrial age, society now depended on supra-local services of co-ordination and surveillance. Unlike agricultural society, it relied (and relies) heavily on the state as a, or rather the, multi-purpose supra-local agency – the most extensive available. Whatever still vaster structures there might be did not and do not have the functional versatility or the authority, not to mention power, of the state.

Of the twin goals that, since the inception of the modern era, the sovereign state had struggled to secure, namely acceptance of its legitimacy and autonomy, the former was served by industrialization at the same time as the latter was being undermined. The state became indispensable – the ultimate claim to legitimacy – because there was no other framework for organizing the large-scale processes of industrial production, but in the long run it could not be large enough, since it could not contain the phenomenon within its borders.

Moreover, while industrialization gave the state unprecedented ability to mobilize, marshal and deploy resources for warfare, by the same token it also gave the state unprecedented (and ever-increasing) vulnerability. This resulted from the growing destructive efficiency of the military means available as well as the growing sensitivity of large-scale (potentially global) economic processes to local or regional disruption. The pre-industrial modern state had essentially been an apparatus for wielding power, defined, and defining itself, not least through its capacity for war-making. The paradox increasingly facing the industrial state was that its war-making capacity now grew in proportion as that same capacity became dysfunctional for society.

This was the crisis to which IR owes its existence, and, importantly, it was a crisis of the state. Even without taking cognizance of the fact, IR theory has always been premised on this crisis of the state. As a result, it has, since the beginnings of the discipline, been constitutionally unable to deal with anything other than the (modern: i.e. sovereign and territorial) state.

The genesis of IR realism

The crisis of the state brought on by industrialization has engendered a double response which is at the bottom of the single most important dichotomy in IR theory since its inception in the late nineteenth century:

the divide between Realist and anti-Realist theory. Realism is the type of IR theory that interprets all aspects of international politics as reducible to a struggle for power, with the state seen as a unitary entity in control (more or less) of its destiny, the main actor but conditioned in its behaviour by the 'international anarchy', the absence of government in the interstate sphere that is regarded as the hallmark of international politics. The state, for Realism, is a power-maximizer in a self-help environment where no one can be trusted and violence is endemic. Non-Realist IR theory is invariably also anti-Realist. It never ignores Realism, but always incorporates a critique of that paradigm to position itself intellectually. This is because Realism is about the state. Since we cannot evade the state, which is everywhere and all around us and the centre-piece of our political cosmology, neither can IR theory evade Realism.

Despite all the talk about 'paradigm shifts', successive 'great debates' and the like, looking back at the century or so of systematic IR theory-making it becomes apparent that at the most basic level there is this single fundamental dichotomy. What, in turn, causes the dichotomy are different ways of dealing with the state. The conservative position (i.e. Realism) defends the sovereign territorial state against all comers; the progressive position is less attached to it.

While it was only in the 1930s that Realist thinking gained academic respectability within the discipline of IR (as well as its current name), as a set of ideas it was in place by about 1900, having quickly developed in the last third of the nineteenth century. Take the preoccupation with war, which according to Realism is the central problem of IR theory. Hitherto, war had not been a favourite topic of political thinkers, being dealt with in the manuals of military craft rather than in political philosophy. If war was philosophized about it was depicted as an evil, though sometimes a necessary one. Some early modern writers, to be sure, took a less negative attitude, but this rarely amounted to anything like a systematic defence of war – until, precisely, the last third of the nineteenth century. It was then that, for the first time, not only war in itself but its defence became a genre of political literature.[3]

This is a key element of emergent Realism. Even early nineteenth-century thinkers like Benjamin Constant had concluded that economic progress was making war obsolete; later, Auguste Comte and Herbert Spencer explicitly based this thesis on sociological analysis of the effects of industrialization. Progressive opinion tended to take this as a given, but, of course, war-making was one of the defining prerogatives of the sovereign state, with the *ius ad bellum* an important facet of the traditional concept of sovereignty.

Those thinkers who viewed the onslaught of industrial modernity on traditional political structures and belief patterns with dismay experienced an increasing need to reassert the right of the state to make war, by positing all manner of wholesome effects of war for society. Not that all their ideas were new (though some, like social Darwinism, were). What was new, however, was the determined and systematic manner in which the defence, indeed the adulation of interstate war, was made a vehicle of conservative opinion.

By 1914 there was a voluminous literature that maintained the obsolescence of war as an instrument of politics, and another that held war to be an inevitable and, indeed, desirable social phenomenon. The pro-war camp was employing standard paraphernalia of Realist IR theory – such as the conception of international politics as essentially and inevitably a struggle for power, the international anarchy as a structural constraint of international politics, and the 'balance of power' as a means of managing the international anarchy – while the progressive camp addressed all this in seeking to develop a counter-position.[4]

When the discipline of IR became an academic subject in its own right from 1919 onwards, the anti-Realist camp at first monopolized it, but was driven into the defensive in the 1930s and 1940s. Rationalized as a reaction to the 'return of power politics' and the failure of Wilsonism, in reality the triumph of Realism in the discipline owed at least as much to the anti-liberal reaction then characterizing the general intellectual climate, with its worship of (state) power that influenced authors as diverse otherwise as E. H. Carr, with his fascination with totalitarianism especially in its Soviet variety, and Hans Morgenthau, whose intellectual outlook was deeply influenced by his study of writers like Nietzsche[5] and Carl Schmitt.[6]

Not only, but also perhaps not least because IR had started its career as an academic discipline in the service of world peace (a goal proclaimed not so much by its early academic representatives – at least in Britain – but by those who financed them, such as the philanthropic millionaires Montague Burton, Andrew Carnegie and David Davies), the new Realist IR personnel did not exactly seek to promote war but did insist that it was inevitable. Yet this position was in fact still a defence of war, albeit a muted, oblique and indeed subliminal one. Again, this defence of war (in the guise of a defence of its centrality to international politics) was really a defence of the state against the challenge, brought about by industrialization to its autonomy and thus to its unfettered political primacy. The political orientation behind it was still very conservative.

Realism and the defence of the state

The fundamental character of Realism as a defence of the state is indicated by a number of the traits of the paradigm. It puts the state, with its specifically modern aspects of (internal and external) sovereignty and territoriality, squarely at the centre of its analytical focus. At the same time, it treats the state as an abstraction similar to the *homo oeconomicus* of economic science. Tellingly, all attributes of the state are left aside, other than the traditional, pre-industrial one of wielder of power and provider of 'security' (somewhat of a misnomer given that the state promises protection from the external insecurity caused in the first place by its own existence). The economic sphere, where the traditional power state was being steadily undermined, is kept out of the analysis.

A further telling feature of Realism is its self-proclaimed timelessness. To give just two examples: according to Morgenthau, '[a]ll history shows that nations active in international politics are continuously preparing for, actively involved in, or recovering from organized violence in the form of war'.[7] Likewise, Kenneth Waltz emphasizes 'the striking sameness in the quality of international life through the millennia',[8] while Robert Gilpin makes it a 'basic assumption' that 'the nature of international relations has not changed fundamentally over the millennia'.[9] Examples of this could be multiplied. This reasoning *sub specie aeternitatis* is a well-known leitmotiv of Realist theory, but though its truth has been impugned, the fundamental oddity has gone unnoticed.

Why make this sweeping claim about remote historical periods? Why is it relevant to twentieth-century Realism whether or not the theory was also true in the days of Thucydides or Hobbes? In heuristic terms this means little; in ideological terms it means quite a lot.[10]

The primary purpose of a twentieth-century theory of interstate politics must surely be to explain interstate politics in the twentieth century. For this purpose it is irrelevant whether any explanation advanced is also applicable to relations among ancient Greek *poleis* or early modern royalty. The fact that this latter concern is so prominent in Realist theory betrays the hidden ideological agenda of defending a conservative general conception of the state as an apparatus for wielding power. Here, as elsewhere in politics, the claim that something is traditional has 'always been like that' has great persuasive force, enhancing logical argument or even rendering it dispensable. The notion that Realism encapsulates the wisdom of the ages is supported by citing political observers from bygone periods – specifically and canonically only three, Thucydides, Machiavelli and Hobbes – who supposedly viewed interstate relations with Realist eyes.

Thucydides (1.22) thought that human nature (το 'ανθρωπινον) being what it is, similar events to those reported by him might happen again in the future, making his analysis a possession for all times (κτημα "ες "αιει). Machiavelli and Hobbes similarly believed in the constancy of human nature and made this a premise of their theorizing. And Hobbes (Leviathan, ch. 13) seems to anticipate Morgenthau with his famous statement that 'in all times, kings, and persons of sovereign authority' have been in a state of permanent if sometimes latent war in their mutual relations.

All this is the basis for an astonishing conceit. In reality, what all three authors share with mid-twentieth-century 'classical' IR Realism is a generally conservative outlook along with the notion of constancy or timelessness of human nature; what they do not share is a theory of international relations. The alleged kinship with late twentieth-century 'neo'-Realism with its rejection of human nature as an explanatory factor consists exclusively of a common conservatism.

None of the three older authors offers any conscious (let alone coherent) theory of anything comparable to modern interstate relations. Their alleged anticipation of IR Realism is extrapolated from a few morsels, isolated from the bulk of their work of which it represents a tiny fraction that, at a pinch, could be described as compatible with Realist IR theory.

There is the one famous statement – enigmatic and very controversial as to its precise significance – in Thucydides (1.23) about the 'truest explanation' of the Peloponnesian War that Thucydides identifies as his own opinion and which, while not enunciating the concept at all, is widely taken to imply some form of 'balance of power' thinking on his part. In fact, the text (here and in related passages such as 1.88 and 1.118) is obscure, more so than many translators make it appear. Taking the 'balance of power' concept for granted, renderings of Thucydides into modern languages project this concept into the text, and in the process taking considerable liberty with the original Greek to make the text fit the concept.

Closer examination of Thucydides' notoriously tricky semantics suggests that Sparta's fear of Athens, which Thucydides identifies as a main explanation of the war, is not simply the result – as it were the flip side – of Athenian power as such, as the majority of modern translators would have it. Rather, Spartan fear and Athenian power are two things, linked but separate, with the latter becoming relevant only as a result of the former developing: Sparta's concern with Athenian power evolves only after, because, and to the extent that, the behaviour of the Athenians gives rise to fear. Nowhere does Thucydides treat power as an (impersonal) factor in its own right as does IR Realism; rather, he is concerned with the spirit in which the Athenians used it.

All other evidence usually adduced to claim Thucydides as a Realist is taken from the speeches he attributes to his protagonists. But little is said in the speeches that is not contradicted by other speakers, and the narrator pointedly abstains from resolving this dialectic tension into any synthesis of his own. Any position advanced by the speakers must also be held against the outcome of their actions. Thus, the Athenians (and they alone) famously proclaim the right of the stronger in their dealings with others. No one else in Thucydides invokes this maxim, and, before accepting it as the timeless political wisdom that many have claimed it to be, it should be remembered that it is the Athenians who fail. Thucydides' unspoken agenda is after all to throw light on the utter disaster towards which the Athenians are headed, and he is really concerned with the role which arrogant recklessness plays in this outcome.

Similarly, there is the one phrase in Hobbes (already referred to) about the behaviour of kings, intended in the context of its chapter of which it is part to prove a point about the behaviour of individuals uncontrolled by a higher power. Hobbes does not speak of 'state' behaviour. Arguably (though not self-evidently) the two may be construed here as equivalent, but if so, it is a step that Hobbes does not take – it would rather spoil his point about the behaviour of individuals. As with the passages in Thucydides, any IR theory here remains implicit.

Finally, with regard to Machiavelli, there is nothing in his political writings that so much as alludes to some element of modern Realist IR theory; efforts to credit him with such implicit theorizing – like, to name just one typical example, the attempt by Robert Sullivan to portray him as a theorist of the 'balance of power'[11] – are obvious projections, whose alleged textual basis does not bear scrutiny.[12]

The concept of the 'balance of power', though later than Machiavelli and absent also from Hobbes, is indeed pre-industrial, and a key element of Realism. A further link is that the rise of the concept in political literature is coeval with the consolidation of the sovereign territorial state central to Realism. But quite apart from the fact that the concept has many, and in part contradictory meanings,[13] it is simply sloppy to suggest that because the eighteenth century had the 'balance of power' concept it also had Realism.

I am disputing the Realist 'immutability thesis' – as Andrew Linklater has called it[14] – so as to show that Realism is ideological in character. Ideology lives on projections. While progressive ideology projects forward, Realism, like any conservative ideology, projects its current political concern backward. The postulate thus runs: if Realism is true, the state, in its conservative, power-political conception, is historically safe; that is, it will be safe in the future also. Not as a theory purporting to explain international relations today (for which purpose this undertaking would at best be of secondary interest), but in its capacity as a conservative ideology Realism hinges on the assumption that what it says is there has always been there, from which it is but a small step to infer that it must and will always be there.

'It' – among other things but most importantly – here means the sovereign territorial state. According to Realism, this must have existed throughout history at least in a basic, generic form. As a result, the state (never defined, but the more easily implied to be, in its essence, comparable to the modern state) becomes the central explanatory concept for all history. In the event that it is really too difficult to discover in a given era, such as the Middle Ages, it is invariably found to have at least been under construction.

This interpretative overlay for making sense of history and which consists in making the state timeless is so potent precisely because it is not made explicit; for this 'discourse of eternity', as R. B. J. Walker has called it,[15] takes its strength not from being convincing but from being taken for granted. It is not, of course, specific to IR authors, and nothing that they purposely developed, but something they unreflectingly absorbed from their intellectual environment.

IR Realism is but one manifestation, and application, of a larger social phenomenon. The state-centred view of history that it has inherited from the late nineteenth century is, after all, simply the one espoused by almost all modern historians until quite recently, and by most of the reading public (not to mention government officials or other beneficiaries with a vested interest in maintaining the system) up till today. Realism is appealing because it is in tune with our traditional political cosmology.

Beyond Realism

The phenomenon of taking as the basic parameters of interstate politics – as well as the assumption that inter*state* politics is what should matter to IR as historically immutable – has been branded by a recent wave of anti-Realist IR theory-making as 'positivistic'. What is criticized here is the habit of treating the current framework of international politics as an empirical given independent, in its existence and essence, of the subjective perception and/or the interests and aims of those aware of it (while – paradoxically for a scientific theory, but not for an ideology – also seeking to vindicate this framework in the face of challenge). By contrast, recent 'post-positivistic' IR theory such as Constructivism, or approaches to IR based on the Frankfurt School critical theory or postmodernism, insists on the character of this framework as historically contingent. Indeed, in the case particularly of Constructivism, emphasis is on its character as a collective mental construct where – political structures being intangible – there is no reality other than what is collectively perceived to be.

This insight (or emphasis) is not as new as might be assumed. Among the many misunderstandings of early twentieth-century non-Realist IR theory (often referred to as Idealist or Liberal) is the view that it was just the more progressive flip side of the Realist paradigm with which it supposedly shared its state-centred nature. In reality, pre- and post-First World War anti-Realist IR authors regarded the sovereign territorial state as historically obsolescent while also interpreting it as the more or less malleable expression of what might now be called a prevalent discourse – what Angell in what is really his central metaphor refers to as the 'public mind'.[16]

All this, however, has at best dented popular belief in, and adherence to, The State As We Know It. The concept of the sovereign territorial state is a powerful totem of contemporary civilization, atavistic as, on reflection, its pre-industrial origin may make it appear. Its quality as a totem is not undermined by the frequent claim that the state is itself being undermined, particularly by 'globalization'; R. B. J. Walker reminds us that constant reiteration of the thesis that a concept, such as state sovereignty, is about to disappear actually tends to perpetuate it by continuously reaffirming its centrality.[17] Indeed, a certain old-fashioned flavour may be part of the charm that the state possesses. People cling tenaciously to selected pre-industrial belief patterns; as with religion – itself pre-industrial – the reason for this may be the emotional comfort afforded by anything seen as timeless, traditional and stable in a world that is in constant and fairly rapid transformation.

In addition, the modern state is in fact a hybrid thing, part-atavistic but also part-functional in its capacity as a provider of supra-local services to industrial society, not to mention as a powerful and as yet unrivalled focus of ('national') community. Its basic problem – and by extension that of IR theory – may be that the state has difficulty in making the transition from its traditional role and perception as essentially an apparatus for wielding power, to the role now required of it only as provider of services (among which the provision of 'security' against the kind of threat arising from clinging to its ancient power role must be regarded as an anachronistic remnant, relevant while and to the extent that not every state has made the transition fully). The state – meaning its leaders, but also the majority of the general public that to a greater or lesser extent continues to subscribe to the traditional view of the state – is still tempted to hang on to the old power-political frills of state sovereignty (witness, for example, the fact that official visitors on state visits, even if for some perfectly civilian purpose, are invariably received with 'military honours').

This hybrid nature of the state, the inability (or indeed disinclination) to distinguish and separate its functional role from its pre-industrial power role, would appear to be a major cause for the predominance of Realist over anti-Realist IR theory in the last hundred years or so. The difficulty or failure to grasp the true nature of the state is in turn linked to the fact that we feel guilt about 'betraying' the state. Our political education impresses on us that we should be loyal, indeed emotionally attached to the (our) state (which may hide behind some other concept, such as 'the nation'). We are certainly not taught to regard it as simply an agency providing services to society. If we openly regarded it as the mere institutional apparatus that it really is that would be frowned upon; it would smack of heresy.

Research on the impact of mentalities on international relations (or whatever, in a given era, takes their place) might well start here. It is the hegemony of the Realist paradigm over the contemporary 'public mind' which explains why so little research has as yet been invested in exploring, from an IR point of view, historical alternatives to the sovereign territorial state. Since for Realist theory such alternatives could not (or must not) have existed (or if they did, must be undeserving of attention), research of that kind is futile (or dangerous). And since, as an ideology, Realism cannot tolerate belief systems other than its own and for that reason discourages belief in belief systems, research and reflection in that area have not really progressed much beyond the positing, against Realism, of its importance.

This is as true of early twentieth-century anti-Realist IR theory as it is of late twentieth-century IR 'postpositivism'. While some forays have been undertaken, much remains to be done; the history of our civilization is still waiting to be explored from an IR-oriented, but non-Realist point of view. For example, I know of no application of the Constructivist interpretation of (political) reality to other historical periods than the present. But how did people in other, particularly pre-modern periods interpret and thus construct their own political reality (when they did not have present-day Realist-inspired historians do it for them)? What was the constitutive discourse underlying their political structures? Can we reconstruct it at all? How and why did it change? In what way did it affect the political process, and how different did that make it from what we observe in our own era?

Nor have critical theory or postmodernist approaches to IR as yet had much to say about the past. What little there is tends to focus, like conventional historical sociology, on the evolution of the modern state or the international system of which it was part, going back no further than the late Middle Ages. Greater comparative knowledge, from an IR perspective, of periods other than the modern era (and thus not focusing on the modern state) is likely to make an important contribution to the development of non-Realist IR theory applicable to the present.

To be able to compare periods in the first place – which, as we have seen, Realism does not do, claiming that from an IR point of view they are all the same anyway – we of course need a theory of 'international' relations (or what better term will eventually be found) that is more than simply the extension to all historical time of current notions of interstate relations. Conversely, bringing history back in (after Realism had really excluded it) would almost certainly transform present IR theory.

Notes

1 A. Osiander, 'The interdependence of states and the theory of interstate relations: an enquiry into the history of political thought', *Law and the State*, 1996, 53/54, pp. 48–50, and idem, 'Rereading early twentieth-century IR theory. Idealism revisited', *International Studies Quarterly*, 1998, 42, pp. 409–32.
2 N. Angell, *The Great Illusion*, London, Heinemann, 1913, p. 50; J. von Bloch, *Die wahrscheinlichen wirtschaftlichen und politischen Folgen eines Krieges zwischen Großmächten*, Berlin and Bern, Edelheim, 1901, p. 79; K. Riezler (published under the pseudonym 'J.J. Ruedorffer'), *Grundzüge der Weltpolitik in der Gegenwart*, Stuttgart and Berlin, Deutsche Verlagsanstalt, 1914, p. 184.
3 M. S. Anderson, *The Rise of Modern Diplomacy 1450–1919*, London and New York, Longman, 1993, pp. 270–3; W. Janssen, 'Friede: Zur Geschichte einer Idee in Europa', in D. Senghaas (ed.), *Den Frieden denken*, Frankfurt, Suhrkamp, 1995, pp. 259–60.
4 For evidence see Osiander, 'Rereading early twentieth-century IR theory'.
5 C. Frei, *Hans J. Morgenthau. Eine intellektuelle Biographie*, Bern, Haupt, 1994, pp. 96–117.
6 A. Söllner, 'German conservatism in America. Morgenthau's political realism', *Telos*, 1987, 72, pp. 161–72.
7 H.-J. Morgenthau, *Politics among Nations*, 6th edn, New York, McGraw-Hill, 1985 (first published 1948), p. 52.

8   K. N. Waltz, *Theory of International Politics*, New York, McGraw-Hill, 1979, p. 66.
9   R. Gilpin, *War and Change in World Politics*, Cambridge, Cambridge University Press, 1981, p. 211.
10 The term 'ideological' is used here in its Mannheimian sense of something to which its proponents themselves subscribe, without being aware that it reflects political preference rather than critical insight.
11 R. R. Sullivan, 'Machiavelli's balance of power theory', *Social Science Quarterly*, 1973, 54, pp. 258–70.
12 See my observations on Machiavelli in Osiander, 'The interdependence of states'.
13 See E. B. Haas, 'The balance of power. Prescription, concept or propaganda?', *World Politics*, 1952/53, 5, pp. 442–77; M. Wight, 'The balance of power', in H. Butterfield and M. Wight (eds), *Diplomatic Investigations: Essays in the Theory of International Politics*, London, Allen & Unwin, 1966, pp. 149–75.
14 A. Linklater, 'The achievements of critical theory', in S. Smith, K. Booth and M. Zalewski (eds), *International Theory. Positivism and Beyond*, Cambridge, Cambridge University Press, 1996, p. 282.
15 R. B. J. Walker, 'International relations and the concept of the political', in K. Booth and S. Smith (eds), *International Relations Theory Today*, University Park, PA, University of Pennsylvania Press, pp. 306–27.
16 Angell, *The Great Illusion*; F. Delaisi, *Political Myths and Economic Realities*, London, Noel Douglas, 1925; L. Woolf, *The Way of Peace*, London, Ernest Benn, 1928; A. Zimmern, *Internationale Politik als Wissenschaft*, Berlin and Leipzig, Teubner, 1933.
17 Walker, 'International relations', p. 322.

Part I

War and peace in classical antiquity

Introduction

Hans van Wees and John Rich

Archaic and classical Greece

The traditional picture of the early Iron Age in Greece (*c.* 1100–800 BC) as a Dark Age of primitive technology, poverty, political chaos and cultural isolation is becoming ever less gloomy in the light of archaeological discovery. Even so, it remains true that the character of Greek political organization underwent a transformation from the eighth century BC onwards. Settlements became larger and more numerous, the first fortifications and monumental buildings – mostly sanctuaries – appeared, and Greeks began to trade and settle all over the Mediterranean (and soon afterwards around the Black Sea as well). This is when the characteristic Greek form of political organization, the city-state (*polis*), began to emerge. The process was slow and uneven, and, on a strict definition, the *polis* perhaps never quite reached the point where it was worthy of the name 'state'; yet by the beginning of the classical period (*c.* 500 BC) at the latest, most Greek communities had enough of a centralized and formalized form of government to warrant loosely calling them 'states'.

It is likely that the emerging *poleis* staked territorial claims where boundaries had earlier been only vaguely drawn, if at all, and that this sparked off border warfare. The earliest conflict of which we have any record (other than the wars of heroic legend) is the First Messenian War, probably fought in the early seventh century, which ended with the Spartans occupying their neighbours' territory and making serfs of its inhabitants, an event unique in Greek history. Perhaps at about the same time, Eretria and Chalcis, two Euboean cities, waged the Lelantine War over the plain between them, a clash which became famous for the many allies that both sides brought into the conflict. The evidence for this, as for other early conflicts, however, is late and patchy. Contemporary poetry leaves no doubt about the prominence and frequency of war in the seventh and early sixth centuries BC, but does not allow us to reconstruct a military history in any detail.

An important development of the mid-sixth century was the formalization of relations between *poleis*. The earliest surviving inscribed treaties of alliance and friendship between states date to this period, and it appears to have been at about this time that Sparta created for itself the system of bilateral alliances known as the Peloponnesian League (since it covered most of the southern Greek peninsula, the Peloponnese). The Spartans, with both a large population of serfs and a large number of subordinate allies to call on, were now the dominant Greek power and able to intervene well beyond the Peloponnese. They accepted alliances with the King of Lydia, and perhaps the Pharaoh of Egypt, and in 545 BC are said to have offered at least a token challenge to the meteoric rise of the Persian Empire – which went on, regardless, to conquer the Greek cities in Asia Minor (modern Turkey). The Athenians, meanwhile, fought wars against all their neighbours, engaged in small-scale overseas expansion, and showed signs of wanting to play a leading role in international politics when they in turn challenged the Persians by sending a fleet to support the eastern Greek cities in a doomed attempt to throw off Persian rule (499 BC).

In 490, Persian expansion reached mainland Greece and suffered a setback when the Athenians defeated a force which had landed at Marathon. A vastly greater expedition followed in 480, commanded in person by the new king, Xerxes. Many, but by no means all, Greek *poleis* formed a defensive alliance led by Sparta. The allied fleet, dominated by the Athenian navy, scored a surprise victory at Salamis, after which the bulk of the Persian forces retreated; in the following year the allied army defeated the remaining Persian troops at Plataia. A Greek campaign of retaliation ensued, but Sparta and its Peloponnesian allies soon lost interest, allowing Athens to create a new alliance under its own leadership, the Delian League. The Athenians made more strenuous demands on their allies than did the Spartans, and early on began, in effect, to turn their league into an 'empire' and their allies into tribute-paying subjects.

For some time, Sparta and Athens appear to have had an understanding that they could be joint 'leaders of the Greeks' (a notion periodically revived afterwards), but the ambitions of both sides led to a series of great 'hegemonic' wars in which the two powers sought to establish their dominance once and for all: the First Peloponnesian War (461–446), the two phases of the (Second) Peloponnesian War (the Archidamian War, 431–421, and the Ionian or Decelean War, 413–404), and the Corinthian War (395–386). For much of the fifth century, the Athenians were successful and confident enough to get embroiled in more distant wars as well, most notably an attempt to support an Egyptian revolt from the Persian Empire and an expedition to gain control over Sicily, both ending in disaster. Sparta ultimately gained Persian financial support, enabling them to defeat Athens and its allies twice. In the late 380s, Sparta was the unchallenged hegemon of Greece, and more powerful than ever.

However, new challengers for the leadership soon emerged, including the Boeotians, Arkadians and Thessalians, while Athens revived some of its old power by creating a Second Athenian Confederacy. Further conflicts broke out, in which constantly shifting alliances under changing leadership fought for hegemony with less and less lasting success. In order to fund their war efforts, city-states often appealed to the governors of the nearest provinces of the Persian Empire, just as they appealed to the Persian king to lend his authority to a whole series of short-lived attempts to impose a 'common peace' on all Greeks. The Spartans were decisively defeated at Leuktra in 371, and subsequent wars, as an exasperated Xenophon said, left Greece in ever greater disorder, without any recognized leading power at all (*Hellenika* 7.5.26–7).

In the 350s, the unification, reorganization and expansion of the kingdom of Macedon under Philip II established a new force to the north of Greece, with material and manpower resources that none of the city-states could begin to match. Philip II was quickly drawn into Greek politics as an arbiter and ally to some, an expansionist rival to others. His army ended up defeating a broad Greek coalition at Chaeronea in 338 BC, and he made himself the hegemon of a new organization of Greek city-states, the League of Corinth. After the famous conquests of Philip's son and successor Alexander the Great, this league found itself as no more than a small part of a vast empire, stretching from Macedonia and Egypt to India, and although the empire disintegrated soon after Alexander's death in 323, the Macedonian-ruled kingdoms which emerged from it were still far more powerful than any of the city-states. For centuries afterwards, Greek *poleis* continued to assert their claims to status and independence whenever possible, by any means at their disposal, but they were reduced to minor players, if not mere extras, on an international scene now dominated by the Hellenistic monarchies and ultimately by the Roman Empire.

Roman expansion

In its early centuries Rome was no more than one (albeit the most important) of the cities of the Tiber plain. This changed dramatically *c.* 343, when the Romans embarked on a series of wars against the Samnites and other Italian peoples. By the 270s they had conquered all of Italy south of the Po Valley. About a quarter of the free population of Italy had now been incorporated into the Roman citizen body, occupying a broad swathe of territory extending across the peninsula. The rest of the communities of Italy south of the Po Valley were nominally independent, but allies of the Romans, bound to supply them with troops on demand.

The Roman conquest of Italy was immediately followed by conflicts with overseas powers, beginning with Carthage, a Phoenician city in north

Africa which had built up an empire in western Sicily, Sardinia and southern Spain. In 264 the Romans responded to an appeal for help from Messana in eastern Sicily, which led to war with Carthage (the First Punic War). The Romans rapidly won over the cities of eastern Sicily and then became locked into a protracted struggle over the rest of the island, in the course of which they built their first fleets. The war ended in 241 with the Carthaginians' withdrawal from Sicily, and in 237 the Romans took advantage of the Carthaginians' difficulties with their mercenaries to prevent them from recovering Sardinia. The Carthaginians, under the command of successive members of the Barcid family, then turned to expanding their power in Spain. The Romans responded by taking an interest in Spain themselves. In 219 Hannibal attacked Rome's friend Saguntum, and this led to the outbreak of the Second Punic War in 218.

At the start of this war the Romans expected to be fighting in Spain and Africa, but Hannibal surprised them by crossing the Alps, and in 218–216 won a series of brilliant victories. Any other power would have been crushed, but the Romans' resilience and huge resources of manpower enabled them to fight back. The war continued not only in Italy, but also in Spain, Sicily, Greece and eventually Africa. Scipio decisively defeated Hannibal at Zama (202), and in the ensuing peace settlement (201) the Carthaginians were reduced to a small territory in north Africa.

The former territories of Carthage became the first Roman provinces: Sicily, Sardinia, Hither and Further Spain. The term *provincia* originally meant the sphere of duty of a magistrate. In its developed form a province was a territory with a resident Roman governor responsible for security, some jurisdiction and the levying of taxes. Although provincials were some-times used as troops, the main means by which they were exploited (in contrast to the Italian allies) was by taxation. It was once believed that the provincial system was introduced into the former Carthaginian terri-tories as soon as the Carthaginians were expelled, but it now seems more likely that it evolved only gradually over the later third and early second centuries.[1]

In the early second century the Romans were engaged in wars on several fronts. In Spain they fought a long struggle down to *c.* 178 to establish their control, in the process extending their power far into the hinterland. In the same period, they completed the conquest of northern Italy, which had been begun in the late 220s, in retaliation at the Gallic invasion of central Italy in 225, but interrupted by the Second Punic War. Their most notable wars, however, were in the Greek East.

The Romans had first crossed the Adriatic in 229 in response to Illyrian piracy, and several communities on the Adriatic seaboard had then submitted to Rome. In 215 King Philip V of Macedon had allied with Hannibal, forcing the Romans to open a new theatre-of-war in Greece, and in 206-205 they had been obliged to accept a compromise peace. In 200, in response to appeals from various Greek states who were suffering from Philip's aggression, the Romans renewed war with Philip (the Second Macedonian War). They soon declared their war aim to be the expulsion of Philip from Greece, and their victory at Cynoscephalae (197) forced Philip to agree to their demands (196). The Roman commander Flamininus then proclaimed the freedom of the Greeks and in 194 brought back all his forces across the Adriatic.

By then, however, the Romans were already at odds with Antiochus III, of the Seleucid dynasty of kings, whose wide territories centred on Syria. Antiochus had used the opportunity of Philip's discomfiture to take various cities on the Asia Minor seaboard and west of the Dardanelles. Lengthy negotiations followed, which eventually broke down over Antiochus' refusal to withdraw from the territory he had occupied on the European side of the straits. In 192 he initiated war by crossing to Greece at the invitation of the disaffected Aetolians. The Romans easily drove him out of Greece and then pursued him to Asia Minor, where they defeated his motley army at Magnesia in 189. At the ensuing peace settlement he was obliged to cede all his extensive territories in Asia Minor north of the Taurus mountains. Once again the Romans retained no territories for themselves: some of the cities were declared free, and the rest of the ceded territories were assigned to their friends, the Rhodians and the King of Pergamum.

The Romans had now defeated the last power in the Mediterranean world which could be thought capable of challenging them. During the peace negotiations following the battle of Magnesia, a Rhodian ambassador is said to have told the Senate that 'the gods have subjected the inhabited world to your sway' (Polybius 21.23.4). This outcome was reinforced two decades later when the Romans went to war against Philip's son Perseus, who in their view had been destabilizing the settlement in Greece (171). The Third Macedonian War began badly but the Romans won a decisive victory at Pydna and captured Perseus soon afterwards (168). There had been much disaffection in Greece to which the Romans reacted sternly, deporting many politicians to Rome (including the future historian Polybius) and enslaving 150,000 Epirots. But they still avoided annexation, instead turning Macedonia into four republics.

A comparatively peaceful period followed, and Polybius (32.13.6) claims that in 156 the Romans welcomed the opportunity for war with the Dalmatians because they feared that Italian men were becoming enfeebled by the long peace. However, soon afterwards war broke out on several fronts. Serious warfare began again in Spain in 155 and dragged on until 133, with the Romans suffering several humiliating defeats. In addition, in 149–146 there were revolts in Macedonia and Greece, and the final war with Carthage. The latter arose out of quarrels between Carthage and its neighbour, the Numidian King Masinissa. The Romans maintained that the Carthaginians had violated their treaty and were again a threat to Rome. The Carthaginians submitted and were ordered to move to a different site; this provoked their last desperate resistance, which ended in the sacking and destruction of the city by Scipio Aemilianus (with his friend the historian Polybius looking on). Two new provinces were created in 146, namely Africa, from the former territory of Carthage, and Macedonia: the rebellion in Macedonia finally obliged the Romans to give up their attempt to avoid establishing provinces in the East.

Thereafter the Romans' imperial commitments regularly provided them with further wars to fight in various theatres. From time to time new provinces were created, beginning with Asia (the former kingdom of Pergamum, bequeathed to Rome in 133) and Transalpine Gaul (southern France, *c.* 120). At the end of the second century a serious threat from marauding Germanic tribes, the Cimbri and Teutones, was finally repelled under the leadership of Marius. In the first century there were major eastern wars against King Mithridates VI of Pontus (89–82, 73–63), which led to a further huge extension of Roman power through new provinces (Bithynia, Syria) and client kingdoms.

Mithridates was emboldened to challenge the Romans by their own internal conflicts. Discontent had been simmering since the late second century. In 91 the Social War broke out, in which a large group of Italian allies rebelled because they had been denied citizenship. The Romans won this war at the cost of conceding the franchise, but it was immediately followed by two bouts of civil war (88–87, 83–82). Sulla won these wars and imposed a harsh settlement which he hoped would prevent further popular agitation, but he died in 78 and his settlement had unravelled by 70.

In the turbulent post-Sullan years a succession of commands was conferred on Sulla's former henchman Pompey, culminating in the war against Mithridates. In 62 Pompey returned from the East to a triumph of unprecedented splendour. The Republic might have survived if the Senate had been ready to accommodate him, but in fact they thwarted his wishes, particularly land allotments for his troops. This drove him to make common cause with Caesar, the consul of 59, and with his old rival Crassus. Caesar's reward was an extended command in Gaul. He made brilliant use of this opportunity, seizing various pretexts to conquer the rest of France. Crassus sought to do the same against Parthia, but was defeated and killed at Carrhae (53). With Caesar's return in prospect, Pompey buried his differences with the Senate. As the poet Lucan (1.125–6) put it, 'Caesar could not endure a superior or Pompey an equal'. In the ensuing civil war (49–45) Caesar defeated first Pompey and then the remnants of his supporters.

Appointed dictator, Caesar soon made it clear that he had no intention of giving up power. This led to his assassination (44) and a renewed series of civil wars. Caesar's adopted son Octavian emerged as the victor from the last of these in 31–30, and then proceeded with consummate skill to fashion a monarchical system under a republican guise, taking the name Augustus (27) and reigning until his death in AD 14. The successful management of war and external relations played a key part in the establishment of his regime. Egypt was annexed as a result of the last civil war. In the East, Augustus avoided war with the Parthians, settling for a policy of peaceful co-existence which he represented as Parthian submission. In Europe he extended the empire further than any of his predecessors, pacifying northern Spain and the Alps and extending Roman power to the Danube and the Elbe. Augustus also completed the replacement of the old citizen militia with a professional, standing army, stationed in frontier provinces. From then on, until the empire's collapse, warfare and military service played little part in the lives of the rest of the population.

A disastrous defeat in AD 9 led to the loss of Germany, and this marked the end of the steady Roman expansion which had proceeded over the previous three and a half centuries. Some emperors made new conquests (notably Claudius' invasion of Britain and Trajan's annexation of Dacia), but most preferred to consolidate.[3] In the third century AD the empire came under intense pressure, both internal and external. A new stability was established in the fourth century, but in the fifth the empire collapsed in the West.

The whole of Antiquity probably poses most problems for us in terms of source material: the histories we know are particularly sophisticated, while there is a particularly striking lack of any documentation of the mindset of ordinary people, be they free or slaves.

In their contributions, Simon Hornblower and Hans van Wees point out the importance of kinship and kinship diplomacy between city-states and their imaginary or real colonies; of prevalence, hegemony and honour (intimately connected with rank), of loyalty to a league and of piety. Religion was obviously important, even to the highly intellectual historiographers Thucydides and Polybius. But the nexus we take for granted in the world marked (however faintly, at the beginning of the third millennium AD) by Christianity, between a sinless life and the prospect of a pleasant afterlife (and concomitantly, between a sinful life and long-lasting punishment after death) was made rarely, if ever. Collective piety was seen as influencing the gods' attitude towards collectives of people, but the assumption of individuals into the Olympian heavens on account of their impressive life (impressive, note, not necessarily flawless!) was a special treat preserved for the likes of Hercules, or the Roman emperors, but not even for especially virtuous priests, nor for especially successful generals. What the Edda later referred to as the sole feature that survived the dead, namely the glory of their deeds, was perhaps central to the concerns of great leaders or kings, but could hardly render the individual hoplite immortal. At the other end of the spectrum, Ducrey thinks that not even the gods were believed universally in Ancient Greece to be able to change the future (and thus, to influence events), but that they could tell the future, which differentiated them from mortals.[4] How then could it be a consideration how one fought or sacrificed oneself, if either way it could not change one's own or one's group's destiny?

Simon Hornblower shows the importance of myth and historical examples and role models for Greeks (including Macedonians), which Ruth Stepper shows for the Carthaginians. Time and again leaders from the Graeco-Roman world felt called upon to fashion themselves on and to copy quite consciously mythical or historical heroes.

(For literature on the subject, see the select bibliography at the end of this volume.)

Notes

1 See especially J. S. Richardson, *Hispaniae: Spain and the Development of Roman Imperialism, 218–82BC*, Cambridge, Cambridge University Press, 1986.
2 For this date and interpretation see J. W. Rich, 'Roman aims in the first Macedonian War,' *Proceedings of the Cambridge Philological Society*, 1984, vol. 210, pp. 126–80.
3 On the reasons why Roman expansion ended see T. J. Cornell, 'The end of Roman imperial expansion', in J. W. Rich and G. Shipley (eds), *War and Society in the Roman World*, London and New York, Routledge, 1993, pp. 139–70.
4 Pierre Ducrey, *Guerre et Guerriers dans la Grèce Antique* (originally published 1985), 2nd edn Paris, Pluriel/Hachette, 1999, p. 241.

3   War and peace in ancient Greece

Hans van Wees

The modern image of war, peace and international relations in ancient Greece is very much the image that the historian Thucydides sought to project in his history of the Peloponnesian War (431–404 BC): a world in which every state was always out to increase its power at the expense of others and where unscrupulous power politics had reduced all ethical concerns to mere pretence; a world in which war was the norm and annihilation the price of defeat. Ancient Greece thus seems to fit perfectly the extreme 'realist' scenario of an anarchic system of states constantly struggling for survival and power. Yet Thucydides' own account of the war shows that the hard-nosed analyses which he offered were one-sided, and other evidence confirms that Greek international relations were much more complex, and rather less brutal, than he suggested. There was indeed constant tension and frequent warfare between the city-states throughout the archaic and classical periods (*c.*700–500 and 500–300 BC), but we cannot follow Thucydides or modern realists in attributing this to simple 'laws of human nature'. Relations between political communities in Ancient Greece were shaped by a culture which did much both to encourage and inhibit the eruption of armed conflict.

Hellas: an international society of city-states

As a system of many communities, the Greek world – which consisted of several hundred city-states (*poleis*, πόλεις), situated not only in Greece itself but all around the coasts of the Mediterranean and the Black Sea, with heavy concentrations on the coasts of the Aegean, Sicily and southern Italy – had two notable characteristics. First, although the city-states took some pride in being different from one another in dialect, script, cults, political institutions and material culture, they believed that they shared certain essential characteristics which set them apart from all other cultures as Greeks (or 'Hellenes', as they called themselves). Intercommunity relations among the city-states accordingly differed from those between Greeks and non-Greeks. Second, despite intense rivalry between communities, they were bound to one another by such a variety of relationships that it is much more appropriate to think of them as a 'society' of states than as a purely anarchic political system.

Some sense of a distinctive Greek identity already emerges in the earliest surviving Greek poetry, and it grew ever more pronounced. By the end of the fifth century BC, theories were in circulation which explained that Greeks were by nature superior to their 'barbarian' neighbours in Asia, Africa and Europe. These other peoples, it was argued, were born to be slaves, whether literally or metaphorically as subjects of autocratic rulers, whereas Greeks were innately 'free' and born to rule others. Such ideas not only legitimated wars of aggression against, and enslavement of, barbarians, but also supported the view that, among Greek city-states, all should enjoy political independence (*autonomia*, αὐτονομία) without undue interference by more powerful neighbours – let alone by barbarian kingdoms such as the Persian Empire – and that in war no Greek should enslave another Greek.[1]

It is true that the city-states often failed to live up to these conventional, as opposed to legal, and ideal rules of conduct between communities. To some extent, all the most powerful states infringed the autonomy of a greater or lesser number of towns on their borders (the so-called *perioikoi*, πεϱίοικοι, 'dwellers-around'), cities within the region, or more distant allies. Moreover, during the classical period, about two dozen Greek city-states suffered the extreme fate of annihilation by Greek enemies: all adult male citizens were executed and the rest of the population was sold into slavery. Nevertheless, the rules did exist and did matter. The autonomy of Greek city-states was taken seriously enough for the greater powers to make a habit of announcing that their goal in war was the 'liberation' of the weaker, and the taboo on enslaving other Greeks was strong enough to cause an outcry whenever it was broken.[2]

A remarkable feature of relationships among the city-states is the notion that each community had ties of kinship (*syngeneia*, συγγένεια) with others. At the most general level, all Greeks were believed to be 'of the same blood' (Herodotus 8.144.2) as descendants of Hellen, son of Deukalion. The four main dialect groups – Dorians, Ionians, Aeolians and Achaeans – were thought to be kin groups as well, each with a son or grandson of Hellen as common ancestor. Particularly close ties of kinship existed between a 'mother-city' and her 'colonies'; that is, the independent settlements abroad for which in historical or mythical times she had, or claimed to have had, provided settlers, or at least an official founder. For Herodotus, these affiliations were important enough to specify in almost every entry in his catalogue of Greek forces at the Battle of Salamis ('the Aeginetans are Dorians from Epidaurus', 'the Naxians are Ionians from Athens', and so on; 8.43–8), and to cite repeatedly as a motivation in international relations. The Athenians, for example, regarded it as 'proper' to send military aid to Miletus, since according to legend they had founded it hundreds of years ago (5.97). They took to heart the subsequent sack of Miletus as 'their *own* misfortune' to the point of banning a play on the subject and fining its author (6.21). Some years later, they blocked a Spartan proposal to resettle the inhabitants of a range of cities in which the Athenians had also played a legendary role as founders, on the grounds that the Spartans 'ought not to be making decisions about *their* [the Athenians'] colonists' (9.106).

In an extraordinary extension of the concept, some non-Greeks claimed kinship with the Greeks, or so Herodotus reports. Among them was allegedly a king of Persia who claimed that it was appropriate for the Persians and the city of Argos to form an alliance since they were descendants of Perses, son of Perseus, a legendary Argive hero: 'We are your descendants, and it is not proper for us to campaign against our ancestors, or for you to support others and become our adversaries' (7.150). The story is unlikely to be true, but it expresses very clearly the Greek notion that kinship between communities should be a major consideration in interstate relations.[3]

Thucydides, by contrast, went out of his way to argue that kinship was only a nominal factor in international politics. Thus he insisted that 'the truest reason' for the Athenians' interventions in Sicily – officially in defence of kindred cities – was their desire for strategic advantages and, later, for the conquest of the whole island (3.86.4; 6.6.1). At the culmination of Athens' Sicilian expedition, he presented a catalogue of the assembled forces, specifying, in an echo of Herodotus, their kinship affiliations; his purpose, however, was to show that 'they took sides *not* primarily in accordance with justice or *kinship*, but according to either expedience or coercion, as the circumstances dictated in each case' (7.57.1). He accordingly noted all instances of kinsmen fighting one another along the lines of 'these Aeolians fought under compulsion against Aeolians, their founders', or 'the Argives, . . . for their private gain, as Dorians followed the Ionian Athenians against Dorians' (7.57.5, 9). The fact that Thucydides felt the need to argue this case against the likes of Herodotus shows that many Greeks did believe kinship was a major factor in international politics. He himself conceded that it could play a part: Leucas and Ambracia supported Corinth 'on the basis of their kinship' (7.58.3). Thucydides' playing down of the role of kinship is in keeping with his realist ideas, but does not do justice to the more complex reality of his world.[4]

The range of relations other than kinship is summed up in the phrase 'peace, alliance, and in addition great friendship and closeness to one another' (Thucydides 4.19.1). That two cities might be 'friends' or 'close', even without concluding a formal state of peace and alliance, was recognized throughout Greek history: not only did Thucydides regularly refer to the 'closeness' (*oikeiotês*, οἰκειότης) of states, but before him Herodotus and even Homer (*Odyssey* 16.427) spoke of communities being, or not being, 'harmonious' (*arthmios*, ἄρθμιος) in their relations with one another. Formal treaties usually stipulated that the parties should enjoy 'friendship' (*philia*, φιλία) as well as alliance (*symmakhia*, συμμαχία), and indeed some of the earliest examples to survive imposed nothing but friendship, without specific conditions or obligations, or imposed an 'alliance' in such broad terms as to amount to friendly relations all round: 'The Sybarites and their allies and the Serdaioi united in friendship faithful and guileless forever' (*c*.550–25 BC); 'The agreement of the Anaitioi and the Metapioi: friendship for fifty years' (*c*.550 BC); 'The agreement of the Eleans and the Heraians: let there be an alliance for a hundred years, starting this year; if there is any need, whether for words or for deeds, let them stand together in everything, and especially in war' (*c*.550–500 BC).[5]

We are afforded no more than glimpses of what counted as a basis for friendship between city-states, but that a history of mutual military assistance was part of it seems obvious. The Samians, for instance, could claim that the Spartans had sent forces to help them 'in order to return a favour', since a century or so earlier the Samians had sent troops to help Sparta conquer their neighbours (Herodotus 3.47). Less tangible forms of support also mattered. The cities of Sybaris and Miletus 'were more closely bound together by friendship than any we know', and all adult Milesians 'shaved their heads and put on great mourning' when Sybaris was sacked. Herodotus remarked on the failure of the surviving Sybarites to 'repay in kind' when Miletus was sacked in turn: he evidently felt that a reciprocal gesture would have been appropriate. Throughout the classical period, appeals to services rendered by one community to another in the legendary past were a staple of the rhetoric of negotiation. In a particularly striking example, an Athenian envoy to Sparta in 371 BC reportedly argued that, since the Spartans had received a mythical gift of seed-grain from an Athenian hero, 'it would be right for us never to bear arms against one another' (Xenophon, *Hellenika* 6.3.6). Thucydides had the Athenians dismiss such 'fine words' and 'long, dishonest speeches' (5.89), but their persistence and constant repetition shows that for most Greeks reciprocity was a meaningful principle of behaviour in intercommunity relations.[6]

Shared membership of a so-called Amphictyonic League might constitute another tie between city-states. These organizations united communities which shared the use of, and responsibility for, sanctuaries of more than local importance. Although there were several such leagues, only the amphictyony responsible for the administration and protection of the Delphic oracle made much of an impression on the historical record, since its dozen members fought a number of 'Sacred Wars' over the sanctuary. When member-states fought one another, they were supposed to practise restraint and not cut off the opponents' water supply or seek to destroy their city (Aeschines 2.115).

Finally, bilateral military alliances (symmachies) were continually forming, breaking up and re-forming between the Greek city-states. The limited evidence suggests that the nature of alliances developed dramatically during the archaic period. In the epic poetry of Homer (*c*. 700 BC),

allies were called *epikouroi* (ἐπίκουροι, 'helpers'), a term later used for mercenaries, and they offered military support on an *ad hoc* basis rather than
on the basis of an established alliance. In other words, they were not under
a permanent, collective obligation to render assistance, but were recruited
to fight a specific war. The first formalized and long-term relations of
alliance and friendship are attested by 550 BC, as already mentioned.
Initially these were only vaguely defined, but they soon became much
more specific. By 450 BC, treaties of alliance might include stipulations
about such matters as procedures for communal decision-making, shared
rituals, means of settling disputes, rights of plunder, and the provision of
supplies and money. The normal form of alliance, the symmachy
(συμμαχία), was both offensive and defensive, but *epimachy* (ἐπιμαχία), a
purely defensive alliance, also existed.[7] The development of international
politics in this respect suggests a change from informal relations of reciprocity, where one community supports another as a 'favour', often
motivated by kinship or friendship between the cities or their leaders, to
an ever more contractual relationship, with ever more precise, and limited,
mutual obligations.

The main sanction for breaking an alliance was the divine retribution
called down upon oath-breakers, sometimes reinforced by the imposition
of a fine payable to a sanctuary. One should not underestimate the power
of this deterrent. Even Thucydides, who plays down the role of religion
at large, accepts that the Spartans suffered from poor morale during the
first phase of the Peloponnesian War because they had been the first to
break their alliance with Athens and feared divine punishment (7.18.2) –
despite having sent a series of embassies to Athens precisely in order to
manoeuvre themselves into a position where they could declare war without
being seen to be the aggressors (see below).

Although Greek city-states were bound together by kinship, friendship
and alliances on a basis of notional equality, some were inevitably more
powerful than others. The smallest of these communities had territories
of only a few square kilometres inhabited by perhaps a thousand people,
while the largest covered several thousand square kilometres and housed
up to a quarter of a million inhabitants, including slaves or serfs. Superior
resources could be translated into a recognized, but informal, position of
'leadership', *hêgemonia* (ἡγεμονία) or *arkhê* (ἀρχή). (It is not clear that ancient
sources distinguished between these two terms, despite modern scholars'
habit of taking the latter to mean 'empire' as opposed to mere 'hegemony'.) Leadership was exercised in the first instance over immediate
neighbours and allies, but could lead on to the status of 'leader of the
Greeks'. To our knowledge, Sparta was the first state to build up such an
extensive network of alliances that, from about 550 BC onwards, the city
was regarded as the hegemon, not only of its own Peloponnesian League
but of Greece at large. During the classical period, only Athens and, briefly,
Thebes seriously challenged Sparta for this position, but there were many

other, less successful contenders. The Greeks' perception of their cities as part of an international society also affected their ideas of leadership, which was not seen as a matter of mere domination, but as entailing certain responsibilities. Leaders were supposed to be 'champions' (*prostatai*, προστάται) of their followers' interests. Thus Sparta was repeatedly asked to liberate Greek cities from Persian control, on the grounds that this was a leader's rightful duty.

The most tangible expression of Greek unity were the pan-Hellenic sanctuaries, the temples frequently visited by members of all Greek city-states to offer sacrifice, consult oracles, and to compete in the games at the periodic festivals. At these festivals, above all at the Olympia in Elis, the Greek world was represented in microcosm. Non-Greeks were strictly excluded from attending. A king of the 'barbarian' Macedonians had to prove the Greek descent of his family before he was allowed to compete in the Olympic Games (5.22; 8.137–9). Among the Greeks, a truce suspending all hostilities enabled representatives of each community to attend and to acknowledge kindred cities, 'colonies' and friends with invitations to feasts and shares of sacrificial meat. Alongside a show of unity, however, these festivals also offered more than a hint of what drove Greek cities to war: the intense competitiveness of individuals and cities.

Attitudes to war and peace

At the beginning of *Laws*, Plato's final dialogue, one of the speakers declares that 'what most people call "peace" is nothing but a word, and in fact every city-state is always, by nature, in a state of undeclared war with every other city-state' (626a). This comment, combined with the fact that peace was generally concluded for a limited period of time (often between only thirty to fifty years), has inspired the view that for the Greeks war was the *normal* state of affairs in international relations, and peace a temporary aberration. Popular as it is, this view is quite wrong.[8]

The context in which the sentiment expressed by Plato's speaker occurs leaves no doubt that the state of war in question is purely theoretical. It is an intellectual's analysis of the underlying tensions in international relations, not a perception shared by politicians, soldiers or the general public, let alone the perception of an actual war. The speaker admits as much when he sneers at 'the stupidity of the masses in not realizing that everyone, thoughout his life, is always engaged in a continuous war against all the other city-states' (625e). Not all intellectuals agreed: Plato himself argued that constitutions should be geared towards peace (628de), as did Aristotle (*Politics* 1333a31–1334a16), and Xenophon attributes to a contemporary ambassador to Sparta the view that 'if it really has been fated by the gods that mankind must wage wars, then it is up to us to be as slow as possible to start one, and, if one breaks out, to end it as soon as we possibly can' (*Hellenika* 6.3.6).

As for the limited duration of peace treaties, it is vital to remember that most of these treaties did more than merely establish relations of non-aggression: they created alliances, binding the parties to support one another in war, whether defensive or offensive. As it was put by a Corinthian envoy who sought peace but was offered an alliance into the bargain: 'an alliance does not mean peace, but a change of war' (Xenophon, *Hellenika* 7.4.10). It is hardly surprising if states set a limit on such agreements rather than commit themselves indefinitely to fighting on behalf of their allies. In the fourth century BC, many attempts were made to forge a 'common peace' embracing *all* Greeks, and these multilateral treaties, which did not entail military obligations to any single city-state, were *not* limited in time.[9]

Apart from a few seventh-century poems composed as battle exhortations, Greek literature did not glorify war. The *Iliad*, the archetypal martial epic, speaks of abominable, bad, baneful, bloody, cruel, destructive, dreadful, harsh and tearful war, and has only one, if crucial, positive epithet to offer: 'glory-bringing'. Whether in poems, plays or prose, war was commonly denounced as an evil and peace extolled as a time of prosperity and pleasure. In the comedies of Aristophanes, produced during the Peloponnesian War, it was peace which was glorified, as a time when country festivals could be celebrated without fear, and food, drink and sex were abundantly available. More soberly, proverbial wisdom shows that for the Greeks, as for us, war was abnormal and peace represented the natural order of things: 'in war, the sleeping are woken by trumpets; in peace, by the birds' (Polybius 12.26.2; Plutarch, *Nicias* 9.2); 'in peace, sons bury their fathers; in war, fathers bury their sons' (Herodotus 1.87).

Greek states were therefore scrupulous about starting wars, and went out of their way to be able to cite legitimate cause for opening hostilities. In 432/1 BC, the Spartans sent three embassies to Athens with 'complaints', 'so that they might have the greatest possible reason to wage war' (Thucydides 1.126.1). The first claimed that Sparta wished to 'avenge the gods' (127.1) and insisted that Athens should 'drive out the curse of the goddess'. This meant that the Athenians would have to exile their leading politician Pericles, and all his relatives on his mother's side, on the grounds that their ancestors had committed an act of sacrilege two centuries earlier (126.2–127.3). The Athenians countered this by demanding that Sparta should expiate the curses of Taenarus and of the Bronze House, both incurred as a result of similar acts of sacrilege, committed within the last generation or so (128.1–135.1). Odd as these manoeuvres may seem, it was important for a Greek state to be able to cite a religious offence in justification for declaring war. Many an enemy was accused of misusing sacred land, and the long-running feud between Athens and Aegina, for instance, was traced back to the Aeginetans' one-time refusal to make the annual sacrifices they owed to Erechtheus and Athena Polias at Athens (Herodotus 5.82–4). In their campaigns against the Persian Empire, the Athenians advertised their concern to avenge the Persians' destruction of

Greek temples (Herodotus 8.144) by punishing with extreme severity a captured official found guilty of desecrating a shrine – he was crucified while his son was stoned to death before his eyes (9.120) – and by leaving their own temples in ruins as a reminder of the need for revenge.

The second Spartan embassy complained about Athenian treatment of three particular cities, which was deemed to be in breach of existing treaty terms (Thucydides 1.139; cf. 67). Such specific, secular disputes – concerning forcible seizures of property, access to and control over sanctuaries, territorial claims, and the imposition of political control by one city over another – were no doubt most commonly cited in justification, and they were certainly given most space by Thucydides himself in his account of the origins of the Peloponnesian War. A state wanting to fight but unable to cite a plausible grievance might even create a problem rather than open hostilities without justification: the minor border dispute between Locris and Phocis which sparked off the Corinthian War in 395 BC was, according to Xenophon, staged at the behest of Thebes (*Hellenika* 3.5.3–4). A well-established alternative to war as a means of dealing with grievances was arbitration by a third party – a state, a sanctuary or a prominent individual – and it was seen as wrong to refuse arbitration when it was offered. The Spartans' refusal to go to arbitration in 432/1 BC, and their breaking off of the alliance with Athens (noted above), long weighed on their consciences. They felt, Thucydides tells us, that 'it was only natural that they should suffer misfortune' as a result, and they 'took to heart' every defeat (7.18.2).

The third and final Spartan embassy again raised a different issue. It asked the Athenians to 'let the Greeks have autonomy' (Thucydides 1.139.3). This accusation could usually be thrown right back at the accuser, and the Athenians replied that they would let their allies be autonomous if Sparta would do the same for its own allies (1.144.2). Nevertheless, the claim to be fighting for the independence of Greek states was in this case, as in others, quite effective. At the start of the Peloponnesian War, Thucydides claims, 'people felt much goodwill towards the Spartans, especially since they said that they were liberating Greece' (2.8.4), and at the end the walls of Athens were pulled down 'to the music of pipers', as if in celebration, 'since they thought that this day was the beginning of freedom for Greece' (Xenophon, *Hellenika* 2.2.23). It did not escape the Greeks that the self-appointed champions of autonomy were the very states which posed the greatest threat to it – including Persia and Macedon which, as parties to 'common peace' treaties, were supposed to help enforce the freedom of all Greeks. Yet the irony does not seem to have detracted much from the feeling that liberation was a just and noble cause for war.

So much for the factors inhibiting warfare: the manifold relationships between states, the glorification of peace, and the sense that one should not declare war without abundant, preferably religious, justification. Why, then, was war so common?

Motivations and goals in international relations

Thucydides put his finger on a fundamental cause of Greek wars when he had an Athenian say: 'We believe that it is divine, and know for certain that it is universally human, by natural compulsion, to rule whatever one can' (5.105.2; cf. 1.76.2). An explanation of the psychology, found in all three surviving classical historians, is that a community which enjoys prosperity will form a high opinion of itself (*phronêma*, φρόνημα) and develop aggressive contempt (*hybris*, ὕβρις) towards others, which will inspire a 'desire for more' (*pleonexia*, πλεονεξία). Herodotus says as much about sixth-century Spartans and Aeginetans (1.66; 5.81); Thucydides has others say it about fifth-century Corcyreans and Mytilenaeans as well as about states in general (1.25.4, 38.6; 3.39.4–5, 45.4); Xenophon reports in the same terms on fourth-century Olynthians and Arkadians (*Hellenika* 5.2.16–18, 38; 7.1.23–6, 32). Expansionism was thus a structural characteristic of Greek states, as the oath sworn by young Athenians on first joining the citizen army confirms: 'I shall not hand on the fatherland [to the next generation] in a reduced state, but *larger and stronger*' (Tod no. 204).

Greek expansionism had two remarkable features. The first is that it did not usually aim at territorial conquest, but at attaining a recognized position of leadership – the *hêgemonia* (ἡγεμονία) or *arkhê* (ἀρχή) already alluded to – among at least notionally independent city-states. An ambitious state might seek recognition as a regional power, or as 'ruler of the sea' (*thalassokratôr*, θαλασσοκράτωρ), or as the dominant state in Greece at large. The second feature is the double motivation said to underlie the 'desire for more'. On the one hand, there is high self-regard, the awareness that one has superior resources and is capable of taking on even more. On the other hand, *hybris* (ὕβρις), a peculiarly Greek concept meaning unprovoked aggression, seeks primarily to humiliate the victim and thus deprive him of honour, rather than make material gains at his expense.[10] These two motives correspond to two goals: material advantage, or 'profit' (*ôphelia*, ὠφελία), and immaterial prestige, or 'honour' (*timê*, τιμή). International relations in the Greek world can only be understood if we recognize that the object of Greek expansionism was not primarily territory, and that other forms of material gain were no more important than 'honour', i.e. a high status acknowledged by other communities' respectful behaviour.[11]

Thus, in defence of their *arkhê* (ἀρχή), Thucydides says, the Athenians explained that they acted 'above all out of fear, then for the sake of honour, and later for the sake of profit', adding that 'we have not done anything out of the ordinary or against human nature, if . . . we have succumbed to the three greatest things, honour and fear and profit' (1.75.3, 76.2). Similarly, in Thucydides' analysis of the Peloponnesian War, it was fear which 'forced' the Spartans to declare war on Athens (1.23.6, 33.3, 88), while Xenophon implied that in this war their goals, shared by their allies but attained only by the Spartans themselves, were 'leadership, honour, and possessions' (3.5.12).

The first motive, fear, seems easy to translate into the language of 'realist' theories of international relations as the equivalent of what Americans call 'national security'; but Greek city-states did not fear quite the same things as modern states. The ultimate risk in war, of course, was the complete destruction of the community. In practice this rarely happened, but the mere possibility, however remote, would have affected the way in which military threats were assessed. Annexation of defeated communities was also rare, at least in wars between Greeks: Sparta's conquest of neighbouring Messenia, turning its inhabitants into serfs, was unique. Territorial annexation, if any, was normally confined to rather small, disputed areas on the borders between two cities. Other than that, losing a war usually meant nothing worse than being forced to join an alliance on terms dictated by the victor. At their most severe, such terms could be quite intrusive – financial 'contributions', destruction of fortification walls and warships, and constitutional changes might all be imposed – but commonly the only demand was for military support in time of war. The autonomy of a city-state would thus often be compromised, but it would hardly ever be lost altogether.

In the major wars about which we are best informed, the city-states' 'fear' was not for their survival or independence but for their position of leadership. Sparta had been content to see Athens' power grow, but only until it 'touched their own symmachy' (Thucydides 1.118.2): it was the risk of losing some of their allies and thereby some of their international power and prestige which drove them to war. Half a century later, they declared war on Olynthos for very similar reasons. Although remote and no immediate threat, the Spartans decided to strike pre-emptively before this expansionist city could challenge its hegemony (Xenophon, *Hellenika* 5.2.12–20). All the major powers waged frequent wars against allies whose loyalty was suspect, or who openly wished to end the alliance. Their main concern, it would seem, was to ensure that their status as leading powers should not be questioned. Athens went so far as to destroy a neutral city, Melos, merely because its very independence was felt to constitute a challenge to Athenian dominance (Thucydides 5.97). The Greek concept of 'national security' clearly extended well beyond survival to include the pre-emptive defence of a city-state's position in the international pecking order.

It follows from this that the material 'profit' and 'possessions' to be gained through war were rather limited. Even when a city was destroyed and its territory occupied, it was rarely integrated into the victorious state; instead, a new, formally independent community was normally established on the site. This new community did not necessarily comprise settlers from the conquering state: more than once, the occupied land was handed over to faithful allies who had lost their own land. The region of Kynouria, for instance, was one of the most hotly disputed in the Greek world, with a history of several centuries of disputes and wars over the area between Sparta and Argos. However, when the Spartans were in control of the territory, they gave much of it away to refugee Aeginetans, to reciprocate their previous military support and general loyalty (Thucydides 2.27.2; 4.56.2). The case of Kynouria is also interesting for the almost ritual quality of the repeated clashes over it. In the mid-sixth century, both sides sent select bodies of 300 'champions' to contest possession (Herodotus 1.82), and in the late fifth century, the Argives only agreed to conclude an alliance with Sparta if the treaty allowed them, whenever there was no other war (or plague), to challenge their new allies to a fight over Kynouria (Thucydides 5.41.2). It seems obvious that control of this territory was important not so much because of its resources – which were limited, unremarkable, and evidently for Sparta easily dispensable – but because of its significance as a symbol of military superiority.

Border territories, towns and sanctuaries were the subject of long-running disputes throughout Greece and Greek history, but there has rarely been any suggestion that the main issue was an urgent need for agricultural land or the other resources of the region. There is much justice in the ancient observation that, as a rule, the Greeks fought for small material stakes, 'little bits of not particularly good land and tiny boundaries' (Herodotus 5.49). As in the case of Kynouria, the explanation is surely that the material value of the land mattered less than the opportunity to test one's neighbours in a trial of military strength: the chief goal was status rather than wealth.

With regard to material goals other than territory, the Athenians were unusual in exploiting their military power to extort money from neighbouring islands during and shortly after the Persian invasions, and subsequently imposing on their allies what was in effect a regular tribute, although officially the payments were supposed to be 'contributions' to collective military expenses. Sparta, by contrast, never demanded more than *ad hoc* contributions – which, as we know from an inscription (Fornara 132), one ally paid in raisins rather than money. All successful Greek armies did take booty (primarily grain, livestock and slaves), but this rarely amounted to a significant source of revenue. Most campaigns took place in the summer months, and an invading force would find the enemy's grain harvest already gathered, all people and animals evacuated from the countryside and even the woodwork of the farmhouses removed for safe-keeping (Thucydides 2.14). Greater plunder was to be had only on those rare occasions when an army managed to either take the enemy completely by surprise, or to sack a town, or capture the camp of some ostentatious Persian dignitary.[12]

Since the Greeks were motivated more by 'fear' for the status of their community in the society of city-states than by the community's physical or political survival, and since the tangible 'profits' of war were usually quite small, it is not surprising that 'honour' was cited so prominently, after security but before material gain, as a third major goal in international relations. The importance of the honour of a city-state – which depended on its representatives being treated with respect in international diplomacy, at pan-Hellenic events, and during allied congresses and expeditions – is illustrated by the Corinthians' declaration of war on the Corcyraeans in 433 BC. The formal reason given was a dispute over control of the city of Epidamnus, but the main cause, according to Thucydides, was Corcyra's refusal to 'honour' Corinth and treat it as their 'leader', which as 'colonists' they were expected to do (1.38.2–3): 'they did not give them the conventional privileges at common religious festivals and did not serve the first portion of sacrificial victims to a Corinthian, as other colonies did' (1.25.3–26.1). For all his realist inclinations, Thucydides treats not the territorial dispute but the 'neglect' and 'contempt' implied by the withholding of signs of deference (of great symbolic but negligible material value) as the true, and valid, cause for war.

The story of Sparta's fraught relations with its neighbour Elis similarly turns on points of honour. In a series of diplomatic and military manoeuvres, both sides tried to gain control over the border town of Lepreon. None of these events led to war, but the most serious crisis, according to Thucydides, came in 420 BC when the Eleans banned Spartans from competing in the Olympic Games and whipped a prominent Spartan citizen who had entered surreptitiously (5.31. 43–50). When war did break out almost twenty years later, notionally over the 'liberation' of dependent towns, this episode was still one of Sparta's major grievances against Elis. The only other incident that was singled out as an additional cause for war, in spite of numerous other incidents that took place in the interim, was the Eleans' refusal to let the Spartan King Agis carry out a sacrifice at the altar of Zeus in Olympia (Xenophon, *Hellenika* 3.2.21–2).

Modern historians tend to ignore these accounts of insult and retaliation as 'silly', and focus on border territories and strategic advantages as more plausible causes for war. The latter were no doubt also important, but it must be stressed that, here and elsewhere, our sources present the insults as the genuine causes of the conflict, and the power political issues as mere excuses.[13] This will seem less surprising if we bear in mind that the Greeks liked to think of themselves as different from barbarians in 'competing not for money but for excellence' (Herodotus 8.26), and that Xenophon went so far as to single out the striving for 'honour' as the distinguishing characteristic of human beings as opposed to dumb animals, and of 'real men' as opposed to mere human beings (*Hiero* 7.13). We should take our sources seriously and accept that, in a culture where honour is all-important, the urge to defend or enhance communal prestige might at times override concerns for communal security and other advantages.

Striking a balance between the demands of honour and the demands of material self-interest in international relations was always a problem for the city-states. The clearest exposition of their dilemma is the so-called

Mytilenean Debate, a pair of speeches in which Thucydides has two Athenian speakers advocate different ways of dealing with the city of Mytilene on Lesbos, and with rebellious allies in general. The first speaker, Kleon, sees hostile actions as acts of *hybris*, and argues that it is essential and 'just' to respond to such aggression with extreme anger and violence. One must strike back at once, before one's anger is 'blunted', or, if there is a delay, one must remind oneself of how strong one had felt initially (3.38.1, 39.4–6, 40.4–7). The other speaker, Diodotus, counters that, although an angry response is indeed 'just', it may not always be compatible with self-interest, and a less emotional response, tempered with 'good sense', will be less costly in material terms (3.42.1, 44.1–4, 46.4, 47.5). The choice was between following Kleon in taking the issue as a matter of honour and annihilating Mytilene, or following Diodotus in calculating costs and benefits and confining retaliation to the politicians most directly responsible. Honour ultimately lost out in this case, but its appeal was strong enough to let Kleon win the first vote and to allow Diodotus only a narrow majority in a second vote when the assembly was recalled.

The surviving works of classical Greek historians are full of references to states making calculations of political self-interest as well as to the 'anger' and 'hatred' felt by one community for another which had treated it with *hybris* and a lack of respect. The Mytilenean Debate shows that both types of motivation could play a part at the same time, and that they might be precariously balanced. In analysing Greek international relations we should clearly give full weight to both sets of motivations.

Conclusion: 'Realism' and the causes of war in Ancient Greece

Just as modern Realists' theories seem to have been shaped by the most traumatic political and military developments of our day,[14] so too was Thucydides' attempt at a universally valid analysis of human behaviour skewed by contemporary events and trends. His personal experience of the social breakdown caused by several years of the virulent epidemic which killed one in three Athenians, his experience of exile, his awareness of the massacres committed in the civil wars which were breaking out all over the Greek world, his active role in warfare, his familiarity with current intellectual trends which sought to question all traditional values – all of these factors would have predisposed him to be sceptical about religion, ethics and convention, and to see the ruthless pursuit of self-interest in action everywhere. But this was not the full picture.

The competition for leadership and power was of great importance in Greek culture, but, whether in relations within communities or relations between communities, it had to contend with the demands of kinship and friendship, with general moral constraints and with specific contractual obligations. Moreover, leadership and power were matters of prestige and symbolic deference as much as of material advantage. To assume that naked self-interest always prevailed over ethical concerns or that self-interest was in the final analysis always a matter of financial, territorial or strategic gains is to impoverish our understanding of ancient Greek international relations. Thucydides, for all his emphasis on the pursuit of self-interest, especially in his portrayal of the Athenians, did acknowledge that such things as kinship and honour *could* play a real part in politics. Modern historians have often gone beyond even Thucydides' realism, banning such motivations from their analyses altogether. To do so is to turn the history of Greek international relations into a caricature.

Notes

1 For Greeks and barbarians see especially E. Hall, *Inventing the Barbarian*, Oxford, Clarendon Press, 1989, and also S. Hornblower, Chapter 4, this volume. The earliest references to 'a distinctive Greek identity' are in Homer's *Iliad* and hint at the Greeks' superior discipline in battle: H. van Wees, 'Heroes, knights, and nutters', in A. B. Lloyd (ed.), *Battle in Antiquity*, London, Duckworth, in association with the Classical Press of Wales, 1996, pp. 59–60.

2 The concept of autonomy: M. Ostwald, *Autonomia: Its Genesis and Early History*, Chico, CA, Scholars Press, 1982; M. H. Hansen, 'The "autonomous city-state", ancient fact or modern fiction?', in M. H. Hansen and K. Raaflaub (eds), *Studies in the Ancient Greek Polis*, Stuttgart, Steiner, 1995, pp. 21–43. Dealings with defeated communities: P. Ducrey, *Le traitement des prisonniers de guerre dans la Grèce antique*, Paris, École Français d'Athènes, 1968; P. Karavites, *Capitulations and Greek Interstate Relations*, Göttingen, Vandenhoeck and Ruprecht, 1982.

3 Kinship and ethnicity: J. M. Hall, *Ethnic Identity in Greek Antiquity*, Cambridge, Cambridge University Press, 1997.

4 Thucydides' treatment of kinship in international relations: S. Hornblower, *A Commentary on Thucydides, Vol. II: Books IV–V.24*, Oxford, Clarendon Press, 1996, pp. 61–80; L. G. Mitchell, *Greeks Bearing Gifts*, Cambridge, Cambridge University Press, 1997, pp. 23–8; C. P. Jones, *Kinship Diplomacy in the Ancient World*, Cambridge, MA, Harvard University Press, 1999.

5 Interstate friendship as distinct from alliance, discussion of the usage of *arthmios*, and the full Greek text of the three treaties: R. A. Bauslaugh, *The Concept of Neutrality in Classical Greece*, Berkeley, University of California Press, 1991, pp. 56–64.

6 Reciprocity in interstate relations and Thucydides' realist attitude towards it: G. Crane, *Thucydides and the Ancient Simplicity. The Limits of Political Realism*, Berkeley, University of California Press, 1998.

7 A survey of treaty-making and diplomacy in Ancient Greece: F. E. Adcock and D. J. Mosley, *Diplomacy in Ancient Greece*, New York and London, Thames & Hudson, 1975; cf. the collection of articles in E. Olshausen and H. Billet (eds), *Antike Diplomatie*, Wege der Forschung 462, Darmstadt, Wissenschaftliche Buchgesellschaft, 1979. International relations in the Homeric epics: K. A. Raaflaub, 'Politics and interstate relations in the world of early Greek poleis: Homer and beyond', *Antichthon*, 1997, vol. 31, pp. 1–27.

8 A recent statement of this view: M. M. Sage, *Warfare in Ancient Greece: A Sourcebook*, London and New York, Routledge, 1996, p. 129: 'A hostile relationship was assumed to be the norm', and peace was 'an abnormal state that could not be expected to last indefinitely'.

9 Common peace: T. T. B. Ryder, *Koine Eirene. General Peace and Local Independence in Ancient Greece*, Oxford, Oxford University Press, 1965; M. Jehne, *Koine Eirene. Hermes Einzelschriften*, 1994, vol. 63, Stuttgart.

10 This is the ancient meaning of *hybris*, not to be confused with the modern sense of 'overreaching arrogance', as demonstrated by N. R. E. Fisher, *Hybris. A Study in the Values of Honour and Shame in Ancient Greece*, Warminster, Aris & Phillips, 1992.

11 For the Ancient Greek concept of honour, see J.-C. Riedinger, 'Remarques sur la timè chez Homère', *Revue des Études Grecques*, 1976, vol. 89, pp. 244–64; H. van Wees, *Status Warriors. War, Violence, and Society in Homer and History*, Amsterdam, J. C. Gieben, 1992, pp. 69–77. For the role of honour and revenge in Greek war (and civil war), see especially the chapters by J. E. Lendon and N. Fisher in H. van Wees (ed.), *War and Violence in Ancient Greece*, London, Duckworth, 2000.

12 On the limitations of agricultural devastation: V. Davis Hanson, *Warfare and Agriculture in Classical Greece*, 2nd edn, Berkeley, University of California Press, 1998. The evidence for booty: W. Kendrick Pritchett, *The Greek State at War*, esp. vol. 5, Berkeley, University of California Press, 1991.

13 'Silly' causes (supposedly attributed in imitation of Homer): A. Momigliano, 'Some observations on the causes of war in ancient historiography', *Studies in Historiography*, London, 1966, pp. 112–25; also G. E. M. de Ste Croix, *The Origins of the Peloponnesian War*, London, Duckworth, 1972, p. 218 ('oddities'). For an analysis of the dispute between Corinth and Corcyra: G. Crane, 'Power, prestige, and the Corcyrean affair', *Classical Antiquity*, 1992, vol. 11, pp. 1–27. For alternative analyses of Spartan motivations in the Elean War, see C. Falkner, 'Sparta and the Elean War, c.401/400: revenge or imperialism?', *Phoenix*, 1996, vol. 50, pp. 17–25; J. Roy, 'Thucydides 5.49.1–50.4: the quarrel between Elis and Sparta in 420 BC', *Klio*, 1998, vol. 80, pp. 360–8; J. Roy, 'Spartan aims in the Spartan–Elean War of c.400: further thoughts', *Electronic Antiquity*, 1997, vol. 3, no. 6.

14 See e.g. J. W. Honig, 'Totalitarianism and realism: Hans Morgenthau's German years', *Security Studies*, 1995/6, vol. 5, pp. 283–313.

4 Greeks and Persians

West against East

Simon Hornblower

Introduction

My story is of war (*polemos*, πόλεμος) between West and East, specifically between the Greeks (Hellenes) and the Persians (whom the Greeks sometimes called 'Medes', even though Medes and Persians were ethnically distinct). This story has its origins in ancient myth rather than history proper, and developed over many centuries. By the story's end, the participants had changed their identity completely: the Romans had inherited the role of the Greeks, and the Achaemenid Persians had been identified with the Parthians (and after that with the Sasanid Persians). Long though it is, the theme of East and West is itself a mere episode in a larger phenomenon, which in the second millennium AD became that of 'Orientalism', the Western conception of the Orient.[1]

We shall concentrate here mainly on two important (and by ancient standards reasonably well-attested) phases of actual conflict:[2] first, the Graeco–Persian Wars of the early fifth century, an initially defensive struggle from the Greek point of view, and their more aggressive aftermath, the formation of the Delian League or Athenian Empire (*arkhê*, ἀρχή) and its early years of campaigning against the Persians; and second, the conquering war of Alexander the Great between 334 and 323 BC.

How far did idealism, sentiment and anti-barbarian (βάρβαρος) fervour count in all this, and how far were the combatants after booty, an idea whose importance is reflected by the wide range of different ancient Greek words for it (the nouns λεία, λάφυρα, σκῦλα, ὠφέλεια and the verb συλᾶν)?[3] Until very recently,[4] modern historians have tended to dwell on the former set of motives to the almost complete exclusion of the latter, although the ancient sources take the profit motive for granted, for all that they report the discourse used by and about the Greek and Macedonian combatants. Is the newer and more cynical scholarly view correct? Before addressing these questions, I shall discuss the sources and then offer a narrative flagging the chief points of dispute.

The sources: history, myth and poetry

The sources are complex. First, they are mainly literary and were produced by highly literate élite individuals; this means that it is hard to gauge how far they are representative of collective mentalities.[5] Second, the sources are in effect exclusively Greek, despite an accretion of new bureaucratic Persian material, especially from Persepolis. The extent to which documentary Persian material was available to Greek writers is uncertain, but in any case the interesting possibility has recently been raised that what *was* available was mediated by Greeks in Persian service but with Greek ways of interpreting events and governmental structures.[6] This means that anything said about Persian motives in the following pages is either modern speculation or derived from Greek sources. The surviving Greek literary sources may however be based on good local information: there is increasing evidence for cultural interaction between Greeks and Persians, especially in Asia Minor, and Greeks like Herodotus and Xenophon could have spoken to bilingual (δίγλωσσοι) – Persians, or to Greek feudatories, or to Greek-speaking feudatories.

The Greek narratives of the two main wars are soon listed: for the Persian Wars we have the *Histories* of Herodotus of Halicarnassus in Asia Minor, supplemented by some poetic evidence and perhaps some genuine local traditions preserved in minor writers. The first phase of the Athenian Empire (the *pentekontaetia*, πεντεκονταετία or fifty years from 480–430 BC) was recorded summarily by the Athenian Thucydides, Herodotus' younger contemporary, in an excursus early in his detailed but incomplete account of a later war: that fought between the Athenians and Spartans from 434–431 BC (the 'Peloponnesian War'). A third Greek writer, Xenophon, participated in and recorded (in the *Anabasis*) an expedition into the Persian Empire in about 400 BC.

Alexander's campaigns, another *anabasis* (ἀνάβασις) or march eastwards from the sea, were reported by contemporaries and military colleagues, notably Ptolemy I, the later ruler of Egypt. These contemporary accounts are now lost, but were drawn on by writers of the Roman period like Diodorus of Sicily, Quintus Curtius, Arrian and Plutarch. Identifying and characterizing the strictly lost originals is no easy task, but the main lines of the campaigns, and many of the details, are agreed.

The complexities arise when we examine the sources for the ideology of these conflicts, because we are plunged back into the epic world of the Homeric heroes. Because Homer was centrally installed in Greek education, any Greek or Macedonian military operations against the peoples to the east of them were liable to be represented, and in a psychologically real sense justified, as reruns of the mythical or nearly mythical ten-year Trojan War. That war, or a short episode in it, was the theme of Homer's *Iliad*. Agamemnon and Achilles are two of the leaders of a pan-Greek expeditionary force against Troy in north-west Asia Minor.

The abduction by Paris of Helen of Sparta was the *casus belli*.[7] Herodotus opens his account of the 'Persian Wars' of 500–479 BC with a series of mythical abductions of women, some carried off from East to West, others from West to East. Helen is one of them, a West-to-East traveller; but so is Medea, whose abduction by Jason belongs to the saga of the Argonauts who sailed in their talking ship, the *Argo*, from Thessaly in Greece to the east coast of the Black Sea. For Herodotus this was no mere whimsical introduction to real events: he knew that the East–West polarity had a hold on policy-making as well as on the imagination. By using Helen to introduce a narrative about the Persian Wars, Herodotus was making a comparison, in terms of theme, scale and importance, between the Trojan and the Persian Wars, which were already some five decades in the past when he was at the height of his powers. The parallel was spelt out even more clearly by a famous poet who was nearly contemporary with the Persian Wars, Simonides of Keos.[8] Simonides' poem begins with a hymn to Achilles and continues with a narrative about Plataia and the victory won by the Greek commander (*strategos*, στρατηγός), Pausanias the Spartan, who is thus painted as the new Achilles.

Not only were the Persian Wars seen as a rerun of the Trojan; Alexander's expedition was too. The young king is represented, like Pausanias, as the new Achilles, though it is hard to be sure how far this was his own self-image and how far it was imposed on him by later writers like Arrian, who explicitly compared himself to Homer. But history acquires extra layers, like the stratigraphy of an archaeological site, and Alexander's expedition had a 'Persian War' as well as a 'Trojan War' aspect; his invasion was represented as revenge for 480 as well as a reprise of the war for Troy.

The events

The Graeco–Persian Wars of 500–479 BC were not fought between two simple political entities, 'Greece' and 'Persia'. The combatants on the Persian side were admittedly led by a Persian king and Persian divisional commanders, in pursuit of Persian-formulated objectives, but the armies and fleets were manned by an imperial conglomerate of subject peoples, including some Asiatic Greeks. On the opposing side, the 'Greeks' were even less of a unity. The Greek mainland and islands contained a large number of separate and in many ways independent city-states. Although they combined to repel the invaders, the coalition was fragile and temporary: some communities '*medized*', i.e. they took the Persian side,[9] often (it would seem, and as Herodotus believed, 8.30) out of dislike of a more patriotic Greek neighbour. Thus the medizing Thebans, Argives and Thessalians were long-standing enemies of the patriotic Athenians, Spartans and Phokians respectively. The unity which enabled the Greeks to win was partly cemented by, precisely, the Persian threat, and it cracked as soon as that threat receded, so that 'the Greeks' (*hoi Hellenes*, οἱ Ἕλληνες) became once again 'the Athenians' (*hoi Athênaioi*, οἱ Ἀθηναῖοι), 'the Spartans' (*hoi Lakedaimonioi*, οἱ Λακεδαιμόνιοι) and so on. But in part that unity was based on real, though episodically operative, factors making for a feeling of Greekness (*to Hellenikon*, τὸ Ἑλληνικόν). Herodotus, in a famous passage (8.144), identifies these as shared blood, customs, religion and language. He does not add, but in his narrative takes for granted, another cementing factor, namely mythical kinship or *syngeneia* (συγγένεια, that is, supposed descent from a shared mythical founder) between particular groups and cities.[10] This kind of charter myth, or myth of origins, is widespread in the ancient world. The most famous myth of origins is the story that Rome was founded by Aeneas, a refugee from Troy after Troy was sacked by the Greeks; cities which wished to ingratiate themselves with the Romans, like Lampsacus near Troy in the early second century BC, would stress the Trojan heritage which they shared with the Romans.[11] But here we should note that 'kinship' could also be used to justify *medismos* (μηδισμός), thus the Argives and Persians are both said to have been descended from the mythical hero Perseus.[12]

By Alexander's time, a century and a half after the Persian retreat from mainland Greece, the Greeks were only slightly less divided, culturally and politically (the Spartans stood superciliously aside from Alexander's expedition); and the feudally organized Macedonians themselves were not part of the Greek city-state (*polis*, πόλις) tradition. 'Standard Greek' or *koine*, κοινή (to confine ourselves to language, which is the most precisely traceable of Herodotus' four factors constituting Greekness) had begun to spread, but the process was not complete; and though Macedonian itself is now thought to have been akin to north-western Greek,[13] it remained a distinct dialect at this time. Alexander's own expedition was in some ways a counterpart not to the defensive Greek coalition of the early fifth century but to the Persian invading army of 480 BC, that is to say it was an invading multicultural conglomerate led by a feudal king newly come to the throne. As Austin has stressed for the period of Alexander and after, there was always, in ancient history, a particular need for *young* kings to prove themselves by conquest.[14]

Numbers of combatants are hard enough to establish for Alexander's expedition (the best two sources offer discrepant totals of 30,000 and 40,000 for Alexander's infantry, *pezhoi*, πεζοί) but practically impossible for the armies of the early fifth century. Herodotus gives the total of the Persian army, including non-combatant camp followers, as over 5,000,000, and it is better to simply admit ignorance than try to scale figures of this sort down rationalistically. For similar reasons it is unwise to estimate reinforcements or casualties, either for 500–479 or for 334–323. Alexander, by denuding Macedon of manpower, may have weakened it long term for the eventual struggle against Rome, so that the Persians had a sort of delayed revenge.[15] However, there may also have been significant voluntary emigration from Macedon to the new cities founded during and after Alexander's conquests.

The Persian Empire

The Persian Empire was relatively young when its leaders attacked the Greek mainland in the early fifth century BC. Cyrus the Great had founded it in the mid-sixth century; in 546 the Lydian kingdom of the cultural *philhellene* (φιλέλλην, 'Greek-loving') Croesus, including the Asiatic Greeks of the east Aegean seaboard, succumbed to Cyrus. Thereafter annexation followed annexation, most importantly that of Pharaonic Egypt in the mid-520s.

By 500 BC, this conquering pattern was so well established that it seems otiose of Herodotus to look for a special motive for the attack on the Greeks of the mainland, notably on the Athenians. He found it in an event strictly internal to the Persian Empire, the so-called Ionian Revolt of 500–494 BC. This was the name of a rising by the western Asiatic Greeks, aided by the Athenians, who claimed to have supplied the original Greek settlers or *apoikoi* (ἄποικοι) of Ionia. That is, the Athenians thought of themselves as the 'mother-city' or *metropolis* (μητρόπολις) of Ionia. Here is a very early example of 'kinship' in action, one that is difficult cynically to reinterpret as mere desire for booty.

Four years after the end of the revolt, in 490 BC, the Persian king Darius I struck at Athenians and the nearby Eretrians in ostensible revenge for the help they had given to the Ionians; but as we have seen, this may be 'over-determination' imposed by a historian deeply preoccupied with reciprocity (*tisis*, τίσις, literally 'requital') and revenge (*timoria*, τιμωρία), because Greece was hardly the first country to be so attacked by a Persian king. The invasion ended in a Persian defeat on the plain of Marathon near Athens (490 BC). The victory was not quite an Athenian monopoly – they had some *symmachoi* (σύμμαχοι, allies, literally fellow-fighters) from Plataia in Boiotia (central Greece, north of Athens). The Plataians were the perennial enemies of their more powerful fellow-Boiotian neighbours the Thebans, but it was at Athens that the victory was turned into myth.[16] Away from Athens, at the great temple complex of Delphi, the Athenians celebrated Marathon and the Athenian *strategos* (στρατηγός) Miltiades even more directly than was possible back home in semi-democratic Athens where local jealousies would have got in the way. Talk of 'propaganda' is always tricky where the ancient world is concerned,[17] but the Athenian exploitation of their Persian War role, especially Marathon, comes close to justifying the use of this modern word.

The Persians returned ten years later, by which time Darius had been succeeded by his son Xerxes whose much bigger enterprise was not just a punitive attack on Athens and Eretria but was aimed at the conquest of the whole of mainland Greece. With some help from the natural elements (part of the Persian fleet was destroyed by a storm before the battle of Artemisium, 480 BC), the Greeks won a crushing pair of naval victories. Salamis, near Athens, was the climax (also 480), fought in narrow waters which neutralized the advantage of the lighter and more manoeuvrable warships (*triereis*, τριήρεις, 'triremes') on the Persian side and turned the fighting into something resembling land fighting. By land the Persians were defeated in 479 at Plataia by an army led by the Spartan Pausanias. Greek weaponry was superior and decisive: heavily armed infantrymen (*hoplitai*, ὁπλῖται) fought against light-armed. The Persians retired from Greece, leaving behind them a smouldering heap of temples on the Athenian *akropolis* (ἀκρόπολις) or citadel. This uncharacteristic act of desecration – the sanctity of temples (*hiera*, ἱερά, literally 'sacred things/places') was normally respected by Persian commanders and governors (*satraps*, σατράπαι) – was to be of importance in the next century because it would be invoked (or exploited) by Alexander and his historians as the justification (or pretext) for the attack on Persia.

Very soon after Plataia, the Greeks, led by the Athenians, went on the offensive against the Persians. The Greeks of the east Aegean region were still vulnerable, not just from the Persians but from Pausanias, so they turned to the Athenians to ask them to take the hegemony; this marked the beginning of the Athenian empire or *arkhê* (ἀρχή). Thucydides gives a negative motive for the Greek appeal, fear of the violent (*biaios*, βίαιος), Pausanias (Spartans were often physically violent people so the word should be given some literal content), and a positive one, Ionian kinship. A prosaic and a sentimental motive: which should be preferred?

Thucydides then gives an explanation in terms of reparation for the Athenian assumption of the 'offered' hegemony, ἡγεμονία (were they merely responding to appeals?), and for their organization of the military and financial side to the new alliance. The pretext – as Thucydides calls it (*proschema*, πρόσχημα) without offering any other explanation – was to exact reparation for what they had suffered at the hands of the Persians. Morally justified booty, then, was the objective. The language of pretexts suggests, however, other and perhaps deeper motives, and these have been sought in Athenian hostility against their rivals the Spartans, or in their hypocritically concealed desire to coerce and dominate their allies or *symmachoi* (σύμμαχοι).[18] However, other evidence may suggest that Thucydides also passed over the idealistic programme of liberation (*eleutherosis*, ἐλευθέρωσις) from Persian oppression. The recently liberated peoples must also have sought means to defend themselves collectively.

Amidst the fighting over the following decades, the high point for the Greeks was the battle of Eurymedon in southern Asia Minor (early 460s); the low point was in the middle of the following decade when a huge Athenian fleet was destroyed in Egypt. Peace (*spondai*, σπονδαί, literally 'libations', a religious concept in origin) between Athenians and Persians, the so-called Peace of Kallias, seems to have been made in 450 and renewed 25 years later.[19] Peace between the Persians and Spartans was longer coming; in a sense hostilities were not terminated until 411, when the Spartans needed Persian money to defeat the Athenians. But the Athenians, not the half-heartedly imperialistic Spartans,[20] were the main enemy the Persians had to reckon with, and to that extent the Peace of Kallias is the real watershed. The 411 deal between the Persians and Spartans was finalized only in 386, by the King's Peace, which settled that Sparta's hegemony in Greece would be recognized by the Persian king on condition that Asia Minor was acknowledged as Persian property. This was the diplomatic state of affairs still obtaining when Alexander crossed to Asia in 334 BC. Eleven years later, when he died in his thirty-third year, he had conquered everything as far as the north-west frontier of India. (India itself had been a Persian satrapy or province in the time of Darius and Xerxes, but had slipped away from Persian control by the second half of the fourth century.)

Reasons for Alexander's wars

Alexander 'inherited' his father's war, just as Xerxes had inherited that of Darius. Alexander of Macedon did not himself initiate the war with the Persian Empire; he invaded it because his father Philip (assassinated in 336 BC) had already planned and begun the invasion. But dead people's decisions can be reversed, and as with Xerxes' invasion of 480 we cannot be solely content with the idea of an inherited war. Other motives were given or can be suggested. For instance, the Macedonian overrunning of Asia can be seen as a response to a fourth-century BC population explosion such as had happened some centuries earlier when the Macedonians settled Phrygia in central Anatolia;[21] thus Alexander's expedition was just another eastward movement of overly populous peoples, but this time the basic cause was justified in terms appropriate to an age with a developed consciousness of myth, literature (Alexander as Achilles) – and history. Thus one essential element in Alexander's justificatory manifesto was the concept of revenge for what the Persians had done in 480, especially the burning of the Athenian temples. That is, a religious motive was present, even though Polybius (see p. 62f) claimed this was a mere pretext, giving the perceived weakness of the Persian Empire as the real reason. Modern enquirers[22] have pushed the implications of this further and insisted on the booty factor. This hardly conflicts with the Homeric image of Alexander, because the epic poems are themselves full of references to spoils, ransom and the material perquisites of victory, above all chattel slaves (*douloi*, δοῦλοι).[23] Alexander's great victories, above all those at Granicus (334), Issus (333) and Gaugamela (331), gave him control of huge but unfortunately unquantifiable accumulated riches, specifically bullion. The conquest was not only justified in terms of traditional Greek religion; it also changed that religion. The god Dionysus' main traditional provinces were theatre, wine, ecstatic possession and the afterlife. In the Hellenistic period, after Alexander's death, he acquired a fifth and entirely new aspect by becoming associated with the conquest of India in particular and with Alexander's Eastern conquests generally, and thence by extension with Eastern imperial aspirations by successors of Alexander.[24]

By 331 BC the Persian Empire had ceased to exist, or rather Alexander had taken it over; but Persians continued as a social presence in the Near East and beyond:[25] this was not a war of extermination, rather it involved the demotion of an élite,[26] and the Persian Wars lived on, in cult and commemoration. Plataia, the home of the Athenians' helpers at Marathon in 490 and the site of the great military success of 479, became a place of virtual pilgrimage. In the third century BC, as we know from an inscription on stone published as recently as 1975, there was a cult of 'Zeus the Liberator [*Eleutherios*, Ἐλευθέριος, i.e. from the Persian threat] and the concord [*homonoia*, ὁμόνοια] of the Greeks' and an athletic contest (*agon*, ἀγών) 'which the Greeks celebrate on the tombs of the heroes who fought against the barbarians for the liberty of the Greeks'.[27] The notion of *homonoia* (ὁμόνοια) was an adaptable one; the Persians had become a convenient vehicle for aspirations of Greek solidarity in the face of new and different threats (the context of the inscription is the Chremonidean War, fought against Macedon by Athens, Sparta and other Greek *poleis* (πόλεις) with the support of Ptolemy II of Egypt). The Romans perpetuated the theme further: the poet Horace, writing in the time of the Emperor Augustus (sole ruler from 31 BC to AD 14), could describe the Parthians as 'Persians' without mental dislocation, and both he and his contemporary Virgil draw on the theme of Alexander-as-Dionysus as a way of pointing their own ruler in the direction of Eastern campaigns, or simply of flattering him as if he had already been an Eastern conqueror. (Actually Augustus' successes against the Parthians were diplomatic not military, the retrieval of some military standards, *signa*, humiliatingly lost in the previous generation.) It has been suggested that one reason why the Romans adopted the 'Persian Wars tradition' so energetically was to make themselves more acceptable to their Greek subjects; the anti-barbarian torch had passed to a new civilization.[28]

Causes and motives

To a twentieth-century materialist or 'Realist' view of international relations, it may seem naive and absurd that the above sections permit the slightest doubt about the central relevance of booty and desire for territorial annexation, perhaps driven by demographic pressure. Just as the Macedonians had spilled over into Anatolia centuries before Alexander, a similar long perspective is available for the understanding of the eastward movement of Greeks into the new city foundations of Asia Minor, the Levant and Egypt, in and after the late fourth century BC (see above,

p. 52). Greece was a poor country and it was natural for its inhabitants to look east for fertile land. The Greeks had settled in Ionia early in the first millennium BC; the Athenian pamphleteer Isocrates, in 346 BC, had urged a similar policy of western Anatolian conquest and colonization on Alexander's father Philip (5.120). Alexander's conquests made it possible.

Materialistic, narrowly selfish explanations appeal to 'Realist' interpreters of ancient imperialism, especially those who derive their knowledge of the politics and warfare of ancient Greece from a reading[29] of Thucydides with his apparent modernity, sophistication and secularism. It is, as the sociologist and ancient historian Moses Finley remarked,[30] to Thucydides (6.24) that we owe one of the most explicit ancient statements of the booty motive for undertaking an ancient war, the Athenian expedition against Sicily in 415 BC. But first, it is a great mistake to regard the usually sceptical Thucydides as a typical Greek or even a typical Athenian in his attitude to religion.[31] The Greek for 'religion' was *to theion* (τò θεῖον); thus Thucydides says, 'the Spartans marched to the sound of flutes not for the sake of τò θεῖον. but to keep in step' (5.70). There is admittedly some reason to believe that the generality of Athenians was more 'enlightened' than that of say Corinthians or Spartans. But it is the same Thucydides who reports, with perhaps embarrassed brevity (5.32), that in 420 BC the Athenians reinstated some evicted Delians on Apollo's sacred island of Delos because they were mindful of their reverses in the Peloponnesian War so far and because the god Apollo had told them to do so. Second, Thucydides is a slippery writer with more than one literary and emotional register, certainly capable of pages of brisk, shrewd and factual military narrative, but equally capable of superstitiously asserting in his own person (i.e. not merely when reporting a speech or a collective decision) that the Peloponnesian War was accompanied by an unusual number of *earthquakes*. Most relevant of all to our present enquiry, he is aware of kinship diplomacy and refers to it casually and often.[32]

Sentimental, mythical and religious motives have featured extensively in the narrative above; they do not exclude factors like desire for booty, but they deserve some weight – more than even Polybius was prepared to grant. If more attention has been paid to them – and in particular to 'kinship diplomacy' – in the past decade or so, that has been because of the chance of epigraphic finds, in which the theme of kinship is stressed as a motive for action.[33] But the literary evidence has always been there (see n.32 above). Moreover, the New Simonides entitles us to insist, more forcefully than before, that the Persian Wars were from a very early date perceived as a reprise of the Trojan. Alexander's imitation of Achilles may have been posturing by him or flattery by his historians, but his actual treatment of the Asia Minor cities shows that one clearly identifiable principle was especially favourable treatment of those with a 'good record' from the time of the Ionian Revolt.[34] In addition, Alexander's desire for the Athenian fleet or at least Athenian neutrality in the impending war may be relevant to his altruistic desire to avenge the impiety perpetrated on the temples of the Athenian acropolis so long ago.

In this or any other historical enquiry about the motives for collective action, one must doubt that groups of people act from identical motives even when they agree on a course of action (and not even Darius or Alexander are represented as in sole control of events, without benefit of advisers). Complexity of motive means two things: the same person usually acts from a mixture of motives, and two or more people act from motives different from each other, or blended in different proportions. This may seem obvious, but it is surprising how often this fact is ignored by historians and international relations theorists, especially the self-styled 'Realists'. One answer to our problem then, and a plausible one, is that at Athens and Sparta, and perhaps Persia too, there were some who were more keen on booty and others who genuinely saw things in terms of kinship, Homer, revenge or whatever. Thucydides, in the passage about Sicily and 415 BC mentioned above, does in fact attribute different motives to different groups, including desire for the sight of exotic foreign places; he confines the enrichment motif to the masses. This is a rare acknowledgement of a mass motive. On the whole the information we have from the ancient world about motives for undertaking wars relates to élites; we have little information about collective mentalities. The Classical Athenians came closest[35] to involving the whole (male, citizen) population in its decision-making processes, but even here there is dispute about how far foreign policy decisions were a matter of genuine popular decision[36] and how far they were determined by political leaders.[37] A compromise view stresses the influence and advice of regional experts.[38]

Can we then (to take this line of approach further) say that sophisticated élites and leaders thought and behaved in one selfish way, but felt it necessary to ice the cake with myth and religion for consumption by the superstitious masses? Cynical leaders there certainly were, but there are clear counter-cases: Thucydides says that Perdikkas, late fifth-century king of Macedon, acted in a certain way because the Argives (the people of Argos in the Peloponnese) were doing so, 'and he was ancestrally an Argive' (5.80). As the myth of Argive descent applied only to the Macedonian kings, not to the mass of their subjects, no cake was being iced here. In any case, there are occasions (see above, p. 52, for the Athenian help to the Ionian Revolt in 500 BC) where both leaders and led seemed to act for sentimental or religious reasons which did not obviously serve their own narrow interests.[39] And it would (see n.5 above for classical Athens) be a mistake to suppose that arguments in terms of mythology can have appealed only to élites.

Another explanatory route is to stress development of attitudes over time. We have seen that Herodotus and Simonides talk in terms of chronic East–West conflict; was this picture of hostility (*echthos*, ἔχθος),[40] true to the reality of attitudes? An influential monograph, whose title *Inventing the*

Barbarian says it all, has argued the contrary; that there were, so to speak, no barbarians in the world before the fifth-century Persian Wars generated the idea, and polarized Greek and non-Greek.[41] There are difficulties with this, such as Homer's reference to 'barbarian-speaking Carians' in Asia Minor, and his distinctive treatment of Trojan ritual, but we can accept that attitudes evolved. It has even been argued[42] that the East–West, Greek–Persian stereotypes were being challenged as early as Herodotus, though Herodotus is a writer of prodigious and exceptional sophistication, and the challenge would make no sense unless the stereotype was itself very prevalent. In the decades before Alexander, there is plenty of evidence (e.g. in Xenophon) that Greek (especially Spartan) and Persian élites found themselves naturally and comfortably on the same cultural wavelength;[43] but again, ordinary Greek attitudes may have been different. As for Alexander, he may have started out with the idea of a pan-Hellenic (all-Greek) crusade against Persia, but he soon claimed to be the new legitimate king of Persia and heir to the Achaemenids, and by the end of his short life he had moved some way towards integrating the Persian ruling class (see n.26 above). Finally, we have seen that by the Roman period new enemies could be defined as Persian long after the Persian Empire proper was dead.

In conclusion, the East–West, Greek–Persian conflict is more than the history of an idea: real blood was spilt at Plataia and Gaugamela; real booty was carried off after those battles. But in evaluating the causes and course of the conflict it would be wrong to deny force to considerations of myth and religion, or to treat kinship diplomacy as merely sentimental decoration.

Notes

1 E. Said, *Orientalism: Western Conceptions of the Orient*, Harmondsworth, Penguin, 1979.
2 For readable and recent modern accounts of the Persian Wars see J. F. Lazenby, *The Defence of Greece*, Warminster, Aris & Phillips, 1993; P. Green, *The Greco–Persian Wars*, Berkeley, University of California Press, 1996; for Alexander's campaigns see A. B. Bosworth, *Conquest and Empire*, Cambridge, Cambridge University Press, 1988, or more briefly in D. M. Lewis, J. Boardman, S. Hornblower and M. Ostwald (eds), *Cambridge Ancient History*, vol. 6, 2nd edn, Cambridge, Cambridge University Press, 1994, chs 16 and 17.
3 W. K. Pritchett, *The Greek State at War*, 5 vols, Berkeley, University of California Press, 1971–90, vol. 5, pp. 68–152.
4 M. I. Finley, *Ancient History: Evidence and Models*, London, Chatto & Windus, 1985; M. M. Austin, 'Hellenistic kings, war and the economy', *Classical Quarterly*, 1986, vol. 36, pp. 450–66 and M. M. Austin, 'Alexander and the Macedonian invasion of Asia: aspects of the historiography of war and empire in antiquity', in J. Rich and G. Shipley (eds), *War and Society in the Greek World*, London and New York, Routledge, 1993, pp. 197–223.
5 The question of decision-making is related (see below): was it always carried out by élites and individuals, or was there mass involvement? (The latter possibility really arises only for democratic Athens.) The two questions are related because

some of the themes (e.g. themes drawn from mythology) which we find in ancient Greek orators and historians, and adduced as motives for action, might be assumed to have élite rather than popular appeal. But for Athens, at any rate, this is only an assumption: Greek tragedies were almost entirely mythical in content and their performances were attended by five-figure audiences whose make-up was similar to those of the political assemblies.

6 O. Murray, 'Herodotus and oral history', in H. Sancisi-Weerdenburg and A. Kuhrt (eds), *Achaemenid History II: The Greek Sources*, Nederlands Instituut voor het nabije oosten, Leiden, 1987, p. 110, drawing on D. M. Lewis, 'Persians in Herodotus', in P. J. Rhodes (ed.), *Selected Papers in Greek and Near Eastern History*, Cambridge, Cambridge University Press, 1997 (originally published 1985), pp. 345–61.

7 Helen was wife of Agamemnon's brother Menelaus (and became 'Helen of Troy' only as a result of the abduction).

8 Whose substantial fragment of a narrative poem about the battle or *mache* of Plataia (the culminating Greek victory over Persian forces, in 479 BC) was published in only 1992 from a papyrus copy; see P. J. Parsons, '3965. Simonides, Elegies', *Oxyrhynchus Papyri* 59, 1992, 4–50; D. Boedeker and D. Sider (eds), *The New Simonides*, New York, Oxford University Press, 2001, including S. Hornblower, 'Epic and Epiphanies'.

9 See above, p. 48, for the way the Greeks sometimes used 'Mede' to mean 'Persian'.

10 C. P. Jones, *Kinship Diplomacy in Greco–Roman Antiquity*, Harvard, Harvard University Press, 1999; O. Curty, *Les parentés légendaires entre cités grecques: catalogue raisonnée des inscriptions contenant le terme* ΣΥΓΓΕΝΕΙΑ *et analyse critique*, Geneva, Droz, 1995; S. Hornblower, 'Propaganda', in S. Hornblower and A. Spawforth (eds), *Oxford Classical Dictionary*, Oxford, Oxford University Press, 1996, pp. 61–80.

11 E. S. Gruen, *Studies in Greek Culture and Roman Policy*, Leiden, Brill, 1990, p. 14.

12 In this paragraph I have written, for instance, of 'the Argives', not of 'Argos'. This is in order to avoid the misleading suggestion that decision-making in these communities was monolithic. Even 'the Argives' is usually misleading shorthand for 'a majority of decision-making male Argives'. The ancient Greeks themselves were inconsistent in their terminology; they usually spoke, for example, of 'the Athenians' (not 'Athens') as the agent, but equally Thucydides can say 'Stagiros [not 'the Stagirans'] revolted from Athens' (4.88).

13 O. Masson, 'Macedonian language', in S. Hornblower and A. Spawforth (eds), *Oxford Classical Dictionary*, Oxford, Oxford University Press, 1996.

14 Austin, 'Hellenistic kings, war and the economy' (above, n.4).

15 Diodorus (18.12.2), drawing on a good near-contemporary source, Hieronymus of Cardia; A. B. Bosworth, 'Alexander the Great and the decline of Macedon', *Journal of Hellenic Studies*, 1986, vol. 106, pp. 1–12.

16 J. Boardman, 'The Parthenon frieze: another view', in *Festschrift für Frank Brommer*, Mainz, 1977, pp. 39–49 for the idea that the 192 horsemen (ἱππεῖς) of the Parthenon frieze represent the Athenian dead at Marathon, though other interpretations are also and perhaps simultaneously possible.

17 Hornblower, 'Propaganda' (above, n.10).

18 S. Hornblower, *The Greek World 479–323 BC*, 2nd edn, London, Routledge, 1991, p. 26; see also S. Hornblower, *A Commentary on Thucydides*, vol. 1, Books i–iii, revised paperback edn, Oxford, Oxford University Press, 1997, commentary on Thucydides i. 96 and 97, where the extensive modern literature is cited.

19 There is some uncertainty because Thucydides, our main and best source, does not mention either the peace or its renewal where we would expect. See 'Callias, peace of' in S. Hornblower and A. Spawforth (eds), *Oxford Classical Dictionary*, Oxford, Oxford University Press, 1996, and G. L. Cawwell, 'The peace between Athens and Persia', *Phoenix*, 1997, vol. 51, pp. 115–30.

60   *Simon Hornblower*

20 A. Andrewes, 'Spartan imperialism?', in P. Garnsey and C. R. Whittaker (eds), *Imperialism in the Ancient World*, Cambridge, Cambridge University Press, 1976, pp. 91–102.

21 S. Hornblower, 'Epilogue', in D. M. Lewis, J. Boardman, S. Hornblower and M. Ostwald (eds), *Cambridge Ancient History*, 2nd edn, vol. 6, Cambridge, Cambridge University Press, 1994, pp. 876–81.

22 Austin, 'Alexander and the Macedonian invasion of Asia' (above, n.4).

23 It was a quarrel between Achilles and Agamemnon about allocation of human booty of this sort which led Achilles to sulk in his tent and so provide the plot of the poem. Fifth-century Greek tragedy, which owes so much to epic, likewise insists that war entailed the transfer of human property; Euripides' play *Trojan Women* (415 BC) is the starkest expression of this motif.

24 Therefore images of Dionysus feature so prominently in the precious surviving account of an imperialistically boastful πομπή or procession celebrated by Ptolemy II at Alexandria in the third century BC; see E. E. Rice, *The Grand Procession of Ptolemy Philadelphus*, Oxford, Oxford University Press, 1983.

25 See the inscription from Afghanistan cited in S. Hornblower, *The Greek World 479–323 BC*, 2nd edn, London, Routledge, 1991, p. 275.

26 The extent to which Alexander and his successors aimed at or achieved integration between the higher echelons of Greeks and Macedonians on the one hand and of Persians on the other is a disputed topic: A. B. Bosworth, 'Alexander and the Iranians', *Journal of Hellenic Studies*, 1980, vol. 100, pp. 1–21, reacting against the excesses of Sir W. W. Tarn; but see D. M. Lewis, *Sparta and Persia*, Leiden, Brill, 1977, pp. 148–52. The scholarly fashion has swung away from acceptance of a 'policy of fusion' towards seeing the measures in question as repressive devices overinterpreted by modern panegyrists; but there is no doubt that Alexander adopted some elements of Persian dress and favoured those of his friends and subordinates who followed him in 'going Persian'.

27 M. M. Austin, *The Hellenistic World*, Cambridge, Cambridge University Press, 1983.

28 A. Spawforth in S. Hornblower (ed.), *Greek Historiography*, Oxford, 1994, pp. 233–47.

29 See e.g. K. Waltz, *Theory of International Politics*, Reading, MA, Addison Wesley, 1979; R. Gilpin, *War and Change in World Politics*, Cambridge, Cambridge University Press, 1981; J. Nye, Jr., 'Neorealism and neoliberalism', in *World Politics*, January 1988, vol. 40, no. 2; R. Jervis, 'Realism, game theory, and cooperation', in *World Politics*, April 1988, vol. 40, no. 3; R. N. Lebow and B. S. Strauss (eds), *Hegemonic Rivalry: From Thucydides to the Nuclear Age*, Boulder, CO, Westview Press, 1991; D. Kagan, *On the Origins of War*, London, Pimlico, 1995; R. O. Keohane (ed.), *Neorealism and its Critics*, New York, Columbia University Press, 1996; S. Constantinides and A. Platias, 'Thucydides: the classical theorist of international relations', *Hellenic Studies*, Autumn 1998, vol. 6, no. 2.

30 Finley, *Ancient History*, p. 77.

31 S. Hornblower, 'The religious dimension to the Peloponnesian War, or, what Thucydides does not tell us', *Harvard Studies in Classical Philology*, 1992, vol. 94, pp. 169–97.

32 S. Hornblower, 'Propaganda', in S. Hornblower and A. Spawforth (eds), *Oxford Classical Dictionary*, Oxford, Oxford University Press, 1996, pp. 61–80. For example, Thucydides tells us that Anaxarchos the Theban, i.e. a Boiotian, was put in command of exiles from Methymna on the island of Lesbos, 'because of kinship' (8.100), taking for granted that we know that in the prehistoric period of Greek history the Boiotians supposedly colonized the north-east Aegean island of Lesbos and the mainland opposite, and so counted as the 'mother-city' (*metropolis*) of the Methymnans.

33 The chief new text is a late third-century BC inscription found at Xanthos in southern Turkey, Curty: *Les parentés légendaires* no. 75, concerning an appeal for financial help to the Xanthians by the people of Kytinion in central Greece. Kinship arguments feature prominently.

34 E. Badian, 'Alexander the Great and the Greeks of Asia', in E. Badian (ed.), *Ancient Society and Institutions: Studies Presented to Victor Ehrenberg*, Oxford, Blackwell, 1967, pp. 37–69; Bosworth, *Conquest and Empire*, p. 250f.

35 The Macedonian army assembly had certain attested powers (acclaiming kings, rejecting proposals, acting as a criminal court) but these powers limited the power of the monarch only on rare occasions.

36 P. Harding, 'Athenian foreign policy in the fourth century', *Klio*, 1995, vol. 77, 105–25; J. Ober, *Mass and Elite in Democratic Athens: Rhetoric, Ideology, and the Power of the People*, Princeton, NJ, Princeton University Press, 1989.

37 L. Kallet-Marx, 'Money talks: rhetor, demos and the resources of the Athenian empire', in R. Osborne and S. Hornblower (eds), *Ritual, Finance, Politics: Athenian Democratic Accounts Presented to David Lewis*, Oxford, Oxford University Press, 1994, pp. 324–31, and L. Kallet-Marx, 'Institutions, ideology and political consciousness in ancient Greece: some recent books on Athenian democracy', *Journal of the History of Ideas*, 1994, pp. 307–35, criticizing Ober.

38 S. Hornblower (ed.), *Greek Historiography*, Oxford, Oxford University Press, 1994, p. 147f.

39 See H. Popp, 'Die Einwirkung von Vorzeichen, Opfern und Festen auf die Kriegführung der Griechen im 5. und 4. Jahrhundert v. Chr' (diss. Erlangen, 1957); A. J. Holladay and M. Goodman, 'Religious scruples in ancient warfare', *Classical Quarterly*, 1986, vol. 36, pp. 151–71, for the dynamics of religious scruples in ancient warfare.

40 The adjective and adjectival noun corresponding to this abstract noun is *echthros*, one of the two standard words for 'enemy', the other being *polemios*, from *polemos*, 'war'.

41 E. Hall, *Inventing the Barbarian*, Oxford, Oxford University Press, 1989.

42 C. Pelling, 'East is East and West is West – or are they? National stereotypes in Herodotus', *Histos*, 1997, vol. 1.

43 D. M. Lewis, *Sparta and Persia*, Leiden, Brill, 1977, pp. 148–52.

5 Warfare and external relations in the middle Roman Republic

John Rich

Introduction

The course of Roman expansion has been outlined above (pp. 27–31). The focus in this chapter will be on the warfare of the period 264–133 BC, for several reasons. First, this was the period of the decisive wars which established Roman mastery of the Mediterranean world. Second, it was a period of political stability. The aspirations of individual members of the elite were already an important element, but these were held in check by their rivals and by the collective interest. In the first century, by contrast, the unfettered ambitions of individual dynasts like Pompey and Caesar were a major motive force in the wars of expansion. Third, the period is comparatively well documented (although our information does have tantalizing gaps and limitations, notably the shortage of contemporary Roman witnesses).[1]

A few relevant documents (e.g. treaty texts) survive for the warfare of 264–133, on inscriptions or cited by historians. For the most part, however, we are dependent on historical writers, above all the Greek Polybius (*c.*200–120 BC), who wrote a universal history for the years 264–146. Polybius was a very well-placed observer. He was also an intelligent and enquiring writer, and, although generally favourable to the Romans, does not hesitate to criticize them on occasion. Unfortunately, his history is intact only for the period down to 216, and thereafter survives only in extracts. More of his work is preserved indirectly by Livy, who under Augustus wrote a vast history of Rome, one of the surviving portions of which covers the period 218–167. On internal events and warfare in Italy and the West, Livy mainly used earlier Roman historians of the first century BC, who were only too ready to improve the record for rhetorical effect or the greater glory of Rome. Where neither Polybius nor Livy are extant, we have to make do with inferior sources, such as Diodorus, Appian and brief epitomes of Livy.

Was it inevitable that, having conquered Italy, the Roman Republic would go on to fight and defeat the other powers of the Mediterranean world? Or was this development a contingent event, which owed as much to chance and to the actions and attitudes of their enemies as to the Romans themselves? These questions, and the related issue of the Romans' motives for undertaking their mid-republican wars, have been debated since Polybius' day. He several times enunciates the theory that the Romans in the years 218–167 pursued and achieved the goal of world rule. However, even in the fragmentary state in which his work has survived, it seems clear that he did not establish full coherence between this theory and his detailed interpretations of individual wars.[2]

In modern times, it was until recently orthodox to hold that mid-republican Roman imperialism was essentially defensive. The principal factor which led the Romans to undertake their wars was, it was held, the fear (sometimes well-grounded, sometimes mistaken) of powerful neighbours. Some writers also stressed the importance of accident and misunderstanding.[3] A thoroughgoing attack on this view was mounted by Harris.[4] Stressing the Romans' habituation to continuous warfare and minimizing the defensive motive, Harris argued that the most important factor in bringing about the wars was their desire for the glory and economic benefits which successful warfare conferred. Harris' work has sparked off a lively debate: the old 'defensive imperialism' view still has its champions, but for many, Harris' thesis continues to have a powerful appeal.[5] In my view, both of these interpretations share the same defect: both offer too monocausal an explanation of a highly complex phenomenon.[6]

Enemies of Rome

Rome's enemies in their wars of the mid-republican period differed greatly in their level of political organization and cultural development. In the north and west, their opponents were mainly tribal societies. Elsewhere there were more complex entities – there was Carthage, like Rome itself a city-state ruling an empire, and there were kings ruling portions of the former empire of Alexander. The Romans knew nothing of the language and little of the culture of most of the societies with whom their wars brought them into contact, except when dealing with Greeks, first in southern Italy and Sicily and later in the Greek east. Rome had been receptive to Greek cultural influences from very early times, and by the later third century their impact had become profound: by then many, if not most, elite Romans had some knowledge of Greek, and the first Roman literature was being produced on Greek models.[7]

The Romans themselves behaved quite differently towards tribal enemies than towards the more highly developed entities. In areas where a province had already been established (as in second-century Spain), decisions about warfare against tribes were normally taken by the commander on the spot without consulting the authorities in Rome, and the war aim was generally to secure unconditional surrender (*deditio*). By contrast, wars against enemies like Carthage and the Hellenistic kings were normally preceded by diplomatic exchanges and authorized by war votes passed in the Senate and in the assembly of the Roman people, and commonly ended with a formal peace treaty.[8]

The Romans' wars against Hellenistic kings were fought out in the world of the Greek city-states, some of them subject to the kings, others either independent or members of leagues. Few of these states counted for much militarily, but Greek sensitivities could hardly be ignored. This, rather than (as the proponents of the 'defensive imperialism' thesis maintained) a reluctance to annex, is the reason why the Romans avoided establishing provinces east of the Adriatic for so long. For them to have retained territory would have played into the hands of those who denounced them as barbarian conquerors. Instead, they were able to seize the high moral ground by claiming to be liberators of Greece, in conformity with a long-established Greek tradition. At the same time, they made it clear that, in return for this benefaction, they expected loyalty from their Greek friends. The liberation policy was thus the means by which the Romans established their hegemony over the Greek world.

Roman sources generally represent all their wars as a response to enemy aggression. These claims are often heavily distorted, but expansionism and belligerence on their enemies' part was certainly one factor in bringing about many of the wars. At least some, and perhaps most, of their wars against tribal societies were a response to enemy raiding. In my view, Polybius was right to hold that the Barcids' aim in expanding the Carthaginian empire in Spain after the First Punic War was to equip Carthage for an expected renewal of the conflict with Rome.[9] Most Hellenistic kings aspired to be successful military leaders,[10] and it so happened that those whom the Romans encountered in their first involvement in the East, namely Philip V and Antiochus III, were among the most restless and enterprising monarchs of the Hellenistic period.

It was no accident that none of their opponents proved a match for the Romans. The Republic was a unitary state with a strongly developed civic ethos, well-organized and disciplined armies, and huge resources of manpower. All free-born citizens who met a (low) property qualification were liable to serve in the legions, and a similar duty was imposed on the Italian allies. By contrast, Carthage had a much smaller citizen body and formed her armies mainly from mercenaries and subject allies. The Roman victories in both the First and Second Punic Wars were due above all to the fact that they had greater resources than Carthage to survive a war of attrition. Only the Macedonian kings had at their disposal a national army comparable to that of Rome, but their manpower resources were not on the same scale, and their victory at Pydna finally proved the superiority of the legion over the phalanx.

The human cost of Rome's wars for their enemies and the peoples over whose lands the wars were fought, though unquantifiable, was immense. This appears most vividly in their treatment of captured cities. The Romans (unlike the Greeks) regarded themselves as under an obligation (which they

usually observed) to respect the lives of the inhabitants when the unconditional surrender (*deditio*) of a city had been accepted. But when a
city was taken by force, its inhabitants were usually subjected to the full
rigours of the laws of war, recognized by all the peoples of the ancient
Mediterranean world. What distinguished the Romans' conduct in such
cases was the maintenance of discipline, though this was doubtless exaggerated in the famous account of Polybius (10.15–16). The sack began
with a killing spree in which, according to Polybius, not even animals were
spared. Then, after a signal from the commander, the troops turned to
the systematic collection of plunder. The survivors, unless ransomed, were
sold into slavery.[11]

A society geared for war

From the mid-fourth century onwards, the forces of the Roman Republic
were engaged in warfare almost every year, sometimes in several spheres
at once. It has been estimated that from the later third century to the end
of the Republic, the median size of the Roman army amounted to some
13 per cent of all adult male citizens, with significantly higher proportions
being attained at peak periods like the Hannibalic War and some years
in the early second century.[12] No other state in history has sustained so
high a level of military participation over so long a period.

In the Second Punic War, the Romans suffered heavy casualties, particularly in the early years.[13] Serious casualties were also suffered at times in
the second-century wars, notably in the mid-century campaigns in Spain
and at Arausio in 105 at the hands of the Cimbri. Long terms of military
service will have undermined the viability of some peasant farms. None the
less, most Roman citizens of the middle Republic probably did well out of
the constant warfare. In most of the second-century wars, Roman casualties were probably light. Successful war brought booty, and down to the
170s there was regular allotment of lands confiscated from defeated enemies in Italy. Some of the proceeds which accrued to the state treasury from
booty, indemnities and provincial taxes were used for the citizens' benefit,
on public works at Rome and, from 167, the remission of direct taxation.

Only once did the assembly of the Roman people reject a war vote,
namely against Macedon in 200. This reflected war-weariness after the
long struggle of the Second Punic War, and the assembly was soon talked
round. All the other war votes were passed unopposed, and in 264 the
assembly is said to have overruled the Senate in deciding to send help to
Messana, enticed by the prospect of booty.[14] Resistance to the levy occasionally occurred when wars were going badly, but, when a lucrative war
was in prospect, men rushed to hand in their names.[15]

Among the well-to-do, many were able to enrich themselves from army
supply contracts, from which senators were debarred.[16] But the greatest
rewards of continuous war went to the political elite, who held the

magistracies and (after attaining junior office) sat in the Senate. Although outsiders were not excluded, this elite had a strongly hereditary character: most senators were of senatorial family, and over the period 200–50 BC some four-fifths of those who held the consulship, the highest magistracy, had a consular ancestor.[17] Until the first century, all members of this elite had extensive military experience: the completion of ten years' service was a prerequisite for candidates for political office. Military command was normally exercised by the senior magistrates (there was no separate military class at Rome). Commanders were entitled to retain a share of their booty for their personal use, and there were great opportunities for enrichment (legitimate and illegitimate) from provincial revenues. There is a good deal of evidence for the increased wealth of the elite, expended on conspicuous consumption or invested principally in land, in the second century, and even larger fortunes were amassed in the first century. However, the rewards of successful warfare were not only material. Within the elite, there was intense competition, both for office and for personal glory, and the aristocratic ethos put strong pressure on individual elite members to excel, and by so doing to enhance their family's distinction. Although honour could also be won in civil life, for example, through oratory, the pre-eminent way to win glory was in war, in youth as a valiant soldier and later as a victorious commander. Victory in war was celebrated by a triumph, in which the returning victor processed through the city followed by his troops and a parade of his booty, and many went on to build a monument, usually a temple, from their spoils.[18]

Roman society in the middle Republic was thus geared to war. There was a war (usually successful) almost every year, and men at all levels in society, and particularly in the political elite, expected to continue to enjoy the benefits of victorious war. These factors must have played a very important part in accounting for the wars themselves: if they had not been so habituated to successful war and its benefits, the Romans would not have been so ready to discern and take up occasions for war. However, other factors also played a part, and the contribution of Roman militarism to the causation of their wars has been exaggerated by Harris and North.[19] I have discussed this at length elsewhere,[20] and can only indicate some of the main points here.

By the second century, there was no need for the Romans to seek out wars: their far-flung imperial commitments ensured that there was generally no shortage of wars for them to fight. Roman warfare and expansion was not as continuous a process as is sometimes suggested. There were some comparatively peaceful periods, and overall there was less warfare and fewer triumphs in the period 167–91 BC than in the early second century. Some regions long escaped Roman attentions, for example, northern Spain and the Alps, which could have been a fertile source of triumphs, but in fact remained unpacified and virtually ignored until the reign of Augustus. Aristocratic emulation was a factor which cut both ways: individuals might aspire to military glory, but their rivals might seek to deny it to them. Only one in four second-century consuls celebrated a triumph, and the right to triumph was often hotly disputed.

As we have noted, wars against tribal enemies were commonly initiated by the commander in the region, for example, in Spain. There was a natural temptation for a commander to pick a fight with a tribe in the hope of winning booty and a triumph. We know of some instances where this happened (sometimes causing a scandal) and a substantial number of others must have occurred. None the less, it is striking that many commanders in provinces which might have offered such opportunities appear to have passed their time in office peacefully: for example, there was little warfare in Spain in the years 178–154 and again after 133. Why this should be so is not clear; one factor may be commanders' fear of scandal.

The most important wars, for example, against Carthage and the Hellenistic kings, were decided at Rome in the Senate, with the assembly rubber-stamping the decision. Very often the Senate's decision came after a lengthy diplomatic process, which may in the end have left them little choice. We are very poorly informed about senatorial debate on issues of war and peace, but it seems likely that it was conducted mainly in terms of ethical and prudential considerations. Whatever views they expressed, many senators' votes in favour of war may in fact have been coloured by their expectation of profit for themselves or their friends. At each such meeting, however, there would have been more senators who did not stand to profit, and some for whom war would mean the advancement of their personal enemies. It therefore seems likely that in most decisions which led directly or indirectly to war, most senators' votes were determined less by the hope of personal advantage than by their judgement of what was right and/or in the public interest.

Religion, justice and the public interest

Religious observances played an important part in every aspect of Roman warfare, from the departing commander's vows in the temple of Jupiter on the Capitol, to the dedication in that same temple which formed the culmination of a returning victor's triumph.[21] Roman religion was primarily a matter of ritual and observance, and the Romans had no hostility to other people's gods; indeed, they occasionally used a special ritual, *evocatio*, to bring to Rome the gods of communities they had destroyed.[22] Accordingly, religion never played a part in bringing about their wars, apart from the exceptional case of the Jewish revolts in the imperial period: the exclusive monotheism of the Jews, unique in the Roman world, led to intermittent conflict with their pagan neighbours and with the Roman authorities' demands for cultic demonstrations of loyalty.

The Romans had special priests, the *fetiales*, responsible for external relations, whose duties included the solemnizing of treaties and declarations of war. According to our sources, the ritual for declaring war opened with a Roman demand for satisfaction for enemy offences, and, if this was refused, continued with an appeal to the gods as witnesses to the justness of the Romans' cause. This ritual may have originated in very early times as a means by which the Romans and neighbouring communities controlled private raiding, and it had ceased to be observed long before the over-seas wars began.[23] None the less, the fetial tradition continued to affect Roman conceptions of the just war. Cicero fused these with Greek influences in passages in his philosophical works, which, mediated by Augustine, helped to shape the medieval just war theory. Roman historians were eager to represent Rome's wars as just, often by flagrant distortions of the evidence. We need not doubt that at Senate meetings which decided on wars, those who voted for war were convinced of the justice of their cause. At least one war, the Third Punic War, seems to have been delayed by scruples over its justice.[24]

The Romans also set much store by their reputation for Faith (*Fides*), already celebrated on a third-century coin of the southern Italian city of Locris, and the occasion for a number of their wars was provided by an appeal for assistance from a new or established friend. The roles of Messana and Saguntum in the first two Punic Wars are notable instances, though in the latter case Rome did not act until it was too late for Saguntum. Cicero made one of the speakers in his dialogue *On the Republic* claim that 'our people gained possession of the world by defending allies'.[25]

Polybius frequently attributes Roman actions to fear, and it is clear from Roman writers that claims that another power was a threat were a common part of the discourse of their external policy. Sometimes such claims were disingenuous, as when Caesar used them to justify his wars of conquest in Gaul.[26] There is no reason, however, to doubt that such beliefs were sometimes sincerely held by the Romans and played a significant part in bringing about some of their wars. Sometimes their concern was well founded,[27] as over Barcid expansion in Spain. At other times it was ground-less, but none the less sincere: to my mind that is the only way to account for the Romans' deplorable order for the destruction of Carthage, which led to the Third Punic War.

An inevitable victory?

I close by returning to the question posed earlier: Was it inevitable that, once they had conquered Italy, the Romans would go on to conquer the Mediterranean world? The Romans themselves certainly came to think so: Vergil's *Aeneid* is only the most eloquent expression of their belief and pride in their imperial destiny.[28]

The rapidity with which the Romans came into conflict with the other major powers in the late third and early second centuries owes much to their enemies. If the Carthaginians had acquiesced in the outcome of the

First Punic War, instead of embarking on an ambitious expansion of their power in Spain under the Barcids, the two republics might well have reverted to their earlier friendly co-existence. If the Macedonian and Seleucid monarchies had been in the hands of rulers less enterprising and more pacific than Philip and Antiochus, the Romans would not have been drawn into Eastern affairs so soon after their great struggle with Hannibal. In the course of the tortuous negotiations which preceded the war with Antiochus, the Romans offered to make a friendly settlement if he would withdraw from Europe. Considerations of prestige prevented Antiochus from making the territorial concession, but there is no reason to believe that the Roman offer was not sincerely meant.

Thus, but for the Romans' opponents, their expansion might well have been much slower. However, one may wonder whether the remarkable military machine which the Roman Republic had fashioned would in any circumstances have been able to co-exist indefinitely with the other Mediterranean powers.

The Romans' victory was facilitated by the opposition's divisions. Hannibal won over many of Rome's allies in southern Italy, Hieronymus of Syracuse and Philip of Macedon, but none of them gave him much assistance, and the Carthaginian home government provided little support. Antiochus sought to profit from Philip's defeat, and Philip assisted the Romans in defeating Antiochus. It may be doubted, however, whether any combination would have been effective. Hannibal recognized that to defeat the Romans it was necessary to destroy their alliance system in Italy, but he never came near to succeeding.

Notes

1 For the best available short history of Rome, see T. Cornell and J. Matthews, *Atlas of the Roman World*, Oxford, Phaidon, 1982. For a more detailed account see *Cambridge Ancient History*, 2nd edn. The following are important regional studies: E. S. Gruen, *The Hellenistic World and the Coming of Rome*, Berkeley, Los Angeles and London, University of California Press, 1984; S. L. Dyson, *The Creation of the Roman Frontier*, Princeton, NJ, Princeton University Press, 1985; J. S. Richardson, *Hispaniae: Spain and the Development of Roman Imperialism 218–82 BC*, Cambridge, Cambridge University Press, 1986; J. S. Richardson, *The Romans in Spain*, Oxford, Blackwell, 1996. On Roman warfare and expansion, see also W. V. Harris, *War and Imperialism in the Roman Republic 327–70 BC*, Oxford, Clarendon Press, 1979; J. Rich and G. Shipley (eds), *War and Society in the Roman World*, London and New York, Routledge, 1993. On the Roman army, see L. Keppie, *The Making of the Roman Army*, London, Batsford, 1984, repr. London, Routledge, 1998.

2 See F. W. Walbank, 'Polybius and Rome's eastern policy', *Journal of Roman Studies*, 1963, vol. 53, pp. 1–13, repr. in his *Selected Papers*, Cambridge, Cambridge University Press, 1985, pp. 138–56; P. S. Derow, 'Polybius, Rome and the East', *Journal of Roman Studies*, 1979, vol. 69, pp. 1–15; Harris, *War and Imperialism in the Roman Republic 327–70 BC*, pp. 107–17.

3 Notable expositions of this view include T. Mommsen, *A History of Rome*, trans. W. P. Dickson, London, Richard Bentley & Son, 1877–80, especially 2.312–14;

T. Frank, *Roman Imperialism*, New York, Macmillan, 1914; M. Holleaux, *Rome, la Grèce et les monarchies hellénistiques*, Paris, E. de Boccard, 1921; Walbank, 'Polybius and Rome's eastern policy'; E. Badian, *Roman Imperialism in the Late Republic*, Oxford, Blackwell, 1968; R. M. Errington, *The Dawn of Empire: Rome's Rise to World Power*, London, Hamish Hamilton, 1971. For an illuminating discussion of its intellectual origins, see J. Linderski, '*Si vis pacem, para bellum*: concepts of defensive imperialism', in W. V. Harris (ed.), *The Imperialism of Mid-Republican Rome*, Rome, American Academy, 1984, pp. 133–64.

4 Harris, *War and Imperialism in the Roman Republic 327–70 BC*.

5 '"Defensive imperialism" defended: A. N. Sherwin-White, "Rome the aggressor?"', *Journal of Roman Studies*, 1980, vol. 70, pp. 177–81; Gruen, *The Hellenistic World and the Coming of Rome*; Dyson, *The Creation of the Roman Frontier*; A. M. Eckstein, *Senate and General: Individual Decision-Making and Roman Foreign Relations, 264–194 BC*, Berkeley, Los Angeles and London, University of California Press, 1987. For a favourable critique of Harris, see J. A. North, 'The development of Roman imperialism', *Journal of Roman Studies*, 1981, vol. 71, pp. 1–9.

6 J. W. Rich, 'Fear, greed and glory: the causes of the Roman war-making in the middle Republic', in Rich and Shipley (eds), *War and Society in the Roman World*, pp. 38–62.

7 For the Roman reception of Greek culture and its effect on Roman policies in the third and second centuries BC, see especially J.-L. Ferrary, *Philhellénisme et impérialisme. Aspects idéologiques de la conquête romaine du monde hellénistique*, Rome, Ecole Française, 1988; E. S. Gruen, *Studies in Greek Culture and Roman Policy*, Leiden, Brill, 1990; E. S. Gruen, *Culture and National Identity in Republican Rome*, Ithaca, NY, Cornell University Press, 1992.

8 On Roman war votes, see J. W. Rich, *Declaring War in the Roman Republic in the Period of Transmarine Expansion*, Brussels, Latomus, 1976, pp. 13–17. The modern term 'Hellenistic' denotes the period in the history of the Greek east from the death of Alexander (323 BC) to Octavian's defeat of Antony and Cleopatra (31–30 BC).

9 J. W. Rich, 'The origins of the Second Punic War', in T. Cornell, B. Rankov and Ph. Sabin (eds), *The Second Punic War: A Reappraisal*, London, Bulletin of the Institute of Classical Studies, 1996, supplement 67, pp. 1–37. For other views, see B. D. Hoyos, *Unplanned Wars: The Origins of the First and Second Punic Wars*, Berlin and New York, Walter de Gruyter, 1998; and Ruth Stepper, Chapter 6, this volume.

10 M. M. Austin, 'Hellenistic kings, war and the economy', *Classical Quarterly*, 1986, vol. 36, pp. 450–66.

11 On the Roman sacking of cities, see A. Ziolkowski, '*Urbs direpta*, or how the Romans sacked cities', in Rich and Shipley (eds) *War and Society in the Roman World*, pp. 69–91 On enslavements, see H. Volkmann, *Die Massenversklavungen der Einwohner eroberter Städte in der hellenistisch-römishchen Zeit*, 2nd edn with additions by Gerhard Horsmann, Stuttgart, Franz Steiner Verlag, 1990.

12 K. Hopkins, *Conquerors and Slaves*, Cambridge, Cambridge University Press, 1978, 31ff., based on the estimates of P. A. Brunt in *Italian Manpower 225 BC–A.D 14*, Oxford, Clarendon Press, 1971, reissued 1987.

13 Brunt, *Italian Manpower 225 BC–A.D. 14*, pp. 54, 419–20, estimates that some 50,000 citizens were lost in 218–15, one-sixth of all adult males.

14 Polybius 1.11.

15 Rich, 'The supposed Roman manpower shortage of the later second century BC', *Historia*, 1983, vol. 32, pp. 287–331, at 316–18.

16 E. Badian, *Publicans and Sinners: Private Enterprise in the Service of the Roman Republic*, Oxford, Blackwell, 1972; T. J. Cornell, 'Warfare and urbanization in Roman Italy' in T. J. Cornell and K. Lomas (eds), *Urban Society in Roman Italy*, London,

UCL Press, 1985, pp. 121–34. P. Erdkamp, *Hunger and the Sword: Warfare and Food Supply in Roman Republican Wars (264–30 BC)*, Amsterdam, J. C. Gieben, 1998, where, on pp. 112–19, he argues that large-scale contractors did not normally play an important part in supplying corn to the armies, but they were certainly used for the supply of clothing and horses.

17 On the composition of the political elite, see P. A. Brunt, 'Nobilitas et Novitas', *Journal of Roman Studies*, 1982, vol. 72, pp. 1–17; K. Hopkins and G. Burton, in Hopkins, *Death and Renewal*, Cambridge, Cambridge University Press, 1983, pp. 31–119. In general on the political system of the middle Republic, see F. Millar, 'The political character of the Classical Roman Republic, 200–151 BC', *Journal of Roman Studies*, 1984, vol. 74, pp. 1–19; and A. E. Astin, 'Roman government and politics', in *Cambridge Ancient History*, 2nd edn, vol. 10, Cambridge, Cambridge University Press, 1989, pp. 136–96.

18 Elite attitudes to, and benefits from, war are analysed well by Harris, *War and Imperialism in the Roman Republic, 327–70 BC*, pp. 10–41, 74–93.

19 Ibid.; North, 'The development of Roman imperialism'.

20 Rich, 'Fear, greed and glory: the causes of the Roman war-making in the middle Republic'.

21 J. Rüpke, *Domi Militiae: Die religiöse Konstruktion des Krieges in Rom*, Stuttgart, Franz Steiner Verlag, 1990.

22 Ibid., pp. 162–4; M. Beard, J. North and S. Price, *Religions of Rome*, Cambridge, Cambridge University Press, 1998, vol. 1, pp. 34–5, 133–4.

23 Rich, *Declaring War in the Roman Republic in the Period of Transmarine Expansion*, 56ff.; Rüpke, *Domi Militiae: Die religiöse Konstruktion des Krieges in Rom*, 97ff.

24 Polybius, 36.21; Livy, *Epitome of Books*, 48–9. On the *ius fetiale*, see also T. Wiedemann, 'The *fetiales*: a reconsideration', *Classical Quarterly*, 1986, vol. 36, pp. 478–90; J.-L. Ferrary, '*Ius fetiale* et diplomatie', in E. Frézouls and A. Jacquemin (eds), *Les relations internationales*, Strasburg, Université des sciences humaines de Strasburg, 1995, pp. 411–32. See my remarks on A. Watson's *International Law in Archaic Rome*, Baltimore and London, Johns Hopkins University Press, 1993, in *Classical Review*, 1994, vol. 44, pp. 322–4. Cicero's views on the just war are discussed well in J. Barnes, 'Cicéron et la guerre juste', *Bulletin de la Société française de la Philosophie*, 1986, vol. 80, pp. 41–80. Roman conceptions of the just war and their relation to Roman practice have been discussed in several recent monographs, although a satisfactory treatment is yet to be reproduced: S. Albert, *Bellum Iustum*, Kallmunz, Verlag Michael Lassleben, 1980; S. Clavedetscher-Thürlemann, *Polemos Dikaios und Bellum Iustum: Versuch einer Ideengeschichte*, Zurich, Juris Druck, 1985; M. Mantovani, *Bellum Iustum: Die Idee des gerechten Krieges in der römischen Kaiserzeit*, Bern, Peter Lang, 1990; M. Kostial, *Kriegerisches Rom? Zur Frage von Unvermeidbarkeit und Normalität militärischer Konflikte in der römischen Politik*, Stuttgart, Franz Steiner Verlag, 1995.

25 Cicero, *On the Republic*, 3.35.

26 *Gallic War*, 1.10.2; 2.1.

27 Rich, 'The origins of the Second Punic War'.

28 On the Romans' pride in empire, see Brunt, 'Laus imperii', in P. D. A. Garnsey and C. R. Whitaker (eds), *Imperialism in the Ancient World*, Cambridge, Cambridge University Press, 1977, pp. 159–91, repr. in his *Roman Imperial Themes*, Oxford, Clarendon Press, 1990, pp. 288–323. On the development of the Romans' conceptions of empire, see J. S. Richardson, *Imperium Romanum*: empire and the language of power', *Journal of Roman Studies*, 1991, vol. 81, pp. 1–9.

6 Roman–Carthaginian relations

From co-operation to annihilation[1]

Ruth Stepper

The three wars waged by the Romans and Carthaginians against each other constitute a prime example of conflict between two powers in antiquity. The overall conflict – spanning several generations, and interrupted only by occasional periods of peace – escalated in its intensity as well as in terms of the war aims. The dogged struggle for victory in the first two wars, both ending in favour of the Romans, lent the Roman–Carthaginian confrontation particular momentum. The Romans, encouraged by military success, were striving for ever greater gains after each victory. Exploiting the successful repulse of the Carthaginians in the First Roman–Carthaginian War, Rome merely sought to weaken the enemy. Yet after the Second Roman–Carthaginian War, Rome aimed for Carthage's complete annihilation. Thus these three wars against Carthage, with their clear pattern of escalation, spectacularly reflect the phases in which Rome built its empire at the expense of its neighbours.

The parties to the conflict

The first Carthaginians were Phoenicians who migrated to North Africa, and came to be known as Punic.[2] The Roman and Carthaginian cultures were strongly influenced by Greek/Hellenic culture and tradition. Examples of Greek influence on Rome abound, but there is also archaeological evidence of such influence on Carthaginian culture, crafts, jewellery and technology; the Carthaginian upper class spoke Greek fluently, and its men frequently married Greek women (e.g. from Syracuse). We will discuss a case of Greek influence on Carthaginian religion and mythology below.

At first, Rome and Carthage were comparable powers. Rome was a city-state that lived originally from the agriculture of the surrounding area, and was run by a land-owning aristocracy whose power was founded on the monopolization of public offices. Accordingly, Rome's social and political power was concentrated in the Senate – an assembly of the most influential and distinguished heads of Roman families. The structure of the constitution corresponded to the military requirements of an expansionist society (with a people's assembly, the *comitia*, and representation of the economically dominating class, the *equites*, who initially included also knights and senators). Civil and military powers were not separate, but rather found their expression in the highest authorities. Consuls were not only the highest bearers of office, but were simultaneously in possession of *imperium*, originally meaning absolute military command.[3] In Carthage, by contrast, there was a division between the two spheres. The *sufets* took care of civil magisterial duties, while the most senior posts of military command were occupied by *strategoi* (the Carthaginian word corresponding to this Greek term is not known).[4] Carthage also owed much of its wealth to agriculture, with thriving estates on Cape Bon, but to an increasing extent maintained trading connections with the whole western Mediterranean basin. Carthaginian *emporia* were situated on Ibiza, Sardinia and Sicily. The Carthaginian ruling class was divided into owners of *latifundia* and tradesmen. This city's greatest asset was the sea, which the Romans, as a traditionally land-based power, still had to conquer.[5]

Rome expanded across Italy in increasing concentric circles. It was natural for the early Romans, as peasants, to seek to enlarge their territory, and expansionism soon became a habit, whether or not individual campaigns were described as defensive. The system of rule was based on a web of treaties (*foedera*) with Italian allies (referred to as *amici et socii populi Romani* – friends and associates of the Roman people).[6] Due to the lack of Carthaginian sources, we cannot say how the Carthaginians perceived the Romans. We can, however, reconstruct Roman views of their enemies on the basis of Roman sources[7] which are biased, as they were formulated both during and after the Roman–Carthaginian conflict: the Carthaginians are described in Roman sources as greedy, avaricious, cruel and unreliable (Punic, i.e. Carthaginian, 'faith' or rather perfidy, *fides punica*, became a bad byword). Roman war propaganda made out that the Carthaginians were not only dangerous, but also morally corrupt.

Not surprisingly, Roman self-descriptions are positive. Rome's political greatness is accounted for by the Romans' piety, their particularly close relationship with the gods (*pietas*). In their opinion, the Romans waged exclusively just wars (*bella iusta*),[8] i.e. wars conducted in self-defence or in defence of an ally, and considered themselves to be the stronghold of justice and morality. Cultural differences between the Romans and other groups did not matter as long as there was no other conflict of interests between them. Only in wartime were such differences seen as important, and would be used by both sides to differentiate themselves from the enemy.

The degree of political, social and economic development of both adversaries was comparable. Rome's strength was founded on the citizen army (legions), and on allied contingents (according to the *formula toga-torum*[9] there was a 700,000-man recruitment pool in 225 BC).[10] Initially, the Roman fleet played a subordinate role. Carthage, on the other hand, as a maritime power, possessed a powerful fleet. The army consisted of citizen militia – which in view of the low number of Carthage's citizen body was of limited scale – augmented by recruited mercenaries.[11] In contrast to the Roman-ruled Italian military co-operative, Carthage could not always count on the contingents of its Libyan and Numidian neighbours who supplied important troops, especially cavalry. From time to time, the Carthaginians had to fear betrayal by them. While Romans had come to be seen as Italian natives by the third century BC, Carthage remained a Punic colony on foreign soil, the issue of a colonialism driven by the search for raw materials, new markets and an outlet for a Punic population surplus.[12] Unlike the Romans, the Carthaginians were not interested in gaining land for agriculture or in enslaving other peoples.

Despite their domination by the aristocracy, both polities were constitutional republics. While the formation of political opinion took place within the ruling class, decisions of consequence, in particular questions of waging war and peace-keeping, required the formal blessing of the people, whose authority was always invoked in such circumstances. The *res publica* (public affairs, a precursor, one might say, of the modern concept of statehood) was too abstract a concept to be used by the Romans in declarations of war or the conclusion of treaties:[13] only the *populus* could do this. The Roman Senate was in this context seen as an adjunct to the people: *Senatus populusque Romanus*.

Relations between Rome and Carthage – which can be traced back to the sixth century BC – initially were peaceful for an extended period of time.[14] The attempt was made to distinguish spheres of interest and to form trade relations by mutual agreement, benefiting both sides. However, as the development of trade and industry was not an appropriate subject for historiography in the eyes of ancient historians, only sparse observations are to be found in literary sources.[15] A few years before the outbreak of the First Roman–Carthaginian war, the previous benevolent neutrality was even turned into a military alliance when a common enemy appeared: King Pyrrhus of Epirus.[16] Yet the outcome of this jointly fought war (280–272 BC) contributed to the subsequent estrangement of Rome and Carthage as allies, indeed to their antagonism, since Roman power now extended to the borders of Sicily, which had belonged to the Carthaginian sphere of influence for two centuries. The tug of war over the possession of this rich island was soon to become the main reason for the imminent military conflict between Rome and Carthage.

The First Roman–Carthaginian War

The First Roman–Carthaginian War (264–241 BC)[17] was triggered by Roman expansionism into Sicily.[18] Even Polybius (I.10) does not deny that Rome intervened without good legal grounds, claiming that it was countering Carthaginian encirclement of Rome at a time when Carthage did not yet have possessions in Spain. This Roman intervention on behalf of their allies, the Mamertines, who in turn had maltreated the Messenians and the Rhegians, might have been limited in time and space but in fact turned into an exhausting war of many years' duration. The Romans initially made rapid advances, extending their war aims from the simple amassing of booty to territorial conquest.[19] This in turn provoked the Carthaginians into extreme resistance, as they were now facing a serious challenge not only to their lootable property but to their political control of Sicily. Due to the parity of resources mustered by both sides, military operations led to a stalemate.[20] Both adversaries had to adapt to the opponent's preferred way of war: the Romans were forced to wage war at sea which was unfamiliar to them, while the Carthaginians had to withstand a ground war on Sicily and in northern Africa. Yet under the influence of advanced Greek military technology (the Spartan Xanthippos reformed the Carthaginian army), the Carthaginian land forces operated very successfully, while the Romans transferred their ground war tactics to maritime conflict and equipped their ships with boarding planks. Probably the most conspicuous difference in the belligerency of both parties was the importance of mercenaries in the Carthaginian army. In view of their limited citizen manpower, the Carthaginians had to entrust a large part of the fighting to hired professional soldiers, mainly from Spain, Gaul, Italy, Greece and North Africa.

Exhaustion finally led to the conclusion of this generation-long struggle. Rome, the warring party with the larger reserves, prevailed. As the theatre-of-war (Sicily) lay outside the original sphere of activity of both opponents, the effects of military action on Rome and Carthage was limited, and there were relatively few casualties among the belligerents' civilian populations. Yet the extreme length of the war eroded support for it on both sides, finally forcing them to agree to a peace settlement which favoured Rome.

The Romans took many prisoners in Sicily and sold formerly free citizens captured on conquered enemy territory as slaves, a standard practice in warfare at the time,[21] but this was enough to establish an irreconcilable hostility between both camps. The victorious Romans displayed their superiority mercilessly, showing little interest in restoring amicable relations with Carthage. The peace treaty ending the First Roman–Carthaginian War (the so-called Lutatius Treaty of 241 BC) was ambivalent:[22] its conditions fired Carthaginian wishes for revenge. Carthage was not just committed to paying hefty reparations, it also lost Sicily and a large part of its fleet. Subsequent Roman behaviour – the Romans exploited Carthage's weakness during the subsequent mercenaries' revolt and annexed the previously Carthaginian-dominated Sardinia without legal foundation when Carthage lost control – boded ill for a renewal of peaceful co-existence.

The Carthaginians now looked for a new sphere of activity to compensate for their losses, finding it in the Iberian Peninsula, where trade connections had long existed and rich metal deposits promised great profit.[23] The

Romans subsequently attempted to contain the successful Carthaginian expansion in Spain, which they regarded with suspicion, by means of an agreement with Hasdrubal in about 226 BC, generally known as the Ebro Treaty.[24] But the treaty did not bring peace for long.

The Second Roman–Carthaginian War

The antagonism which had smouldered after the peace treaty of 241 BC finally escalated into a new war (218–201 BC)[25] because the Romans, on the one hand, continued to meddle in the Carthaginian sphere and because the Carthaginians, on the other, were determined to defend their position in Spain. The Spanish city-state of Saguntum attacked the Torboletae, allies of Carthage. To avenge its allies, Carthage's new Supreme Commander in Spain, Hannibal, in turn attacked Saguntum. At first, the Saguntines made futile requests to Rome for help, which only material-ized when Hannibal's troops conquered Saguntum: the Romans then rushed to drive them out again, unwilling to tolerate this growth of Carthage's power.[26] Hannibal's conquest of Saguntum (around the end of December 219 BC) was thus the *casus belli* for the Romans. They declared war on Carthage, arguing that Hannibal had broken the so-called Ebro Treaty, according to which Saguntum belonged to the Roman sphere of influence and could, as an ally of Rome, lay claim to its protection.[27] Both Carthage and Rome therefore acted on behalf of their allies, while simul-taneously using this occasion to challenge each other's power on the Iberian Peninsula.

Hannibal drew on propaganda to strengthen his cause. The pro-Roman account of events (Livy) describes how Hannibal used religion in this context. Before setting out for Italy, Hannibal visited the shrine of Melkart in Gades where he asked for divine assistance in his future operations against the Romans (Livy XXI.21.9). The god worshipped in Phoenician–Carthaginian culture as Melkart was known as Heracles/Hercules in the Greek and Roman world. Since the times of Alexander the Great, who had made Hercules the leading deity in his spectacular campaign against Persia, the powerful mythological hero had been used to justify campaigns of conquest. Hannibal's youth, like Alexander's, was associated with Hercules: at the age of 26, Hannibal was recipient of Carthage's highest military office. One of the twelve acts of Hercules was invoked as a partic-ularly apposite myth: when Hercules was herding the defeated Geryon's cattle through Spain and Gaul across the Alps and into Italy, Cacus – a giant residing on the Aventine – attempted to steal the animals, but was slain by Hercules. Like Hercules, Hannibal would now march into Italy in order to punish the Romans for their presumptuous conduct in Spain over the matter of the Carthaginian–Saguntine conflict.

Hannibal's mobilization of a leading deity was useful publicity for the Carthaginian cause. The devotion displayed towards Melkart/Heracles by

Hannibal[28] would have appealed not only to the West Phoenicians (particularly the Carthaginians), but equally to the Greeks.[29] Roman encroachment into the Greek east was merely a matter of time after the elimination of Carthage in the west. Hannibal sought to emulate Alexander the Great as the liberator of Greek civilization from foreign oppression: in the case of Alexander, the oppressors were the Persians; in the case of Hannibal, the oppressors were the Romans. Hannibal's aim was the formation of an anti-Roman alliance with the Greeks against the Romans. The success of his propaganda is shown in the fact that well-known Greek states and cities did indeed join his struggle against Rome: Macedonia under Philip V (in 215 BC),[30] Syracuse (in 215 after the death of Hieron)[31] and Tarentum (which fought with Hannibal from 212–209 BC before once again falling to the Romans after being betrayed).[32] Livy reports (XXII.61.12) that Greek cities, particularly on the Appenine Peninsula, joined Hannibal. He appealed to the Greeks and West Phoenicians to remember their own ancient culture and to cast off the shackles of the barbarian Romans. For him, the issue at stake in this war was the preservation, if not discovery, of an independent identity.[33] The image Hannibal constructed of the Romans during the course of the war was therefore that of exploiters, oppressors and power-hungry parvenus who should be put in their place. In response, freedom was the battle-cry. Neither the Greeks nor the Carthaginians wanted to give up their place in ancient world politics without a fight.[34]

The reaction of the Romans proved that this huge propaganda campaign did not fail to have an effect on the enemy. A contemporary of the war and Rome's oldest historian, Q. Fabius Pictor, felt called upon to write an entire history in defence of Rome.[35] The readership he targeted becomes clear from the fact that the work was published in Greek. Unfortunately, nothing of this original work is preserved,[36] but from what we know indirectly from his account, Fabius Pictor argued that Rome waged exclusively legitimate wars in order to protect its allies (here the Saguntines) and that it was morally superior to the Carthaginians. The Roman narrative formed by such accounts paints a thoroughly negative image of Hannibal that is difficult to revise in the absence of any surviving pro-Carthaginian historiography. Livy described Hannibal as an uncivilized monster: 'His cruelty was inhuman, his perfidy worse than Punic; he had no regard for truth, and none for sanctity, no fear of the gods, no reverence for an oath, no religious scruple' (Livy XXI.49). The ideological campaign of the Romans was limited to fairly stylized polemics against the Carthaginians, aimed above all at frightening their own allies, whose loyalty to Rome was severely tested. Fear alone prevented them from risking a union with the Carthaginian intruders and, in the face of horrifying reports of cannibalism and other barbaric brutalities (Livy XXIII.5.11–12) circulated by the Romans, the allies' perceived need for protection by Rome was increased.

Hannibal's liberation rhetoric not only called upon the Greeks but also on Rome's Italian allies to follow Carthage's lead in this campaign for freedom. In view of Hannibal's significant military successes, such talk represented a serious threat to Rome.[37] Capua, the most powerful city in Campania, became Carthage's ally from 216–211 BC.[38] Other cities followed suit, joining the anti-Roman coalition forged by Hannibal. Even though his military operations – which were designed to restrict the Roman sphere of influence to Italy, or indeed to reduce Rome's power even within Italy by depriving it of its allies and clients – ultimately failed,[39] Hannibal's ideological campaign was clearly persuasive; otherwise the Romans would not have resorted to such a hate campaign against him.[40]

Compared with the first, there was an increase in the intensity of military operations in the Second Roman–Carthaginian War, as it was conducted on the territory of both warring parties close to the two warring city-states.[41] In Italy, the struggles became protracted, and the war left behind significant scars: Hannibal is alleged to have destroyed 400 towns and cities. Thousands of civilians were imprisoned and sold into slavery; the first years of the war alone led to the loss of 100,000 soldiers on the side of Rome.[42]

The Roman quest for unlimited domination: the Third and last Roman–Carthaginian War

The Hellenistic monarchies in the Greek eastern territories had a tacit understanding which had proved its worth in the ancient world: power should be shared by them, rather than monopolized by one.[43] In the struggle for the legacy of Alexander the Great, the competition for power was crucial to the development of the individual Hellenistic monarchies: none of them could assert itself entirely at the expense of another, but they had to take each others' interests into consideration in order to prosper.[44] By contrast, the rise of Rome can early on be linked to an *absolute* will for power. It becomes apparent from the prehistory of the Third Roman–Carthaginian War (149–146 BC) how unsatisfactory the strategy of merely weakening Carthage was to the Roman leaders. Tolerance of another possible competitor apart from itself contradicted the Roman concept of rule.

The Carthaginians successfully used the fifty-year peace prior to the Third and final Roman–Carthaginian War to stabilize their economic situation, even though they had to come to terms with the loss of their position as a great power. They were particularly troubled by the Numidian prince Masinissa, favoured by Rome, who repeatedly attacked Carthaginian territory. When Carthage defended itself against Masinissa, it provided the Romans with a pretext to advance against it for a final time. Cato the Elder urged this Roman advance, with the express aim of annihilating the Carthaginians. Few voices in Rome called for peace.

Carthage, although capable of regeneration, was admittedly no longer an evenly matched opponent.[45] Thus, while Rome's involvement in the First and Second Roman–Carthaginian Wars was construed as defensive, the allegation of pro-Roman historians that Rome started the third war to pre-empt an attack by (the economically at best stabilized) Carthage lacks any such persuasiveness.[46] Rome's leaders desired the annihilation of Carthage with Cato the Elder's famous mantra, frequently repeated by him before the Senate, '*Ceterum censeo Carthaginem esse delendam*'.[47] Here we see no respect for the Hellenistic sharing of power that respects the right to live on all sides, with co-equal interaction of independent entities, but rather a model of world domination without competition: anyone who refused to be assimilated into the Roman system, be it because of their desire for self-assertion or their prosperity, was annihilated.

In contrast to the preceding wars, then, the Third Roman–Carthaginian War did not witness a gradual buildup of tension prior to, or an escalation during, hostilities.[48] There was no long legal debate either. Given the inequality of the two sides in this war, its outcome was hardly in doubt. The power struggle had long been decided in Rome's favour. The Third Roman–Carthaginian War resembled an execution rather than a war. The outcome – the annihilation of Carthage – was certain long before the opening of hostilities and was realized to the letter. It was neither possible nor intended to spare the Carthaginian population. The plan for a complete destruction of Carthage implied the annihilation of a large section of its inhabitants. Roman troops went around murdering and looting Carthage for several days,[49] having resolved that the city – which they defined as cursed – should henceforth be uninhabited wasteland, while its territorial possessions were to be governed by Roman pro-magistrates. The Carthaginian Empire was thus utterly destroyed.[50] Rome did not wish to be reminded of the former greatness of her erstwhile partner and later rival for power. The Roman will for power knew no compromise.

War, legitimacy and ethics in the Roman–Carthaginian wars

What else do the three Roman–Carthaginian wars tell us about collective mentality and its influence on war and peace? The fact that only war was seen as a subject worthy of ancient historiography speaks for itself. In this respect the Greeks and the Romans do not differ from one another.[51] Yet warfare was limited by considerations of legitimacy: contemporaries were concerned not to be seen as greedy conquerors attacking the enemy without a legal basis for their action. It was important to put forward good reasons for entering into a war;[52] usually assistance for allies under attack, based on a treaty obligation, was cited. In the case of the First Roman–Carthaginian War, both the Romans and the Carthaginians reacted to a call for help from the Mamertines of Messina. In the Second Roman–Carthaginian War,

Hannibal rushed to the aid of the Torboletae when they were under attack from the Saguntines, while Rome assisted Saguntum. In the Third Roman–Carthaginian War, Rome came to the defence of the Numidian prince Masinissa. The issue of war guilt preoccupied not only the historians of subsequent generations, but also the very participants in the wars, in which each side attempted to assign the blame to the other. This issue was taken so seriously that it became central to historiography.

As an integral part of politics, wars always had to be declared and undertaken in accordance with the gods representing the interests of state.[53] In this, Romans and Carthaginians were very similar. Hannibal enlisted the entire Carthaginian Pantheon in his ranks. The endeavours of the Romans – who were sticklers for formalities – to obtain divine backing for their policies are especially apparent in all rituals connected with war, including declarations of war, cease-fire and peace agreements, as well as interstate treaties by the *fetiales*.[54] Another rite was the opening of the gates of the temple of Janus, which symbolized the state of war. The closing of the temple gates, signalling the beginning of a period of peace, was the exception rather than the rule.[55] According to Palmer, Janus was a deity worshipped by the Carthaginians. After the Romans had won their first great sea battle against Carthage in the First Roman–Carthaginian War, they built a temple for Janus in Rome. In bringing the gods of the enemy back to Rome, the Romans sought to assure themselves of the most comprehensive divine protection possible.[56] Triumphal processions up to the Capitol (Temple of Jupiter Capitolinus) in Rome[57] also had ritualistic functions. They celebrated the successful conclusion of a campaign, rather than the peace achieved after the end of the war: thus prisoners of war were paraded alongside the booty.

The extent to which the Roman authorities considered waging war to be a priority can be seen in the names given within the Roman ruling class. Many prominent Romans increased their prestige by conquering foreign territories, the names of whose (defeated) ethnies then became part of the Roman family names, for example, Publius Cornelius Scipio *Africanus* (the victor over Hannibal), or Publius Cornelius Scipio Aemilianus *Africanus Numantinus*, the conqueror of Carthage in the Third Roman–Carthaginian War. Therefore, allusions in names to military victories were often the only distinguishing feature between the frequently identical names of the members of a Roman *gens* (or clan).

Nevertheless, war was not allowed to pervade all aspects of Roman society. Civilian society and the military community (*domi militiaeque*) were consciously separated spacially. The city of Rome was demilitarized. The ban on carrying weapons was most noticeably demonstrated by the Lictors – representatives of the municipal authorities – who had to deposit their axes and fasces outside the city walls. It was assumed that Rome's military might was always directed outwards: external enemies, rather than Roman citizens, had to fear it.

Notes

1 *Pedro Barceló quinquagenario.*
2 W. Huß, *Geschichte der Karthager*, Munich, Beck, 1985, p. 55.
3 J. Bleicken, *Die Verfassung der Römischen Republik*, Paderborn, Schöningh, 1993, 6th edn, pp. 74–83.
4 G. C. Picard, 'Le pouvoir suprême à Carthage', in E. Lipinski (ed.), *Studia Phoenicia. VI: Carthago*, Leuven, Uitgeverij Peeters, 1988, pp. 119–24; B. Wollner, *Die Kompetenzen der karthagischen Feldherrn*, Frankfurt, Bern, New York and Paris, Peter Lang, 1987; Huß, *Geschichte der Karthager*, pp. 458–80.
5 P. Barceló, 'Zur karthagischen Überseepolitik im VI. und V. Jahrhundert v. Chr.', *Gymnasium*, 1989, vol. 96, pp. 13–37; S. Lancel, *Carthage*, Oxford and Cambridge, Blackwell, 1995, pp. 110–33; E. C. González Wagner, *Fenicios y Cartagineses en la Península Ibérica: Ensayo de interpretación fundamentado en un análisis de los factores internos*, Madrid, Editorial de la Universidad Complutense de Madrid, 1983, pp. 178–283; C. R. Whittaker, 'Carthaginian imperialism in the fifth and fourth centuries', in P. D. A. Garnsey and C. R. Whittaker (eds), *Imperialism in the Ancient World*, Cambridge, Cambridge University Press, 1978, pp. 59–90.
6 T. Hantos, *Das römische Bundesgenossensystem in Italien*, Munich, Beck, 1983.
7 E. Burck, 'Das Bild der Karthager in der römischen Literatur', in J. Vogt (ed.), *Rom und Karthago. Ein Gemeinschaftswerk*, Leipzig, Koehler & Amelang, 1943, pp. 297–345; F. Càssola, 'Tendenze filopuniche e antipuniche in Roma', *Atti del I Congresso Internazionale di Studi Fenici e Punici*, vol. 1, Rome, 1983, pp. 35–59. In addition, see P. Barceló, 'The perception of Carthage in classical Greek historiography', *Acta Classica* XXXVII, 1994, pp. 1–14.
8 S. Albert, *Bellum iustum. Die Theorie des 'gerechten Krieges' und ihre praktische Bedeutung für die auswärtigen Auseinandersetzungen Roms in republikanischer Zeit*, Kallmünz, Lassleben, 1980; M. Kostial, *Kriegerisches Rom? Zur Frage von Unvermeidbarkeit und Normalität militärischer Konflikte in der römischen Politik*, Stuttgart, Steiner, 1995.
9 The name of the list which was put up every four years giving information on the military strength of Rome and its allies. Cf. Polybius II. 23, 8–24, 17.
10 P. A. Brunt, *Italian Manpower 225 BC–AD 14*, Oxford, Oxford University Press, 1971, repr. 1987, p. 44 ff. On the subject of the Roman army during this period, see L. Keppie, *The Making of the Roman Army. From Republic to Empire*, London, Batsford, 1984, pp. 14–40.
11 W. Ameling, *Karthago. Studien zu Militär, Staat und Gesellschaft*, Munich, Beck, 1993, pp. 183–225.
12 H. G. Niemeyer, *Das frühe Karthago und die phönizische Expansion im Mittelmeerraum*, Göttingen, Zürich, Vandenhoeck & Ruprecht, 1989.
13 H. Drexler, *Politische Grundbegriffe der Römer*, Darmstadt, Wissenschaftliche Buchgesellschaft, 1988, pp. 1–30.
14 R. E. A. Palmer, *Rome and Carthage at Peace*, Stuttgart, Steiner, 1997, pp. 15–30.
15 Polybius III. 21, 9–26, 7; Aristotle, *Politics*, 1280a, 36–8.
16 D. Flach, 'Das römisch–karthagische Bündnisabkommen im Krieg gegen Pyrrhos', *Historia*, 1978, vol. 27, pp. 615–17; B. Dexter Hoyos, 'The Roman–Punic Pact of 279 BC: its problems and its purpose', *Historia*, 1984, vol. 33, pp. 402–39; R. E. Mitchell, 'Roman–Carthaginian Treaties: 306 and 279/8 BC', *Historia*, 1971, vol. 20, pp. 633–55.
17 On the course of the First Roman–Carthaginian War cf. Huß, *Geschichte der Karthager*, pp. 222–51; H. H. Scullard, 'Carthage and Rome', in *The Cambridge Ancient History*, vol. 7, no. 2, 2nd edn, Cambridge, Cambridge University Press, 1989, pp. 537–69, and J. F. Lazenby, *The First Punic War: A Military History*, London, University College London Press, 1996.
18 Cf. P. Barceló, *Hannibal*, Munich, Beck, 1998, pp. 42–3.

19 On the extension of Roman war aims, see Polybius I. 20.

20 B. H. Warmington, *Carthage*, New York, Frederick A. Praeger, 1960, pp. 152–64; Huß, *Geschichte der Karthager*, pp. 230–47.

21 Huß, *Geschichte der Karthager*, pp. 234–8.

22 H. H. Schmitt, *Die Staatsverträge des Altertums III*, Munich, Beck, 1969, no. 493, pp. 173–81; B. Scardigli, *I Trattati Romano-Cartaginesi*, Pisa, Scuola Normale Superiore, 1991, pp. 205–43.

23 P. Barceló, *Karthago und die Iberische Halbinsel vor den Barkiden*, Bonn, Rudolf Habelt, 1988, pp. 115–32.

24 On the geographical determination of the border mentioned in this treaty, cf. P. Barceló, 'Die Grenze des karthagischen Machtbereichs unter Hasdrubal: Zum sog. Ebro-Vertrag', in Eckart Olshausen and Holger Sonnabend (eds), *Geographica Historica 7*, Stuttgarter Kolloquium zur Historischen Geographie des Altertums 4, 1990, Amsterdam, Adolf M. Hakkert, 1994, pp. 35–55.

25 On the subject of the course of the war, see Barceló, *Hannibal*, pp. 32–93; J. Seibert, *Hannibal*, Darmstadt, Wissenschaftliche Buchgesellschaft, 1993, pp. 63–495, and J. F. Lazenby, *Hannibal's War: A Military History of the 2nd Punic War*, Warminster, Aris & Phillips, 1978.

26 J. Seibert, *Forschungen zu Hannibal*, Darmstadt, Wissenschaftliche Buchgesellschaft, 1993, pp. 117–62; Huß, *Geschichte der Karthager*, pp. 285–93; D. Kagan, *On the Origins of War and the Preservation of Peace*, New York, London, Toronto, Sydney and Auckland, Doubleday, 1995, pp. 232–80; and J. Rich, 'The origins of the Second Punic War', in T. Cornell *et al.* (eds), *The Second Punic War: A Reappraisal – Bulletin of the Institute of Classical Studies*, London, supplement 67, 1996, pp. 1–37.

27 On this much-discussed problem, cf. P. Barceló, 'Rom und Hispanien vor Ausbruch des 2. Punischen Krieges', *Hermes*, 1996, vol. 124, , pp. 45–57.

28 On Melkart as Hannibal's leading deity cf. W. Huß, 'Hannibal und die Religion', in C. Bonnet *et al.* (eds), *Studia Phoenicia IV: Religio Phoenicia*, Namur, Société des Études Classiques, 1986, pp. 234–8.

29 Ibid., p. 237.

30 Livy XXIII. 33 and Polybius V. 105; VII. 9.

31 Hieronymus of Syracusse, cf. Livy XXIV. 6. 3ff. and Polybius VII. 2f.

32 Livy XXV. 7. 10ff. and Polybius VIII. 26.

33 Livy. XXIV. 6. 8: Hieronymus of Syracuse was courted with a view to fighting for the Carthaginians as he was related to the famous King Pyrrhus.

34 On the Greeks' concept of the enemy, the 'barbaric Romans', cf. J. Deininger, *Der politische Widerstand gegen Rom in Griechenland 217–86 v. Chr.*, Berlin, New York, Walter de Gruyter, 1971, pp. 23–37.

35 P. Bung, 'Q. Fabius Pictor. Der erste römische Annalist', MS D. Phil., Cologne, 1950.

36 Fabius Pictor's work survives chiefly through Polybius.

37 Livy (XXIII. 42. 4 and XXIII. 43. 10f). conveys an impression of Hannibal's skill in dealing with Roman allies.

38 On Capua's break with Rome cf. Livy XXIII. 6–10. On the motto of freedom used by Hannibal cf. Livy XXIII. 10. 7f.

39 At the decisive battle at Zama (North Africa) in 202 BC. For the Carthaginians the peace agreement of 201 BC brought with it the loss of all overseas holdings, the handing over of their fleet and the payment of high reparations to the Romans. Rome now controlled Carthaginian foreign policy and Hannibal was relieved of his military command.

40 Livy himself confesses this at the beginning of his expositions on the Second Punic War: 'The animosity, too, with which they fought was almost greater than their strength' (XXI. 1. 3).

41 The immediate threat of an independent state increased with the terror cry of the Romans: 'Hannibal ad portas!' (Livy XXIII. 16. 2).

42 Appian, *Hannibalica* 25, 100; Seibert, *Hannibal*, pp. 493–4.

43 For a criticism of the notion that people at the time conceptualized a 'balance of power', see E. Badian, 'Hegemony and independence: prolegomena to a study of the relations of Rome and the Hellenistic states in the second century BC', in J. Harmatta (ed.), *Actes du VIIe Congrès de la Fédération Internationale des Associations d'Études Classiques*, vol. 1, Budapest, Akadémiai Kiadó, 1984, pp. 397–414. For a summary of the debate on this subject, see H.-J. Gehrke, *Geschichte des Hellenismus*, Munich, Oldenbourg, 1990, p. 197f.

44 On the 'balance of power' as characteristic of the Hellenistic states of that period, see P. Klose, *Die völkerrechtliche Ordnung der hellenistischen Staatenwelt in der Zeit von 280 bis 168 v. Chr. Ein Beitrag zur Geschichte des Völkerrechts*, Munich, Beck, 1972, pp. 35–92.

45 On Roman foreign policy see Seibert, *Forschungen zu Hannibal*, pp. 329–39, with a discussion of recent research.

46 Huß, *Geschichte der Karthager*, pp. 436–9; Warmington, *Carthage*, pp. 200–3.

47 'But I propose that Carthage be destroyed' (Plutarch, Cato Major 27).

48 W. V. Harris, 'Roman expansion in the west', in *The Cambridge Ancient History*, vol. 8, 2nd edn, Cambridge, Cambridge University Press, 1989, pp. 142–62.

49 The lives of 50,000 men and women who gave up their opposition were spared. See Huß, *Geschichte der Karthager*, pp. 455–6.

50 See V. Krings, 'La Destruction de Carthage. Problèmes d'Historiographie ancienne et moderne', in H. Devijver and E. Lipinski (eds), *Studia Phoenicia X: Punic Wars*, Leuven, Uitgeverij Peeters, 1989, pp. 329–44.

51 Homer sang the praises of the Trojan War, Herodotus supplied a portrayal of the Persian Wars and Thucydides was the critical commentator of the Peloponnesian War. Roman historiography began wholly in this tradition with the Second Roman–Carthaginian War.

52 On the diplomatic preliminaries before the beginning of a war cf. J. W. Rich, *Declaring War in the Roman Republic in the Period of Transmarine Expansion*, Brussels, Latomus, 1976, pp. 56–118.

53 On the relationship of war and religion in Rome see J. Rüpke, *Domi militiae. Die religiöse Konstruktion des Krieges in Rom*, Stuttgart, Steiner, 1990.

54 See T. Wiedemann, 'The "fetiales": A reconsideration', *The Classical Quarterly*, 1986, vol. 36, pp. 478–90.

55 Thus Emperor Augustus could boast in his *res gestae* (RG 13) of having made possible the closing of the Janus Temple, which had only occurred twice since Rome's foundation. Against the backdrop of a general desire for peace after the long years of civil war, peace was considered valuable and was used accordingly by Augustus as propaganda. However, this peace was always to be understood as a 'victorious peace': only when Rome ruled could there be peace. Rüpke, *Domi militiae*, p. 141.

56 See Palmer, *Rome and Carthage at Peace*, pp. 57–9.

57 H. S. Versnel, *Triumphus. An Inquiry into the Origin, Development and Meaning of the Roman Triumph*, Leiden, Brill, 1970.

Part II

War, peace and faith in the Middle Ages

Introduction

Julian Chrysostomides and Beatrice Heuser

Part II treats the theme of war and peace over a period which spans a thousand years, from the aftermath of the fragmentation of the Roman Empire in the West to the fall of Constantinople, the capital of the eastern half in 1453.

After Constantine the Great recognized Christianity as one of the official religions of the Empire, it went on to be accepted by the end of the fourth century as the one true faith to the exclusion of all others. This section spans the time until the Reformation and the Religious Wars, which arguably began around 1400 with the Peasants' Revolt in England (with its religious element) and the Hussite Wars in Bohemia. Historical periods are never neatly self-contained, and there is inevitably much overlap with the mentality of preceding and ensuing cultures. Thus the late Roman Empire and the Byzantine world carried important elements of ancient Greek philosophy and of the pagan Roman world. At the other end of this period, the Hundred Years' War had much in common with the dynastic wars so typical of the Early Modern period. Nevertheless, comparing these strongly Christian cultures with those of the other periods covered in this book, what is striking is the intensity of men's preoccupations with matters spiritual, with the afterlife of the soul. Thus it seems that more than in the other eras, the European Middle Ages are characterized by the particular religion that provided the systemic framework of reference for beliefs about the divinely ordained *ordo mundis* or world order, about good and evil, war and peace, friend and foe.

By the end of the fifth century, as a result of the Germanic migrations, the Empire's western half (*pars occidentalis*) was fragmented giving its place to a new order. By contrast, the eastern half (*pars orientalis*), with its capital in Constantinople, succeeded in maintaining its centralized character. With the fragmentation of the imperial structure and the emergence of a new political order in the West, the Church gradually grew in importance as the bishops of Rome assumed responsibilities which in the past were exercised by the secular government. In addition, the Church in the West, as the repository of the Latin language, culture and Roman political concepts, developed its own distinct theology and modes of thought that influenced the newcomers, and in particular the Franks. By contrast, the eastern Roman Empire, with its imperial framework intact and its culture rooted in the Hellenistic tradition, developed along different lines to evolve into what we now call the Byzantine Empire. After the unsuccessful attempt of the Emperor Justinian I (527–65) to restore the *imperium romanum* by recovering the lost territories in the West, the Empire concentrated on defending its lands in the east and in the Balkans, and spreading its cultural influence among the Slavs. Yet the vision of the Roman Empire, encouraged by the papacy, exercised a strong appeal to the nascent political entities of Europe, as we shall see.

As Bernhard Zeller shows (Chapter 8), the Germanic newcomers had brought with them their own customs, but also absorbed and evolved new structures and identities which affected their political outlook and their mode of pursuing war and peace. In this new order the Papacy remained a potent centre of authority despite the tension between the secular and ecclesiastical elements. Hence its instrumental role in the creation of the crusading movement, the redefinition of the Augustinian concept of the just war into holy war, and the moral and juridical restrictions imposed on the combatants undertaking this armed pilgrimage in defence of Christendom. The complexities of this movement, which insisted on the just cause of any military expedition and which was directed not only against Muslims but also against Christian heretics, are discussed by Jonathan Riley-Smith (Chapter 10).

The concepts of war and peace, which were entertained in the West, also had their counterpart in the East. Julian Chrysostomides (Chapter 7) shows that, developed by the early Fathers of the Church in the fourth century, Sts Athanasius and Basil, they remained not only part of the Byzantine canon law but also affected secular political thought. But unlike the West, eastern Christendom never developed the idea of holy war despite its familiarity with the concept of *jihad*, and later with the western crusading movement.

Empire, kingdoms and principalities

The Roman Empire proved to be so powerful that the idea of such an empire, spanning all of Christianity, survived its actual demise in the West in two forms: the eastern Roman Empire which never ceased to see itself as the direct successor of Rome, and the twofold re-invention of the Roman Empire in the West, once applied to Charlemagne and his heirs and by extension to their possessions, and once to those of Otto the Great and his successors. (Both Charlemagne and Otto III were also influenced by the Byzantine tradition as the motto '*renovatio imperii Romanorum*' they used attests.) From Otto I in the tenth century a direct line of continuity can be traced through the Middle Ages and Early Modern periods until the formal dissolution of the Holy Roman Empire, by now firmly in the hands of one family, the Habsburgs, in 1806. Charlemagne was crowned Roman Emperor by the Pope in 800 AD, but for him and his direct descendants, the Germanic tradition of dividing up one's heritage among one's heirs predominated over any consideration of keeping the Empire together beyond their personal reign. Thus the territory held by Charlemagne and the Franks was divided up several times, first at the treaty of Verdun (843), confirming the pattern of Regnalism, i.e. of loyalty to a particular king or other ruler, rather than to a clearly defined territorial entity. Alongside the idea of universal empire, the order of the European world was dominated by Regnalism until the end of this period and in many cases beyond. Side by side with the Empire, entities began to emerge which either came within its jurisdiction, such as further acquisitions by war or inheritance of its princes, or which refused to accept the suzerainty of the Empire and emphasized their distinctness, such as the kingdom of the Western Franks – the later France (despite its erstwhile inclusion in Charlemagne's realm), England (notwithstanding Richard I's enforced oath of allegiance to the emperor), the Scandinavian and Iberian kingdoms.

Ever since Otto I refounded it in 962 with his own imperial coronation, the Empire had aspirations of universality, and successive emperors behaved as though they were at least *primi inter pares* among the princes of Europe. The Holy Roman Empire tried to extend its sway over neighbouring countries, successfully in the case of Bohemia, unsuccessfully in the cases of Hungary, Poland and Denmark. Nevertheless, it was with the emperors in particular that the popes entered into a contest of power which repeatedly became manifest in outright war, with princes and towns taking sides. These contests, which started in the eleventh century, permitted the rise of other powers and served to undermine those of both emperor and pope, albeit not to the point of total erosion. Indeed, the Holy Roman Empire was to rise to new heights of power in the Renaissance under the Habsburgs, and the institution of the Papacy is with us still today. It meant, however, that the migrant peoples' tradition of loyalty to their respective leaders became transformed into the aforementioned Regnalism, each prince being regarded in a Christian context as chosen by God, each with his or her own mystique of medieval rule. The latter elevated it to a great taboo to raise one's hand against the prince, and although there were civil wars that challenged a ruler's position, these usually hinged on rivalling claims to the crown. Once monogamy became the norm again among the nobility (the migrant peoples had often practised polygamy), the families of the princes, the dynasties, intermarried and provided both peaceful fusion of principalities and contesting claims to the succession. The period of the Hundred Years' War between the English and French crowns which is treated in this book by Anne Curry (Chapter 11) is an example of both. Other examples include the succession of the Stauffian emperor Frederick II to the Norman kingdom of Sicily through his mother, or the succession of Henry the Proud, Duke of Bavaria, to the Duchy of Saxony, again through his mother.

Warfare in the Middle Ages

Up to the twelfth century, warfare was dominated to no small extent by the great migrations which led ever new waves of warriors, often accompanied by their entire clans, to flood the Roman Empire and kingdoms and other principalities which established themselves within its frontiers as Rome and Constantinople progressively lost control of their provinces. The age of the great migrations is often taken to be from 375, when the Huns first raided the Roman Empire, to 568. Even though, after the fall of Rome in 476, Constantinople held out until 1453, and even though parts of Rome's old possessions were reconquered several times by Constantinople or indeed by regnal entities perceiving themselves as the heirs of Rome, the influx of Germanic, Hunnic, Gothic and Slav tribes who came to despoil but also to settle coloured warfare from the Danubian plains to the British Isles. In fact there were further waves of belligerent invasions by – significantly – often non-Christian tribes not influenced by the principle of restraint of Christian just war theory: the Hungarians troubled the empire in the tenth century, the (admittedly Christian) Normans and other Vikings spread their campaigns over the seas surrounding the continent, beginning with the plunder of the Loire Valley in 834 and leading to the conquest of Sicily in the eleventh century. The Byzantine Empire was successively or simultaneously threatened by the Persians, the Arabs, the Pechenegs and the Selchuk Turks. The Mongols and in their wake the Turks pushed into the east of Europe, getting as far as attacking Hungary and Bulgaria in the thirteenth century, and, in the case of the Turks, conquering much of the Balkans in the fourteenth century, nibbling away at the Byzantine Empire until its fall in 1453. The Arabs pushed into Europe both from the east and the south, besieging Constantinople in 674–78 and 717–18 and conquering most of Spain by 711 in the Battle of Guadalete. All these were wars imposed on Europe from the outside, with adversaries who did not adhere to Christian theoretical constraints on war.

For many of the tribes who came in the great migrations to settle in Europe, as Jan Willem Honig has noted in Chapter 9, warfare was an economic pursuit which did not come to an end with the tribe's establishment but became an almost annual enterprise, much to the disapproval of the Church. Warfare with the intention of looting persisted into the fifteenth century, as the chevauchées of the Hundred Years' War demonstrate. This was a second form of warfare endemic in the Middle Ages.

The Church sought to regulate this warfare which, as Christianity was spread among the invading tribes, increasingly pitted Christians against Christians, thereby offending the teaching of the Church. As Jonathan Riley-Smith shows, the crusading movement which started in 1099 with the call to the first Crusade was a way in which popes sought to channel their flock's energies for war into directions which could be seen as beneficiary to Christianity: the purpose was to free Christians from non-Christian oppression and to liberate the holy places from the infidel. Both preceding the Crusades and in parallel with them, wars of colonization and forced Christianization were carried on, first towards the European east, going back to Charlemagne's campaigns against the Saxons, and then towards the south. This third form of warfare in the minds of successive Spanish princes came to include the *reconquista* of the Iberian Peninsula from the Arabs (which arguably began in 722 with the battle of Covadonga, the first Arab defeat, or more properly in the eleventh century, and which ended with the fall of Granada in 1492).

Gradually a fifth form of war began to establish itself, however: warfare for dynastic reasons, which was already an element of the Norman Conquest of England, and by the time of the Hundred Years' War was a widespread pattern underlying the wars of Christian princes against each other. As such, it remained a pattern until well into the eighteenth century, and to the extent to which the German emperor played a role in the origins of the First World War, the contest for supremacy among cousins (here with Edward VII and George V of the United Kingdom) still mattered in the early twentieth century.

The elective process by which popes and emperors were chosen gave rise to a sixth form of warfare: the repeated election of two popes or emperors by rival factions often led to a showdown on the battlefield if not to prolonged wars. Likewise, the long contest between popes and emperors prompted princes and cities to take sides, leading to armed opposition nearly every time an emperor-elect proceeded to Italy to have himself crowned king of Italy and emperor in Rome.

A seventh form of warfare was that of the centralization of nascent kingdoms and later proto-states. Arguably the wars in which a single ruler tried to enforce his superiority over other rivalling princes of the same culture started in Gaul with Clovis in the fifth century when he eliminated other Frankish rulers, and continued up to the Hundred Years' War, if not to the time of Louis XIV with his non-martial centralizing measures of bringing together his nobility at Versailles. The wars of centralization in the British Isles came to an end only when James VI of Scotland inherited the English crown, and even then, the Stuart rebellions ensued.

An eighth form of warfare was roughly religious. Where it was conducted against heretics – the Cathars in the Albigensian Crusade (1209–29), or the Hussites in Bohemia (1419–36) – it had the support of the Church, but where it was low-level butchery in the form of the anti-Jewish persecutions, most notably in periods of pestilence (e.g. 1348–50), it did not, even though its perpetrators felt justified on religious grounds. Religious wars persisted well into early modern times, as Aline Goosens (Chapter 12, Part III) shows, and there are instances of it even today.

A ninth form of warfare concerned rivalling claims to territory, often, however, with a dynastic claim attached. This form of war often involved the kingdoms and principalities which shared borders, and accounts for much of the warfare between the Empire and France, or Denmark, or Poland. Sicily and southern Italy were chiefly contested areas, between the Byzantine Empire, Arabs, Normans, the Empire particularly under the Hohenstauffen dynasty, Aragon and the French dynasty of the Anjou. On a small scale, particularly in northern Italy, where they had long taken sides either with the popes or the emperors or the factions of the Guelfs and Ghibellines, the city-states disputed each other's privileges and territory, warring against each other which led to the rise of the *condottieri* or war lords particularly in the first half of the fifteenth century.

Perhaps the earliest manifestation of local movements towards independence is demonstrated in a tenth form of warfare, symbolized by the victory for Flemish independence imposed by foot soldiers organized in guilds on the French cavalry at Courtrai in 1302, the Swiss campaigns of independence both against the Habsburgs with the Swiss pikemen's victories of Morgarten (1315) and Sempach (1386), and against the Duke of Burgundy with the Swiss victories of Grandson, Murten (both 1476) and Nancy (1477), where Lorraine and Alsace came to the help of the Swiss. Again, Aline Goosens' chapter shows that these local movements for greater self-rule had much in common with those of later periods.

Throughout the Middle Ages wars seemed to have been the norm rather than peace, and many were thus campaigns that not only pitted Christians against Arabs, but also Christians against Christians. Instigators of the latter were, however, perpetually in search of religious justifications for their actions, arguing that God and justice were on their side. Battles were regarded as divine judgements and were thus largely avoided for fear that one's own side's sinfulness, notwithstanding the justice of the cause, might lead God to bestow victory upon the rival side. The mental reference to God and to his eternal judgement was eternally present in the minds of medieval men.

7   Byzantine concepts of war and peace

Julian Chrysostomides

This chapter will examine the concept of war and peace and the structures existing within the Byzantine Empire for waging war and the pursuit of peace. The material is mainly based on the records of the middle Byzantine period (ninth to eleventh centuries), though reference will occasionally be made to earlier sources.

The emperors of the eastern half of the Roman Empire (Byzantine Empire), after the fall of Rome to the Goths, saw it as their duty to bring about the restoration of the western half. This remained an active preoccupation at least until the early seventh century, the most spectacular attempt at restoration being that of Justinian I (527–65). As inheritors of the Graeco–Roman world, they saw their *politeia* (πολιτεία, state or empire) as a civilizing force. The continuous warfare in defence of its borders against the migratory and often destructive tribes emphasized this conception of themselves and their role *vis-à-vis* the outside world. As these change with times and circumstances so does their own perception of themselves and of others.

The political ideas, entertained by the rulers in this period, are expressed by historians or found in the official documents, emanating from the seat of authority, whose centre was the emperor. Based on the Roman concept of authority but modified by Hellenistic ideas of monarchy, the terrestrial kingdom was seen as a μίμησις (*mimesis* = imitation) of the heavenly kingdom, the κόσμος (*cosmos* = universe) which governed by λόγος (*logos* = reason). It therefore becomes imperative for a ruler to imitate God in the realm of governance, and as the embodiment of law (ἔμψυχος νόμος) he promulgated laws guided by reason. Thus the concept of authority and imperial power was no longer conceived simply in terms of military supremacy but also in terms of reason, further endowing the ruler with the attributes of love of mankind (φιλανθρωπία) and devoutness (εὐλάβεια). These Hellenistic ideas were transplanted into a Christian context by Eusebius,[1] and would remain the political theory of the empire throughout its history. It would act as a theoretical paradigm of what a well-ordered body politic or empire (πολιτεία or βασιλικὸν πολίτευμα) should be. This implies that the Byzantines were fostering an awareness of themselves as a community, which linked them with, or differentiated them from, their neighbours or opponents. This differentiation, of 'them and us', may be an element in confrontations, but not always the cause of war. The complex interplay of other factors, such as economic interests, quest for power and glory, religious divergence, revenge or even long-standing hostility, arising from past historical experience going back centuries, may contribute to the outbreak of war, but certainly not all are wars of expansion. For example, the hostility between Persia and Byzantium during Justinian I's reign was not a conflict for territorial expansion as such. The preoccupation of both powers was to bring peoples along their frontiers – Armenia, Georgia, Lazica and the tribes bordering the Caucasus – within their sphere of influence in order to create buffer states. This not only enhanced their respective territorial integrity, providing them with 'a weapon' which could be unleashed against one's enemies, but also gave them access to the trade routes through the Caucasus to Central Asia. Nevertheless, in the course of such an attempt hostilities broke out and violence was perpetrated, for example, in 527, when Persia became apprehensive at the Byzantine encroachment in that area.

Given the realities of force, how did Byzantine political theory, imbued as it was with Christian ideas, reconcile the dichotomy between the belief that man is endowed with rationality by virtue of his being made in the image of God, and the irrationality of war and violence?[2] This problem intensely preoccupied the early Fathers of the Church. They saw the root of conflict and war in man's appetites, his desire for glory, wealth, luxury and greed, thus unleashing violence within himself, which eventually spilled out against his fellow men.[3] The dilemma facing them was whether it was admissible to use violence in order to curb violence. St Athanasius (*c.*295–373), for example, examining society's attitude to 'murder' and 'killing in war', adopted a relative approach. He pointed out that society differentiated between the two. Those who killed in battle in defence of their country, far from being considered murderers, were honoured as heroes.[4] In other words, the motive behind an action determined its essence. St Basil (330–79) too recognized the necessity to fight in defence of prudence and devotion (σωφροσύνη καὶ εὐσέβεια). Although he agreed with St Athanasius' distinction, he nevertheless admonished that it would be prudent for those who had killed in war to abstain from receiving communion for three years, on the grounds that their hands had been polluted with blood.[5] St Basil's verdict established a principle which was to be the guiding rule, at least until the fifteenth century. For example, when the Emperor Nicephoros Phocas (963–69), most probably influenced by the ideas of *jihad*, proposed to enrol as martyrs those who had fallen in battle, it was rejected outright by the Patriarch and his council on the basis of St Basil's statement.[6]

The early Church had succeeded in finding a *modus vivendi* with the existing norms and structures of society. However, in turn, its tenets exercised a strong influence on the secular interpretation concerning the contradiction between good and evil; that is, man's inherent inclination towards good, love and peace, and his capacity for evil, exemplified in war, violence and cruelty. Within these parameters, the Church gave support to war as a last resort for the containment of evil, but it always stressed that it was imperative to employ φιλανθρωπία (*philanthropia* = love of mankind) and οἰκονομία (*oikonomia* = moderation) in the use of force. This theological influence is attested by the preamble of the military treatise, the *Tactica*, written by the Emperor Leo VI (886–912).

In theory, Leo insists, man, as God's creation made in His image, ought to espouse peace, and succour his fellow-men, but the existence of evil (the devil), which is inimical to humankind, incites man, contrary to his nature, to destroy his own species. The only remedy against this evil is for man to take the field with the sole aim of restoring and maintaining peace, and opposing those who are bent on befouling the earth with kindred or foreign blood. War, therefore, can only be excused when it is undertaken in defence of one's country and is waged on behalf of justice, but never when it is perpetrated in order to despoil neighbouring peoples. Its aftermath should be accompanied, as far as possible, by the establishment of peace with one's enemies.[7] In other words, war must be undertaken for the restoration of the terrestrial order, which is a reflection of the heavenly one. To achieve this mission, the knowledge of military science and how one should conduct war becomes imperative.

The *Tactica*, an extensive manual for would-be generals, gives detailed instructions on all aspects of war. It explores strategic planning, military techniques, armaments, ranging from weapons to espionage, and gives detailed observations on the character, strengths and weaknesses of the enemies of the empire and the different combat methods required in any confrontation, depending on one's foe. These have constantly to be updated, for once they have been used and become known to the enemy, they are obsolete.[8]

Apart from practical considerations, Byzantine military texts cast light not only on the characteristics of their opponents, but more importantly on themselves. They reveal to us their own perceptions, prejudices and strengths. Surveying the various peoples with whom the Byzantines were at war they make a distinction between the Persians and the Arabs on one hand and the Turkic tribes on the other. The Persians, apart from differences in tactics, discipline and structure of their armies, displayed different habits and characteristics. Though highly suspicious and subservient to the will of their rulers, whom they served out of fear, they entertained deep patriotic feelings, to the extent that they were prepared to suffer all sorts of hardship out of love for their country. They were formidable when besieging, but more so when they were themselves besieged, for they could hide and endure distress to such a degree that they could transform the situation by their endurance and, though themselves reluctant to put forward proposals for a treaty, they accepted it when it was offered to them.[9] Once such a treaty had been concluded, on the whole it was respected. In contrast to the Persians, each Arab tribal leader fought on his own account, either for glory or booty, but from the point of view of tactics and methods of fighting, the Byzantines regarded them as their most formidable enemy. Leo VI derived his information on the Arabs, not only from the imperial records, from generals and earlier emperors, but in particular from his own father, Basil I (867–86), who had led a number of expeditions against them.[10]

The nomadic tribes, on the other hand, insofar as keeping agreements was concerned, were a far cry from the Persians, as the Byzantines discovered in their dealings with those bordering their frontiers. Though the empire was prepared to pay a yearly tribute in gold, for example, to the Tzani in the Euphrates, on condition that they did not plunder the area, this was not successful. For the Tzani, having accepted the gold and sworn according to their customs to keep the peace, would break their agreement and return to plunder. A similar situation occurred at a later period with the Turkic tribes, who out of greed for money easily broke their oath and did not honour the treaties.[11] Faced with such a dilemma, the Byzantines were forced either to strike an agreement with the foes of their opponents, or try to bring them within their sphere of political and cultural influence.

Both approaches worked fairly well for a time. For example, in the late ninth and early tenth centuries, they were able to stem the incursions of various tribes by befriending the ethnie (ἔθνος) of the Pechenegs with gifts and imperial honours. The fear of a counter-attack by the Pechenegs put a check on the Bulgar and Russian attacks; at the same time, it stopped the Pechenegs themselves from plundering imperial territory.[12]

Tribute to prevent war was paid not only to tribes but also to the Persians and Arabs. Peace was often concluded with the payment of a fixed sum, since in this way the destruction of cities and populations was avoided. It is true that such a policy at times proved a double-edge sword. The policy may have had its opponents; for example, Procopius in his *Secret History* accused Justinian I of being too ready to buy peace from the Huns, thereby encouraging the tribes to send their compatriots to pillage imperial lands in order to elicit more money 'from a man, who, for no good reason wished to purchase peace'.[13]

The second approach, namely that of bringing potential foes into the Byzantine political orbit, was practised widely by the empire. This led to the Christianization of, among others, the Tzani in the sixth, the Serbs and Bulgars in the ninth and the Russians in the tenth centuries.[14] This, however, did not always eliminate military conflict. King Symeon of Bulgaria (893–927), for example, brought up in Constantinople and aspiring to sit on the imperial throne, reversed his father's policy of co-operation and embarked on a military conflict with Byzantium. Despite

Byzantine diplomatic efforts to call upon the Magyars to attack the Bulgars in the rear, the war dragged on with a few interruptions for thirty-three years, ultimately coming to an end with Symeon's death.

The art of war demanded knowledge in weaponry, tactics, construction for the erection of siege engines and fortresses, logistics, astronomy and medicine. It was considered essential for the general in charge of an expedition to take advice from experienced veterans who had distinguished themselves in war but also that he should have some knowledge of these disciplines. This presupposed the support of a staff with particular expertise, including scientists, tacticians, engineers and accountants as well as craftsmen. Knowledge of astronomy, for example, was not only essential for gauging their position on the ground, but also the weather, climatic changes and direction of the wind, which could affect a battle.[15] The advance knowledge of a solar eclipse was used by Alexius I Comnenus (1081–1118) against the Pechenegs, by portraying it as a divine omen of their planned perfidy, thus forcing them to honour their commitment to a truce.[16] Vigilance along the borders was essential for the defence of the empire, but also for projecting an image of invincibility in order to preempt hostilities.

In the event of war becoming inevitable, military preparations demanded the involvement of the entire country. Constantine VII Porphyrogenitus (913–59) gives an interesting account of his father's preparations for the expedition against the island of Crete in 911, then under Arab occupation. Throughout the littoral and islands of the empire ships were fitted out, and sailors and soldiers recruited. Provisions came from all over the empire. Similarly, factories in different districts were ordered to manufacture a quantity of weapons of every type: arrows, shields, lances, nails, and mattocks, to produce tin, bronze, lead and other metals used in shipbuilding, and to make ropes, oars, sails, and measures of cotton for Greek fire and caulking ships.[17] These preparations involved not only the administrative authorities but also merchants and craftsmen and a large section of society, which created a sense of unity. This is clearly reflected in Patriarch Nicholas I Mystikos's letter to the metropolitans with regard to the Bulgarian hostilities in 920. 'Dangers, which threaten the community' he wrote, 'require that the community shall assist: for circumstances affecting us all cannot be amended unless all of us to the best of our power take a hand in their amelioration.' Echoing the Platonic argument, he goes on to say, 'that if the community is saved, then each will certainly preserve his own along with it, but if the whole is ruined, there can be no salvation left for the individual'.[18]

In fact, unity was considered so essential that generals were advised to group together brothers and friends so that during battle they would not abandon each other, but out of love would stay and fight with greater tenacity to defend each other.[19] Fear was deemed to be the enemy within. Therefore, if some of the soldiers before or during battle were seized by fear and feigned sickness, they were sent away from the battlefield and allotted guard duties in fortified places, or given other tasks that did not carry danger to prevent others from being affected in the same way.[20] It was the general's task to inspire loyalty and sacrifice, not simply with stirring words, but by sharing all hardships with his men.[21] An example of outstanding leadership was shown by Basil I during his campaign against Germanikeia in Syria in about 873, when his army had to cross the river Paradeisos at the dead of night. Surrounded by torchlight, the emperor stood in the middle of the river encouraging his men to cross and came to the rescue of those who were in danger of being swept away.[22]

This sense of cohesion, strengthened by common language and religion, engendered a certain caution towards other groups recruited into the army as mercenaries, particularly those who did not share the same religious beliefs. Secrets were to be withheld from them, and measures taken to ensure that the number of foreign mercenaries did not exceed those of their own soldiers. In the event that foreign troops happened to belong to the same tribe as the enemy, they had to be moved to another part of the country, so that they were not given the opportunity either to fight against their own people or unite with them to the empire's detriment.[23] Experience on many occasions confirmed the validity of this observation, for example, at the battle of Mantzikert in 1071, and the capture of Nicaea in 1333. Such views displaying wariness of the 'other' must not be identified with racism. Byzantine society, barring religion, was an open, multi-ethnic society, given that a number of individuals and families of foreign extraction rose to the highest positions, including that of the imperial office, and even founded imperial dynasties. Nevertheless, it would be important to explore to what extent these views influenced their behaviour towards their enemies in battle, their treatment of prisoners and conquered populations.

Though war inevitably engenders violence, it is important to stress that the essence of good leadership, as the Byzantines conceived it, was to minimize bloodshed on either side. Hence, often a pragmatic and an ethical approach seems to have been intertwined with the advice given on the conduct of soldiers on the battlefield. For example, in engagements with marauding Arabs, the soldiers were instructed to shoot not only at the riders but also at the horses with poisoned arrows, for Arab horses were so valuable that their loss would discourage the marauders from future expeditions.[24] The same approach is reflected on the advice given about investing a castle or a town. To avoid a long drawn out siege, onerous for both sides, the commander in charge would persuade the inhabitants to surrender either through released prisoners, or by letters shot over the wall on arrows, promising the inhabitants that they would be left free and unharmed.[25] If, however, the castle or town was captured after a battle, only those carrying weapons were to be put to death. These conditions were announced in the local dialect, so that all could understand the message and be given the chance to throw their weapons down. Such methods, they believed, turned an enemy into a suppliant to the advantage of the conqueror.[26] Once a castle or town had surrendered, those wishing to leave should be allowed to do so, otherwise they might be driven to despair and transform themselves into a hostile army. The same should apply to a captured contingent, for this was considered to be the most practical and profitable solution, since it would be difficult to keep guard on such numbers.[27] Similarly, in a protracted siege, if any of the inhabitants were captured outside the walls, the young males should be detained, but the women, children and old people should be released and allowed to take refuge in other towns. There were two reasons for adopting such a course. First, they would not have to be fed, and second, the captors would have demonstrated their humanity (φιλανθρωπία), which ultimately might split the views of the besieged and lead to surrender. But beyond these practical considerations, a general should show humanity both to the conquered in their suffering, and to his own men for enduring hardships.[28] The just and humane treatment shown by General Nicephorus Phocas in his campaign in Lombardy in about 876 reflected these qualities, for not only did he succeed in recovering lost territory from the Arabs, but above all he won the allegiance of the people by granting remission of taxes and personal burdens. Such a policy aimed both at the glory of the empire and the welfare of its people.[29]

The issue of the treatment of prisoners forms another important subject in the military treatises. There was no question of their being maltreated or put to death. According to Eusebius, Constantine the Great exhorted that prisoners of war should not to be killed. The tradition survived, at least in principle, as is attested by the *Tactica* and the letters of Patriarch Nicholas I Mystikos.[30] On the other hand, captives were paraded together with booty in triumphal processions amid acclamations to stress the might of the empire, as, for example, in 831, when Emperor Theophilos commemorated his victory over the Arabs.[31]

Prisoners of war were an invaluable source of information concerning the layout of enemy country, numbers of troops and other secrets which enabled a general in charge of the operation to plan more efficiently his defence or attack. They were made to taste food and drink water or wine, in order to find out whether these had been poisoned by the retreating enemy, as happened during the Persian campaign under Maurice, when a large number of Byzantine horses perished after having eaten poisoned barley.[32] Prisoners were also used as human shields when marching under attack through hostile country, in the hope that the enemy would not shoot at their own people.[33] A ploy to boost the morale of their troops was to send the healthy, strong and well-armed prisoners away from the camp. Instead they paraded the mean and badly equipped ones, making them plead for their lives, thus giving the impression that the enemy was to be pitied rather than feared.[34] Similarly, the treatment of spies on the battlefield had a propaganda purpose. If, for example, the position of the imperial army was strong, any spy caught was to be released unharmed, since he was expected to inform the enemy about the situation; but if the imperial army was in a dire position, the spy would either have had to be killed or sent in safety away from the front.[35] To minimize losses and prevent long drawn out wars, propaganda also played an important role in the diplomatic field. Special treatment was given to visiting ambassadors in the hope that this would give rise to suspicion among the enemy that they had been bribed. As far as possible, misleading impressions were created and false information relayed, for the Byzantines knew that, apart from their official capacity, ambassadors were not averse to intelligence gathering.[36]

Reflecting on their attitude to war and treatment of captives, one has to differentiate between theory and practice. Though atrocities occurred in battles or during the capture of cities, these were actions and decisions taken by individuals in the heat of the moment or otherwise. Constantine V (741–75), for example, during his Bulgarian campaign in 763, is said not only to have eliminated his enemies on the battlefield, but to have brought a considerable number of captives to Constantinople and delivered them to the circus factions to be killed in cold blood. Another example is Basil II (976–1025), and the blinding of the Bulgarian soldiers in their hundreds, or the revenge which the Byzantine general Eumathios Philokales (*c.*1108) wreaked on the Turks at Lampe for having reduced to rubble the flourishing city of Adramyttion some years earlier.[37] Such examples of brutality can be multiplied, but there is no evidence to suggest that these inhuman acts were part of, to use a modern term, an ideology. On the contrary in the military treatises the approach is fundamentally different. It was axiomatic that a successful war was conducted with prudence and humanity as far as it was possible. Chroniclers and historians, on the whole, by their condemnation or factual reporting, confirm this view. And it is indicative that after his victory over Bulgaria in 1018, Basil II granted that country extensive privileges, thereby eliciting Michael Psellus' remark that he was 'more of a villain in war time, more of an emperor in time of peace'.[38]

Ultimately, the ravages of war, the slaughter, the displacement of populations, the untold misery and the depletion of resources, forced opponents to put an end to hostilities and begin negotiations for peace. There was a well-established protocol for this. The negotiations began first with the exchange of envoys between generals of opposing parties. On this point, the *Tactica* advises the general not to be intransigent, but to accord them every respect, for theirs is a sacred task, and by endangering their lives the actual office is put in jeopardy, thereby depriving ethnies (ἔθνη) of the benefits they provide.[39] Indeed, ambassadors were protected by customary law and enjoyed immunity. It was therefore considered an act of barbarism to retain envoys, as King Symeon of Bulgaria was in the habit of doing.[40]

Once these preliminary negotiations had proved successful, they were taken up at a higher level between governments, and in this second instance it was appropriate to exchange gifts.

One of the main points in negotiations with the Arabs concerned the exchange of prisoners. This usually took place along the border on the River Lamos. The system adopted was to construct two bridges, one for the Greeks and the other for the Arabs, so that simultaneously each side sent a prisoner across, the stipulation being that the number exchanged would be exactly the same. In 845, however, the exchange did not proceed according to plan. The Muslims detained by the Byzantines totalled 3000 men, and 500 women and children. The prisoners held by the Arabs were fewer in number, and the Byzantines were not prepared to accept old men in exchange for young ones. The Arab officials had to scour the markets of Baghdad and Raqqa to buy Greek slaves to make up the number, but as these were not sufficient, Khalif Watiq had to release some Greek women from his harem.[41] The more prominent prisoners were held in Constantinople, and in 922 an Arab delegation visited them to ascertain their condition.[42] Negotiations for the signing of treaties were not always easy, and diplomacy had to be exercised. Even the seating arrangements of delegates became important; hence the round table the Byzantines provided for their negotiations with the Arab emirs in 946.[43]

As stated at the beginning of this chapter, the aim of war was to re-establish peace among peoples in accordance with the divine order, and to cease shedding the blood of one's own people or of others, for it was the duty of everyone and particularly of a leader to do his utmost to secure peace, 'that inestimable prize left by Christ', for all mankind.[44] The question is: How could peoples divided by language, and above all by religion, as in the case of the Arabs, and by the memory of atrocities, establish if not total and lasting peace, at least a truce? The answer lay in understanding each other on a cultural, spiritual and everyday level. Embassies of purely cultural and commercial nature contributed towards such an understanding. The exchange of sumptuous gifts, besides their propaganda value, gave an idea of the cultural standing of their opponent. The despatch by Constantine VII of a manuscript of Dioscorides' *materia medica* to the Khalif of Cordova at his request casts light on these attempts to understand each other. In addition the presence of eminent prisoners, both in Constantinople and Baghdad, played a significant role in fostering an appreciation of each other's culture. It was a student of Leo the Mathematician, who, taken prisoner by the Arabs, told his master about his teacher's profound knowledge of Euclidean geometry.[45] The Khalif of Mamun then wrote to Theophilus, 'from the fruit we have known the tree, from the student the teacher', and invited Leo to Baghdad, though the emperor, an ardent admirer of Arab culture, refused to let him go.[46]

It was in this sharing of cultural experiences and understanding that the road to peace lay. It is therefore appropriate to close this chapter with the words of Nicholas Mystikos in his letter to the Emir of Crete. Speaking about the friendship that existed between his predecessor, Photios, and the emir's father, he writes:

> although the barriers of religion stood between us, yet a strong intelligence, wit and character, a love of humanity, and all other qualities which adorn and dignify man's nature, arouse in the breast of good men an affection for those to whom the loved qualities are found. And so he loved your father, who was endowed with the qualities I speak of, even though the difference of religious faith stood between them.[47]

Notes

1 N. H. Baynes, 'Eusebius and the Christian Empire', *Mélanges Bidez*, Annuaire de l'Institut de philologie et d'histoire orientales, vol. 2, 1933–34, pp. 13–18, repr. in *Byzantine Studies and Other Essays*, London, Athlone Press, 1960, and cited here, pp. 168–72.

2 The subject of violence and its various aspects is being explored by my student Andreas Meitanis in his doctoral thesis, *Violence in Byzantium*, for the University of London.

3 Gregory of Nazianzus, *Or.* 19.14, ed. J. P. Migne, *Patrologia Graeca*, 1863, vol. 35, Paris, col. 1061A; J. Chrysostom, *Hom. 7.1. in 1 Timotheum*, *Patrologia Graeca*, vol. 62, col. 534; idem., *Exp. in Ps. 119:7*, *Patrologia Graeca*, vol. 5, col. 343.

4 Athanasius, *epistula ad Amunem*, *Patrologia Graeca*, new edn, 1887, vol. 26, col. 1173B.

5 Basil, *epistula 188 can 13*, *Patrologia Graeca*, 1886, vol. 32, col. 681.

6 J. Zonaras, *Epitomae Historiarum*, ed. M. Pinder, *CSHB*, Bonn, 1897, vol. 3, p. 506.

7 Leo VI, *Tactica*, *Patrologia Graeca*, 1863, vol. 107, col. 673B–C; col. 1080B, no. 14.

8 *Tactica*, col. 1009D, no. 63.

9 *Das Strategikon des Maurikios*, ed. and trans. by G. T. Dennis and E. Gamillscheg, Vienna, Öster. Akad. d. Wissenschaften, 1981, pp. 354, *9–14*.

10 *Tactica*, col. 976A, no. 123.

11 Procopius, *History of the Wars*, ed. and trans. by H. B. Dewing, London, Heinemann, 1954, vol. 1: I. xv. 21, p. 136; *Tactica*, col. 957B–C, no. 47.

12 Constantine VII Porphyrogenitus, *De administrando Imperio*, ed. and trans. by Gy. Moravcsik and R. J. H. Jenkins, Washington, DC, Dumbarton Oaks, 1967, pp. 48–56.

13 Procopius, *Secret History*, vol. VI: x. 5–7, pp. 130–2.

14 Procopius, *Wars*, vol. 1: I. xv. 21–5, p. 136; *Tactica*, col. 960D no. 61.

15 *Tactica*, cols. 1088A–1092; 1084A, no. 33.

16 Anna Comnena, *Alexiad*, VII. 3, ed. L. Schopen, Bonn, ed. Weber, 1839, I, p. 338. English translation by E. R. A. Sewter, London, Penguin Books, 1969, p. 221.

17 Constantine VII Porphyrogenitus, *De cerimoniis*, ed. J. J. Reiske, Bonn, Weber, 1829, pp. 657–60.

18 Nicholas I Mystikos, Patriarch of Constantinople, *Letters*, ed. and trans. by R. J. H. Jenkins and L. G. Westerink, Washington, DC, Dumbarton Oaks, 1973, 92, pp. 354, *1–3*, 356, *9–21*.

19 *Tactica*, col. 708B, no. 39; col. 1056B, no. 160.
20 *Strategikon*, p. 274, no. 29; *Tactica*, col. 1021B–C, no. 30; col. 1057A, no. 165.
21 *Tactica*, cols. 1013C–1016A.
22 Ibid., col. 772A, no. 13.
23 *Strategikon*, p. 242, *1–4*; *Tactica*, col. 1037C–D, no. 89.
24 *Tactica*, col. 952B, no. 23; col. 980A, nos. 135–6.
25 *Strategikon*, p. 272, no. 21.
26 *Tactica*, col. 892D, no. 22.
27 *Strategikon*, p. 274, no. 25; *Tactica*, col. 1021A, no. 28.
28 *Tactica*, cols. 892D–893A, no. 23; cols. 897D–900A, no. 45.
29 Ibid., cols. 896D–897A, nos. 38–9; cf. J. Skylitzes, *Synopsis Historiarum*, ed. J. Thurn, Berlin, Walter de Gruyter, 1973, 4, pp. 262–3.
30 *Life of Constantine*, ed. I. A. Heikel, Leipzig, 1902, II, ch. 13, p. 46; *Tactica*, 1021A, no. 28; Nicholas Mystikos, *Letters*, 102, p. 376, *57–64*; cf. 2, pp. 14, *36*–16, *62*.
31 Constantine Porphyrogenitus, *De cerimoniis*, pp. 504–5.
32 *Strategikon*, pp. 318, *94–5*; 320, *122–7*; *Tactica*, col. 929C–D, nos. 68–9; John of Nikiou, *Chronique*, ed. and trans. H. Zotenberg, Paris, Imprimerie Nationale, 1883, ch. 96, p. 408.
33 *Strategikon*, p. 324, *47–51*; *Tactica*, col. 780D, no. 49.
34 *Tactica*, col. 844C, no. 4.
35 *Srategikon*, pp. 282–4, no. 29.
36 Ibid., p. 272, no. 17.
37 Nikephoros, Patriarch of Constantinople, *Short History*, ed. and trans. by C. Mango, Washington D.C., Dumbarton Oaks, 1990, 76, pp. 148–50; Skylitzes, p. 349, *35–9*; Anna Comnena, *Alexiad*, Bk. 14, ch. 1, II, p. 250, English translation by E. A. R. Sewter, p. 437.
38 Michael Psellus, *Chronographie*, ed. and trans. by E. Renauld, Paris, Budé, 1926, I, 34, p. 21, English translation by E. A. R. Sewter, p. 47.
39 *Tactica*, cols. 1021D–1024A, no. 33.
40 Nicholas Mystikos, *Letters*, 28, p. 192, *32–6*.
41 A.A. Vasiliev, *Byzance et les Arabes*, Institut de Philologie et d'Histoire Orientales, 1935, I, pp. 199–202: Arab sources cited.
42 Nicholas Mystikos, *Letters*, 102, pp. 372–80.
43 Constantine Porphyrogenitus, *De cerimoniis*, II. 15, p. 594.
44 *Tactica*, cols. 692D–693A, no. 49.
45 Vasiliev, *Byzance et les Arabes*, II, p. 186.
46 Theophanes continuatus, *Chronographia*, ed. E. Bekker, Bonn, Weber, 1838, pp. 185–90.
47 Nicholas Mystikos, *Letters*, 2, pp. 14, *21–7*.

8 Collective identities, war and integration in the Early Middle Ages

Bernhard Zeller

In the Early Middle Ages, ethnic groups were established primarily on the basis of common mythical traditions which were handed down orally in tales of gods and mythical figures. Tales of legendary origins and glorious history created a group's identity. Such constituent myths represented the beginning of a collective historical consciousness which manifested itself in the belief in a biological community of origin. This played a decisive role in ethnogenesis, the gradual process of forming and stabilizing a people,[1] through the creation of a collective self-consciousness and a specific group identity.[2] Reinhard Wenskus rightly argued that the ethnic existence of a community only began when it developed its own historico-ethnic tradition.[3] Admittedly, this ethnic consciousness did not apply to all members of the *gens* to the same extent and at all times. On the contrary, it seems frequently to have been concentrated around representatives of the leading families within the ethnic unit, who made a pronounced contribution to the tradition of the *gens*. Through this they were further able to substantiate their claim to power, as they embodied the historical continuity of their people and thereby also that of its ethnic existence.[4]

The emergence of an Early Medieval *gens*

The tradition of each individual *gens* bound people to an imagined ethnic unit which could fluctuate in its composition, since early medieval societies were dynamic rather than static entities. Hence it often came about that smaller groups split off from an ethnic community.[5] This may have been determined by economic conditions, as the barbarian economy ran at a loss and was unable to make a profit from the available settlement area. In the Early Middle Ages, barbarian clans lived from hand to mouth. Unforeseeable events such as natural disasters could necessitate tribal fission. Admittedly, this was more frequently determined by a combination of factors within the nobility, for life in an early medieval tribe was hardly romantic and harmonious. Barbarian societies rarely knew peace: one constantly found oneself in a state of war. Peace constituted an exception and had to be contractually determined.[6] As soon as one group had

come into being through splitting off from another, it left its old homeland and formed a new tribe or people. The inverse – integration of units
into larger wholes – was more difficult to achieve. Upon joining larger
groups, small ethnic groups tended to give up their own tribal tradition
completely and thus disappeared as units; others were able to maintain
their ethnic identity when joining larger groups. Hence early medieval
peoples often manifested themselves as polyethnic migrational entities.
Examples include the large army of Theoderic the Great, in which
Rugians, Vandals, Alans, Heruls, Sciri, Suevi, Sarmatians, Gepids and
Alamanni fought alongside the Goths,[7] or the Lombards, led into Italy by
Alboin in 568, whose ranks included Gepids, Heruls, Thuringians, Saxons,
and even people from the provinces of Pannonia and Noricum.[8]

War, peace and integration

Scholars have long held the migrant Germanic peoples to be responsible
for the destruction of the Roman world. This idea was for the most part
linked with the image of a clear chronological break between Antiquity and
the Middle Ages. In earlier historiography, numerous papers portrayed Late
Antiquity as the twilight of the gods. Other scholars saw the Early Middle
Ages as the dawn of a new age.[9] More recent research into the period of
transformation presents it as an unstable image which can appear sometimes as Late Antiquity and sometimes as the Early Middle Ages.[10] Along
with this, there has been a change in the historical assessment of various
barbarian groups (above all that of the Germanic peoples), who in fact neither destroyed the Roman Empire nor revived it, but rather settled within
it and transformed it.[11] Many sought a share in the empire, which they were
either granted or which they seized by force. Barbarian kingdoms thus
dissolved Roman universal statehood, and Roman–barbarian kings became
heirs, as it were, to the universal empire. This does not mean that the political demise of the Roman world empire should be denied, and it certainly
does not allow the replacement of the old catastrophe theory with a naive
hypothesis of continuity: the transformation of the Roman world was
neither a peaceful process, nor did it merely constitute the change of land-
ownership,[12] nor was it determined solely by the victory of the barbarian
gentes (tribes, ethnies) which seldom conquered imperial territory. It was
more frequently the case that the Romans allowed them, under contract,
to settle in territories situated on the border of the empire. Thus, a *modus
vivendi* arose between Rome and a section of the barbarian *gentes*, which
inaugurated the transformation of the Roman world in Late Antiquity.

War, armament and warfare in the age of migration

Jordanes, a sixth-century historian who wrote a history of the Goths based
on the works of the Roman statesman and scholar Cassiodorus, describes

104 Bernhard ZE Zeller

the battle at Nedao, an unknown river in Pannonia at which the Huns and their allies were decisively defeated by a barbarian coalition under the leadership of the Gepids in 454. In his account, he assigns particular weapons to some of the peoples involved in the clash. However, his statements contradict the testimony of other historians of Late Antiquity. It is thus less easy to claim that weapons had ethnic associations.[13] The great scholar Isidorus of Seville (d. 636) associated the *francisca* (battle-axe) with the Franks in his *Etymologiae*, an encyclopaedic work that attempted to include the entire knowledge of Antiquity.[14] His claim was not entirely without foundation, for excavated graves prove that this weapon was part of the standard equipment of Frankish warriors. Nevertheless, it was not used exclusively by the Franks.[15] A similar point may be made with regard to the *sax*, a small sword. As Widukind of Corvey (d. after 973) asserts in his history of the Saxons, the name 'Saxon' ought to be associated with this particular weapon,[16] although this is not to say that it was used solely by this people.[17]

If weapons did not constitute an ethnologically specific characteristic, the variations in weaponry and methods of fighting among military units of Late Antiquity and the Early Middle Ages need to be considered in a wider context. Thus, western European peoples can be differentiated from those on the lower Danube and in the Pontic steppe area, albeit with some reservations. While the foot soldiers of the former – armed with spears, swords and shields – were merely reinforced by mounted units, the latter always fought on horseback, although this does not necessarily mean that the Goths, Huns and Avars did not possess infantry. Of course there were foot soldiers who had certain specific tactical functions, but mounted soldiers – who carried the *contus* or lance, sword and circular shield – were responsible for striking the decisive blow.[18] Due to the military effectiveness of such heavy mounted units, they soon became an indispensable part of the military contingent in western Europe also. In contrast, light cavalry – armed with the reflex bow – remained a speciality of peoples from the eastern and southern European areas due to climactic reasons.[19]

The barbarians were originally organized in battle according to families, clans and tribes. Caesar's account of his clash with Ariovistus in 58 BC reveals that as the barbarians prepared for battle with Roman legions, they were deployed by tribe.[20] However, Caesar also tells us about proto–feudal links, which in time increased in importance.[21] At the time of the migration, such hierarchically organized units dominated the communities of origin, even though the clan was still recognized as the legal community. Tribal armies, which at that time were principally organized according to allegiance, were made up of approximately 3,000 men. They were therefore almost as strong as late Roman legions, whose mainstay during this period was no longer heavily armed foot soldiers, but rather the all-decisive cavalry. Hence there was only a minimal difference between the late Roman/Byzantine armies and those of the tribal units, a fact that was reinforced by close contracts between the two sides. While barbarians frequently belonged to the Roman armed forces as confederates, numerous officers who had been tactically and strategically trained in the Roman army served with barbarian forces. Naturally these lacked the basic infrastructure of the Roman legions, but under appropriate leadership their logistical advantages could be decisive. Over the course of the fourth and fifth centuries, the rising importance of the Roman, or Byzantine, military led to their increasingly carrying out civil functions. Wolfram has emphasized the fact that the army became an instrument for the remodelling of the Roman world.[22] The extent to which this analysis can be endorsed is illustrated in the example of the Late Antique policy of the Romans towards their confederates.

Peace and integration: the foedus[23]

By binding contractually the *gentes* to Rome and thus making them confederates, a constructive link was created between the classical world and that of the barbarian peoples. The allies undertook to respect Roman imperial borders, to send warriors and tributes from time to time, in return for payment and general protection. Theoretically, Rome's contractual position was on the whole more favourable than that of its partners, although it should be remembered that the *foedera* made a limited contribution to the solution of military and political problems. Treaties with barbarian peoples usually became void upon the death of the current emperor. Thus it is little wonder that the barbarians were considered disloyal by the Romans.

The roots of a policy towards confederates were already laid in the second century. For example, treaties were concluded in the Rhine area between Romans and barbarians. Admittedly, they were not overly effective, as the Franks and Alamanni were not monarchies in the third and fourth centuries, but rather were composed of several small groups. The Franks – the Germanic peoples on the right bank of the Lower Rhine who had merged in around 200 AD and were still free from Roman rule – mainly threatened the area to the left of the Lower Rhine with recurrent raiding. From the third century onwards, this could occasionally penetrate deep into the Roman Empire. The frontier was continuously attacked, plundered and devastated by barbarian hordes. Tongres, for example, was destroyed during this period and Trier suffered the same fate a little later. Roman defensive measures were only minimally effective. On numerous occasions they were indeed successful in ambushing the enemy, surrounding them and inflicting heavy losses upon them, yet ultimately they failed to beat them.

At around the same time, the Alamanni begin to appear in our sources. As in the case of the Franks, we are dealing with a unit of various small ethnic groups of Suebian origin. In a relatively short time, they succeeded in advancing in the west over the Rhine to Trier and in the south across the Danube to the northern foothills of the Alps. The Roman army was once again able to repel them after a while, but the pressure of Alamannic looting on Roman imperial territory increased to such an extent over the following years that the Roman defence along the route of the Rhine, Lake Constance, the Ill and the Danube was withdrawn and the area of the Decumanti abandoned to the savage Alamanni. It is notable that from the Roman point of view this did not constitute a conquest, as the territory was ceded for tactical reasons and the claim to rule it was not relinquished.

The Goths were the Romans' greatest enemy on the Lower Danube in the third century. In the middle of the century they attacked the Balkan Peninsula and Asia Minor in a series of raids. The Goths and a number of other tribal groups of both Germanic and Sarmatian origin were under the leadership of a king by the name of Cniva, and were thus a monarchy unlike the Franks and Alamanni. The Goths were victorious, and made a killing in both human and material terms, invading the Roman Empire again in subsequent years in order to rob and pillage. In 268, Gothic attacks reached previously unknown heights. A few months later, however, the Roman Emperor Claudius II (268–70) won a decisive victory over the enemy at Naissus-Niš, which can be viewed as being relevant to the later fission of the Goths. Further successes can be attributed to his successor Aurelian (270–75). These peaked in 271 when Aurelian and his army crossed the Danube and were able to defeat the Goths several times on their own territory. He was thus able to avert the barbarian threat for some time.

The fact that the administrative relinquishing of Trajan's Dacia took place in this period shows that this development was not immediately associated with the Gothic assault, but rather with the fact that the situation on the Danube was to be stabilized. The Romans were also successful in the Rhine area during the last quarter of the third century, where Emperor Probus (276–82) succeeded in re-establishing imperial borders despite heavy exchanges with the Franks. Prisoners of war who were taken during these clashes were enslaved by the Romans and transported to the Black Sea, where they were to be settled as dependent farmers. These plans failed when prisoners seized some ships and, after an adventurous journey through the Mediterranean and the Straits of Gibraltar, returned to their homeland on the Lower Rhine. The battles continued there and the Romans were able to record further successes under the leadership of Maximian (286–305). The emperor and his army twice crossed the Lower Rhine and were victorious against the Franks. One of their kings by the name of Gennobaudes submitted, making a pledge of peace to the victorious Romans and handing over numerous prisoners of war. In return, Maximian granted him a proper *foedus*, though it did not have much effect.

The first workable treaties were concluded with the Goths, who were probably already Roman confederates in the third century. The first unambiguous evidence for the conclusion of a treaty originates from the time of Emperor Constantine (306–37), who successfully launched an offensive in the Lower Danube area in 328. Four years later, Constantine concluded a *foedus* with the Gothic chieftain Ariarich, according to which the Goths were to provide a particular number of reinforcements in exchange for annual cash payments. However, the treaty did not long prevent bands of Gothic raiders from invading Roman imperial territory south of the Danube. After the middle of the century, the intensity of the clashes increased. When the Goths, under the leadership of Athanarich, intervened in Roman domestic policy and supported the usurper Procopius against Valens (364–78), the latter, after having eliminated his competitor, campaigned against them from 367 to 369. The conflict saw the Romans once again crossing the Danube, without inflicting serious damage on the enemy; it ended with a treaty where both parties were equal.

Valens' older brother Valentinian (364–75) who governed in the west, had greater success in his wars against the Alamanni, who had plundered Mainz in 368. In a large-scale counter-offensive, the emperor advanced over the Rhine into enemy territory and was able to inflict a major defeat on his enemies, whereby Rome's position on the Rhine frontier was decisively consolidated. Even after this victorious undertaking, there is evidence of resistance against the empire. Nevertheless, the extent to which Roman policy had the situation in hand at this point can be illustrated by the example of Macrianus, an Alamannic chieftain who was initially not prepared to accept Roman supremacy, but who was nevertheless persuaded to conclude a treaty which rendered him an ally of the empire. Henceforth he became a loyal confederate until he finally fell victim to Mallobaudes, a Frankish king in Roman service.

The attack by the Huns in the last quarter of the fourth century upset the newly gained stability on the Rhine and the Danube. The empire tried to continue the traditional policy, but this policy acquired a new emphasis as major *gentes* were now settled in the empire more frequently. The prerequisite for this was the *deditio*, i.e. submission of foreigners, whereby weapons were surrendered and an oath was demanded by which they agreed to be settled as subjects (*colonii*) liable to tax, according to the will of the emperor. In such cases where the requirement was not fulfilled, the situation could escalate within a very short period of time. This occurred in 376 when the main group of Danube Goths was settled in Thrace under the leadership of Fritigern, but could neither be disarmed nor could their status as *colonii* be established. When supply problems set in soon after, there were severe disturbances, and the situation spun out of control. The Romans lost the initiative, and murder, fatal beatings, war and devastation finally took over. Valens sought a military solution to the problem but failed: the Goths were victorious at the battle of Adrianople in 378.

Even though the Goths were able to take only limited advantage of their victory, Roman policy towards those barbarians belonging to the empire changed: henceforth it had to show greater respect for assimilated groups, even if these had been defeated. This gave rise to the settlement of Fritigern's Goths in Thrace by means of a treaty in 382, which specified that the foreigners became citizens of the empire, but without possessing a *connubium* with the Romans. They acquired, principally in the Moesia II and in the north-east, in Dacia ripensis, tax-free land for settlement between the Danube and the Balkans which, according to Roman law, did not constitute their property but still remained Roman sovereign territory. The Goths lived there alongside Roman provincials. Reasonable levels of tax probably financed their supplies and they also received money annually. In exchange they were committed to providing military service to the Romans.

The *foedus* with the Goths from 382 became a model for a whole series of treaties, which were concluded with other *gentes* right into the sixth century. It was in this way that the threat posed by the barbarians was to a certain extent brought under control through at least partial integration into the Roman world. One of the best examples of this is the settlement of the Visigoths in southern Gaul in the second decade of the fifth century. At that time they did not enter the country as conquerors, but rather by order of the imperial government and in agreement with the local élite. They were needed for the reinvigoration of the country, which had been destroyed by the Vandals, Alans and Suebi. The Gothic army arrived as a Roman confederate army, which remained in the country over the long term and formed the basis of a kingship and ultimately a kingdom with fixed territory. This Visigothic model went beyond the previous and consistently unsuccessful attempts to settle internal Roman confederates through military billeting, to feed and finance them. It became the model for a series of later settlements by barbarian tribes on Roman soil, for example, for the *foedus* of 488, concluded between the (East Roman) Emperor Zeno and Theoderic the Great. The treaty allowed the Gothic king to march to Italy and put an end to Odovakar's rule in his capacity as an imperial representative with the rank of a supreme army commander at the head of his tribe, which comprised approximately 20,000 warriors and in total probably around 100,000 people. Theoderic was to rule thereafter in place of the emperor until Zeno himself arrived in Italy, i.e. the Gothic chieftain was to reign as vicar of the legitimate emperor. Theoderic complied with the treaty even after Zeno's death. The *foedus* thus had a transpersonal quality, in that it did not automatically expire upon the death of a contractual partner.

In March 493, Theoderic was proclaimed king by his army without any imperial agreement. Hence his status grew *vis-à-vis* the emperor in Constantinople, on whose behalf he had gone to Italy. The Byzantines now called Theoderic a usurper.[24] Nevertheless, the memory remained alive of Theoderic being sent to Italy as a Roman patrician and consul, in order to avenge Romulus Augustulus by overthrowing Odovakar and ruling his country. This strengthened the authority of Gothic rule in Italy.[25] As in the case of the integration of other barbarian tribes into the late classical world, the *foedus* was thus of great significance for the Goths. It marked the beginning of the transformation of the Roman world, at the end of which stood a more or less durable Germanic kingdom on imperial territory. This could only survive intact if legitimized by the emperor (the demographic imbalance between Romans and foreigners alone left no alternative).[26] Yet integration was not merely a legal matter. It required a high degree of adaptation, above all on the part of the foreigners.

It was necessary to restructure the tribal make-up of the migration periods, which was characterized by strongly military kingship and strict allegiance. In the end, however, the military kingship was successful only when it 'annulled' itself, 'in other words, when the kings succeeded in subordinating their peoples to Roman statehood and integrating them into larger units (*patriae*)'.[27] The traditional migrational kingdom had to be transformed into a territorial kingdom, which was not only capable of integrating the members of the Germanic *gens*, but also the resident provincial population. The initiative had to come from the king himself, and this proved to be a dangerous balancing act. The concomitant repression of the old tribal structure gradually called into question the traditional legitimation of the king. If he was unable to establish himself in time as a ruler of a 'new' people, composed of members of his *gens* and the Roman population (which was in the majority), this more often than not meant the end of his rule and sooner or later the end of the military unit he led and represented. Theoderic, King of the Goths, pursued a policy whose aim was a lasting settlement of his polyethnic tribal unit in Italy. Full of determination, he pursued the integration of his people into the Roman world, which was quite obviously also in the interest of Constantinople. This was suggested by the aforementioned *foedus* of 488. The agreement made the Goths imperial allies and thus an extension of Roman imperial power. In terms of the constitution, its Italian empire was both an independent and a subordinate part of the unified empire.[28]

There is no doubt surrounding how Theoderic understood his rule in Italy, as illustrated by his royal title, which was not *Rex Gothorum*, for instance, but typically, *Flavius Theodericus rex*. As Herwig Wolfram was able to demonstrate in his study of Latin royal titles up to the end of the eighth century, the emergence of the title 'Flavius' was a result of an assimilation of Roman tradition.[29] In having this title, Theoderic placed himself in a tradition which dated back to the third century AD. Even Claudius II (268–70) attempted to trace his origin to the famous imperial family of the first century. This example was followed by Constantine the Great, in making his father a descendant of the famous victor over the Goths. Members of the non-Roman aristocracy, or rather those alien to the empire who classified themselves as belonging to the Flavian royal house, took up this tradition. The first signs of a link between the name Flavius and the functional title *rex* must have appeared at the time of Odovakar, even though the first clear evidence occurs in the case of Theoderic.[30] Ostrogothic adoption of Roman imperial traditions did not, of course, remain restricted to the royal house; it was expanded across the whole *gens*. This is confirmed in the *Getica* by Cassiodorus/Jordanes – a history of the Gothic people and its Amalian dynasty, probably commissioned by Theoderic. In this work the history of the Goths was quite purposefully and pseudo-logically placed on the same level as that of the Geti, a Dacian people, which had been regarded as a part of the Roman world at a much earlier point in history. Hidden behind this grandiose-grotesque construct, as Wolfram described it, was strong political motivation.[31] The issue at stake was to render the history of the Goths a part of Roman history and thus to anchor the barbarian tribe in the Roman world. Theoderic's claim to rule in Italy would thereby be legitimized.

The Gothic kingdom in Italy was based on tribal and Roman elements. Theoderic's kingdom in Italy bridged the two spheres. As Wolfram made clear in his book on the Goths, the kingdom was on the one hand orientated towards the empire of Late Antiquity; on the other, his kingdom possessed relatively strong tribal elements which cannot simply be ignored, as his position within his polyethnic unit of warriors was based on his Amalian descent. This, however, remained an unused asset in the unprecedented rise from chief of a wandering Balkan tribe to the representative of the emperor and ruler of Italy.[32] Theoderic's grand scheme was eventually unsuccessful as none of his followers was able to continue his adroit policy with regard to Constantinople. Athalaric, the heir apparent, was just 10 years old when he assumed power under the tutelage of his mother Amalasuitha. Such a combination of individuals provoked a power struggle at the heart of the Italian Empire and led to a general destabilization, which was to remain a distinguishing feature of Gothic history until 552. It was self-evident that this situation could not fail to have an effect on the politics of great powers. Above all, the war with Constantinople, which was of many years' duration, had serious consequences, and could not be prevented by Theoderic's successors: it ended with the defeat of the last Ostrogothic army between the *Mons Lactarius* and the River Sarno.[33]

The foundation of a Frankish Empire in Gaul proved to be more durable. It was initiated by Clovis, who succeeded his father both as Salic Frankish king of Tournai and administrator of the Roman province Belgica II.[34] The conversion of Clovis and his people to Catholicism made the equalization of *Franci* and *Romani* considerably easier, as the Frankish king adopted the religion of the majority of the Gallic population, although this admittedly had a decisive effect only in the centuries after his death. However, during his lifetime he was able to rely on support from the Roman ruling class with respect to church policy, administration and indeed perhaps even the military.[35]

Clovis' own political activity, however, was barely influenced by his conversion to Christianity. This can be illustrated in the consistency of his actions towards other Frankish kings, whom he eliminated in a cold-blooded fashion after his major success against the Alamanni, Burgundians and Visigoths, i.e. after he extended his rule to large areas of Roman Gaul.[36] In 508, Clovis was appointed honorary consul by a Byzantine envoy in Tours. The Frankish king controlled the most powerful military machine in Gaul, as well as what had once been imperial provincial territory, which meant that he controlled the budget as well as the mint, to say nothing of the royal demesne. He also dominated the Church and was in a position to convene synods.[37] Another indication of integration may be found in the development of the Frankish myth of origin. Fredegar, writing in the seventh century, placed the origins of the Franks in Troy.[38] The significance of this myth enabled the assertion of the mutual descent of the Franks and Gallic Romans, using the older Roman Trojan tradition of Vergil. This integrated the history of the Franks into a world history which had become canonical.[39] The transcription of the Trojan legend, which had become 'the common property of Frankish historical consciousness',[40] illustrates the unique success of Roman–barbarian integration, which ultimately failed in the other cases we have looked at.

Notes

1 W. Pohl, 'Die Gepiden und die Gentes an der mittleren Donau nach dem Zerfall des Attilareiches', in H. Wolfram and F. Daim (eds), *Die Völker an der mittleren und unteren Donau im 5. und 6. Jahrhundert*, Vienna, Verlag der Österreichischen Akademie der Wissenschaften, 1980, p. 240.
2 W. Pohl, 'Conceptions of ethnicity in early medieval studies', *Archaeologia Polona*, 1991, vol. 29, p. 40.
3 R. Wenskus, *Stammesbildung und Verfassung: Das Werden der frühmittelalterlichen Gentes*, 2nd edn, Vienna and Cologne, Böhlau, 1977, p. 54.
4 Wenskus, *Stammesbildung und Verfassung*, p. 54.
5 H. Wolfram, *The Roman Empire and Its Germanic Peoples*, trans. T. J. Dunlap, Berkeley, Los Angeles and London, University of California Press, 1997, p. 8.
6 Wolfram, *Empire*, p. 8; cf. H. Wolfram, *Die Germanen*, 3rd edn, Munich, Beck, 1997, p. 20. See also R. Wenskus, 'Probleme der germanisch-deutschen Verfassungs – und Sozialgeschichte im Lichte der Ethnosoziologie', in H. Beumann (ed.), *Historische Forschungen für Walter Schlesinger*, Vienna and Cologne, Böhlau, 1974, p. 34.
7 H. Wolfram, *History of the Goths*, trans. T. J. Dunlap, Berkeley, Los Angeles and London, University of California Press, 1987, p. 8.
8 Wolfram, *Empire*, pp. 285–6.
9 P. E. Hübinger, 'Spätantike und frühes Mittelalter. ein Problem historischer Periodenbildung', in idem., *Zur Frage der Periodengrenze zwischen Altertum und Mittelalter*, Darmstadt, Wissenschaftliche Buchgesellschaft, 1969, p. 167. See also W. Goffart, 'The theme of "The Barbarian Invasions" in late antique and modern historiography', in E. K. Chrysos and A. Schwarcz, *Das Reich und die Barbaren*, Vienna, Böhlau, 1989, pp. 93–4.
10 Hübinger, 'Spätantike und frühes Mittelalter', p. 165.

112   *Bernhard Zeller*

11 Wolfram, *Empire*, p. 313.
12 W. Pohl, 'Barbarenkrieger – Wahrnehmungen und Wirklichkeiten', in C. von Carnap-Bornheim (ed.), *Beiträge zu römischer und barbarischer Bewaffnung in den ersten vier nachchristlichen Jahrhunderten*, Siegmaringen, Thorbecke, 1994, p. 167; H. Wolfram, 'Landnahme, Stammesbildung und Verfassung', *Deutsches Archiv für Erforschung des Mittelalters*, 1996, vol. 52, pp. 161–9.
13 W. Pohl, 'Telling the difference: signs of ethnic identity', in W. Pohl and H. Reimitz (eds), *Strategies of Distinction: The Construction of Ethnic Communities 300–800*, Leiden, New York and Cologne, Brill, 1998, p. 27.
14 Isidor of Seville, *Etymologiarum sive originum libri XX*. 18.6.9.
15 Pohl, 'Telling the difference', pp. 33–4.
16 Widukind, *Res gestae Saxonicae*, pp. 1, 6–7.
17 Pohl, 'Telling the difference', p. 37.
18 Wolfram, *Goths*, pp. 302–3.
19 Wolfram, *Germanen*, p. 69.
20 Caesar, *De bello gallico*, I. 51.2; Wolfram, *Germanen*, p. 67.
21 Caesar, *De bello gallico*, I. 48.5; Wolfram, *Germanen*, p. 68.
22 Wolfram, *Germanen*, pp. 70–5.
23 For the following summary, see Wolfram, *Empire*, pp. 41–50, 57–67, 79–89, 108, 147–9; and idem., *Goths*, pp. 62, 67–70, 133, 223, 279, 285–6.
24 H. Wolfram, 'Gotisches Königtum und römisches Kaisertum von Theodosius dem Großen bis Justinian I', *Frühmittelalterliche Studien*, 1979, vol. 13, p. 23; *Empire*, p. 108.
25 Wolfram, *Empire*, p. 108.
26 Wolfram, 'Gotisches Königtum', p. 26.
27 Wolfram, *Goths*, p. 9.
28 Wolfram, *Goths*, pp. 287–8; *Germanen*, p. 98.
29 H. Wolfram, *Intitulatio I. Lateinische Königs- und Fürstentitel bis zum Ende des 8. Jahrhunderts*, Vienna and Cologne, Böhlau, 1967, pp. 56–76; see also R. Wenskus, 'Zum Problem der Ansippung', in H. Patze (ed.), *Festschrift Reinhard Wenskus*, Sigmaringen, Thorbecke, 1986, p. 85.
30 Wolfram, *Intitulatio I*, pp. 57–8.
31 H. Wolfram, 'Einleitung oder Überlegungen zur Origo gentis', in H. Wolfram and W. Pohl (eds), *Typen der Ethnogenese unter besonderer Berücksichtigung der Bayern 1*, Vienna, Verlag der Österreichischen Akademie der Wissenschaften, 1990, p. 26.
32 Wolfram, *Goths*, p. 290.
33 See Wolfram, *Goths*, pp. 332–62; *Empire*, pp. 224–39; *Germanen*, p. 99.
34 Wolfram, *Empire*, p. 196; *Germanen*, p. 106.
35 Wolfram, *Intitulatio I*, p. 112.
36 Wolfram, *Empire*, p. 216.
37 Wolfram, *Intitulatio I*, p. 110.
38 Fredegar, *Chronicae* 3.2.
39 See E. Zöllner, *Geschichte der Franken bis zur Mitte des 6. Jahrhunderts*, Munich, Beck, 1970, p. 5; R. Wenskus, 'Religion abâtardie: Materialien zum Synkretismus in der vorchristlichen politischen Theologie der Franken', in H. Keller and N. Staubach (eds), *Festschrift Karl Hauck*, Berlin and New York, Walter de Gruyter, 1994, p. 223.
40 Zöllner, *Geschichte der Franken*, p. 5.

9 Warfare in the Middle Ages

Jan Willem Honig

The conduct of war in the Middle Ages has given military historians a great deal of trouble. Medieval warfare does not appear to meet what they generally take to be the benchmark of good strategy. In the words of Hans Delbrück, the 'father' of academic military history writing:

> The first natural principle of all strategy is to concentrate forces, to seek out the main forces of the enemy, to defeat them and to exploit the victory until the defeated party submits to the will of the victor and accepts his conditions, in the extreme case up to and including the occupation of the enemy's entire country.[1]

If this is what strategy is about, then it is difficult to find clear medieval examples of the single-minded pursuit of decisive battle and the uncompromising imposition of one party's will on another. Battles, as Hans Delbrück and a host of others who studied the subject quickly discovered, were few and rarely decisive in the Middle Ages.

Why was this? To Delbrück, the answer lay in the immaturity of political institutions. In feudal Europe, power was too fragmented for medieval rulers to be able to organize disciplined, combined arms units that could follow orders and execute tactical and strategic designs:

> The knight is too much of an individualist to be a leader, and his arms too specific to allow the application of the term 'tactics', and without tactics there is in turn no strategy.[2]

The nineteenth-century German obsession with the rise of the state was not equally shared everywhere in Europe, however. Delbrück's British near-contemporary, Sir Charles Oman, sought the solution to the absence of decisive battle in a different direction, namely that of mental immaturity. Take his judgement on the Crusades: 'Nowhere are more reckless displays of blind courage, or more stupid neglect of the elementary rules of strategy and tactics to be found, than in the great expeditions to the Levant.' Further, although he adds, 'we have also had to observe among the more capable leaders of the crusading armies a far higher degree of intelligent generalship than was usual among their contemporaries in the West', the overall picture was not impressive: until the resurgence of infantry and the introduction of gunpowder in the fourteenth century, 'tactics and strategy make comparatively small and slow progress'.[3]

The popularity of Delbrück's and Oman's explanations for its medieval absence may have waned,[4] but the basic idea that decisive battle consti- tutes the essence of good strategy still reigns surprisingly supreme.[5] The major, widely accepted, explanatory modification over the past forty years posits that a lack of means precluded battle-seeking strategies, rather than political or mental immaturity. This is the key idea in the work of the great Belgian medieval military historian, Jan-Frans Verbruggen. He was able to undermine fatally a key tenet of Delbrück's theory by proving convincingly in his magisterial 1954 work, *De krijgskunst in West-Europa in de Middeleeuwen*, that medieval armies had been tactically well organized, displaying discipline and manoeuvre on the battlefield.[6] When it came to strategy, however, Verbruggen still clung to the conventional strategic paradigm. In contrast with the positive tenor of the rest of the book, one can detect a slightly apologetic tone in his conclusions regarding strategy:

> offensive strategy was not in general well developed in the Middle Ages. Owing to the small size of medieval states and their armies it was extremely difficult to wage offensive warfare on a grand scale. In any event, it was virtually impossible to conquer castles and fortified towns in any number. War aims, therefore, had to be limited, and many campaigns necessarily took on the character of mere plundering expeditions.[7]

The thesis that medieval warlords were aware of the critical strategic aim of overthrowing their enemies, and occasionally tried, but were usually doomed to failure because of a lack of means, is a respectable one. However, it leaves many characteristics of medieval warfare unexplained. Let us look briefly at one example from the Hundred Years' War. The 1339 campaign is typical of medieval warfare in general in that it involves extensive plundering and no battle is fought.[8] It also reveals a number of typically puzzling features.

In September 1339, the English king, Edward III, concentrated an army of perhaps 12,000 men in the territories of his Low Countries' allies, Brabant and Hainault. The army marched into the bishopric of Cambrai, an ally of the king of France, on 20 September. A two-week siege of Cambrai ensued (where Edward deliberately made his camp just across the Scheldt 'within the march of France'). Raiding parties, meanwhile, fanned out into the region. As the king wrote to his son: 'on the Monday, the Eve of the Feast of Saint Matthew [20 September], the troops began to burn in the Cambrésis and they burned there for the whole of the following week so that the whole territory was laid waste and quite stripped of corn, cattle and everything else.'[9] When the siege made little progress Edward decided to move on and, on the evening of 9 October, advanced into France proper. This had given the French king, Philip VI, ample time to call up his army and order it to join him at Compiègne, some forty miles from the border. On Edward's invasion, the French army advanced to Péronne, just inside the border. What followed is typical of medieval campaigns. While Edward's army laid waste to a twenty-mile-wide strip of French countryside, plundering and burning hundreds of villages,[10] Philip shadowed the invaders at close (generally half a day's) distance. The armies quickly established formal contact via messengers, and challenges to battle were sent back and forth. On 14 October, Edward made a sally towards Péronne and that evening the armies were within a mile of each other. Battle appeared imminent. But Edward quickly moved away again eastwards, crossing the Oise river and plundering the territory south of the river. The French army followed along the northern bank of the river, threatening to interpose itself between the English and the border. The English, however, managed to turn northwards ahead of the French and, having earlier accepted the challenge to battle, halted on the evening of 21 October between La Capelle and La Flamengrie, just inside France. The French arrived the following day and both sides drew up in battle order. Battle was expected for 23 October. The armies faced each other all day, but nothing happened. At nightfall the English marched out of France. The next day, Edward once more arrayed his forces for battle, but the French failed to pursue him across the border. Thus ended the campaign.

Campaigns such as this one puzzle historians.[11] There appears to be, especially on the French side, a remarkable lack of initiative in defence of their land. Why did Philip not try to relieve Cambrai[12] or, failing that, confront Edward as soon as he invaded and round up his dispersed forces? These failures are all the more surprising if one takes into consideration that Philip's army seems to have been at least twice the size of Edward's. The balance was even more favourable to the French because some 7,000 out of the 12,000 troops in the English army were supplied by Edward's allies from the Low Countries and their loyalty was in serious doubt. Edward was finding it exceedingly difficult to pay them, and many of the allies, like the Duke of Brabant and the Count of Hainault, were vassals (and relatives) of the King of France who were hesitant about upsetting their lord (indeed, the Count of Hainault, who was Edward's brother-in-law, changed sides, joining his uncle, the King of France, on the eve of the invasion of France). One could therefore reasonably have expected an aggressive strategy from Philip.

Although the (mostly English) historians who have analysed the campaign are most critical of Philip, one must observe that Edward behaved strangely as well. It seems foolhardy to spread out one's army to burn and plunder in the face of a numerically superior opponent whose forces are close by and concentrated. Indeed, this act offends against one of the 'timeless' principles of strategy, concentration of force.[13] In addition, by crossing the Oise and allowing the French army a chance to cut the English off from the border, Edward seems seriously to have compounded the error. Historians assume that Edward's objective was to seek battle and the plundering was meant to taunt Philip.[14] If this was so, it is remarkable that Edward was not more aggressive. Although early on in the campaign he moved towards Philip and got very close, he then backed off just as quickly. At the end of the campaign, near La Capelle, Edward had another chance. Even though the armies were actually arrayed opposite each other, neither attacked. If Edward wanted battle, surely this was his chance, and if the French refused to attack, should he not then have taken the initiative?[15]

How are these events more convincingly explained, other than by reference to gross failures in leadership and a basic lack of understanding of the fundamentals of strategy? For a better answer, we have to turn away from military historians. It has really been the preserve of non-military, specialist medieval historians to develop the critical ideas for understanding the fundamentals of medieval strategy.[16] My aim in the rest of this short chapter is to extract from these historians the two fundamental elements which provide the basic context in which medieval warfare has to be understood.

The first key feature is that a central objective in war was the acquisition of loot. When one surveys the campaigns from the period of the great migrations to the Hundred Years' War they all exhibit the same trait: armies cut, like giant lawnmowers, through wide swathes of enemy territory, penetrating deeply and burning and looting everything in their path. The Germanic tribes that finally brought down the Roman Empire in the fifth century were attracted by the prospect of such vast hoards of loot as could never be collected in the primeval forests of central Europe. The fantastic itineraries of tribes such as the Vandals and the Goths (whose names continue to live on in our collective memory as barbaric destroyers of civilization) were driven by a combination of a constant desire for riches, of which more always lay beyond the horizon, and an inability to stay in one place once local resources had been exhausted. The campaigns of Charlemagne, three hundred years later, may have turned the direction of the campaigns outward, away from the renewed *imperium Romanorum*, but the objective stayed the same. Saxons, Avars, Lombards, Moors and Bretons all suffered, year after year, in monotonous repetition, the depredations of the Franks. Charlemagne's biographer, Einhard, still marvelled, decades later, at the success of the 795–96 campaigns against the Avars, in which, for the loss of 'only two Frankish magnates':

> All money and treasures heaped together [by the Avars] over a long period were plundered. No war brought against [!] the Franks, which human memory can record, increased their riches and power more.[17]

Not surprisingly the Byzantines had a proverb, quoted by Einhard with quiet satisfaction: 'If the Franks are your friend, they are not your neighbour.'[18] Moving forward another six hundred years to the Hundred Years' War, as already pointed out, the English campaigns or chevauchées in France displayed the same characteristics.[19] Ravaging and pillaging remained the main preoccupation of soldiers well into the Early Modern period and were only slowly recognized as an illegal activity.[20]

Armies engaged in this activity, not, as many historians have it, by default, but, as Georges Duby has written, 'out of habit'.[21] This habit, throughout the Middle Ages, was often stronger (one is tempted to say, habitually stronger) than the desire for peace. In 575, for example, the Austrasian army is said to have told their king, who had just made peace, '[d]o as you promised and give us a chance to fight and take plunder, otherwise we won't go back home'.[22] Things had not changed fundamentally by 1390, when, according to the chronicler Jean Froissart, the Duke of Gloucester complained about a proposed peace with France because, for one thing, 'the poor knights, squires and archers of England, who are idle and sustain their estate by war, are inclined to war'.[23]

Despite our modern belief that war does not pay, these quotations suggest a different reality for the Middle Ages.[24] Although there were obviously many individuals for whom war did not work out, the general perception, and reality, for many men of war was that it was profitable. In a desperately poor society, as was most of Europe in the Middle Ages, the modern observer can readily understand that people resorted easily to force to augment their rudimentary existence. But the phenomenon was more complex than a simple rational cost–benefit calculation on the part of mostly poor people. What must be noted is that not everyone participated fully or equally in the pillaging business. The venture came to be dominated by a noble class which, by its very nature, was not the poorest in society. The story of the Early Middle Ages is a tale of the gradual emergence of a class of heavily armoured, mounted 'knights', who, by the eleventh century, dominated society militarily, and thus economically, politically, socially and, in many ways, culturally. This was a completely different situation from Late Antiquity, when the Roman Empire had been invaded and brought down by tribes that were essentially 'nations-in-arms', in which all able-bodied men fought, usually on foot. How and why 'chivalry' rose (and declined again with the emergence of the new merchant class and mercenaries) need not concern us here. What matters is that plunder did, of course, have some strategic rationale for this elite. First, it was critical to the provisioning of armies. Second, it weakened an opponent by causing economic damage and calling into question his ability to protect his subjects. But, more importantly, the quest for plunder is not necessarily a sign of anarchy: by being the preserve of a relatively wealthy class, plunder did not just follow from pure strategic or tactical necessity, but instead reflected a certain mentality that appreciated plunder for other reasons as well.[25]

Plunder was a fundamental part of a peculiar economic system, 'an economy of pillage, gift and generosity'.[26] Nobles and their followers accumulated in order to give. There was a constant redistribution of what limited wealth there was. In a very different sense from our own, this was an excessively materialistic, selfish, but at the same time intensely ideological activity. Medieval people gave to the Church to assure their place on God's right hand in the afterlife. At the same time, they sought to assure that the Church – as a critical social, political and legitimating power – stood by their side in this earthly life. But, most directly, largesse provided the means by which secular social networks were created and maintained. Largesse tied people together into what the Belgian historian Jan Dhondt has called, with a deliberate modern analogy, 'gangs'.[27] Lords gave to their followers, creating, to use Late Medieval terms, an 'affinity' with 'retainers'. But followers also gave to their lord. Thus society was bound together in a network of reciprocal ties of dependence.[28]

The critical prerequisite for the ability to give, and continue to give, was war. In 796, when one of Charlemagne's margraves captured the hoard of the Avars, he sent it to his king in Aix-la-Chapelle:

> After he [Charlemagne] had accepted these [treasures] and thanked God, the giver of all goods, this prudent, generous man and steward [dispensator] of God sent a large portion to Rome, the gateway of the apostles . . . the rest he gave to his magnates, lay and secular, and his other faithful men.[29]

Here is a crucial paradox of the Middle Ages: war built social order. War gave access to a critical commodity that was needed to build a network of mutual loyalties. The depth and strength of these loyalties was closely tied to success of the gang in war. Success, in turn, relied heavily on the qualities of the gang leader. Charlemagne's success as ruler resulted in large part from his outstanding ability to lead in wars of plunder. Equally, the striking alternation, for example, in the domestic and foreign political fortunes of the English kings of the Hundred Years' War was clearly related to their military qualities: the militarily successful Edward III and Henry V were strong kings, whereas the unhappy, unsoldierly kings Richard II and Henry VI were deposed by an increasingly restive nobility. On the French side, the pattern was the same. King John struggled to re-establish his authority after his capture at the Battle of Poitiers. The mentally unstable Charles VI almost lost France to the combined forces of his envious close relatives and the King of England.

The intricate customs surrounding looting and giving suggest that the Middle Ages do not present an example of Hobbesian struggle of all against all. War is made an even more ordered process by the second key feature of medieval war: the idea that war was a continuation of justice by other means.[30] Or, to be more precise, war was the continuation of the defence of rights by forceful means:

> pure violence . . . offends against the very special sense of law [*recht*] of the Middle Ages. This is a very special sense, as said, not one of justice [*rechtvaardigheid*], but of right [*recht*]. And this is understandable: that slowly organising society of the Middle Ages faces in anarchy its greatest threat: if whoever takes whatever, whenever circumstances happen to permit, life is no longer bearable for anyone. Therefore there is a sort of agreement: whoever can take whatever, but only if he has legal cause. . . . What medieval princes are after are 'rights'.[31]

These rights often, but not exclusively, involved rights to territory. Princes and lesser nobles obtained these rights as the result of marriage. Marriage was like acquiring a ticket in an exclusive lottery. For one or the other family it might ultimately lead to a prize, a claim to the other's territories. To give one small, typical example: between 1425 and 1428, Philip the Good, Duke of Burgundy, and his cousin Jacqueline of Bavaria, Countess of Holland, Zeeland and Hainault, fought a bitter war over who should rule Jacqueline's possessions. Philip's claim went back forty years, to the day when his father had married Jacqueline's aunt. Philip was offered an irresistible opportunity to claim his prize because Jacqueline lacked a male protector without whom, in the general opinion of the Middle Ages, a woman could not rule. After a very effectively conducted war, Philip forced his cousin to appoint him her 'protector' (*ruwaard*) in July 1428.[32] Sadly, the ticket which Jacqueline's grandfather had acquired by marrying his son to Philip's aunt on that same day in 1385 did not pay out. Holland, Zeeland and Hainault went to Burgundy, rather than the other way around.

Wars of succession were one of the most common types of conflict in the Middle Ages and the Early Modern period. They were inevitable because of the combination of centuries of noble interbreeding and a certain idea of right. But not all wars were over territory, either as cause or as object. Land was very important. In an agricultural society, it was the ultimate source of food and thus wealth. Even so, territory did not always need to be an object because plunder provided a more dynamic, though transitory, source of income, and there were many other legal justifications for resorting to war which did not involve contested land. In the mid-fourteenth century, the exemplary knight Geoffroi de Charny summed these up in his *Livre de Chevalerie*: knights could go to war 'to defend their honour and their inheritance' and that of 'their intimates' or fight for 'their rightful lord in his wars'.[33] 'Honour', of course, is a concept requiring explanation. Many consider it so vague that it allowed for a resort to force under practically any circumstance. That, however, is an exaggeration.

The juxtaposition of 'honneur' with 'heritage' indicates that medieval honour was more tangible than its modern equivalent and not largely concerned with behaviour. It had an important material connotation: actions affecting a noble's heritage, that is, his possessions or patrimony, affected his honour. Extrapolating from this, one can say that what made up the position of a person in society constituted his honour. As Gerd Althoff has written:

> *Honour* determines rank, and rank is something vitally important – not only in the Middle Ages, but here in a special way – because on it depends all possibilities of cooperation, exertion of influence and structuring in the social and political order of the Middle Ages. *Honour*, the position in such hierarchies, is therefore logically not something static, but is contested, defended and attacked. . . . Disputes over injured honour are in the Middle Ages, in large part, hidden or explicits contests over rank.[34]

Honour thus encapsulated an enormous variety of potential conflictual issues from (in our view) minor ones, like the way one was greeted or where one was seated at a banquet, to major ones, like the power to rule. None the less, the number of these issues was not limitless. There was no written code, but rather an intricate body of customs, norms and values with which nobles were imbued from the day they were born. Open to interpretation, it was exposed to exploitation as well as mistakes, but within bounds. The major corrective and restraint was the need for social support. No noble could undertake action (unless he was suicidally inclined) without the support of his 'gang'. Cause for conflict was thus constantly debated – and thus restrained.

In addition, the conflicts that ensued were not pursued without limit. Because the forceful response to an insult led to a counter-insult which legitimately allowed, or rather necessitated, a forceful reaction, a resolution to the conflict that completely satisfied one injured party still left the other with a legitimate injury in need of repair and thus cause for continuing the fight. Compromise was therefore the order of the day.[35] When in the 1120s the Count of Flanders exacted the common punishment on one of his unruly subjects, named Borsiard, of burning and destroying his stronghold 'to its foundations', the count, after the intercession of mediators acting on behalf of Borsiard's clan elders, also promised to compensate him 'with a house [read: stronghold] that was even better', albeit in a different location. In this way, the count attempted to nip in the bud the feud that was bound to arise with Borsiard's clan.[36]

The example of Jacqueline and Philip illustrates also, in another way, that medieval ideas of right did not incorporate the pursuit of an exclusionary, absolute form of justice. Instead, as the envious princes and nobles were caught in such a complex web of competing and overlapping rights, only relative justice could be achieved. One cannot conclude that this sense of right was only a fig-leaf designed to cover uncomfortably the unrestrained pursuit of power. Dynastic conflict, like all other forms of conflict, was constrained by legal concerns. The most striking example is that not everyone could compete for the apex of power, but only those who were born into the established ruling dynasty. Furthermore, losers to a struggle for succession, like Jacqueline of Bavaria, did not usually lose their life, or even their title, as a modern observer might readily have expected.[37] Complex constitutional constructs were drawn up which sought to more or less respect everyone's rights.

Because of the inbred need for compromise, much medieval conflict was demonstrative and ritualistic. Players went through the violent motions of defending their honour because the maintenance of their position (both materially and immaterially) required it, while constantly on the lookout for a mutually satisfactory compromise. Yet it was precisely also this ritualistic quality that allowed for so much conflict to occur. Since the ritual circumscribed the use of force, it also had the effect of limiting the physical transaction costs of the use of force. Paradoxically, the restraints made war more possible and frequent.

A further limitation, which reinforced the ritual and legal dimensions of war, was the influence of Christianity. In a society which believed that an omnipotent and omniscient God determined the course of history, ultimately for good and not ill, there naturally arose the problem of knowing the will of this supernatural being. Means were sought of inviting God to divulge His intentions. One means was the trial by battle. This idea fused seamlessly with a Germanic tradition that saw war in legalistic terms, as a trial and an ordeal (in the sense not only of test, but also of 'Urteil' or judgement). Battle was not a simple test of strength, but a test of divine favour and justice.[38] It was surrounded by ritual to ensure that the solemnity and importance of the occasion was clear to all; hence such acts, strange to modern eyes, as the invitation to battle, the naming of date and place, and so on.[39] A *iudicium dei* was the ultimate court of appeal. Combatants were understandably fearful about taking such a momentous step.[40] It tested the strength of the belief of both parties in the justness of their cause – and who could be certain of being totally right if no one was without sin and indeed the shedding of blood was a sinful activity?

This fact goes a long way in explaining the rarity of battle and the extensive and tortuous manoeuvring in campaigns, as in the example of 1339 related above. Both Edward and Philip had to be seen to be convinced of the justness of their cause and thus exhibit a willingness to invite a judgement. Battle was the focus of the campaign. Whereas inviting each other to do battle may have been a relatively easy step to take, actually fighting one was not. Here is another paradox of medieval warfare: battle was feared by being potentially too decisive. The best (and rare) example of decisive battle was Hastings in 1066 in which Harold the pretender, in a clear sign of divine disfavour, was killed.

To sum up, many still think of medieval warfare as anarchic struggles of all against all. In fact, warfare was organized, regulated and limited. None the less, war was often brutal and never more so than warfare between classes, between religions and in sieges. The nobility fought hard to keep warfare as their profitable privilege and fought pitilessly against peasant, mercenary and burgher interlopers. Equally, Christian ideology mandated that heretics be dealt with harshly. And in sieges, laws going back to Deuteronomy (XX, 10–14) prescribed that, if a town that had resisted surrendered, 'you shall put all males to the sword' and 'divide the loot among the army'. Yet, even in these cases, the mentality that regarded war as a business venture and a legal compromise-seeking procedure often intruded and exerted its restraining effects, preventing them from becoming genocidal or total. In the struggle between the noble pretenders for the Countship of Flanders in 1128, the victorious side in the battle of Axspoele held to ransom nobles – and burghers.[41] No Christian knight raised an eyebrow when King Louis of France – Saint Louis – was held to ransom by his Muslim opponents during the disastrous crusading expedition to Egypt in 1250.[42] In the sacking of towns, the lure of loot habitually distracted from the formal obligation of killing of the inhabitants.

Medieval warfare remained limited as a result of an ultimately inextricable combination of material interest and collective mentality. War gave access to that critical commodity, loot, which so effectively maintained and extended social relationships and thus built order. War was a legal procedure that served to defend rights by forceful means. In this framework, strategic aims had to differ radically from modern ones. Imposing one's will on an opponent by destroying his means of resistance in battles of annihilation was not one of them; but then, peace was not meant for this medieval world either.

Notes

1 'Das erste natürliche Grundgesetz aller Strategie ist, die Kräfte zusammen zu nehmen, die Hauptmacht des Feindes aufzusuchen, sie zu schlagen und den Sieg zu verfolgen, bis der Besiegte sich dem Willen des Siegers unterwirft und seine Bedingungen annimmt, äußersten Falls also bis zur Besetzung des ganzen feindlichen Landes.' H. Delbrück, *Geschichte der Kriegskunst im Rahmen der politischen Geschichte*, Bk IV, *Neuzeit*, Berlin, Walter de Gruyter, 1962 (originally published 1920), p. 334.
2 'Der Ritter ist zu sehr Persönlichkeit, um Führung zu haben, und seine Bewaffnung zu einseitig, so daß zunächst der Begriff der Taktik fast unanwendbar wird und ohne Taktik wiederum gibt es auch keine Strategie.' Ibid., p. 126. See also H. Delbrück, *Geschichte der Kriegskunst im Rahmen der politischen Geschichte*, Bk III, *Mittelalter*, Berlin, Walter de Gruyter, 1964 (originally published 1923), pp. 339–46.
3 Sir Charles Oman, *A History of the Art of War in the Middle Ages*, 2 vols, London, Methuen, 1978 (originally published 1924), vol. 1, pp. 355, 358. As the work was an expanded version of Oman's Oxford BA thesis, one might be tempted to con-

clude that some of the judgements in his work are a sign of his own immaturity. However, Oman's was a popular nineteenth-century thesis which saw the development of European history as reflecting the ages of man. Such a view, for example, can also be detected (albeit in a rather more subtle version) in Johan Huizinga's 1919 classic *Waning of the Middle Ages: Herfsttij der Middeleeuwen: Studie over levens- en gedachtenvormen der veertiende en vijftiende eeuw in Frankrijk en de Nederlanden*, in J. Huizinga, *Verzamelde Werken*, vol. 3, Haarlem, Tjeenk Willink, 1949.

4 It must be noted, though, that Delbrück's emphasis on the interrelationship between political structures and war is making a comeback in the Anglo-American academic world, albeit without any clear awareness of its continental European genealogy: e.g. B. M. Downing, *The Military Revolution and Political Change: Origins of Democracy and Autocracy in Early Modern Europe*, Princeton, NJ, Princeton University Press, 1992, and C. J. Rogers, 'The military revolutions of the Hundred Years War', in C. J. Rogers (ed.), *The Military Revolution Debate: Readings on the Military Transformation of Early Modern Europe*, Boulder, CO, Westview Press, 1995, pp. 55–93.

5 See R. L. O'Connell, *Of Arms and Men: A History of War, Weapons, and Aggression*, New York, Oxford University Press, 1989, pp. 5–6: 'Neither tactical and strategic ends nor the nature of military organizations has proved greatly changeable – only technology'; A. Jones, *The Art of War in the Western World*, New York, Oxford University Press, 1987, pp. 145–6, 172–3, 670–2 and 690–704; G. Parker, *The Military Revolution: Military Innovation and the Rise of the West, 1500–1800*, 2nd edn, Cambridge, Cambridge University Press, 1996, p. 43; cf. also J. Keegan, *The Face of Battle*, London, Jonathan Cape, 1976, pp. 30, 335.

6 J. F. Verbruggen, *De krijgskunst in West-Europa in de Middeleeuwen (IXe tot begin XIVe eeuw)*, Brussels, Academie van Wetenschappen, 1954. The work has been published in English twice: in 1977, in a heavily truncated version, without its critical footnote apparatus, and, still incomplete but with more text and footnotes, by Boydell in 1997.

7 J. F. Verbruggen, *The Art of Warfare in Western Europe during the Middle Ages*, trans. S. Willard and S. C. M. Southern, Amsterdam, North Holland, 1977, p. 285. The quotation does not appear as such in the original, but the general meaning does not differ; cf. Verbruggen, *Krijgskunst*, p. 541.

8 The most detailed, modern account, which I follow for convenience's sake, is J. Sumption, *The Hundred Years War*, vol. I: *Trial by Battle*, London, Faber, 1990, pp. 278–89. Note that similar campaigns, to mention the main ones in the first half of the Hundred Years' War, took place in 1340, 1342, 1346, 1355, 1356, 1359–60, 1370, 1373 and 1380. The 1346 and 1356 campaigns are exceptional in that battles (Crécy and Poitiers) were fought.

9 Letter from Edward III to his son, quoted in Sumption, *Hundred Years War*, vol.I, p. 281.

10 For a map showing the extent of the destruction, see P. Contamine, *La guerre au Moyen Age*, Paris, PUF, 1980, pp. 372–3.

11 A. H. Burne, though, claims not to be puzzled, and simply judges the campaign to be 'ridiculous' and ending 'in disappointment and almost in farce': *The Crécy War: A Military History of the Hundred Years War from 1337 to the Peace of Bretigny, 1360*, London, Greenhill, 1991 (originally published 1955), pp. 49–50.

12 Sumption (pp. 279–80) suggests that Philip did not try to relieve Cambrai because it was on imperial territory and threatened to antagonize the emperor as well as stiffen the lukewarm support of Edward's German allies. However, Cambrai being on the Scheldt and the Scheldt being the border meant that merely a march towards Cambrai would have forced Edward, who was camping on French territory anyway, to consider his position.

13 Cf. Verbruggen, *Krijgskunst*, pp. 462–3, who sees concentration of force as a critical feature of the art of war. See also the quote from Delbrück above.

14 Sumption, *Hundred Years War*, I, p. 281; Burne, *Crécy War*, p. 46.

15 The English armies, of course, achieved their greatest successes on the battle-field on the defence. The mostly English historians who have described the campaigns of the Hundred Years' War tacitly assume that this is the right tactic under all circumstances, but what good is a tactic that always leaves the initiative to attack to the enemy? Verbruggen, *Krijgskunst*, p. 461, considers it reasonable that Philip avoided battle, because the stakes were too high. Quoting the chronicler Jean le Bel, if defeated, Philip would 'lose his kingdom' whereas the English would 'neither lose land nor possessions'. If this is so, one could turn this argument around and ask again: Why did Edward not attack?

16 Note that, until recently, 'real' medieval military historians were a rare breed (with only mavericks such as Verbruggen, C. Gaier and R. C. Smail). Delbrück and Oman, for example, were generalist military historians who happened to write about medieval military history. This situation has begun to change fundamentally with Philippe Contamine, the doyen of contemporary medieval military history. Yet, in line with more general historiographical trends, his interest has been largely focused on social structures and the organization for war, not the conduct of war, especially not if understood (as here) in the more narrow sense of strategy. Only in the past few years has the conduct of war, still broadly defined, become a subject for research again: e.g. J. France, *Victory in the East: A Military History of the First Crusade*, Cambridge, Cambridge University Press, 1994; M. Strickland, *War and Chivalry: The Conduct and Perception of War in England and Normandy, 1066–1217*, Cambridge, Cambridge University Press, 1996; and R. de Graaf, *Oorlog om Holland, 1000–1375*, Hilversum, Verloren, 1996.

17 Einhard, *Vita Karoli*, in R. Rau (ed.), *Quellen zur karolingischen Reichsgeschichte*, Darmstadt, Wissenschaftliche Buchgesellschaft, 1980, vol. 1, ch. 13, p. 182.

18 Ibid., ch. 16, p. 186.

19 See the map in A. Curry and M. Hughes (eds), *Arms, Armies and Fortifications in the Hundred Years War*, Woodbridge, Boydell, 1994, p. 104.

20 See the excellent work by F. Redlich, *De Praeda Militari, Looting and Booty, 1500–1815*, Wiesbaden, Franz Steiner, 1956.

21 'En premier lieu, ce monde sauvage est tout entier dominé par l'habitude du pillage et par les nécessités d'oblation': G. Duby, *Guerriers et paysans, VIIe–XIIe siècle, Premier essor de l'économie européenne*, Paris, Gallimard, 1980, p. 60.

22 Quoted from Fredegar, III, ch. 71, in T. Reuter, 'Plunder and tribute in the Carolingian Empire', *TRHS*, 5th series, vol. 35, 1985, p. 79.

23 'aussi s'enclinoient à la guerre povres chevalliers et escuiers et archers d'Angleterre, qui avoient aprins les oiseuses et soustenoient leur estat sur la guerre.' Quoted in D. Hay, 'The division of the spoils of war in fourteenth-century England', *TRHS*, 5th series, vol. 4, 1954, p. 91.

24 See the debate between K. B. McFarlane, 'War, the economy and social change: England and the Hundred Years' War', *Past and Present*, July 1962, no. 22, pp. 3–15, repr. in K. B. McFarlane, *England in the Fifteenth Century*, London, Hambledon, 1981, pp. 139–49, and M. M. Postan, 'The costs of the Hundred Years' War', *Past and Present*, 1964, vol. 27, pp. 34–53. Recently, it has been 'discovered' that violence in modern civil wars has an 'economic function': D. Keen, *The Economic Function of Violence in Civil Wars*, Adelphi Papers no. 320, Oxford, Oxford University Press for the International Institute for Strategic Studies, June 1998.

25 Of course, given the chance, the peasantry happily participated in rape and pillage, but this was abhorred by the elite and dealt with ruthlessly. In the late

1350s, the Captal de Buch and his cousin Gaston Phoebus, Count of Foix, both from the South of France and enemies due to their allegiance to opposing sides in the Hundred Years' War, happily went on Crusade in east Prussia together during a lull in the war and, on their return, helped put down the *Jacquerie* in northern France, an area they had no connections with: B. W. Tuchman, *A Distant Mirror: The Calamitous Fourteenth Century*, Harmondsworth, Penguin, 1979, pp. 179–80.

26 'Une économie du pillage, du don et de la largesse.' Duby, *Guerriers et paysans*, p. 69.

27 J. Dhondt, 'Groepsvorming in de verre Middeleeuwen, Vlaanderen in 1127–28, een maatschappij die van uitzicht verandert', in *Geschiedkundige opstellen*, Antwerpen, 1963, pp. 47–83. The main source and inspiration behind this article, the twelfth-century chronicler Galbert of Bruges, used the word 'potentiae'.

28 On the importance of the gift in primitive societies, see the classic by M. Mauss, 'Essai sur le don. Forme et raison de l'échange dans les sociétés archaïques', in *Sociologie et anthropologie*, Paris, PUF, 1950, pp. 143–279.

29 *Annales regni Francorum*, in Rau (ed.), *Quellen*, vol. 1, pp. 64, 796. See also Reuter, 'Plunder', p. 81.

30 The (para)phrase is by M. van Creveld, *The Transformation of War*, New York, The Free Press, 1991, p. 128.

31 J. Dhondt, *Hoe de staat tot stand komt* (s.l., s.d.), p. 19.

32 On the conduct of the war, see J. W. Honig, 'Strategie in de Late Middeleeuwen; of het zonderlinge geval van de afwezige militaire genieën', *Skript, Historisch Tijdschrift*, vol. 8, no. 4, winter 1986/87, pp. 251–61.

33 '[P]our deffendre leur honneur et leur heritage . . . leurs amis charneulx . . . leur droit Seigneur en ses guerres.' R. W. Kaeuper and E. Kennedy (eds), *The Book of Chivalry of Geoffroi de Charny*, Philadelphia, University of Pennsylvania Press, 1996, pp. 86–8.

34 '*Honor* bestimmt . . . den Rang, und der Rang ist – sicher nicht nur im Mittelalter, aber hier in besonderer Weise – etwas existentiell Wichtiges, weil von ihm alle Möglichkeiten der Mitwirkung, der Einflußnahme und Gestaltung in den Lebens- und Herrschaftsordnungen des Mittelalters abhängen. Der *honor*, die Stellung in solchen Rangordnungen, ist daher logischerweise nichts statisches, sondern wird umkämpft, verteidigt und angegriffen . . . Streitfälle um verletzte Ehre sind im Mittelalter zu einem Gutteil verkappte oder gar nicht verkappte Rangstreitigkeiten.[34].' G. Althoff, '*Compositio*, Wiederherstellung verletzter Ehre im Rahmen Gütlicher Konfliktbeendigung', in K. Schreiner and G. Schwerhoff (eds), *Verletzte Ehre, Ehrkonflikte in Gesellschaften des Mittelalters und der Frühen Neuzeit*, Cologne, Böhlau, 1995, pp. 63–4.

35 See Althoff, '*Compositio*', for one view on this hitherto neglected topic.

36 Galbert of Bruges, *The Murder of Charles the Good, Count of Flanders*, trans. James Bruce Ross, New York, Columbia University Press, 1960, pp. 105–7.

37 When one surveys European medieval history, it is striking how few princes were executed or even assassinated and to what extent many victors compromised. Of course, there are exceptions, but in those cases the sense of discomfort in successors and observers is palpable. The 'palace coup' of 751 that established the Carolingians on the Frankish throne was never quite forgotten in spite of the undisputed success of the dynasty and ample opportunity to rewrite history. The usurpations and assassinations within the English royal dynasty, which begin to occur with some frequency near the end of the Middle Ages, were considered revolutionary acts and did the legitimacy of the usurpers and assassins no good. And how much trouble did the 1407 assassination of the Duke of Orléans, the French king's brother, on the instigation of his cousin, John the Fearless, Duke of Burgundy, and the reprisal assassina-

tion of John on the bridge of Montereau in 1419, cause the reputation of those involved?

38 K.-G. Cram, *Iudicium Belli: Zum Rechtscharakter des Krieges im deutschen Mittelalter*, Münster and Cologne, Böhlau, 1955.

39 See Galbert (*Murder*, pp. 297–301) for the example of the 1128 battle of Axspoele, where the losing party's defeat is ascribed to their failure to observe the proper ritual.

40 G. Duby, *Le dimanche de Bouvines, 27 juillet 1214*, Paris, Gallimard, 1973.

41 Galbert, *Murder*, p. 299: 'and in fact such an enormous amount of money was paid out to redeem our [Bruges'] captives from Count William and his men that in a certain sense our land was again despoiled.'

42 Joinville, *Vie de Saint Louis*, ed. Jacques Monfrin, Paris, Classiques Garnier, 1995. See also the contribution of J. Riley-Smith (Chapter 10, this volume) and M. A. Köhler, *Allianzen und Verträge zwischen fränkischen und islamischen Herrschern im Vorderen Orient*, Berlin and New York, Walter de Gruyter, 1991.

10 The crusading movement

Jonathan Riley-Smith

The Christian environment

Christianity had inherited from Judaism a belief in a single, omnipotent God, the creator not only of the cosmos but also of whatever existed on any other plane, and the conviction that in the distant past something had gone wrong with His creation, so that men and women and the environment in which they lived had been corrupted. It believed, nevertheless, that in God's mind the cosmos had a purpose, and that one day, when this purpose was fulfilled, He would bring it to an end. In the meantime He had delivered messages about Himself and what He wanted of mankind, and had intervened directly in history in the person of Christ to assist mankind in fulfilling what He desired for it and to put right whatever had gone wrong in creation. Latin Catholics and Greek Orthodox were in agreement that Christ was at the same time the one God and a true human being, who had risen from the dead and preceded the rest of mankind to heaven.

Men and women, created for the purpose of loving God, were destined to live eternally. In exile while living here on earth, they had an obligation to prepare themselves for an afterlife in which they would be subject to judgement. If they had wholly alienated themselves from God they would be deprived of His presence for ever in hell. If they had proved themselves they would be welcomed into His presence in heaven. If they ended this life neither wholly alienated nor wholly at one with God they would have to undergo a painful but healing period of purgation, although the consensus that purgatory had a separate location in the afterlife was only achieved in the twelfth century. Strictly speaking, the last judgement would be made when God brought the cosmos to an end and all men and women were resurrected, but it was believed that there were already saints in heaven. Their intercession, particularly that of the Blessed Virgin Mary, Christ's human mother who took part in the redemptive process by agreeing to bear Him, could help mankind here on earth.

For men and women, membership of the Church, the community of the baptized faithful, which, being founded by Christ, was associated with

God's redemptive intervention in history, was necessary for salvation. Christ had endowed the Church with the outlines of a structure, which included a priesthood, the fullness of which was to be found in the bishops, who were the heirs of his chosen companions, the apostles. For Catholics, authority was to be found in the guidance given them by the bishops and especially by the Bishop of Rome, or Pope, who had inherited from St Peter the responsibility of overseeing the whole Church on Christ's behalf through the exercise of jurisdiction, teaching, defining the faith and pronouncing on the morality or otherwise of human actions. The idea of a discrete, identifiable community of the faithful, subject to authoritative guidance, was an essential element in crusade theory.

Crusades

A crusade was a form of Christian holy war, waged, like others, in defence of Christendom against external or internal injury, but distinguished from them in that it was penitential and was authorized by a pope on Christ's behalf. Each crusader vowed publicly to take part as an act of individual penance; in return he (or she) was granted an indulgence and enjoyed certain temporal privileges, the purpose of which was to make the task easier. Crusading bred two mutations: military orders, the members of which, sometimes operating out of their own little order-states, were not crusaders, being permanently, as opposed to temporarily, engaged in the defence of Christendom; and crusade leagues, which were alliances of certain front-line powers, the forces of which were granted crusade privileges.[1] Most, although not all, historians now accept that crusades were fought in many theatres-of-war besides the eastern Mediterranean region: in the Iberian Peninsula, the Baltic region, eastern Europe, North Africa and the interior of western Europe. The enemies were not only Muslims, but also Mongols, pagan Balts, Orthodox Greeks and Russians, heretics of various kinds and opponents of the papacy who were believed to be threatening the interests of the Church (and thus to be offending God).[2]

Crusading was an invention of the papacy. As soldiers of Christ, crusaders were summoned by the popes, who in their role as Christ's vicars provided the legitimate authority that was a necessary criterion for Christian war. They were recruited by preachers authorized by the papacy and their indulgences could only be granted by popes, on whom they also came to depend financially. As penitents and war-pilgrims, they ranked in canon law as temporary churchmen, subject to ecclesiastical jurisdiction. The Church should therefore have had a measure of control over their behaviour, because it could use its existing jurisdictional apparatus for this purpose. Just how limited that control was in practice will become apparent below.

The crusading movement lasted a very long time, from the late eleventh to the late eighteenth century, although towards the end it was regarded with distaste by intellectuals. The heirs of the Enlightenment critics, to whom pious violence seemed a contradiction in terms, were inclined to believe that crusaders must have been motivated by secular considerations, and their attitude was reinforced by the encomia of enthusiastic nineteenth-century imperialists, who saw the Crusades as originating the 'expansion of Europe' which in their view had brought such benefits to mankind.[3] Materialistic explanations are still popular. It is maintained that the early crusades were little more than large-scale plundering expeditions with which western knights were already familiar from their forays into Spain and elsewhere. Or crusading was a colonial enterprise, the purpose of which was to gain land for settlement. Or it was an economic safety-valve: a rising population was forcing land-owning families to take measures to prevent the subdivision of their estates, but these strategies destabilized society and led to a surplus of young men with no prospects, for whom adventure, spoils and land overseas were attractions. These supernumeraries were encouraged to make themselves scarce and a crusade was an appropriate way for them to reduce the burdens which their families faced.[4] Although a group of scholars, mostly French, proposed that the essence of crusading lay in a prophetic, eschatalogical, collective exaltation arising in the peasantry and the urban proletariat – the more radical among them had argued that the only true crusade was the first[5] – they did not gain much support, largely because so little was known about the masses that their ideas were unprovable. It was not until the 1960s that the prevailing view began to be seriously challenged by those who were drawn to ideological explanations of motivation, although all agreed that material or ideological considerations were not mutually contradictory. The weakness of the materialistic position – that evidence for it is ambivalent or non-existent – has been exposed, while the influence of sociology and anthropology has made historians more inclined to take past societies as they find them. In the past thirty years there has been a great deal of work on the ideas, cerebral and popular, which underpinned crusading and on the religious and social aspirations which generated recruitment.[6]

The just cause

The crusading movement is of importance because it was at times genuinely popular. It was much more complex than is often supposed, and developments over time can be traced in the mass of source material it generated. At the same time charismatic and institutionalized, it was used by the popes as an instrument for the defence of Christendom from outside threats and internal disorder: holy war in all religions has a tendency to become introspective, because success against external enemies is perceived to be dependent on the internal purity of the community it represents. This chapter will be concerned with the first three centuries of crusading, the period in which it was most vital and appealed to a wide spectrum of classes and interests. For much of that time western Christendom has almost the appearance of being in a permanent state of war; indeed from the late twelfth to the late fourteenth century there was hardly a year in which a crusade was not being fought somewhere. This is not surprising with respect to crusades against Muslims, since the jihad prohibited the making of a lasting peace with the *dar al-harb*,[7] but Latin Christendom was also engaged against other enemies, many of them non-Muslim, and forces in different regions fighting different enemies could be described as elements in one enormous transcontinental or intercontinental army.[8]

Applying the terminology used throughout this book, crusades were never genocidal, although genocidal actions are sometimes to be found on their fringes, and total war, in the sense of involving a total mobilization of population and economy, could never be waged by a movement essentially dependent on volunteers. Crusades against Catholic enemies of the Church were civil wars and those against heretics were absolute wars: it is noteworthy that crusades against heretics, relying on forces composed of volunteers who had taken temporary vows, all failed.

Most crusading, however, falls somewhere between limited and absolute wars, because while some – the campaigns in the Baltic region or in Spain, for example – had as an ultimate goal the subjugation or recovery of a region, others, such as campaigns for the 'liberation' of Jerusalem or the defence of the Holy Land, had limited aims; and because crusades were supposed to accord with the traditional criteria for Christian public violence, which were restrictive.[9] The just cause, for example, was taken very seriously: in his preaching handbook *De praedicatione sanctae crucis contra Saracenos* (1266–68, but printed in Nuremberg as late as *c.*1495), the distinguished Dominican Humbert of Romans typically maintained that war against Islam was fought in reaction to aggression.[10] He had to write at length about justification, because throughout the history of the crusading movement people needed persuading that the danger to which they were going to expose themselves was worthwhile. This meant that in almost every crusade proclamation there was a laborious explanation why a justifiable reaction to a specific injury perpetrated by the enemy was required.

The enemy

The importance attached to the just cause demanded that those who were perceived to be threatening the community had to be shown to be genuine injurers. Some arguments were less convincing than others: Innocent III's statement that crusading in Livonia was legitimate because 'the church' there – a handful of converts – was coming under threat from indigenous paganism[11] must have struck contemporaries as being as specious as it is to us. But no opponents – except perhaps the Mongols – were unfamiliar and a feature of the propaganda was that, while often hate-filled, it was usually very specific. Islam was believed to be bad in itself and its control of the holy places in Jerusalem 'polluted' them, but it was the 'tyranny' of Islamic rule over Christian people and the usurpation of, or threat to, Christ's patrimony by Muslims that justified waging war on them.[12] One cannot ignore the fact that there was a partially submerged current of missionary fervour as well,[13] but this could be no part of the Church's official teaching, since non-Christians could not be forced to the faith but had to be persuaded by reason.

The gulf between the ferocity of the language, fuelled by the need to demonstrate that there was a just cause, and the policies pursued in practice, can be illustrated with respect to the treatment of Muslims. As Christian reconquest (including crusading) got under way in Spain and the Near East from the late eleventh century onwards some highly experimental measures were put into effect by the Christian rulers. The measures were largely based on existing Islamic *dhimmi* legislation, which regulated the life and semi-independence of Christian and Jewish groups, and enabled Muslims to have their own protected community existence under Christian rule.[14] Within ten years of conquest some of the Christian settlers in the Near East were already allying themselves to Muslim principalities – even against each other. Even more striking were their attitudes towards the practice of Islam and Judaism. Muslim and Jewish travellers in the Levant were struck by the way mosques, synagogues and local shrines, visited by adherents of many religions, still flourished. A mosque-church in Acre had a Frankish eastern apse, incorporating the *mashhad* (oratory) of 'Ali ibn Abi Talib (the prophet's son-in-law), and was used by Muslims, Jews and Christians, who believed that this was the spot where God had created cattle for Adam's use: 'Muslim and infidel assemble there, the one turning to his place of worship, the other to his.'[15] Muslims and Jews were admitted as patients to a Christian hospital for pilgrims in Jerusalem and it is even possible that their dietary laws were respected.[16] While it would be wrong to speak of 'toleration' – a concept which did not come to the fore anywhere until the seventeenth century – it is equally impossible to take too hard a line on 'otherness'.

The Catholic community and the faithful

Underlying crusading was the notion of the theocratic community (*communitas, Christianitas, populus Christianus, gens* or *societas Christiana*) which needed to be defended. Although everyone who considered the matter realized that earthly Christendom comprised both the blessed and reprobate, it was thought of as being an extension on this plane of the only authentic state, ruled in heaven by Christ, and one of the common terms for this state, *Respublica christiana*, continued to be used well into the sixteenth century. This universal, transcendental state, in which earthly bishoprics and kingdoms resembled provinces, formed a political structure authorized by God and provided the only environment in which justice – characterized

by love of God and neighbour – could prevail. It was believed to represent Christ's wishes for mankind and any threat to it or to its citizens was
believed to be directed against His own intentions.[17] The supranational
nature of crusading was one of its defining features. Even when internal
propaganda elevated one national group's contribution over others – as
in works entitled *Gesta Dei per Francos*[18] – and when in practice only one
region was contributing fighters, a crusading army was always treated as
carrying out Christ's business in defence of the whole of Christendom.
The thirteenth-century preacher Eudes of Châteauroux was expressing a
common sentiment when he wrote:

> But someone says, 'The Muslims have not hurt me at all. Why should
> I take the cross against them?' But if he thought well about it he would
> understand that the Muslims do great injury to every Christian.[19]

In this respect the development of crusade leagues from the 1330s onwards
was a departure, because it was an adaptation of crusading to the aspirations
of governments more conscious than hitherto of their freedom of action.

The above quotation might lead one to suppose that the supranational
dimension of crusading was hard for the laity to grasp. But critics often
complained that men and money were being diverted to theatres-of-war
other than their own,[20] and the competition between different theatres
shows that the notion of a single Christendom responding to threats from
whatever quarter was alive. The close association between crusading and
Christendom, viewed as a community and identified with the Church, is
demonstrated further by the way that, from the later twelfth to the sixteenth
century, reform of the Church was believed to be a prerequisite for a
successful crusade.[21] Crusade preaching could arouse popular enthusiasm,
although the prospect of mass recruitment was abhorrent to senior
churchmen. The early campaigns had proved what a nuisance poor,
unqualified non-combatants could be, but they had had to be tolerated
because crusades were also pilgrimages, which traditionally attracted
women, the elderly and the sick, and it would have been impossible for
the Pope or anyone else to have confined a pilgrimage to youngish healthy
males with military training. Crusade redemptions, by which the unsuitable were encouraged to commute their vows to money payments, were
regularized by Pope Innocent III in 1213, although they caused scandal.[22]
The transportation of thirteenth-century crusaders by sea went a long
way towards solving the problem of the unsuitable, who could not afford
the passage and expressed their frustration in movements like the
Children's Crusade of 1212, the Shepherds' Crusades of 1251 and 1320
and the Popular Crusade of 1309, although in the fifteenth century, when
the priority had become the defence of the Balkans against the Turks,
crusades of the poor were revived and popular armies were recruited by
great preachers like John of Capistrano.

The arms bearers, whom the popes normally preferred to recruit, were often less easy to enthuse. No crusade, however large, attracted more than a fraction of the qualified manpower available. Because the vow was in canon law a voluntary act no churchman could make men take the cross (although some crusades were imposed as penances after confession); he had to persuade them to volunteer. From the first, crusading was extremely expensive and the costs rose with advances in technology, equipment and shipping. It was uncomfortable and perilous, with exhaustion, starvation and disease probably accounting for as many deaths as combat, and it could also pose real dangers for the family a crusader left behind, which was often burdened with debt and sometimes exposed to threats from neighbours and collaterals. The task of recruiters was made harder still by the conventions of the society they were addressing, which militated against spontaneity. They had to persuade their listeners to make spontaneous decisions, which did not come naturally to them, committing themselves to enterprises which would disrupt their lives, possibly impoverish and even kill or maim them, and inconvenience their families, the support of which they would anyway need if they were to fulfil their promises.

It is hardly surprising that preachers of the cross went about their task with as much theatricality as possible, indulging in great set-piece public sermons, sometimes delivered to audiences of thousands. The day on which a sermon of this type was to be delivered was often deliberately chosen. On a year-long 2,000-mile preaching journey through France (1095–96), the first official crusade preacher, Pope Urban II, timed his arrival in towns to coincide with great patronal feasts: he was at St Gilles for the feast of St Giles, at Le Puy, the greatest Marian shrine of the time, for the feast of the Assumption, at Poitiers for the feast of St Hilary.[23] In 1188, for his most important sermon in Germany, the crusade preacher Henry of Marcy chose the fourth Sunday in Lent, *Laetare* Sunday, the introit of which begins, 'Rejoice Jerusalem and come together all you that love her. Rejoice with joy you who have been in sorrow.'[24] In 1291 the Archbishop of York, employing Dominicans and Franciscans from thirteen communities, organized preaching rallies in thirty-seven places in his diocese, to be held simultaneously on 14 September, the Feast of the Exaltation of the Cross.[25] The locations for crusade sermons were often dramatic and out-of-doors, while every technique was employed to create an emotional ambience in which spontaneous commitments would be easier to make. In 1146 Bernard of Clairvaux persuaded the King of France to stand wearing his cross on a dais beside him, listening to his address.[26] In the 1190s preachers stood before a huge canvas screen on which was painted Muslims on horseback desecrating the Holy Sepulchre.[27]

Proceedings would begin with Mass being sung in the presence of as many senior ecclesiastics from the region as could be assembled. Then any general letter in which Christians were summoned by the Pope to a particular crusade would be read and translated. This explains the highly emotional words with which so many of these letters opened. The homily itself would be relatively short and would end with an *invitatio*, in which the preacher implored his listeners to take the cross. It would be followed by a hymn or song[28] – in 1100 the Archbishop of Milan had made use of a popular song, '*Ultreia, ultreia*'[29] – which must have been sung as men came forward to commit themselves publicly. Each votary was presented with a cloth cross which he was expected to attach to his clothes at once and to continue wearing until he had fulfilled his vow;[30] at Vézelay in 1146 so great was the enthusiasm that the stock of made-up crosses ran out and Bernard of Clairvaux had to tear his monastic habit into strips to provide additional ones.[31] It is easy to forget how visible these crosses must have been. A mid-twelfth-century sculpture, from the priory of Belval in Lorraine, shows a crusader wearing a cross on his chest made from two-inch strips of cloth and measuring six-by-six inches. The crosses got bigger as the twelfth century progressed.[32]

Preachers knew that they had to express basic Christian ideas in terms which would accord with the aspirations of the people. Crusading as an act of charity was a popular theme from the First Crusade onwards, with a stress on fraternal love: the Christians in the East were the Europeans' brothers and their interests must not be betrayed. Of course all educated churchmen knew that Christian charity involved love of enemy as well as of friend, but most of the faithful would not have comprehended love of enemy in the crusading context, and it is noteworthy that the only surviving sermon to give the rounded picture of love of both friend and enemy was one preached to clergy.[33] If charity posed a problem, so did a widespread belief in the martyrdom of crusaders who died in battle. This had been an established element in propaganda and in popular understanding from the first. It was, of course, one thing for the public to hold to the dubious proposition that a warrior, whose internal dispositions in the heat of battle could not be measured, should be ranked with those who died passively for the faith, and quite another for the Church to include in its calendars those who died in battle. Although local cults could develop around the tombs of crusaders, I know of no case in which martyrdom in battle was officially sanctioned in such a way. Churchmen, nevertheless, could not afford to offend their listeners by denying the idea, and the difficulties faced by even the senior among them are illustrated by two sermons commemorating the deaths of Robert of Artois, the brother of King Louis IX of France, and his companions at Mansurah in Egypt in 1250, preached, probably on the first anniversary of the disaster, by Eudes of Châteauroux, the papal legate on the Crusade. One sermon appears to have been directed at an audience of French lay nobles who had fought in the battle, including perhaps King Louis himself. In it Eudes actually referred to the dead as martyrs, in the context of 'different kinds of martyrdom', but his treatment was restrained, and he allowed himself a way out of his predicament by asking God's forgiveness for those 'who, prevented by fear of suffering, did not perhaps accept death in the state of devotion in which they ought to have been'. In the other sermon, probably delivered before clergy, there is no reference at all to martyrdom.[34]

A striking example of people-pleasing was the way propagandists coped with the concept of missionary war. This has no place in official Christian thought, but the ideal of bashing the infidel into submission to the faith was strongly held at grass-roots level and was pervasive in crusade literature.[35] It was not a powerful enough force in most of Europe to persuade preachers to employ it with regard to campaigns in the East or in Spain, but the Baltic region was different, because muscular Christianity was a feature of popular piety in Germany from where most recruits came, and because there had been a tradition of missionary warfare in the region from the time of Charlemagne. Several leading churchmen, Bernard of Clairvaux and Innocent III among them, sailed very close to the wind when justifying crusades against the pagan Balts to German audiences.[36]

As time went by, the message of the preachers had to be adapted to appeal to the imaginations and preconceptions of new generations. For example, the image of Christ presented to the faithful seems to have changed from that of the father of a noble household to that of a feudal lord, reflecting the importance of lordship in thirteenth-century society. The most radical aspect of crusading – the fact that it was a personal act of penance – was gradually diluted and fused with chivalric values, so that it came to be seen more as service-in-arms for Christ, a much more conventional idea than that of the fighter engaged in an act of penance, with a long history stretching back to Augustine of Hippo around 400. Crusading had originally been only secondarily about serving Christ, or benefiting the Church or Christianity; it had been primarily about benefiting the crusaders themselves, through the imposition of condign self-punishment, and as such it had been an act of self-sanctification.[37] It is evidence of how far ideas had changed that with Humbert of Romans a century and a half later the stress was almost exactly the reverse: Humbert emphasized that the crusade was the performance of service to Christ and that this service could only be effective if it was penitential. Christ was now centre stage and penance had become a means of adequately serving Him.[38]

Crusading remained a penitential activity, however, and this was reflected in the devotional language of thirteenth-century sermons, in which attachment to the cross had become central.[39] It goes without saying that the cross had always been closely associated with crusading thought, but for the first eighty years of the movement the imagery appears to have been less significant in the words of preachers and the minds of crusaders (insofar as one can see into them) than the reality of the Holy Sepulchre in Jerusalem. The triumph of the cross in crusading thought, its transformation from a potent symbol of self-sacrifice to the justification which gave meaning to everything, came about because the central Middle Ages were characterized by growing devotion to the crucifixion and by the appearance of affective imagery relating to it. The emphasis on the cross reflected a popular religion which was becoming more and more cross-centred.[40]

Extra-curricular violence

In comparison with the just cause and legitimate authority, the third traditional criterion for Christian violence, right intention, appears to have been spectacularly ignored. As penitents, of course, the crusaders were expressing right intention, but this should also have meant that the violence they engaged in was circumscribed in such a way that the innocent suffered as little as possible. The early crusaders knew, and were prepared to abide by, the developing conventions of war, such as the custom of sparing from destruction a city which was prepared to surrender; it was the Muslims themselves who reported that the breakdown of negotiations led to the sacking of Ma'arrat in Syria on 12 December 1098.[41] However, one cannot ignore the fact that the history of crusading is punctuated, particularly early on, with atrocities: pogroms against Jews, which heralded almost every major campaign before 1300, examples of ethnic cleansing and collapses in discipline with appalling consequences for the wretches found in an army's path. These were partly the consequence of the theatrical display and the highly coloured language addressed by preachers to a martial society which in the late eleventh and for much of the twelfth century was swept by vendettas. Around 1100, when the dominant binding force in western Europe was the kindred, preachers played on the image of Christ as a noble head of household, calling, sometimes in the language of the blood feud, on His children and relations to help save His patrimony. By preaching the First Crusade in this way they almost certainly contributed to the persecution of the Jews.[42]

The crusades were expressions of a society which was very violent and could voice even its piety in violent forms, but early crusades were also uncontrollable by nature. The composition of the armies depended entirely on the drawing power and personalities of the individuals who chose to respond to the appeals, and this made adequate chains of command hard to establish. Popes could summon crusaders, tax the Church to provide funds, arrange for shipping, work to establish peace in western Europe and discuss strategy with the leaders, but they were helpless once an army was on the move, being dependent for its conduct on the laymen who had taken the cross. Sometimes if one – and it had to be only one – king was involved, he could provide clear, unambiguous leadership. Otherwise, every crusade was run by a committee made up of the great lords together with the papal legate, who as a priest was technically disqualified from military command and could rely only on his personality to influence councils-of-war. It was hard to persuade the often proud and touchy magnates to agree on any course of action, partly because they themselves could never make decisions independently of their own subordinates who, like them, were volunteers and who, unless they were associated with the greater lords by ties of family or clientage back home, were serving in their contingents only because of the ability of the lords to provide for them. All early crusades were characterized by a kaleidoscopic shifting of allegiances as minor figures moved from one contingent to another, or armies and individuals came and went.

With so many volunteers there was always going to be indiscipline, and the emotional penumbra which enveloped every crusade from the recruiting assemblies onwards was heightened by apprehension and fear, by the devotional practices which punctuated the march and by exaggerated chivalric display. On the larger crusades the fighters were exposed to tension and alienation for very long periods of time. Although it is hard to draw lessons from modern combat psychiatry and apply them to situations hundreds of years ago, it is now known that volunteers are more likely to commit atrocities than conscripts[43] and that over-long exposure to stress is bad for efficiency and discipline.[44] The cocktail of idealism, self-righteousness, indiscipline, alienation and stress created almost copybook conditions for expressions of inhumanity.

These problems began to resolve themselves in the thirteenth century. The decision of the papacy in 1199 to subsidize crusaders by raising large sums from the taxation of the Church, which were then allotted to those leaders who were taking the cross, led to improvements in discipline. Although it was common for western kings to make over-optimistic declarations about their intentions in order to get their hands on the money, the system did provide a way of funding crusaders through their commanders and of making them more dependent on them. From the 1230s on, crusade leaders were entering into contracts with their followers, granting them money in return for specified service with a known number of men, and this enabled volunteers to be paid as if they were in the leaders' employment.[45] Even more important was the introduction from the 1330s onwards of the crusade league, because the states in that kind of alliance made use of their 'regular' forces (if one can use that term), combining the benefits of crusading with a more professional, and employed, fighting element.[46] As the professional elements increased, the weaknesses inherent in contingents of volunteers diminished. A huge gulf separates the Christian navy which fought the battle of Lepanto in the sixteenth century or the armies of the Holy League which disputed Hungary with the Ottomans in the seventeenth century from the scratch forces of the twelfth-century crusades.

Conclusion

Crusading was a radical form of Christian holy war, waged by volunteers under the direction of the Church on behalf of the theocratic community that was Christendom. It appealed to at least some of the faithful because at various levels it helped to bridge the gap between the expectations of their ideologies and the extent to which they could meet them in their daily lives. Always concerned about response, however, crusade preachers developed techniques – the use of theatre and symbols, the employment of highly charged language – to try to ensure adequate recruitment, although their efforts contributed to the emotional ambience in which wars of this sort were fought. Once crusading had become institutionalized it appealed to the popes and church leaders because they believed that it could be used both to defend Christendom against external non-Christian enemies and to achieve internal order and uniformity of faith by restricting the activities of heretics and those Christians who were perceived to be attacking the church itself. In this they were mistaken, because the voluntary, charismatic nature of crusading made it a very uncertain instrument, often beyond their control.

Notes

1 See J. S. C. Riley-Smith, *What were the Crusades?*, 2nd edn, London, Macmillan, 1992, *passim*, with the modifications proposed in J. S. C. Riley-Smith, *The First Crusaders*, Cambridge, Cambridge University Press, 1997, pp. 48–52, 63–4.

2 For the debates on definition, see N. Housley, *The Later Crusades*, Oxford, Oxford University Press, 1992, pp. 2–4; J. S. C. Riley-Smith, *The Oxford Illustrated History of the Crusades*, Oxford, Oxford University Press, 1995, pp. 8–12; G. Constable, 'The Historiography of the Crusades', in *The Crusades from the perspective of Byzantium and the Muslim World*, ed. A. E. Laiou and R. P. Mottahedeh, Washington DC, 2001, pp. 1–22.

3 See J. Flori, *Pierre l'ermite et la première croisade*, Paris, Fayard, 1999, p. 10.

4 See Riley-Smith, *The First Crusaders*, pp. 15–21.

5 Constable, 'The Historiography', *passim*.

6 Examples of the new approach are J. M. Powell, *Anatomy of a Crusade*, Philadelphia, Pennsylvania University Press, 1986; S. Lloyd, *English Society and the Crusade*, Oxford, Clarendon Press, 1988; M. Bull, *Knightly Piety and Lay Response to the First Crusade: The Limousin and Gascony, c.970–c.1130*, Oxford, Clarendon Press, 1993; J. S. C. Riley-Smith, *The First Crusade and the Idea of Crusading*, London, Athlone, 1986, and *The First Crusaders*; and Flori, *Pierre l'ermite*.

7 M. A. Köhler, *Allianzen und Verträge zwischen fränkischen und islamischen Herrschern in Vorderen Orient*, Berlin and New York, Walter de Gruyter, 1991, *passim*; P. M. Holt, *Early Mamluk Diplomacy (1260–1290). Treaties of Baybars and Qalawun with Christian Rulers*, Leiden, Brill, 1995, pp. 3–6.

8 See G. Constable, 'The Second Crusade as seen by contemporaries', *Traditio*, 1953, vol. 9, pp. 213–79.

9 Riley-Smith, *What were the Crusades?*, *passim*.

10 Humbert of Romans, *De praedicatione sanctae crucis contra Saracenos*, Nuremberg, c.1495. See P. J. Cole, *The Preaching of the Crusades to the Holy Land, 1095–1270*, Cambridge, MA, The Medieval Academy of America, 1991.

11 Innocent III, 'Opera omnia', comp. J. P. Migne, *Patrologiae cursus completus. Series Latina*, 1844–64, Vol. 214, Paris, cols 739–40.

12 See e.g. Riley-Smith, *The First Crusaders*, pp. 60–2; also Humbert of Romans, 'Opus tripartitum', in E. Brown (ed.), *Fasciculus rerum expetendarum et fugiendarum*, London, 1690, Vol. 2.

13 See B. Z. Kedar, *Crusade and Mission. European Approaches Toward the Muslims*, Princeton, NJ, Princeton University Press, 1984, *passim*.
14 Treated by J. S. C. Riley-Smith in 'Government and the indigenous in the Latin kingdom of Jerusalem', forthcoming.
15 Ibn Jubair, *The Travels*, trans. R. J. C. Broadhurst, London, Jonathan Cape, 1952, pp. 318–19; 'Ali al-Harawi, *Guide des lieux de pèlerinage*, trans. J. Sourdel-Thomine, Damascus, Institut Français de Damas, 1957, p. 57.
16 B. Z. Kedar, 'A twelfth-century description of the Jerusalem hospital', in H. Nicholson (ed.), *The Military Orders, Vol. 2, Welfare and Warfare*, Aldershot, Ashgate, 1998, p. 18.
17 J. A. Watt, *The Theory of Papal Monarchy in the Thirteenth Century*, London, Burns and Oates, 1965, esp. pp. 103–4.
18 See Riley-Smith, *The First Crusade*, pp. 141–2, 147–8; *The First Crusaders*, pp. 64–5.
19 Eudes of Châteauroux, 'Sermones de temporis et sanctis', in J. B. Pitra (ed.), *Analecta novissima*, Paris, 1888, vol. 2, p. 314.
20 E. Siberry, *Criticism of Crusading*, Oxford, Clarendon Press, 1985, pp. 156–89.
21 See J. S. C. Riley-Smith, *The Crusades. A Short History*, London, Athlone, 1987, pp. 241–2.
22 C. T. Maier, *Preaching the Crusades. Mendicant Friars and the Cross in the Thirteenth Century*, Cambridge, Cambridge University Press, 1994, pp. 135–60.
23 Riley-Smith, *The First Crusaders*, pp. 54–60.
24 Cole, *The Preaching of the Crusades*, p. 66.
25 Lloyd, *English Society*, pp. 55–6.
26 Eudes of Deuil, *De Profectione Ludovici VII in Orientem*, ed. and trans. V. G. Berry, New York, Norton, 1948, p. 8.
27 Baha' ad-Din, *Kitab al-nawadir al-sultaniya wa'l-mahasin al-yusufiya*, trans. C. W. Wilson, London, Palestine Pilgrims Text Society, vol. 13, 1897, pp. 207–8.
28 Humbert of Romans, *De praedicatione, passim*.
29 Landulf the Younger of Milan, 'Historia Mediolanensis', *Monumenta Germaniae historia. Scriptores in Folio et Quarto*, 1826ff., vol. 20, p. 22.
30 Riley-Smith, *The First Crusaders*, p. 11.
31 Eudes of Deuil, *De Profectione Ludovici VII*, p. 8.
32 Riley-Smith, *The First Crusaders*, p. 11.
33 J. S. C. Riley-Smith, 'Crusading as an act of love', *History*, 1980, vol. 65, pp. 177–92.
34 P. Cole, D. L. d'Avray and J. S. C. Riley-Smith, 'Application of theology to current affairs: memorial sermons on the dead of Mansurah and on Innocent IV', *Historical Research*, 1990, vol. 63, pp. 230–3, 236–7, 239. The sermons have been published by Cole, *The Preaching of the Crusades*, pp. 235–43.
35 Kedar, *Crusade and Mission, passim*.
36 Riley-Smith, *The Crusades*, pp. 96, 131–2.
37 Riley-Smith, *The First Crusaders*, pp. 68–72, 75.
38 Humbert of Romans, *De praedicatione, passim*.
39 This is true of the sermons of James of Vitry in the first quarter of the century, of those of *Etudes of Châteauroux* in the second quarter and of Humbert of Romans' *De praedicatione* in the third. See Cole, *The Preaching of the Crusades*, p. 206.
40 J. Pelikan, *The Christian Tradition. A History of the Development of Doctrine. 3. The Growth of Medieval Theology (600–1300)*, Chicago, IL, The University of Chicago Press, 1978, pp. 129–44.
41 See C. Hillenbrand, *The Crusades: Islamic Perspectives*, Edinburgh, Edinburgh University Press, 1999, p. 59.
42 Riley-Smith, *The First Crusade*, pp. 50–7. See also R. Chazan, *European Jewry and the First Crusade*, Berkeley, University of California Press, 1987, *passim*.

140   *Jonathan Riley-Smith*

P. Watson, *War on the Mind. The Military Uses and Abuses of Psychology*, London, Hutchinson, 1978, pp. 243, 246.
44 J. Keegan, *The Face of Battle*, London, Jonathan Cape, 1976, pp. 328–9.
45 See Lloyd, *English Society*, esp. pp. 134–9.
46 J. S. C. Riley-Smith (ed.), *The Atlas of the Crusades*, London, Times Books, 1991, pp. 140–1; Housley, *The Later Crusades*, pp. 431–5.

11 War, peace and national identity in the Hundred Years' War

Anne Curry

The fourteenth and fifteenth centuries in western Europe were dominated by major conflict which has been known since the 1860s as the Hundred Years' War (1337–1453). The term is convenient, for it implies at a glance that this was a protracted and essentially insoluble struggle. It is also a helpful term in that it does not name its protagonists directly, for we shall see that it was always much more than a simple fight between two monarchies or two peoples, English and French. At its heart was a dispute between kings. A duke of Normandy conquered England in 1066, and all successive rulers of medieval England were also holders of lands within France. In the late twelfth century, the Angevin kings held not only Normandy but also Anjou, Maine and Touraine, as well as Aquitaine and Poitou. King John (1199–1216) lost most of these territories save for the coastal lands of Aquitaine, commonly known as Gascony. In 1259, the Treaty of Paris confirmed that the remaining lands in France were held by the English king as a vassal of his French counterpart, to whom he was thereby obliged to pay liege homage. Thus, the English king, in his capacity as Duke of Aquitaine, did not have full legal sovereignty over Gascony; his subjects could appeal to the French king. This situation conflicted increasingly with developing notions of the authority of rulers within their own territories, and led to two wars, 1294–97, and 1324–27. There was already a state of Cold War between the English and French kings when an additional cause of dispute arose. This was Edward III's claim that he was the rightful King of France through his mother, Isabella, daughter of Philip IV.

There has been much debate on the seriousness of the dynastic claim: was it merely a bargaining counter aimed at negotiating full sovereignty over Gascony?[1] War had already broken out in 1337 over the issue of vassalage. The formal claim to the throne, advanced three years later, was an irredeemable insult to the French king. A blood right could never be surrendered, so, once taken up, Edward and his successors were obliged to maintain it, and the French kings were equally obliged to resist it, and to restate the fact that the English kings were vassals of the French crown. Edward met with considerable military success, including the capture of the French king, John II, at the Battle of Poitiers in 1356, but as Honig has pointed out, protagonists were prone to seeking 'a mutually satisfactory compromise'.[2] The capture was a double-edged sword: for Edward to ransom John for an enticingly large sum was in effect to admit Valois kingship, and thus to deny his own. This is essentially what happened through the Treaty of Brétigny in 1360 where Edward ostensibly gave up his claim to the throne in return for full sovereignty over an enlarged Aquitaine, Poitou and Calais. However, territorial rights of monarchs were, as with blood rights, difficult to abandon, and it is not surprising that the French should subsequently reassert their sovereignty over the lands ostensibly held absolutely by Edward. Once most of the territories gained had been reoccupied by French armies, the English could do little more than restate the claim to the French throne itself. This situation might have persisted had it not been for divisions within France which paved the way for Henry V's revival of English military success in the second decade of the fifteenth century, and for his acceptance as heir and regent to the crown of France by the Treaty of Troyes in 1420. This envisaged that once the mad Charles VI of France was dead, an English king would rule both kingdoms, and that, through a union of crowns, there would be peace between their peoples. Henry VI was crowned king in both London and Paris in 1429 and 1431 respectively. But by this time the Dauphin had himself been crowned in the traditional French crowning place of Reims, a fact which gave him much greater status; such symbols and links with the historic past were central to the concept of legitimacy in this period. The English were now on the retreat, although it was not until 1449–53 that they lost all their French lands except Calais. Even though Calais did not fall until 1558, and the use of the French royal title was not abandoned until 1801, historians have generally taken the Hundred Years' War as ending in the mid-fifteenth century, for that marked the real end of any credibility in terms of English claims to the crown, or to territorial sovereignty.

Chivalry and codes of conduct

In his general overview of European warfare, Michael Howard discusses the medieval period under a chapter title of 'Wars of the knights'.[3] Conflicts were, in this interpretation, fought with, and for, honour by a warrior elite for whom there was a distinctive and international ethos: chivalry.[4] The Hundred Years' War is a defining moment for the code and practice of chivalry in France and England, and many of the chivalric orders had their origins as a direct result of it. The Order of the Garter was founded by Edward III partly as a commemoration of his victory at Crécy in 1346. In France at the same juncture, the king founded the Order of the Star in an attempt to revive French self-belief in nobility and 'chevalerie' in the face of the humiliation of defeat. Foundations of the Breton order of the Ermine (*c*.1381) and the Burgundian order of the Golden Fleece (1430) reflect attempts by smaller principalities to create a focus for allegiance based upon chivalric principles.

Setting aside for the moment administrative and diplomatic documents produced as a result of the Hundred Years' War, the principal sources for its study are chivalric chronicles. Knights gained renown by virtue of their valiance, generosity and piety. Thus, their activities were deliberately recorded by chroniclers in order to extol the cult of the individual, and to encourage others to emulate the deeds of the good knight. The most famous of these chroniclers of the fourteenth-century phase of the Hundred Years' War, the Hainaulter, Jean Froissart, begins his work thus:

> In order that the honourable enterprises, noble adventures and deeds of arms which took place during the wars waged by France and England should be fittingly related and preserved for posterity, so that brave men should be inspired thereby to follow such examples, I wish to place on record these matters of great renown.[5]

The Burgundian, Enguerran Monstrelet, our main chronicler for the fifteenth-century phase, deliberately began his chronicle from the point where Froissart left off and aimed to follow his predecessor's intentions.[6] Both regale us with stories of *individual* prowess in war, but also show group solidarity. The conduct of the knight both on and off the battlefield was dictated by an expected code of behaviour. The same values, the same definition of prowess (and on the reverse side of the coin, of cowardice and lack of personal worth), prevailed even between men who were enemies. Out of this developed 'laws of war', governing the preliminaries, conduct of military actions and personal conduct. Admittedly these should be seen as *ius* rather than *lex*, but, arising as they did out of a common chivalric mentality, they could be universally accepted.[7] According to the laws of war, the conduct of warfare can appear a contrived, even gentlemanly affair. For instance, once agreement had been reached between besiegers and besieged that surrender would take place unless a town or fortress was relieved and a *journée* (battle) fought, the state of siege could be suspended. Hostages might be delivered to guarantee that the composition would be kept, but there was also a strong sense of chivalric trust that those who had sworn on their honour would not, for the sake of preserving the same, renege upon their promise. Those who transgressed this code were humiliated. This was the fate of Sir John Fastolf, who was seen to have acted in an unchivalric and cowardly fashion at the battle of Patay in 1429 and who lost his garter stall as a result.

The period sees the rise of heralds and other officers of arms who were concerned, among other things, with the conduct of hostilities. In war and diplomacy, in the issuing of summons and defiances, the heralds represented the protagonists. They were appointees of a particular monarch or lord, and bore names which reflected this. Soon after his victory of 1415, for instance, Henry V appointed an Agincourt herald whose missions to France stood as a constant reminder of a defeat so scarring that the French could not call it by name, referring to it as *la maudite journée* (the accursed day). Yet the heralds also stood outside the debate, even literally so, grouping together to observe battle and being considered non-combatants exempt from violence or capture. Importantly too, several heralds wrote chronicles. Jean Le Fèvre, who was appointed king-of-arms of the Burgundian Order of the Golden Fleece in 1431, is a particularly useful example to cite, for, as a young *officier d'armes* of the King of France or Duke of Brabant, he accompanied the English army from Harfleur to Agincourt in 1415, and was thus an eyewitness to the battle.[8] This genre of historical writing is also reflected in an unpublished mid-fifteenth-century chronicle written to extol the military career of Sir John Fastolf, perhaps as a counterweight to his earlier disgrace (especially as it breaks off before Patay). This account contains many lists of battle presences and garrison commands, of the French as much as the English, but all of men of rank and renown, and notes individual acts of prowess and good leadership.[9] Thus when chronicles of this type speak of the warriors involved in the Hundred Years' War, they are interested only in those of gentle status. They presage Shakespeare's famous line on English casualties at Agincourt: 'none else of name, and of all other men/But five and twenty.'[10]

In this belief system, chivalry and nobility were inextricably linked. The code of conduct which chivalry implied percolated through to behaviour in peacetime where there was a similar emphasis on the keeping of one's honour, and to acting as a true knight in terms of generosity and piety. When the Duke of Suffolk was impeached in the English Parliament in 1450, being blamed for the defeats then being suffered at the hands of the French, the charges included offences against the code of honour as well as peculation and collusion with the enemy.[11] While knights were seen as an essential part of the body politic, most usually portrayed as the arms to the ruler's head and the peasantry's feet, they could also be criticized if they were deemed to have failed in their duties as active protectors of the kingdom and people. This is made apparent by the vitriol poured on them in France after the defeats of Crécy, Poitiers and Agincourt, yet there remained a strong link between military service and social status. In France, those who followed arms and were accustomed to serving in the armies were exempt from taxation, as were the *hidalgos* in Spain, a country where it was a mark of respect to be said to be 'living as cleanly as a knight'.[12] Knightly status was the defining norm: this is apparent to us today by visual means, for men throughout western Europe regularly had themselves portrayed on their tombs as warriors even if they had not seen any military service. By extension, in such a value system, prowess and courageous service in military activity was itself ennobling, even by those of lower social status. In at least one case before the French *cour des aides*, there is an explicit statement that all who fought at Agincourt were reputed noble.[13]

At the apex of this came the chivalric warrior king, as is revealed by artefacts such as the armed riding figure on the obverse of seals, the parade helmet of Charles VI now in the Louvre Museum, and the funeral achievements and tomb decoration of Henry V in Westminster Abbey. Honour was paramount in the central conflict between the English and French kings. The English king was bound by honour to claim his rightful inheritance, and the French king was similarly bound to resist. This led to the production of much justificatory material on both sides. The notion also arose that national as much as regal honour was at stake. If the Hundred Years' War began between kings, it developed into conflict between peoples; but how was it possible that war could be waged between two Christian peoples at all?

Wars between Christians

As Jonathan Riley-Smith has indicated, the justification for fighting the infidel or heretic was straightforward. It was possible, therefore, to wage a crusade within one's own kingdom against one's own people if they had departed from the true faith, but was it right to shed *Christian* blood? The crusading ideal never disappeared – indeed it continued to be perceived as a pinnacle of chivalric military service. The Saracen persisted as the archetype of evil and unbridled cruelty; in the French civil war of the early fifteenth century, for instance, the pro-Burgundian author of the *Journal d'un bourgeois de Paris* equated the rival Armagnac faction with the Saracens.[14] However, as the Middle Ages advanced, war between Christian peoples came to predominate in both time and space. Throughout the Hundred Years' War, much attention was given to the concept of the just war, based not only on Thomas Aquinas' preconditions, but also on Roman law and chivalric dictates. We have a plethora of treatises written in the period which show the way in which these three elements were combined.[15] The notion of the crusade also became adulterated so that it could be applied to action against a Christian enemy, as is revealed by the adoption of crusade-style language in justifying and describing what were essentially wars between kingdoms and peoples.[16] This was given an extra fillip during the Papal Schism. With Europe divided behind opposing popes between 1378 and 1417, and England and France on different sides, campaigns in this phase of the Hundred Years' War took the form of crusades, with kings exploiting the possibilities of diverting crusading taxes to their own political ends. The religious dimension of the conflict persisted after the end of the Schism. Both the English and the French portrayed themselves as God's chosen people. Joan of Arc bore the banner of Christ, and was seen as the virgin who would save France or as the limb of the Devil, depending upon which side one was on. The churches were also called upon to approve and promote the war policies of rulers. This they did by prayers, processions and sermons for victory, even at times when, theoretically at least, they were part of a universal Christendom whose pope often set himself up as mediator for peace.[17] This helped make the Hundred Years' War a conflict between peoples and not simply between kings. Another reason for this latter development was the nature of the armies which fought the war.

The armies

While the Hundred Years' War was occasioned by, and conducted according to, concepts of personal and collective honour, the armies were not solely made up of mounted men-at-arms of knightly or armigerous origins. Indeed, this was the 'age of infantry' rather than the 'age of cavalry'.[18] While military leadership remained with the nobility and gentry, and the core of armies throughout Europe continued to be formed from their retinues, armies were boosted in size and changed in nature by the increased deployment of foot infantry and archers. The first real signs of this are seen in the late thirteenth century in Edward I's wars against the Welsh and Scots, and in Philip IV's against the Flemish. In the case of the English, the fire power of massed and well-disciplined archers served to place in disarray a mounted attack before it got close enough to engage.[19] In the fourteenth century, English armies contained about equal numbers of men-at-arms and archers. In the fifteenth century, there were three archers for every man-at-arms, and sometimes the ratio was even greater.[20] Not only were archers cheaper, collecting half the daily rate of pay of a mounted man-at-arms, but there was a greater pool from which to recruit. So we see a broadening of the basis of recruitment away from the traditional chivalric classes, and hence an investment in war by the lower ranks of society. The French were slower to abandon reliance on the traditional military group, to dismount to fight, and were disparaging of the English archers and the Flemish urban militias, to their cost.[21] Here we see an interesting perception of the enemy too, and of warfare as something which was properly the preserve of those who had been born and trained to fight. Victory finally came to the French, however, when they reorganized their army in the 1440s with ordnance companies, contingents of *francs archers* and a more effective artillery train.

We also see the development of a paid army in both countries, with monetary reward being made even to those of noble status. Thus armies (and navies) were increasingly royal not private, and can be traced through the records of state administration. The distribution of pay meant that troops were essentially volunteers in the service of the state rather than obliged to serve by virtue of tenure. Service by obligation never died out, and the level of perceived emergency is revealed by the invocation of the *arrière ban* and *semonces des nobles* in France. Much has been made of mercenaries in this period, yet a close examination of the composition of armies suggests that relatively few foreign soldiers hailed from countries which were *not* in alliance with the ruler in whose cause they fought. Most famously, the Scots fought for the French throughout the entire war. The service of Spanish, Portuguese, Germans and Flemish in English or French armies was occasioned by fluctuating alliances; yet no ruler had a standing army. They could not afford to have one, nor was their power over the nobility enough to allow them to raise armies independently of the latter. This helps to explain the apparent dichotomy of how a king could win a foreign war yet lose in civil conflict at home. What we can suggest, therefore, is that royal absolutism based on military control was still a century or more away, but that changes in military organization, towards a national army, were already tending in that direction.

Wars between kings or wars between peoples

Kings and princes made peace and war as the duty of their God-given position dictated. English kings stated their right to French territory and crown by stressing the *justice* of their claim, and employed teams of lawyers both to investigate their rights and to express them at home and abroad. The peoples of England and France had no reason for conflict save as subjects of their kings. Likewise, the French had collectively no right to attack Flanders, save only in the service of their king who was feudal over-lord of the count. This situation is replicated in all other theatres of the conflict. These were at base dynastic and feudal wars. Attack was justi-fied on the basis of the fact that the people were, by supporting their own ruler, disobedient rebels. The French who resisted were guilty of treason against their natural lord, the King of England. An interesting aspect of this is the public burning of civic records at the capture of towns, symbol-izing the fact that they had been generated under the aegis of illegal authority. In diplomacy this is epitomized by the denial of the title of one's opponent; thus, at the outset of the war, we have 'Philip, who calls himself king of France', and after 1420, Charles 'the so-called Dauphin', while the French denied the English kingship of Henry IV after he deposed Richard II in 1399.

Backed by the weight of law against treason, already a most heinous offence, and with reference to Deuteronomy 20, the use of considerable violence was justified in the case of those who resisted their rightful lord. Burning, pillage, destruction, expulsion – all were acts of war deliberately used by English kings in France and Scotland, justified by emphasis on the rebellion of subject peoples. The few battles were fought between increasingly professional armies, and so affected civilians only vicariously through the loss of relatives and breadwinners. Sieges and raids on land, and licensed piracy at sea, were the main form of warfare. Recent research has suggested that the English *chevauchées* in France and Scotland were deliberately aimed at destruction of the economic base and the consequent demoralization of the population.[22] It was hoped that the latter would realize the folly of continuing to support a ruler who could not protect them, and would therefore accept the authority of the enemy. There is something slightly perverse in this view but it has persisted into many modern wars. In the fifteenth century, the English focused on systematic conquest and occupation, which led to considerable local upheaval as well as to dilemmas over loyalty. Should one accept English rule in order to save one's property? In raids as much as conquest, civilian populations were both target and victim. Although these wars were never aimed at wiping out a native population, many were forced from their homes and their property sequestrated. Trade embargoes and blockades were imposed. Even in periods where hostilities were suspended, informal and unofficial war was carried out by the ex-soldiery, which central power was too weak to prevent.[23]

While wars began between rulers and technically remained so, there is much to suggest that in practice they became wars between peoples. This was partly due to the ruler's manipulation of the concept of defence of the realm. The ruler's rights were not private and personal but stood for the rights of his kingdom as a whole. Thus an assault on them was portrayed as against the kingdom and the people as a whole. The prince was in many ways already 'the state'. The stress on defence was easy enough in France where the English invasions threatened to damage everyone's interests. Thus, for instance, the burning of records at Caen in 1346 and again in 1417 was an obvious insult to the Caennais as well as the French king, but how could the people of England be persuaded of the need to fight for their king as an aggressor overseas? Rewards, pay for military service and the promise of loot or land gains in conquered territory were all useful, but there had also to be a more conceptual underpinning. Defence of the king's rights was defence of the English people as a whole. Consequently emphasis was placed upon French plans to invade England, which were described in parliamentary records from the reign of Edward I onwards as being aimed at 'the destruction of the English tongue'.[24] There were indeed French raids at various stages of the war, but never any real invasion. One has the distinct impression that the English crown did much to cash in on the fear of attack in the creation of the notion of an ancient enemy, meaning not only the French but also their allies, the Scots.

Rulers needed to get their subjects behind them in a way that had never before been necessary. So large-scale and protracted were wars from the late thirteenth century onwards that they led to the broadening not only of recruitment but also the taxation base, and thus affected the civilian population of western Europe to a degree never hitherto experienced. This in turn led to the expansion of administrative systems. Regular revenues were not enough, and so rulers had to have recourse to the estates and parliament for grants of taxation. Arguments put forward therein reinforced the notion of national interests and defence as opposed to the private ambitions of rulers. Such acts made war feel collective and national.

National identity and regional considerations

There is considerable evidence to support the view that the persistence of Anglo–French conflict did much to define the separate identity of the two nations and to change their perceptions of each other. This is revealed by portrayals in literature as much as in the more formal prose of diplomacy. The French were double and false, the English were thugs, 'goddams', who swore and pillaged their way through. Long-standing cultural and linguistic ties between England and France began to be undermined, in some cases deliberately, as happened when English ambassadors refused to negotiate in French in 1418/19, claiming falsely that they had no knowledge of the language. Even in an early fifteenth-century manual for learning French, there was the inclusion of a conversation about Agincourt which would hardly have offered a suitable conversational gambit.[25] It can be no coincidence that the use of the English vernacular increased over the course of the war, most notably in periods of defeat. There is a marked and sudden move to the use of English in official records at both national and local level in the early 1450s, and the late fourteenth century is well known for literary output in English. In France, French was already the language of government and culture before the wars began, but the developing sense of national consciousness is revealed by stress on the legitimacy of the Valois.

So engrained were the concepts of 'France' and 'England' by 1420 that it is difficult to see how the imagined harmony of the two nations in Henry V's plans for a double monarchy could ever have been realized, given that he had spent much of the time leading up to Troyes exacerbating the sense of the English as God's chosen people and the French as the perfidious against whom the Almighty had shown his ire. Long-term enemies could not be made into friends overnight, even by sharing a ruler, and by a marriage to cement the relationship. Henry had also tried to create another imagined community – that of the old Anglo–Norman world – by stressing his own links with William the Conqueror and reviving ancient Norman institutions, hoping to appeal to Norman separatism.[26] Edward III had also hoped to exploit divisions within the kingdom in 1340. The manifesto which he circulated in France soon after his assumption of the title of King of France in 1340 exploited contemporary French concerns that standards of law and order had declined as a result of the partisan and corrupt government of recent years. Edward promised that, as king of France, he would return to the good laws of St Louis and rule with the advice of the nobility.[27]

France was by no means a unified kingdom, however. The war was never a straight fight between the English and French kings and their subjects. Intranational relations also had a role to play. In the late 1330s, Edward III had been urged to attack by none other than the brother-in-law of Philip VI himself, Robert of Artois. In the early 1340s, one of the claimants to the Duchy of Brittany offered his allegiance, with the result not only that Edward ended up being accepted as King of France in parts of Brittany but also that, in the Breton civil war which followed, the French king inevitably gave his backing to the other candidate. Thus a local conflict was caught up in an international war. In the fifteenth century the two parties in the French civil war both negotiated with the English, with the Burgundians entering into formal alliance between 1419 and 1435. By virtue of their tenure of the county of Flanders from 1383, and of an increasing number of provinces in the Low Countries in the early fifteenth century (which later formed the basis of Habsburg power in the north), the Burgundian dukes were rapidly developing into more than simply French magnates. They never ruled a kingdom, remaining technically vassals of the kings of France, but they were powerful enough in political and military terms to pursue their own policies. Even before they controlled Flanders, this particular county played a pivotal role in Anglo–French relations. In the earlier fourteenth century, the situation was further complicated, for while the count, a vassal of the French king, was loyal, the towns of the county, affected by cross-Channel trading links and precocious levels of self-government, pursued their own line in favour of the English. It is no coincidence that Edward III made his formal assumption of the title King of France in Ghent, thereby absolving the leading Flemish towns from what was otherwise a clear act of rebellion against their count and his Valois overlord.

While England was a more unified country, the ostensibly subject peoples in Scotland looked to the French. The 'auld alliance', first created in 1295 and persisting for almost three centuries, was a perpetual thorn in the side of the English. It was war, too, which led to the formulation of a strong sense of Scottish national identity, complete with an appeal to history and to the papacy, and to their survival as a separate kingdom.[28] This is but one example of the added complexity arising out of the involvement of 'client states' which from time to time generated transnational groupings. There were many areas where the local ruler was in practice independent even if he was not a truly sovereign prince. Thus the German princes did not always follow the lead of their emperor, and neither he nor they pursued a consistent policy of support for England or France. Likewise the Spanish kings. The attitude of Pere IV of Aragon was partly dictated by his relations with Castile. In the latter, a succession war created a similar situation in the 1360s and 1370s to the one that had arisen in Brittany, with the English and French supporting rival claimants.

Conclusion

To sum up, some alliances were consistent, others shifting. The central Anglo–French war was caught up in other international and intranational issues. This was one of the factors which contributed to the difficulties of achieving peace, for, even if the principals were able to sort out their differences, albeit temporarily, the conflict could continue vicariously. There were other reasons why true peace was well-nigh impossible, and why the two major treaties of the Hundred Years' War, Bretigny and Troyes, failed. The appeal to history and to justice made it very difficult for either party to surrender, and in both England and France rulers used the threat of an outside enemy to bolster their rule at home. Moreover, as noted at the outset of this chapter, blood claims could never be fully given up for they were integral to one's very existence, hence the longevity of many dynastic wars. Diplomacy became a form of war in itself, fanned by the workings of lawyers and polemicists. War was often advertised as a way to peace. There is a strong feeling that while it was admitted that the shedding of Christian blood was wrong, some had to be shed in order to avoid more being so. The papacy tried to mediate on several occasions, but found itself compromised by its perceived close links with France and by the Schism. Emperors also entertained hopes of acting as peacemakers but found their own interests tended to impel them to partiality.

It was, then, as near as the West had ever come to a pan-European conflict. Of course, it would be wrong to perceive of this period as one of 'total war' by modern standards: there was no systematic genocide even if civilians were the principal victims of *chevauchées* and sieges. The size of armies did not permit the take-over of vast territories, and as the protagonists were relatively evenly matched in terms of technology, it was difficult for one to gain a permanent upper hand. The use of gunpowder was present but still embryonic, often acting as a deterrent rather than as a decisive weapon. Moreover, English fortunes were far too dependent upon political (and military) support in France. Peace, like war therefore, was not wholly dependent upon international relations pure and simple, but on an array of factors, internal and external. There can be no doubt that the claim by one major ruler of the throne of another was a significant contribution to the creation of instability in western Europe both in the later Middle Ages and beyond. Essentially, England and France remained enemies for many centuries to come, even after the English had lost their territorial possessions or any possibility of regal authority in France.

Notes

1 For a survey of the historiography and an outline history of Anglo–French relations, see A. Curry, *The Hundred Years War*, London, Macmillan, 1993; C. T. Allmand, *The Hundred Years War*, Cambridge, Cambridge University Press, 1988, is a wider ranging study.

2 See Jan W. Honig, Chapter 9, this volume.

3 M. E. Howard, *War in European History*, Oxford and London, Oxford University Press, 1976.

4 M. H. Keen, *Chivalry*, New Haven and London, Yale University Press, 1984, provides an excellent survey of the subject, with much of relevance to the period under discussion.

5 Froissart, *Chronicles*, ed. G. Brereton, London, Penguin Books, 1968, repr. 1978, p. 37.

6 L. Douet-d'Arcq (ed.), *La Chronique d'Enguerran de Monstrelet*, 6 vols, Paris, Société de l'Histoire de France, 1857, vol. 1, pp. 2–3.

7 M. H. Keen, *The Laws of War*, London, Routledge, 1965. See also M. Howard, G. J. Andreopoulos and M. R. Shulman (eds), *The Laws of War. Constraints on Warfare in the Western World*, New Haven and London, Yale University Press, 1994.

8 F. Morand (ed.), *Chronique de Jean Le Fèvre, Seigneur de Saint Rémy*, 2 vols, Paris, Société de l'Histoire de France, 1876–81.

9 London, College of Arms MS 9, discussed in B. J. H. Rowe, 'A contemporary account of the Hundred Years War from 1415 to 1429', *English Historical Review*, 1926, vol. 41, pp. 504–13.

10 'King Henry the Fifth', Act 4, scene 8, lines 96–7.

11 *Rotuli Parliamentorum*, v, pp. 176–83.

12 A. Mackay, 'The lesser nobility in the kingdom of Castile', in M. C. E. Jones (ed.), *Gentry and Lesser Nobility in Later Medieval England*, Gloucester, Alan Sutton, 1986, p. 175.

13 Rouen, Archives Départmentales de la Seine Maritime, 3B 1121. I am grateful to Dr Gareth Prosser for this reference.

14 J. Shirley (ed.), *A Parisian Journal, 1405–1449*, Oxford, Clarendon Press, 1968, pp. 107, 115.

15 Ph. Contamine, *War in the Middle Ages*, trans. M. C. E. Jones, Oxford, Blackwell, 1984, pp. 284–92. This book contains the fullest bibliography of the subject of medieval warfare in general.

16 C. Tyreman, *England and the Crusades 1095–1588*, Chicago and London, University of Chicago Press, 1988, esp. chs 6 and 12.

17 W. R. Jones, 'The English church and royal propaganda during the Hundred Years War', *Journal of British Studies*, 1979, vol. 19, pp. 18–130.

18 C. J. Rogers, 'The military revolutions of the Hundred Years War', *Journal of Military History*, 1993, vol. 57, pp. 241–78, repr. in C. J. Rogers (ed.), *The Military Revolution Debate: Readings on the Military Transformation of Early Modern Europe*, Boulder, CO, Westview Press, 1995, pp. 55–93.

19 M. Prestwich, *Armies and Warfare in the Middle Ages. The English Experience*, New Haven and London, Yale University Press, 1996, ch. 5.

20 A. Curry, 'English armies in the fifteenth century', in A. Curry and M. Hughes (eds), *Arms, Armies and Fortifications in the Hundred Years War*, Woodbridge, The Boydell Press, 1994, pp. 45–7.

21 For French military organization, see Ph. Contamine, *Guerre, état et société à la fin du moyen âge. Etudes sur les armées des rois de France, 1337–1494*, Paris and The Hague, Mouton, 1972.

22 C. J. Rogers, 'Edward III and the dialects of strategy', *Transactions of the Royal Historical Society*, 6th series, 1994, vol. 4, pp. 83–102.

23 N. Wright, *Knights and Peasants. The Hundred Years War in the French Countryside*, Woodbridge, The Boydell Press, 1998, chs 2 and 3.

24 See, in general, J. Barnie, *War in Medieval Society*, London, Barnes and Noble, 1974.

25 'Manière de langage 1415', in A. M. Kristol (ed.), *Manières de langage (1396, 1399, 1415)*, Anglo–Norman Text Society, 1995, vol. 53, p. 70.

26 A. Curry, 'Lancastrian Normandy: the jewel in the crown', in D. Bates and A. Curry (eds), *England and Normandy in the Middle Ages*, London, Hambledon Press, 1994, pp. 235–52.
27 A. R. Myers (ed.), *English Historical Documents*, Vol. 4, London, Eyre and Spottiswoode, 1960, pp. 66–7.
28 A. A. M. Duncan, *The Nation of Scots and the Declaration of Arbroath, 1320*, London, Historical Association, 1970.

Part III

War and peace in Early Modern Europe

Introduction

Anja V. Hartmann

The transition from the Late Medieval to the Early Modern era in Europe is marked by three events, none of which is directly related to intercommunity relations, let alone to war and peace. The Protestant Reformation initiated by Martin Luther, Jean Calvin and Huldrich Zwingli (since 1517), the 'discovery' of America by Christopher Columbus and his successors (since 1492) and the publication of Copernicus' book *De revolutionibus orbium coelestium* (1543) all mark the accelerated transformation which took place in European societies around 1500. Though none of these three events was a revolution in the modern sense of the word, each brought about fundamental and far-reaching changes in people's value systems which in turn influenced European foreign and domestic politics as well as European society as a whole. While Copernicus' work challenged the prevailing views on the relationship between the earth and the universe, which were hitherto firmly grounded in the Christian dogma of the earth as the centre of every moving thing in the sky, the 'discovery' of America questioned the role of Europe as the centre of the earth, and, with the coming of the Reformation, even the relationship between men and God was suddenly at stake. Points of reference which had so far been fixed and reliable all at once started to move, and quite naturally the inner structure of the body politic as well as its relations with other entities also began to alter.

Initially, the sixteenth century saw the most successful attempt at universal monarchy that Europe had ever known: the monarchy of the Spanish king and emperor Charles V, whose lands included not only Spain and the Holy Empire but also the New World. The still often proclaimed *Respublica Christiana* came closer than ever to the ideal of being politically united. However, the zenith of the idea of universal monarchy was also the opening to its final disintegration. Although already referred to often in Late Medieval times, dynasty and religion now started to unfold their full power in intra- and intercommunity relations. The struggle for hegemony in Europe between the houses of Valois (in France) and of Habsburg (in Spain and in the empire) continued throughout the sixteenth century, in spite of a number of peace treaties like those of Cambrai (1529), Crépy (1544), or Cateau-Cambresis (1559). Simultaneously, the combination of political and religious goals intensified the Protestants' fight in France and in the Netherlands which threatened the existing institutions of government and produced new ties between communities, based on a common faith rather than on common ancestry. The entwinement of intra- and intercommunity conflicts in the so-called religious wars and the complicated structure of the combatants' interests are illustrated in Aline Goosens' contribution (Chapter 12).

The Thirty Years' War (1618–48) which devastated many parts of Europe was in a way the cumulative apex of the previous centuries' dynastic and religious confrontations, as is shown in Anja V. Hartmann's contribution (Chapter 13). Neither a purely religious nor a strictly dynastic war, the Thirty Years' War combined elements of both, as well as economic and territorial interests. Given the fact that the European state system was heavily restructured in the course of the war, the Thirty Years' War has recently been named a war of state formation (Johannes Burkhardt) which saw the confrontation of several concepts of intra- and intercommunity order within Europe. While neither the ideal of universal monarchy – pursued (consciously or not) at least for a while by the Spanish Habsburgs, the French Bourbons and the Swedish Wasa – nor the notion of quasi-republican estates (*Stände*) – defended in Bohemia and in the Netherlands – was able to triumph definitively, the scheme adopted in the end was the concept of sovereign states, equal in rights and independent from each other on the intercommunity level. The peace treaties of Westphalia (1648), far from founding the 'Westphalian system' dear to political scientists, reshaped many aspects of the inner organization of the Holy Empire, introduced the idea of religious tolerance, put an end to the wars between the emperor, France and Sweden, and recognized the sovereignty of the Netherlands and of Switzerland. Still, the war between France and Spain was to continue until 1659 when the peace treaty of the Pyrenees settled the dispute which had lasted for over 150 years.

While religion lost most of its belligerent force in the course of the Thirty Years' War, dynasty remained an important factor in intercommunity relations. The end of bipolar conflicts – Habsburg–Valois, Habsburg–Bourbon – and the emergence of a multipolar state system which finally centred around the pentarchy of England, France, Prussia, Austria and Russia gave way to a new type of dynastic conflict: the age of the wars of succession began. The French king Louis XIV claimed dynastic rights as a justification for his wars in the Netherlands (1667–68, 1672–78, 1688–97), and the following wars of the Spanish succession (1701–14) and of the Austrian succession (1740–48) as well as the Silesian wars of Maria Theresia and Frederick the Great (1740–42, 1744–45) all originated from dynastic conflicts. Still, dynastic rights often served only as a pretext while underneath the righteous declarations hegemonic, territorial and economic interests were at stake. The concept of a 'balance of power' dominated the theory and practice of intercommunity relations in Europe. At the same time, war aims were usually limited, and conquests were made at the conference table rather than on the battlefield, as Heinz Duchhardt points out in his contribution (Chapter 14). The number of peace congresses especially at the beginning of this period is astonishing, to cite only the most prominent examples: Nijmwegen (1679), Rijswijk (1697), Utrecht/Rastatt (1714). Finally, the *Renversement des alliances* (1756) – the rearrangement of the coalitions between the monarchs of the pentarchy – showed that traditional ties had lost their binding power in intercommunity relations. From then on, co-operation and confrontation between states were to be based on common interests and rational choice rather than on religious or dynastic bonds. Reason of state finally allowed agreements ignoring the interests of minor powers or local populations, such as the exchange of territories or – the most famous example – the divisions of Poland.

Elements of intercommunity relations

The main difference between intercommunity relations in medieval and in Early Modern Europe was produced by the gradual shift from the hierarchical structure led by the Pope and the Roman emperor to a multipolar state system whose members were sovereign states and, as such, equal and independent of each other. The Pope in particular rapidly lost political influence after his rejection of the peace treaties of Westphalia. While he had been able to claim moral as well as political authority in medieval times, he had to abandon even his role as a mediator in intercommunity conflicts after the rise of Protestant powers in Europe. Some monarchies, such as Spain, lost their formerly strong positions little by little, some relocated their main grounds of identification, such as the emperor who acted more and more like an Austrian monarch, and others successfully strengthened their situation and managed to rise, such as Russia or Prussia in the eighteenth century. Nevertheless, the idea of a distinct value system common to all European states persisted throughout the Early Modern era, although its denomination changed from *Respublica Christiana* to 'Europe' and thus finally lost the religious component still present up to the early eighteenth century, especially in the recurring wars against the Ottoman Empire.

Hence, the centuries from 1500 to 1800 saw the emergence of the sovereign monarchical state as the main actor on the stage of intercommunity relations. This development was supplemented by a twofold delimitation of the state's sphere. On the one hand, the states claiming sovereignty disentangled the feudal ties which had previously connected them on various levels, and they fixed their territorial boundaries against each other. The states thus consolidated the limits of their powers against each other. On the other hand, each monarch strove to stabilize the efficiency of his power within his own state, according to a system traditionally known as 'absolutism'. Bureaucracy (including the establishment of a diplomatic corps) and military (a standing army) became the monarch's principal weapons and shields against threats both from without and within. While policy and politics were thus centralized and concentrated, economy and erudition formed networks which held up intercommunity relations on other than state level, as can be illustrated by international merchants' communities as well as by the so-called *République des lettres*.

Despite the gradual dissolution of the traditional hierarchy among the European states, rank and ceremony retained a certain importance in intercommunity relations well into the eighteenth century. First, matters of ceremony implying the mutual acceptance of differences in rank among the sovereigns constituted important issues in planning and in the course of peace congresses. Second, ascending states like Prussia tried to receive title and honour of kingship in order to be acknowledged as 'full' members of the group of sovereign states which gradually excluded communities lacking this formal qualification. Third, the monarch's court became an important arena for the validation of ceremonial and representative models, mirroring the internal structure of the state as well as its external position in relation to others. Still, the traditional grounds for claiming a certain rank and the corresponding ceremonial honours steadily gave way, and were finally replaced by a hierarchy of military power and successful implementation of the 'reason of state'.

The formation of the sovereign monarchical state was accompanied by the institutionalization of diplomacy which had started in Italy in the fifteenth century. The seventeenth and the eighteenth centuries in particular brought about the creation of permanent embassies whose number and splendour became a manifestation of the state's importance and its modernity. States like Russia aiming at recognition as members of the European state system deliberately used diplomatic institutions to establish their positions. However, the diplomats' training still remained largely unorganized, despite the foundation of professional academies in France or Prussia. The status and rights of diplomats slowly became codified as part of the flourishing literature on international rights, and consequently the mistreatment of diplomats and their disengagement often constituted matters of great political importance. All through the Early Modern era, most diplomats remained highly dependent upon their sovereigns' political orders, even more so because foreign policy was regarded as the monarch's privilege, and foreign offices only came into existence at the end of the eighteenth century. On the whole, however, the institutionalization of diplomacy provided the basis for a regular exchange of information between the courts and thus intensified the ties of communication in Europe.

On the field of warfare, the Early Modern era and the centralization of state finances gave rise to the introduction of standing armies replacing the troops of mercenaries led by military entrepreneurs dominant in the Thirty Years' War. Instead of private military leaders who sold their own and their soldiers' services in wartime, the monarchs now formed their own standing armies. Although most soldiers still were mercenaries, uniforms and weaponry were standardized, and the incorporation of specialists of all kinds into the armies drove forward the process of professionalization. As regards the extent of warfare, the Early Modern period can be divided into two. While the sixteenth century and the first half of the seventeenth century were the time of perpetuated wars – the Eighty Years' War between Spain and the Netherlands, the Thirty Years' War – where many different interests were mixed up, the eighteenth century was one of shorter wars usually entered upon for limited aims. This was partly due to the immense costs of prolonged warfare barely sustainable over an extended period even by those who otherwise assisted their allies by paying subsidies, such as France. The French military budget reached 75 per cent of the total state's budget in 1700, a ratio impossible to bear for more than a short interval. Warfare which had been omnipresent, threatening, and often accompanied by cruelties up to the peace treaties of Westphalia, was thus slowly turned into an instrument of the power politics of the sovereign state, set about with clearly defined intentions, limited in scope and extension, and fought out by professional soldiers, often not even in open battle but rather in a continuous struggle of mutual sieges.

12 Wars of religion

The examples of France, Spain and the Low Countries in the sixteenth century

Aline Goosens

The theme of war features prominently, at least in volume, in narrative sources from the fourteenth century onwards.[1] Many medieval conflicts were triggered without much thought or planning, but it would be wrong to think that advance planning was completely alien to medieval governments. For war to be fought well, it was necessary to effectively combine money, men and their equipment, as well as logistical support, on the battlefield.[2] Continual problems with manpower, command, money and supplies had to be dealt with. So few noblemen were willing to join military operations that, until the mid-fifteenth century, war remained an individual venture: gains and losses concerned each combatant, and state intervention was uncertain or marginal. In addition, war was not just for professionals. Everyone had the right to defend himself against aggression, be he in a rural community, town or principality.

Yet a new model, inspired by Ancient Rome and the perpetuity of chivalric idealism, started to emerge in the fifteenth century: the military was to serve the king or state and defend the welfare of the public while strictly observing the law. At the same time, the subjects' right to defend themselves against aggression was heavily disputed in theory and in practice when the rebels in France and the Netherlands claimed it against their kings. Finally, as Jeremy Black points out, two fundamental factors that were often intimately linked must be taken into consideration for all armed conflicts of the sixteenth century: dynasties and, above all, religion. From the beginning, the Reformation was seen as threatening the politico-religious order of Europe.[3] For the whole of the sixteenth century, successive European conflicts betrayed a hidden battle which concerned religion as much as dynasties (notably the Valois and the Habsburgs).[4] However, one must not forget territorial and economic stakes. The Dutch Revolt was a striking example of civil or even private conflict which degenerated into an international war where propaganda played a major role. In addition, an immense psychological effort was required to mobilize the masses.[5]

The failure of the ideal of universal monarchy

Paramount to the world order at the time of the Renaissance was the idea that Christianity, which had been divided since the Great Schism, was threatened in its entirety by the advancing Turks. There was still the underlying conviction on the part of the Catholics that Christendom had to be restored to its universality and homogeneity, while the Protestants accepted more readily the view that different parts of Christianity should follow their different creeds and local preferences. Likewise it was the Catholics who most readily accepted the idea of a universal monarchy (*Monarchia universalis*) – one Christian Church, one pope, one emperor, one Holy Roman Empire. Charles V came closest to this ideal of universal monarchy when he was elected emperor, as the Habsburg lands he inherited also included the united crowns of Aragon and Castile and all their possessions. It is significant that during his reign, centrifugal tendencies barely existed, while the division of the Habsburg territories after his reign deprived Spanish rule in the Netherlands[6] of imperial overlordship, and in deposing Philip II, the princes of the Netherlands merely deposed one king, not the emperor.

Charles V was raised on the model of his ancestors, the Dukes of Burgundy. He spent his childhood immersed in books on the Old World by Burgundian chroniclers such as Chastellain and Olivier de la Marche. The literature centred around bravery and chivalric honour, and drew on the glorious achievements of the Dukes of Burgundy. Charles V aspired to emulate his great-grandfather of military renown, Charles the Bold. The Order of the Knights of the Golden Fleece, founded by Philip the Good in 1430, sought to re-create the Christian chivalry that had led the crusaders to Jerusalem three centuries earlier. Charles V, who throughout his life had been its Master, introduced the order in Spain, and allowed Spanish, German and Italian nobles to join it, thus ensuring their loyalty.

Likewise, he – like many other princes – took recourse to militaristic imagery to enhance his prestige. In the fifteenth and sixteenth centuries, we find a pronounced militaristic culture in this respect. In portraits, princes or potentates were depicted in armour, and made to resemble medieval knights (*miles Christi*) or classical figures. Charles V had himself portrayed (particularly after 1535, when Tunisia was taken by the Turks) as the Christian Hercules on a series of tapestries by Pannemaker in Brussels. Also available are the equestrian depictions of parade armour (see Titian's portrait of Charles V in Mühlberg, and also the bronze and marble statues of the Léoni brothers). Francis I and his successors, as well as Ferdinand I of Habsburg, used similar images for propaganda, for example on the Clouet painting depicting the King of France on horseback and in armour, which is preserved at the Louvre.

Despite the holistic ideal of universal monarchy, there were important parts of Europe which not only remained outside the empire but were also prepared to join the Turks against it – most notably France under Francis I. Accordingly, in France kingship was nominally held in similar veneration as emperorship was within the empire. The King of France was sacred and seen as God's anointed. He was a living symbol of untouchable divinity. As God's chosen, nobody could contest his authority. The rivalry between France and the empire can be traced back to rivalling interpretations of the joint heritage of Charlemagne – on the one hand the imperial, on the other the French royal heritage. The speech given by Gattinara in 1519 is particularly illuminating on this count:

> Sire, God, the Creator, is so clement to have raised you [Charles V] above all the other Christian kings and sovereigns, as he has made you the greatest emperor and king since the division of the empire of Charlemagne, your predecessor, and he has shown you the way towards legitimate worldly hegemony, in order to unite the entire world under the leadership of one guardian.[7]

The idea of a universal monarchy equalled the domination of the entire world, including the new lands of America, rather than just Christian Europe. Yet what Charles V desired most of all was to dominate Europe and to impose himself as an *Imperator Romanorum*. He claimed the moral authority to ensure the cohesion of Christianity and to defend it against its two enemies: the Turk and the Protestant. Still, in practice two obstacles foiled the realization of the universal monarchy. First, it became manifest that, given the size of the territories, they were impossible to govern from one centre. Second, opponents to the scheme argued that it would inevitably lead to abuses of power. During the Dutch Revolt (1567–85), both adversaries were aware that they were all part of the same Christian world order, since both Catholics and Protestants defined themselves as Christians. But this balance of power was divided at the core: whereas most Protestants and the *Politiques* supported the principle of religious pacification and the freedom to choose one's faith, many Catholic leaders wished to restore a uniformly Catholic Europe, either through an adapted catechism or by violence and repression. The Revolt was also an uprising of the nobles, who opposed the hegemonic principles of universal monarchy, and who wished to restore the power of states and of provincial entities. The act by which the General States dethroned Philip II and his sovereign power over the Habsburg Netherlands in 1581 cited these motives while accusing the sovereign of tyranny.[8] The following two extracts from Hubert Languet and Michel de L'Hospital are significant in this respect:

> In the same way that servants are not bound to obey their masters, should they be asked to act against the will of God, so too should subjects not obey their kings, should those want to force [their subjects to] transgress the law of God.[9]

These are not people brought together by foolhardiness, without order, discipline or leaders. These are people who are no strangers to battle, who are determined and reduced to despair; as a consequence they stand together in solidarity and do not allow themselves to be separated, as this union is the basis of their security, life, survival, home, family, honour and social position. They remain steadfast in their resolution to die together rather than to submit to the yoke of their enemies.[10]

The Dutch Revolt and the religious wars in France

A look at the Eighty Years' War (the Dutch Revolt and the Thirty Years' War) will allow us to see the various points that united Henry of Navarre (Henry IV of France), the princes of Orange–Nassau and Elizabeth I. These were not so much ties of blood or friendship, but of a common strong Calvinist faith and an even stronger hatred for the Catholic monarchy of Philip II. Disagreement re-emerged only after the signing of the Treaty of Vervins in 1598, taking on a more economic dimension. According to Jean-Pierre Babelon, three important phases of this alliance need to be distinguished: the period of 1567–88, the subsequent reconquest of the Kingdom of France (1588–98), and finally, the difficult peace (1598–1610).[11]

It is the first period that this study is mainly concerned with, given the coincidence between Catherine de Medici's replication of the repressive religious policy of Philip II, and the Calvinist opposition of Jeanne III (d'Albret), Queen of Navarre and mother of the future King Henry IV of France, in 1567–68, which was encouraged by French Protestant princes. French Huguenot troops left for the Netherlands to fight there against the troops of Philip II. Nevertheless, this military assistance led only to a crushing defeat at the siege of Mons in June 1572. The military ventures of Spa and Mons in 1576 proved failures once again. The return of the southern provinces to Philip II's rule in 1579 changed everything, and despite Henry of Navarre's constant reiteration of his promise to help, he was never able to do so on account of the developments in France and the assassination of William of Orange in July 1584.

French policy oscillated between attempts at reconciliation and peace and the formal banning of the Protestants.[12] When still moderate, the policies of Catherine de Medici were never universally respected; the Dutch Revolt reinforced the Huguenots' determination to have a share in the governing of France. The politico-religious repression by Philip II in the Habsburg Netherlands first spurred the French Protestants and the English Protestants – albeit without the open support of their monarch – into support for the oppressed. Catherine de Medici's reaction was to move towards repressing Protestantism within France, out of fear that a Protestant state would form in the Catholic one. Her political and religious intrigues culminated in the St Bartholomew's Day Massacre.

The two main reasons for the Dutch Revolt can therefore be summed up as follows: first, on a political level, the empire's desire for all administration to be centralized in Madrid caused inhabitants of the seventeen provinces to fear that they would lose their traditional autonomy; second, on a religious level, locals feared the imposition of a strict Catholicism involving the repression of Protestant and especially Calvinist heterodoxy. The combination of these two fears mobilized the whole population, and in particular those who had much to lose: the nobility, who feared for their natural authority and privileges, and the towns, which feared that the interference of the Inquisition would result in the loss of their independence and the repudiation of their customs and laws. This also explains why the war started in the south, where the high aristocracy and the richest and most powerful towns were located.

Still, noble opinion was divided as regards the Revolt. The Orange–Nassau clan brought its large followership into the conflict against Philip II, while a section of the aristocracy was conspicuously active for the king. In 1568, the execution by Philip II of counts Egmond and Horn, who had first served him as loyal Catholics before taking the side of William of Orange in protest against excessive Spanish persecutions, demonstrated the depth of this division. The period 1576 to 1578 proved crucial. The high nobility, conscious that the Dutch Revolt had expanded its aim beyond its original intentions, gradually withdrew from the war and entered into negotiations with the Spanish, in the hope of seeing the situation stabilize and return to the status quo, with the monarchy supported by the local nobility. In contrast, the combatants from the middle class could not face going back to the previous state of affairs, and chose to continue fighting for their own future interests. The division between the two groups enabled the Spanish to initiate a counter-attack which proved victorious in the ten southern provinces in 1585. This was followed by mass population movements, with the town-based middle classes leaving for the provinces in the north – the future United Provinces – in order to join the Revolt. In the south, only the conservative nobility and the Catholic clergy remained, submitting to Madrid's power.

One can only speculate on why the populations accepted sacrifices in the interest of the community. It is hard to understand how the populations of Schieland, Delftland and the Rhineland could accept the flooding of their towns.[13] The suffering of the populations was certainly great. During the worst part of the siege of Leyden and the pillaging of the surrounding area in October 1574, the daily food ration for one person was limited to a half-portion of bread, cheese and one herring.[14] Marnix's description of conditions in the first few years of the war is stirring:

> What pillage of private property! What theft of local money, and sacking of the towns and villages! ... How many murders, killings and massacres of the high nobility, banishments of innocent people,

confiscation of their property, rape of their women and virgins. Pillaging of great and rich properties, profanement of holy places, and the rights and privileges of the country, abolished and trodden underfoot![15]

Were the armies of Alessandro Farnese, governor of the Netherlands on behalf of the Habsburgs (1576–92) and leading general on their behalf during the Dutch Revolt, and the other governors who were to ensure Dutch obedience to Spain, motivated by religion? There are many accounts on the pity towards war victims shown by Farnese, and the religious obligations he imposed on his troops. Symbolically, the Catholic faith was present everywhere: in the chanting of the *Ave Maria* prior to combat, written on battle flags and during the victorious *Te Deum* after victory. The faith did not, however, feature in the heat of the battle and in everyday life, despite the exemplary punishments imposed by Farnese on those who swore, blasphemed, or pillaged churches.[16]

None the less, religion did not always come first, and there were also alliances that ignored it altogether. The aid given by Francis I to the Protestant princes of the Schmalkaldic League and the alliance he concluded with the Turks may serve as examples. Dynastic interests and the struggle for European pre-eminence were therefore two other factors in the war. Still, religion was important in the context of preserving and defending communal life and culture. The Catholics defended the community of believers rather than the beliefs themselves. Of course, political, economic, social and intellectual motivations were also present.[17]

By contrast, in the French wars of religion, religious zeal played a considerable role.[18] Repression and massacres occurred spontaneously, without prior formal declarations and irrespective of the absence or presence of organized armies. This violence appears to have been more common and more aggressive than in other countries that experienced crises at the time of the Reformation. The choice of faith was imposed by the state in a much more radical manner in northern Europe (Sweden, England, the Empire) and in the territories under Spanish control. Nevertheless, it seems that the situation in France was unique. Catherine de Medici's vacillation between a policy of peaceful co-existence and politico-religious repression, as well as the political instability in the succeeding reigns of Francis II and Charles IX (1559–74), served to increase the indecision of local authorities and to favour the creation of factions of nobles, using the religious divide to their advantage.

James B. Woods finds that there were five major obstacles to a swift and definitive royal victory between 1562 and 1576. First, armies had lost control of the war, and massacres sparked off massacres. Second, in 1567, the conflict spread to the south of the Loire into regions far away from royal power, and against Protestant bases that were fortified and determined to hold out. The chronic shortage of money and the poor administrative organization of the armies further complicated the task, whereas the inappropriateness of weapons (above all artillery) was flagrant. Finally, religion helped to support the rebellion, as Protestants received money from abroad which increased their capacity to resist.[19] This was also true for the Habsburg Netherlands, with the slight difference being that there were relatively fewer massacres than in France, particularly in the countryside. Those that occurred usually took place as reprisals for the capture of towns and against very specific groups of people, such as the clergy and Protestants.

Recruitment

We have seen that during the conflicts, the nobility played a distinctive part. As the king's vassal, a nobleman had certain obligations, both personal and as a landowner. He was obliged to raise a specified number of cavalry for the defence of the kingdom. This feudal cavalry was inexperienced, disorganized and badly armed. The preference was growing for a professional army where everyone was equipped with the same arms and divided into companies commanded by experienced captains. But only under Olivares, the leading statesman under Philip IV of Spain, was the traditional military obligation turned into a financial contribution, giving nobles a new weight in political decisions.[20]

In the Habsburg Netherlands[21] there was no permanent infantry, other than a contingent of regular troops set up by its Burgundian ruler, Charles the Bold's, order of 31 July 1471. The need to have a prepared armed defence force at any moment became evident in the 1550s. When the general states refused to pay for a standing army, Charles V was unable to force the creation of two new professional corps with artillery and troops. The monarch subsequently had to raise cavalry and foot soldiers on a temporary basis and was forced to turn to mercenaries. In order to avoid over-dependence on towns, Charles V did not levy rural and community militias except in absolute emergencies.

Recruitment remained a recurring problem in sixteenth-century Spain, on account of high domestic salaries and the harshness of military campaigns both on land and at sea. Recruits complained regularly about having to pay for some of their own needs themselves, whereas superior officers serving with them were paid substantially more. The system in force was one of commission, with each senior officer choosing his assistants and paying them what he saw fit. Thus, at the start of the seventeenth century, for the 150 officers who received a salary from the king, there were some 600 who depended on the goodwill of their superiors.[22] Loyalties were thus likely to be primarily to the senior officer, not to the king. Nor were there strictly 'national' bonds tying all foot soldiers to their monarch. In Philip II's army, which at 100,000 was considered the most numerous in Christendom, only around 30–35,000 soldiers were Spanish, except for a period around 1590, when the number reached 70,000. The remainder came from German-speaking lands including Switzerland, Italy and indeed other parts of Europe.[23]

Two initial attempts to create a permanent army failed, first in 1552 and then in 1562. It was the defeat of the Armada in 1588 that forced the Spanish Crown finally to make a decision. In September 1596, all Spanish Catholic men between the ages of 18 and 44 were registered, and the first defensive conscript army was set up. The system was never really effective however, and began to disappear in the first half of the seventeenth century.[24]

All governments were having difficulties recruiting their subjects at the time. More than ever before, especially for France under Louis XI, it became necessary to resort to mercenary armies, the definitive model of which was Switzerland in the fifteenth and sixteenth centuries. Monarchs often used mercenaries for conflicts against rebellious subjects, when the loyalty of the army could not be guaranteed. The only exception was the Dutch Revolt, when the mercenaries supported the rebels rather than the king, as they were better rewarded by the former.[25] The case of the mercenary Roger Williams is illustrative: during the fourteen years he fought in Flanders between 1572 and 1587, he fought on both the Spanish and the Dutch sides. He was in Dutch pay between 1572 and 1573 and 1578 and 1587, despite serving the Spanish in the interim. Such conduct was common at the time; the two sides fought the English, Scots, Walloons, Germans and Dutch.[26] Mercenaries often sold themselves to the highest bidder and their motivation was mainly commercial. When pay was not forthcoming the troops helped themselves to what they felt was due to them directly by pillaging villages.[27]

Religion and violence: cruelty

Most victims were civilians. The religious wars constituted mainly guerrilla action, as there were few pitched battles. Local populations generally sought refuge inside towns, leaving the countryside to the mercy of errant soldiers or armies in the field, who took and ate what they wished. Many towns were besieged during the religious wars, both in France and in the Habsburg Netherlands. Local populations suffered from the usual ills brought by war itself: famines and malnutrition, diseases and plagues. On numerous occasions, Protestants killed nuns and monks in their monasteries or convents, whereas Catholics decimated the inhabitants of Antwerp during the 'Spanish Fury'. All this had the effect of displacing a large number of civilians and forcing them to take to the European roads, with all the fatal risks that this entailed.

With regard to the question whether Catholic as well as Protestant leaders endorsed attacks on civilians, there is no simple answer. Sovereigns such as Philip II or Catherine de Medici let it be known that as enemies of the state, heretics should be removed. Soldiers and civilians alike were given licence to do so under an exceptional law. With this exception, no leaders – neither the Admiral of Coligny nor William of Orange – appear to have incited killings or massacres. Both men were above all soldiers; they aimed to wage war by opposing the other armies, not by pillaging, raping and slaughtering civilians. As for the Duke of Alba, who had been dispatched to the Habsburg Netherlands in the autumn of 1567 in order to re-instate Habsburg rule, he emphasized in his correspondence to the Spanish sovereign that he was foremost a soldier, and that the repression of a population was an altogether different trade, one which he found repugnant.

The cruelty depicted in various sixteenth-century engravings and paintings (e.g. Bruegel, Cranach and Dürer) is quite unsettling. It must be emphasized, however, that the sixteenth century was still heavily influenced by medieval symbolism. The list of tortures inflicted on convicted prisoners is only a reflection of the crimes committed. In royal law, there was no gratuitous cruelty. Each crime had a corresponding penalty, which was carried out in full view of the public: counterfeiters were burnt just as heretics, common thieves were hanged, blasphemers had their tongues pulled out, profaners had their hands cut off, and so forth. Torturing was part of the judicial process and was only carried out under certain conditions and in accordance with the law. Still, in the event of uncontrolled war, 'non-codified' violence took place which was at times extremely cruel. Infamous examples include the sacking of ancient cities such as Rome (1529), Antwerp (1579) and on St Bartholomew's Night in Paris (1572), the spontaneous violence in the South of France during the wars of religion, which pitted two villages or neighbouring towns against each other, and the massacres of priests and nuns in Germany or the United Provinces. But these situations have nothing to do with the law, and perpetrators were reprimanded by either military authorities or civil judiciaries. Thus, it seems that in general heretics were not treated differently, although it is often difficult to differentiate between those condemned for political offences and those who were heretics. The case of the Council of Troubles – an exceptional tribunal that was held in the Habsburg Netherlands at the beginning of the Revolt between 1567 and 1576 – is revealing: its founding texts spoke of condemning those who disobeyed sovereign authority, yet its statutes on religious matters link religious delicts indissolubly to crimes of disobedience. It was therefore almost impossible to determine the exact reasons for conviction.

As for ascertaining whether people were more or less cruel than today, it is unlikely that human nature has changed much over five centuries. Living conditions have, however: the sight of blood, for example, was then a common occurrence. In the countryside, animals were raised to be eaten, while in towns, although it was less conspicuous, butchers' and skinners' areas were extremely dirty, and butchers' waste littered the roads, especially in the sewage canals. It should also be noted that criminal executions were public and that the corpses remained exposed, sometimes until they had completely decomposed. From this perspective, the sensitivity of the people in the sixteenth century was completely different to today's, and it must not be forgotten that the concept of Human Rights was still non-existent.

Another question that needs to be examined is whether the Dutch war can be considered as being led by the 'Rogues on sea and on land'.[28] Terrorism occurred, particularly between 1567 and 1568, when military action was planned on a large scale. Such acts were committed by Jan Camerlynck, a weaver from Hondschoote in Westkwartier (around Courtrai), and Jack of Heule, a young Flemish Calvinist nobleman who had returned from England to support the rebels in his home town, with assistance from Sandwich, Norwich and London. Their actions included looting and destroying churches, killing clergy, judicial officers and the police, and organizing escapes from prison. Marcel Beckhouse's study notes that all the destruction was caused by about a hundred men from the local textile industry, whose core originated from the area, but who were supported by Flemish co-religionists who had returned from exile in France, Germany, England and the northern provinces.[29]

Schemes of loyalty: towns, states and nations

Together with monarch, ruling dynasty and nobility, towns and loyalty to towns played a major role in the period we are dealing with. The political, administrative and judicial systems of the Habsburg Netherlands, inherited from the Middle Ages, were based on towns. Both the towns and the nobility gradually saw themselves as excluded from their traditional governing role when Charles V continued the centralization of governing structures, passing laws, recording traditional customs, and so forth. Military command was also centralized, the army structure reviewed and authority passed on to the sovereign or his appointed representative. Defence was still organized and paid for by the towns themselves, but it was integrated into the new legal framework. Town militias were in effect an early form of conscription.[30] The towns thus gradually lost their independence in the sixteenth century. The 'bourgeois', to use a contemporary term, now had to be obedient to his town *and* to his king, but it was the latter who was supposed to have pre-eminence. This is illustrated by the attempted rebellion of Ghent between 1538 and 1539 against the authority of Charles V, which was repressed both militarily and judicially. The image of the bourgeois and deputy mayors being forced to make an apology and prostrate themselves before the king clearly portrays the town's defeat in the face of sovereign authority.

The perception of the fundamental unity of the Christian world was offset by loyalty to princes and different creeds, but not by nationalism.

The term 'nation' cannot be used as a synonym for country or geopolitical states before the seventeenth to eighteenth centuries. For the Habsburg Netherlands, the term 'nation' where used refers to a grouping of merchants, tradesmen, students and so on, who shared the same geographical roots but did not constitute what would be called a nation today. The Castilan and Aragonese 'nations' were both Spanish, but they drew on the medieval heritage of two different political entities. The same applies to France (notably with the division between the *langue d'oc* and the *langue d'oil* – the groups of medieval dialects of southern and northern France respectively). It is even more the case in the Habsburg Netherlands, with its two distinct linguistic groups – one comprising the Flemish and Low German languages (ancestors of today's Dutch that was standardized in the nineteenth century), and the other comprising the Walloon languages, including French. In this sense, when a term such as 'Flemish Nation' is used, it signifies not an ethnic entity but only a linguistic one. It was possible for the Flemish and Walloon populations to fight together, as there was no question of ethnicity, inasmuch as there was no feeling of 'nationhood'. A characteristic of religious war in the sixteenth century is that, bar religion, differences were not a problem in the minds of the people. For mercenaries, religion scarcely mattered; they followed whoever paid them. Historical documents call people who live in Flanders Flemings, the people who live in Holland Hollanders, the people who live in Brabant Brabançons and so on. Naming is therefore done on a politico-geographical basis. The term 'Belgian' did not yet exist to designate all those who lived in the provinces as a whole. There was, in fact, no term at all, so texts refer to the 'subjects of King Philip II' or 'inhabitants' of the Netherlands, or they use another literary term, or even a listing of all peoples or provinces. In the heading of any decree or law, reference is made to the sovereign and to all his titles and possessions, so that the reference to his or her person remains central. Where the enemies are concerned, during the Revolt the widely used term is the 'Spanish', even though this is technically incorrect due to the many different ethnies that made up the army. This seems to be the result of Protestant anti-Spanish propaganda, led by the followers of William of Orange.

If we define war as the confrontation between two peoples, and a revolt as the battle for independence against a sovereign state, the religious conflicts of the sixteenth century do not qualify as either. Should we speak of a civil war when two separate political objectives are being pursued? Such a definition would be an over-simplification, as these very long conflicts vary in their objectives, and they mobilized a considerable number of troops, thus quantitatively equalling a traditional war. War theorists have so far been unable to come up with a satisfactory definition of this complex sixteenth-century phenomenon.[31]

Balthazar Ayala describes the Dutch Revolt as a war with a new ideology. For him, it is a battle for independence, and the enemy is a rebellious heretic who is fought passionately. He refuses to speak of war but of police actions carried out on rebellious subjects on the orders of the prince. The enemy is therefore ambiguously portrayed: sometimes as intra-societal, sometimes as international. The prince remains the *princeps legitimus* who opposes the tyrant; the influence of the *Six Livres de la République* by Jean Bodin is evident here. This image was refuted by Hugo Grotius who underlined the fact that the Revolt was a real war, since the Dutch dethroned King Philip II because he had permitted the excesses of the Duke of Alba, thus violating the country's laws. Moreover, he perceived the declaration that dethroned the king as a true declaration of war. Philip II had turned from a legitimate prince into a tyrant; fighting him was not only a right but a duty. Finally, this was not just a civil war but an international one, since the general states formed a virtually independent political entity.[32]

The theory of contract between the king and his people is, beyond any doubt, one of the fundamental contributions the religious wars made to matters of political law, apart from the religious question in itself, of course. During the following centuries, this theory had a considerable impact on European history, as can be shown by citing the examples of the public executions of King Charles I in England and King Louis XVI in France.

Notes

1 F. Tallett, *War and Society in Early Modern Europe*, London, Routledge, 1992; J. R. Hale, *War and Society in Renaissance Europe, 1540–1620*, New York, St Martin's Press, 1985; A. Corvisier, *Armées et sociétés en Europe, 1494–1789*, Paris, PUF, 1976; J. A. Fernandez-Santamaria, *The State, War and Peace: Spanish Political Thought in the Rennaissance, 1516–1559*, Cambridge, Cambridge University Press, 1977.

2 D. Goodman, *Power and Penury: Government, Technology and Science in Philip II's Spain*, Cambridge, Cambridge University Press, 1988; J.-E. Iung, 'L'organisation du service des vivres aux armées de 1550 à 1650', in *Bibliothèque de l'Ecole des Chartes*, 1983, pp. 269–306; J. A. Lynn, *Feeding Mars: Logistics in Western Warfare from the Middle Ages to the Present*, Boulder, CO, Westview Press, 1993.

3 J. Black (ed.), *The Origins of War in Early Modern Europe*, Edinburgh, Donald, 1987, pp. 1–3.

4 S. Adams, 'Spain or the Netherlands? The dilemmas of Early Stuart foreign policy', in H. Tomlinson (ed.), *Before the Civil War*, London, Macmillan, 1983; Ph. Contamine (ed.), *Guerre et société en France, en Angleterre et en Bourgogne, XIVe-XVe siècle*, Villeneuve d'Ascq, Centre d'Histoire de la Region du Nord et de l'Europe du Nord-Ouest, 1991; A. Duke and C. A. Tamse, 'Britain and the Netherlands', *War and Society*, 1977, vol. 6, Den Haag.

5 Y. Cazaux, 'Naissance de la guerre totale et révolutionnaire au XVIe siècle', in M. Baelde (ed.), *De eeuw van Marnix van St Aldegonde*, Ostende, Uitger, Toulon, 1982, p. 63.

6 Brabant, Limburg, Luxembourg, Guelders, Flanders, Artois, Hennegau, Holland, Zeeland, Namur, Lille, Tournai, Malines, Utracht, Overijssel, Groningen and Friesland.

7 See A. Kohler, 'Personnalité et pouvoir', in *Carolus. Charles Quint, 1500–1558*, Gent, Snoeck-Ducaju, 1999, p. 47.

8   Cf. D. R. Kelley, *The Beginning of Ideology: Consciousness and Society in the French Reformation*, Cambridge, Cambridge University Press, 1991; J. Sproxton, *Violence and Religion: Attitudes Towards Militarism in the French Civil Wars and the English Revolution*, London, Routlege, 1995; K. Parrow, *From Defense to Resistance: Justification of Violence during the French Wars of Religion*, Philadelphia, PA, American Philosophical Society, 1993, pp. 38–47.

9   H. Languet, *Vindicae contra tyrannos*, Geneva, 1581, p. 24.

10 M. de L'Hospital, *Oeuvres complètes*, 1823, vol. 2, Paris, p. 177.

11 J.-P. Babelon, 'Une longue fraternité d'armes. Les relations d'Henri de Navarre puis d'Henri IV avec les Pays-Bas', in W. Frijhoff and O. Moorman Van Kappen (eds), *Les Pays-Bas et la France, des guerres de religion à la création de la république batave*, Nijmegen, Gerard Noodt Institut, 1993.

12 See O. Christin, *La paix de la religion: l'autonomisation de la raison politique au XVIe siècle*, Paris, Seuil, 1997.

13 J.-F. Le Petit, *La Grande Chronique ancienne et moderne de Hollande*, 1601, vol. 2, Dordrecht, p. 283; E. De Meteren, *Histoire des Pays-Bas*, Den Haag, 1618; E. Thoen, 'Warfare and the countryside: social and economic aspects of military destruction in Flanders during the Late Middle Ages and the Early Modern period', *The Low Countries History Textbook*, 1980, vol. 13; M. Gutmann, 'Putting crisis in perspective: the impact of war on the civilian populations in the seventeenth century', *Annales de démographie historique*, 1977, pp. 101–28; *War and Rural Life in the Early Modern Low Countries*, Princeton, NJ, Princeton University Press, 1980; J. S. Fishman, *Boerenverdriet: Violence Between Peasants and Soldiers in Early Modern Nederlandish Art*, Ann Arbor, MI, UMI Research Press, 1982; J.-L. Charles, 'Le sac des villes dans les Pays-Bas au XVIe siècle', *Revue internationale d'histoire militaire*, 1965, vol. 24, pp. 43–67.

14 I. W. L. Moerman, *Korte kroniek van Leiden en omstreken, oktober 1573–oktober 1574* in *Leiden '74: Leven in oorlogstijd in de tweede helft van de 16de eeuw*, Leiden, Brill, 1974, pp. 1–12.

15 *Oeuvres de Ph. De Marnix de Sainte Aldegonde*, p. 114.

16 J. Schoonjans, 'Castra Dei: l'organisation religieuse des armées d'Alexandre Farnèse', *Miscellenea historica Van der Essen*, 1947, vol. 1, Brussels, pp. 523–40; L. Van der Essen, 'La psychologie des soldats et des officiers espagnols de l'armée de Flandre au XVIe siècle', *Revue d'histoire ecclésiastique*, 1956, pp. 42–78; A. Vazquez, 'Los sucesos de Flandes y Francia del tiempo de Alejandro Farnese', *Collecion de Documentos ineditor para la Historia de España* 72–74, Madrid, 1879–80; G. Parker, *The Army of Flanders and the Spanish Road 1567–1659*, Cambridge, Cambridge University Press, 1972; R. M. Kingdon, 'The political resistance of the Calvinists in France and in the Low Countries', *Church History*, 1958, vol. 38, pp. 162–85; H. G. Koenigsberger, 'The organization of revolutionary parties in France and the Netherlands during the sixteenth century', *Journal of Modern History*, 1955, vol. 27, pp. 335–51.

17 M. P. Holt, *The French Wars of Religion, 1562–1629*, Cambridge, Cambridge University Press, 1995, pp. 190–1; idem., 'Putting religion back into the wars of religion', *French Historical Studies*, 1993, vol. 18, pp. 524–51.

18 H. Heller, *Iron and Blood: Civil Wars in Sixteenth-Century France*, Montreal, McGill-Queens University Press, 1991, p. 7; D. Crouzet, *Les Guerriers de Dieu: la violence au temps des troubles de religion (v.1525–v.1610)*, Seyssel, Champ Vallon, 1990, 2 vols; Sproxton, *Violence and Religion*; G. Panico, 'Les rites de la violence populaire à travers les troubles et les révoltes en Italie du Sud à l'époque moderne', in *Mouvements populaires et consciences sociales*, 1985, Paris, pp. 185–95.

19 J. B. Wood, *The King's Army: Warfare, Soldiers and Society During the Wars of Religion in France, 1562–1576*, Cambridge, Cambridge University Press, 1996, pp. 4–5.

On the cost of war see F. Tellett, 'Church, state, war and finance in Early-Modern France', *Renaissance and Modern Studies*, 1993, vol. 36, pp. 15–35.

20 I. A. Thompson, *War and Government in Habsburg Spain: 1560–1620*, London, Athlone Press, 1976, pp. 146–8; R. C. McCoy, *The Rites of Knighthood: the Literature and Politics of Elizabethan Chivalry*, Berkeley, University of California Press, 1989; M. H. Keen, 'Chivalry, nobility and the man-at-arms', in Christopher T. Allmand (ed.), *War, Literature and Politics in the Late Middle Ages*, Liverpool, Liverpool University Press, 1976; A. Corvisier, 'La noblesse militaire: aspects militaires de la noblesse française du XVe au XVIIIe siècles', *Histoire Sociale*, 1978, vol. 11, pp. 336–55.

21 M. Beyaert, 'De algemene militaire evolutie sinds de late middeleeuwen en het Zuid-Nederlandse landleger der XVIde eeuw', *Revue belge d'histoire militaire*, 1974, vol. 20, no. 7, pp. 550–73; E. Rooms' articles in *Les institutions du gouvernement central des Pays-Bas habsbourgeois 1482–1795*, vol. 2, Brussels, Archives Generales du Royaume, 1995.

22 I. A. Thompson, *War and Government*.

23 Ibid., pp. 103–4; G. Parker, 'Poner une pica en Flandes: la guerra y Felipe II', in *Felipe II: un príncipe del renaciemiento, un monarca y su época: la monarquía hispanica*, Madrid, Societe Estatal para la onmemoración de los centenarios de Felipe II y Carlos V, 1998, pp. 300–3.

24 R. Cerezo Martínez, *Las armadas de Felipe II*, Madrid, Editorial San Martin, 1988.

25 V. G. Kiernan, 'Foreign mercenaries and absolute monarchy', in Trevor Aston (ed.), *Crisis in Europe, 1560–1660*, London, Routledge & Kegan Paul, 1965, pp. 117–40.

26 Cf. D. W. Davies (ed.), *The Actions in the Low Countries by Sir Roger Williams*, Ithaca, published for the Folger Shakespeare Library by Cornell University Press, 1964.

27 L. de Torre, 'Los motinos militares en Flandes', *Revista de Archivos, bibliothecas y museos*, 3rd series, 1912, vols 21–23, pp. 30–1; J. E. Thomson, *Mercenaries, Pirates and Sovereigns: State-building and Extraterritorial Violence in Early Modern Europe*, Princeton, NJ, Princeton University Press, 1994; M. E. Mallett, *Mercenaries and their Masters: Warfare in Renaissance Italy*, London, Bodley Head, 1974.

28 The *Gueux* – Rogues: nickname given to conspirators of the Compromise of Nobility in 1566 who conspired against the Habsburg rule. By extension, the names were taken by those who resisted the rule of Philip II in the northern Netherlands from the start of the Revolt. There were two types: those who fought on land (land rogues), and those at sea (sea rogues).

29 M. F. Blackhouse, 'Guerilla war and banditry in the sixteenth century: the wood beggars in the Westkwartier of Flanders, 1567–1568' *Archiv für Reformationsgeschichte*, 1983, vol. 74, pp. 232–56.

30 Thompson, *War and Government*, pp. 126–8.

31 See the debate in Jeremy Black (ed.), *The Origins of War*, pp. 11–16; P. Zagorín, 'Prolegomena to the comparative study of revolution in Early Modern Europe', *Comparative Studies in History and Society*, 1976, vol. 18, pp. 151–4; M. E. François, 'Revolts in Late Medieval and Early Modern Europe: a special model', *Journal of Interdisciplinary Study*, 1974, vol. 5, pp. 19–44.

32 For details, see P. Haggenmacher, *Grotius et la doctrine de la guerre juste*, Paris, PUF, 1983; R. Schnur, *Die französischen Juristen im konfessionellen Bürgerkrieg des 16, Jahrhunderts: Ein Beitrag zur Entstehungsgeschichte des modernen Staates*, Berlin, Duckler & Humblot, 1962; O. Yasuaki, *A Normative Approach to War: Peace, War and Justice in Hugo Grotius*, Oxford, Clarendon, 1993; F. H. Russell, *The Just War in the Middle Ages*, Cambridge, Cambridge University Press, 1975.

13 Identities and mentalities in the Thirty Years' War

Anja V. Hartmann

For many parts of Europe and in many respects, the Thirty Years' War was a fiasco, a catastrophe that killed soldiers and civilians, destroyed villages and towns, threatened kings' and princes' thrones, and upset belief systems and world orders. The German poet Andreas Gryphius condensed the experience of this tragedy in one of his most famous poems, 'Die Tränen des Vaterlandes' (Tears of the Fatherland), written in 1636:

> Wir sind doch nunmehr ganz, ja mehr denn ganz verheeret!
> Der frechen Völker Schar, die rasende Posaun,
> Das vom Blut fette Schwert, die donnernde Kartaun
> Hat aller Schweiss und Fleiß und Vorrat aufgezehret.
> Die Türme stehn in Glut, die Kirch ist umgekehret,
> Das Rathaus liegt im Graus, die Starken sind zerhaun,
> Die Jungfraun sind geschänd't, und wo wir hin nur schaun,
> Ist Feuer, Pest und Tod, der Herz und Geist durchfähret.
> Hier durch die Schanz und Stadt rinnt allzeit frisches Blut.
> Dreimal sind schon sechs Jahr, als unser Ströme Flut,
> Von Leichen fast verstopft, sich langsam fort gedrungen.
> Doch schweig ich noch von dem, was ärger als der Tod,
> Was grimmer denn die Pest und Glut und Hungersnot,
> Daß auch der Seelenschatz so vielen abgezwungen.[1]

When Gryphius wrote these lines, the war was to continue to bring destruction for another twelve years, and in many regions the struggle for survival extended well into the period after the peace treaties of Westphalia in 1648. While Gryphius painted a drastic picture of the war's disastrous consequences not only for buildings or food supplies but also for people's bodies and souls, he did not enter upon the subject of the causes which brought about the continuous armed conflicts between 1618 and 1648. Why then did people continuously engage in war during those years in spite of its predictable dangers and damages? How did it actually affect their lives, and how did they manage to survive in spite of the threats? In the following pages I shall address these fundamental questions on three levels, starting with a survey of the population's involvement in the war and its reactions to it, continuing with an analysis of the attitudes of the war's soldiers, officers and armies as well as its diplomats, and ending with a description of the motives and legitimating concepts of the rulers and statesmen.

Popular involvement

While exact figures for death rates among the civilian population are still lacking for most parts of the continent, historians agree on the existence of a 'diagonal belt of destruction' reaching from the far north-east of the German Empire through Thuringia and Saxony to the Palatinate and Wurttemberg. In these regions, often more than 50 per cent of the population lost their lives during the war, whereas other parts of the empire – for example, Westphalia, the location of the peace congress, or parts of Austria – remained largely untouched.[2] There were, of course, well-known massacres like the burning and plundering of Magdeburg by the Catholic army in May 1631 which spared only the cathedral and some seventy houses in its immediate neighbourhood,[3] but there was also the example of Hamburg, flourishing in trade and business during the war and never lodging hostile soldiers within its walls.[4] At any rate, direct effect of the war's battles on the population – like in the case of Magdeburg – was only one of several dangers encountered by civilians. Troops looking for food, shelter or even quarters to occupy during winter sometimes represented a far greater risk for the local population than those actually fighting. Hence famine became one of the most anxiously feared dangers during wartime, and we even know of some cases of cannibalism, and many of starvation and survival by consumption of grasses, herbs and weeds.[5] Finally, illness and disease spread easily under the conditions of war, and the plague that haunted Europe in the 1630s probably killed at least as many men as battle and famine. The apocalyptic foursome of war, hunger, pestilence and death was thus closely interlinked, and one of the four was often followed by its companions, multiplying the threat for the people. However, destruction of the civilian population and its economic resources – tactics of 'annihilation' or burnt earth – did not usually count among the war aims of the belligerents, as they all needed reasonably wealthy villages and towns for their troops' winter camps and for their supply in summer-time.[6]

In spite of the important effects of destruction brought about by war, famine and plague, several strategies of survival based on identity can be identified. Johannes Burkhardt recently enumerated five 'constellations of partnership' that allowed the population to survive the daily dangers of the war: family and community relations, feudal or territorial ties, regional co-operation in matters of information and communication, solidarity within or between religious groups, and collaboration between soldiers and civilians.[7] Thus, far from adopting their rulers' war and embracing its causes and legitimations as offered by publications and sermons, the population chose to defend itself against the destructive forces of wartime by choosing those patterns of identification with other social groups that offered the greatest chances of survival. These could naturally change in the course of time and events, like in the case of the Bavarian town of Wemding that underwent a transformation from Catholic stronghold to Protestant refuge.[8] The attitude of the Bavarian population towards the Swedish troops invading the territory in 1632 – many towns and villages surrendered to the enemy's army and paid high ransoms to escape burning and looting – even provoked the duke's indignation; he accused his people of disloyalty, ingratitude and malice.[9]

Hence positive identities could be adopted according to opportunity and exigency and did not necessarily coincide with the patterns of identity proposed or requested by the secular or religious authorities. On the contrary, the negative ('secondary') identity, i.e. the description of the enemy, was usually rather vague and amorphous. Again, the example of the Swedish soldiers in Bavaria, whose excesses are still cited today, is telling.[10] Correspondingly, the revolt of the Netherlands against the Spanish domination produced the '*leyenda negra*' (the black legend), reanimated each time Spanish armies entered Protestant territories in northern Europe.[11] There was therefore a significant difference between the abstract notion of an enemy like 'the' Swedes or 'the' Spanish, charged with a kaleidoscopic variety of faults and vices, and the concrete and tangible soldier knocking at the house's front door or the town's gates. Little did it matter in the latter case whether the soldier was friend or foe in abstract terms; the important question was whether he would agree on sparing men's lives and possessions. If this could not be assured, the population was often ready to revolt against its own master, like the Bavarian peasants between 1633 and 1634 who protested not against the enemy's troops but against the atrocities committed by Bavarian soldiers.[12]

Military and diplomats

The average soldier of the Thirty Years' War was a mercenary who had more or less deliberately chosen his profession. There were, of course, exceptions to this rule: at the beginning of the Swedish campaign in the German Empire, the conscripted armies of Gustavus Adolphus consisted mainly of Swedish and Finnish soldiers whose maintenance was assured by payments from their home regions, but as time went by, the national component gradually diminished, and already in 1632 the percentage of Swedish and Finnish contingents comprised only one-fifth of the whole army.[13] Moreover, many mercenaries – even if not forced by conscription – took up their career as a result of economic distress or personal danger, and sometimes the armies incorporated whole bands of criminals.[14] By and large, the mercenaries were driven by many different motives among which poverty and fear could play just as dominant a role as family ties or religious and political convictions, for example, Robert Monro, who declared that he entered the war in the Protestant army in order to defend the honour of Elisabeth Stuart, the wife of the 'winter king' of Bohemia.[15] Depending on the weight of the single motives, the mercenary was thus more or less inclined to change sides. For example, the unknown, but none the less famous mercenary, whose diary has been discovered by Jan Peters, started his career in the anti-Habsburg alliance of France, Venice and Savoy in northern Italy, served in the troops of the Catholic league under Pappenheim and thus for the emperor, fought under Swedish command in 1633 to 1634 and finally returned to the Pappenheim regiment after the battle of Nördlingen in 1634.[16]

As a consequence of the mercenary system, the troops of the Thirty Years' War were fairly heterogeneous groups, a well-known Bavarian regiment, for example, gathering soldiers from sixteen different nationalities: German, Italian, Polish, Slovenian, Croatian, Hungarian, Greek, Dalmatian, Lotharingian, Burgundian, French, Czech, Spanish, Scottish, Irish and Turkish.[17] A common identity for the whole regiment, let alone for the whole army, was impossible to establish under such conditions, and indeed personal solidarity developed rather along the lines of clientelism or common experience than according to national or religious ideals.[18] It has to be pointed out that even in battle the identification of the opponents was not as easy as it was to become in times of standing armies and coloured uniforms: in order to be able to distinguish between friend and foe on the battlefield, the soldiers of the Thirty Years' War marked their hats or clothes with ribbons – blue and yellow for the Swedish army, red for the Habsburgs – or even with twigs and leaves, like in the battle of Breitenfeld in 1632.[19]

The military forces were always accompanied by a large train consisting of a regiment of 480 soldiers, 74 servants, 314 women, 3 vendresses and 160 horses.[20] The maintenance of the armies was in general organized and paid for by their leaders, but a large portion of the daily needs of the soldiers had to be covered by contributions from the inhabitants of the area concerned. This arrangement was prone to failure in regions which had been passed over repeatedly and by several armies, or in case of extended battles or sieges. This could easily lead to excesses committed by hungry soldiers, but in general atrocities were heavily punished by the military leaders who were dependent on the goodwill of the local population: during the Swedish campaign in Bavaria in 1632, at least five Swedish soldiers were executed because of their crimes against civilians, and others were sentenced to death.[21] In addition, the fact that simple soldiers were often peasants themselves and therefore shared a common social background with the civilian population facilitated the cohabitation as long as supplies were sufficient for both sides.[22]

Discipline and efficiency of the troops depended largely on the ability of the commanders who were not, in general, officers of a royal army, but military entrepreneurs advancing the money necessary for the maintenance and equipment of the forces. For them, war was not primarily a question of justice or revenge, but a promising bargain that could yield profits in money – once the monarchs paid back their debts – or even land and titles. These military entrepreneurs held key positions in the complicated networks of loyalties built up during the war. On the one hand, the vast majority of the soldiers followed their military commander rather than the ruler the latter was fighting for, and consequently changed sides with his regiment, regardless of political or ideological bonds. The strength of an army therefore rested largely on the ruler's capability to assure the entrepreneur's obedience and faith. On the other hand, the entrepreneur himself could decide to change his employer or even try to wage his own war for his own interests. He therefore represented a continuous threat to those relying on his services. Wallenstein, fighting for the emperor, and Bernhard von Sachsen-Weimar, fighting in turn for the Swedish and French kings, are the most striking examples of such entrepreneurs aiming at more than financial remuneration for their military assistance.[23]

Unlike the officers who were able to preserve a certain degree of independence from their political employer, the diplomats of the Thirty Years' War were highly dependent on their superiors. Again, there are exceptions like Jules Mazarin who started his career as a papal ambassador, was about to be appointed French delegate to the peace congress of Westphalia in the 1640s and finally became prime minister under Louis XIV, but the average diplomat – whether resident or extraordinary – had but little autonomy in his negotiations and decisions. In the event of diplomats acting against the will of their sovereigns, the latter were prone to dismiss the unfortunate ambassador and let him fall from grace. Diplomats therefore had to make their rulers' interests their own in order to advance their careers. Diplomatic procedures and correspondence thus reflect many of the concerns dominating the intercommunity relations in Early Modern Europe on the level of rulers and statesmen. Questions of rank and honour in particular were often fought out between diplomats as the sovereigns themselves hardly ever met each other face to face. Unlike the civilian population, the soldiers and the officers, who all formed their own spheres of identification and separation in contrast to the rulers' and statesmens', the diplomat often faithfully echoed the belief systems promoted by those he was serving.[24]

Princes and statesmen

Kings and princes were sometimes just as afflicted as their subjects by the effects of the Thirty Years' War. Some led their own troops into battle and consequently suffered many of the hardships borne by their soldiers –

Gustavus Adolphus, who even died in battle in 1632, is the most prominent example. Others were forced to leave their residences, like the 'winter king' Frederick of Bohemia who lost not only his new Bohemian crown but also his old territory, the Palatinate, and finally died of a fever in exile in 1632, or Maximilian of Bavaria who had to give up his capital Munich and retreat to Braunau when the Swedish army invaded his lands in the 1630s. Still, the struggle for political and personal survival was usually not the central concern of the rulers and statesmen involved in the war. On the contrary, they were in general thoroughly convinced of the legitimate existence of the communities they governed, and they had certain notions as to how these communities should be treated by others. They thus had precise concepts of how the 'world order' – i.e. the order of the European state system – should be (re-)arranged with a view to the preservation or restoration of the conflicting communities' positions with regard to each other.

Before the congress of Westphalia, which first opened the way for a European state system based on the parity of sovereign states, the prevailing concept depicted a hierarchical order among the rulers. While the traditional leading position of the German emperor was still largely accepted in the seventeenth century, the lower steps of the ladder were less clearly assigned. On the one hand, the positions of ascending states like the Netherlands or Sweden were not agreed upon, and such an agreement would have been structurally excluded by the old order. In this context, the revolt of the Netherlands has even been interpreted as a catalytic element in the process of transition from the hierarchical order to the multipolar system.[25] On the other hand, the traditional powers rivalled each other, such as France and Spain whose respective ambassadors engaged in a far-reaching dispute over questions of rank at the English court in 1619, when the French diplomat claimed not only equality with but precedence over his Spanish colleague.[26] While similar conflicts hardly ever constituted the immediate reasons for the outbreak of war, they were still very powerful in inhibiting the opening and the continuation of peace talks. The beginning of the peace congress of Westphalia was thus delayed for years because of the preliminary negotiations about passports and titles which, far from being a mere pretext, constituted an essential element of the self-esteem of the participants.[27]

The ultimate stage – and somehow a perversion – of a hierarchical world order would have been the universal monarchy, i.e. the absolute domination of one community over the others. None of the belligerents of the Thirty Years' War ever proclaimed the creation of the universal monarchy as his final goal, but several monarchs were accused of pursuing this aim. Hence the fight against a presumed aspirant after the universal monarchy formed a current legitimation for war and a true concern of those engaged in it.[28] The French king and his ministers repeatedly referred to the Spanish and Habsburg ambitions for universal monarchy in order to explain their own bellicose actions and their coalitions with

Protestant powers. Vice versa, the emperor and the Spanish king accused Louis XIII of seeking a predominant position in Europe,[29] and finally the Swedish king was suspected of desiring the emperor's title and crown. For the estates of the German Empire, the *Reichsstände*, the positive concept combined with the fight against the threat of a universal monarchy was the idea of *Libertät*, i.e. a certain kind of sovereignty of the states of the empire. This concept did not necessarily imply complete independence as in the case of the Netherlands, but it contained specific rights in war and peace, especially the right to conclude alliances. France and Sweden both claimed the role as protector of the *Reichsstände*, and both repeatedly enumerated the *Libertät* among the goals they were fighting for.[30]

The identities at stake in the conflicts over hierarchy, universal monarchy, independence and *Libertät* were not intrinsically hostile or antagonistic. On the contrary, the cause of the conflicts lay in the fact that the opponents saw each other as parts of the same world order within which each strove to assure a certain position and the corresponding rights acceptable to and respected by the others. Mutual recognition was therefore a necessary component of any solution to the conflict. The leaders of political entities thus constructed and confirmed their respective identities in the context of the changing state system through a process of permanent communication. War – in the case of victory the ultimate way to prove superiority – was from this point of view a means of communication, and once underway, the refusal of recognition could lead to its perpetuation.

Unlike the notion of a hierarchical state system which raised vertical perspectives of domination and subordination for the single political entity, the idea of dynastic identity could theoretically favour ties between communities regarding each other as equal. The reference to a common dynastic ancestry was often used to justify demands for co-operation or coalition, but even the tight collaboration between the Habsburg monarchs in Madrid and Vienna was never as smooth as its enemies supposed it to be, since particular interests could easily override the dynastic solidarity.[31] At the same time, the violation of dynastic rights frequently led to declarations of war. When Gustavus Adolphus landed at the Pomeranian coast in 1630, the dynastic rights he claimed to the Polish throne counted among the reasons the Swedish king alleged for entering the war.[32] Similarly, the wars in northern Italy centred around the question of who was to be the rightful successor to the Duke of Mantua, a struggle that brought Spanish, imperial and French armies to Italy.[33] But even armed conflict could not extinguish the notion of dynastic affinity: throughout the war, Louis XIII addressed the emperor as 'nostre très cher et tres aimé bon frère et cousin', while the latter answered 'consanguineo, affini et fratri nostro charissimo'.[34] In addition, territorial claims were usually closely linked with dynastic interests, and Richelieu's practice of collecting legal documents to prove French rights to all sorts of territories was a brilliant example of the flexibility of the dynastic argument.[35] Here, as in the case of identity based

on hierarchical order, the validity of the argument depended on its acceptance by others, who where thus necessarily seen as part of the same value
system. Dynastic claims, insofar as they were regarded as just claims,
presupposed a common world order of those making and defeating them
– which of course did not exclude a fierce combat about whose claims
were 'more just'. Dynastic identity thus existed and could be cited in positive and negative ways, but it never constituted a rigid framework of
reference. Obviously, the sheer fact that the monarchs of Europe were all
related to one another via some distant cousin prevented dynasty from
being an unambiguous reason for loyalty.

While the hierarchical order of the state system and the universal existence of dynastic ties both relied on the agreement upon a certain value
system common to all participants, religious identity a priori excluded
such an agreement. In theory, Catholics and Protestants could not live
together or even next to each other within the same world order, as their
ideologies respectively professed universal validity. The papacy rigorously
followed this line of conduct in first denying any negotiations with
Protestant powers and in finally rejecting the peace treaties of Westphalia
because they included the Protestants.[36] In practice, however, no other
power involved in the Thirty Years' War preserved a strictly hostile attitude towards those of a different religion, but this did not mean that
religion did not count in intercommunity relations.

First, many monarchs were profoundly devout believers themselves, and
this often influenced their political decisions. On the Catholic side,
Maximilan I of Bavaria, who spent several hours a day praying and hearing
Mass is a well-known example. As a monarch, he translated his personal
religious convictions into politics, promoting the cult of veneration of the
Virgin Mary and encouraging political measures which served the religious unity of his lands in the sense of confessionalization.[37] A similar
connection between devotion and domestic politics can be found in
Emperor Ferdinand II, who expelled the Protestants from his Austrian
territories.[38] Even the French king Louis XIII, who accepted the Huguenots
in France as long as they refrained from political opposition, is known to
have shed tears when the imperial ambassador told him about the wretched
condition of Catholics and Catholicism in the empire.[39] On the Protestant
side, the elector of Saxony, Johann Georg I, could be mentioned or – of
course – Gustavus Adolphus himself.

Still, in intercommunity matters all the rulers mentioned above – and
many others – showed a certain degree of flexibility in dealing with those
professing a different faith. France's entering into the war on the 'wrong'
side, i.e. on the side of the Swedes and against Habsburg, has often been
criticized by contemporaries because it contradicted religious principles.
Well into the twentieth century, Richelieu has on these grounds been
described as a ruthless advocate of power politics and national interest,
or, as Henry Kissinger put it: 'As the King's First Minister, he subsumed

both religion and morality to *raison d'état*, his guiding light.'[40] But neither were Richelieu's politics completely free from moral and religious considerations, nor was he – as Kissinger claims – 'like a snow-covered Alp in the desert',[41] the only statesman of his time acting against religious imperatives. Certainly, Richelieu's main goal in the Thirty Years' War was to defeat Spain and its presumptive aspirations after the universal monarchy, and in the course of pursuing this goal France also allied with Protestant powers. Nevertheless, Richelieu always inserted articles concerning the preservation of Catholic faith into the treaties concluded with Protestants, and the religious, moral and legal arguments accompanying his political actions have been repeatedly highlighted by historians.[42] Similarly, the emperor acted in disregard of religious principles when he signed the Peace of Prague with the Protestant elector of Saxony in 1635. The peace treaty was supposed to unite the estates of the empire and the emperor against the foreign invaders, namely Sweden and France. Although Ferdinand II was aware of the religious inconsistencies implied in concluding this treaty and although he had considered them at length, he decided in favour of a political solution which could bring peace to the empire.

Thus, religion was a mighty principle of identity which was heavily drawn upon in domestic politics and served as a tool of state-building among others. At the same time, religion never dominated the identities in the intercommunity system. Although religious convictions were never completely abandoned, religious compromise could be integrated into a political line of conduct following non-religious aims. In particular, the idea of a common world order – the still often invoked *Respublica Christiana* – which had to be protected or (re-)established could override the religious disputes between the monarchs. The peace treaties of Munster and Osnabruck finally proved that on the intercommunity level religious tolerance had won out over the paradigms of eternal confrontation.[43]

Conclusion

Obviously, patterns of identity and issues of mentality played an important role in the Thirty Years' War. The people as well as soldiers, officers, diplomats, rulers and statesmen all repeatedly referred to different schemes of identity to justify their conduct in war. The most important sources for conflict on the intercommunity level were disputes over dynastic and religious claims which were often intertwined. But none of the models of identity – not even religion – was strong enough to constitute an overriding line of conduct for everybody. Limited interests of economical, judicial or territorial order as well as the simple struggle for survival often interfered and produced loyalties based on different patterns of identity. Identities and mentalities thus proved to be flexible constructs whose relative importance vacillated, now outweighing other causes and determining decisions, now subject to external influences.

Notes

1 Are we now not totally, indeed more than totally destroyed?
The mass of insolent peoples, the speeding trumpet
the sword, fat with blood, the thundering cannon
have eaten sweat and industry and reserves.
The towers are glowing with fire, the church has been turned upside down
the town hall is destroyed, the strong are cut down,
the virgins are raped, and wherever we look
there is fire, pestilence and death which haunt heart and spirit.
Fresh blood runs through the defences and the city.
Three times six years now have the floods of our rivers
run on, almost jammed with corpses.
And yet I remain silent of that, which is worse than death,
which is grimmer than pestilence and fire and famine,
that so many have been deprived of their spiritual treasure!

Andreas Gryphius, 'Tränen des Vaterlandes anno 1636', in K. O. Conrady (ed.), *Das große deutsche Gedichtbuch von 1500 bis zur Gegenwart*, Zürich, Artemis & Winkler, 1991, p. 39. For general bibliography cf. H. Duchhardt (ed.), *Bibliographie zum Westfälischen Frieden*, Münster, Aschendorff, 1996.

2 Cf. G. Franz, *Der Dreißigjährige Krieg und das deutsche Volk. Untersuchungen zur Bevölkerungs- und Agrargeschichte*, Jena, Fischer, 1940; P. Englund, *Die Verwüstung Deutschlands: eine Geschichte des Dreißigjährigen Krieges*, Stuttgart, Klett-Cotta, 1998.

3 G. Barudio, *Der Teutsche Krieg 1618–1648*, Frankfurt, Fischer Taschenbuch Verlag, 1988, pp. 363–72.

4 Cf. S. M. Schröder, 'Hamburg und Schweden im 30 jährigen Krieg – vom potentiellen Bündnispartner zum Zentrum der Kriegsfinanzierung', *Vierteljahrschrift für Sozial- und Wirtschaftsgeschichte*, 1989, vol. 76, pp. 305–31.

5 J. Burkhardt, 'Ist noch ein Ort, dahin der Krieg nicht kommen sey? Katastrophenerfahrung und Kriegsstrategien auf dem deutschen Kriegsschauplatz', in H. Lademacher and S. Groenveld (eds), *Krieg und Kultur. Die Rezeption von Krieg und Frieden in der Niederländischen Republik und im Deutschen Reich 1568–1648*, Münster, New York, Munich and Berlin, Waxmann, 1998, pp. 3–19.

6 For an exception, see the campaign of Gustavus Adolphus in Bavaria in 1632; cf. D. Albrecht, *Maximilian I. von Bayern 1573–1651*, Munich, R. Oldenbourg Verlag, 1998, pp. 826–9.

7 Burkhardt, 'Ist noch ein Ort'.

8 L. Hintermayr, *Wemding im Dreißigjährigen Krieg*, Wemding, Verein Lebendiges Wemding, 1989.

9 Albrecht, *Maximilian I*, pp. 824–6.

10 Ibid., p. 827.

11 Cf. J. Arndt, 'Der spanisch–niederländische Krieg in der deutschsprachigen Publizistik', in Lademacher and Groenveld (eds), *Krieg und Kultur*, pp. 401–18.

12 Albrecht, *Maximilian I*, pp. 859–61.

13 Cf. M. Roberts, *Gustavus Adolphus. A History of Sweden 1611–1632*, vol. 2, London, Longman, 1958, pp. 201–16.

14 Cf. G. Parker, *Der Dreißigjährige Krieg*, Darmstadt, Wissenschaftliche Buchgesellschaft, 1987, pp. 283–5. (In English: *The Thirty Years' War*, London, Routledge & Kegan Paul, 1984.)

15 Ibid., p. 285.

16 J. Peters (ed.), *Ein Söldnerleben im Dreißigjährigen Krieg. Eine Quelle zur Sozialgeschichte*, Berlin, Akademie Verlag, 1993.

17 F. Redlich, *The German Military Enterpriser and His Workforce, 13th to 17th Century*, vol. 1, Wiesbaden, Steiner, 1964/65, p. 456.
18 For an example see B. R. Kroener, 'Der Krieg hat ein Loch . . . Überlegungen zum Schicksal demobilisierter Söldner nach dem Dreißigjährigen Krieg', in H. Duchhardt (ed.), *Der Westfälische Friede*, Munich, R. Oldenbourg Verlag, 1998, pp. 599–630.
19 Parker, *Der Dreißigjährige Krieg*, p. 382.
20 Albrecht, *Maximilian I*, p. 636.
21 Parker, *Der Dreißigjährige Krieg*, p. 291.
22 Cf. B. Kroener, 'Kriegsgurgeln, Freireuter und Merodebrüder. Der Soldat des Dreißigjährigen Krieges. Täter und Opfer', in W. Wette (ed.), *Der Krieg des kleinen Mannes. Eine Militärgeschichte von unten*, Munich and Zürich, Piper, 1992, pp. 51–67.
23 For an overview see R. G. Asch, *The Thirty Years' War. The Holy Roman Empire and Europe 1618–1648*, Basingstoke, Macmillan, 1997, pp. 155–76.
24 On diplomatic procedure in the seventeenth century see M. S. Anderson, *The Rise of Modern Diplomacy*, London and New York, Longman, 1993, pp. 41–102.
25 Cf. H. T. Gräf, 'Die Außenpolitik der Republik im werdenden Mächteeuropa. Mittel und Wege zu staatlicher Unabhängigkeit und Friedenswahrung', in Lademacher and Groenveld (eds), *Krieg und Kultur*, pp. 481–92.
26 Anderson, *The Rise of Modern Diplomacy*, p. 58.
27 See A. V. Hartmann, *Von Regensburg nach Hamburg. Die diplomatischen Beziehungen zwischen dem französischen König und dem Kaiser vom Regensburger Vertrag (13. Oktober 1630) bis zum Hamburger Präliminarfrieden (25. Dezember 1641)*, Münster, Aschendorff, 1998.
28 Cf. F. Bosbach, *Monarchia universalis: ein politischer Leitbegriff der frühen Neuzeit*, Göttingen, Vandenhoeck & Ruprecht, 1988.
29 Cf. e.g. E. Jarnut and R. Bohlen (eds), *Die französischen Korrespondenzen* (Acta Pacis Westphalicae Serie II Abt. B), Band 3, 1. Teil, Münster, Aschendorff, 1999, p. 471.
30 Cf. Barudio, *Der Teutsche Krieg*.
31 H. Ernst, *Madrid und Wien 1632–1637: Politik und Finanzen in den Beziehungen zwischen Philipp IV. und Ferdinand II*, Münster, Aschendorff, 1991.
32 Parker, *Der Dreißigjährige Krieg*, p. 200.
33 Cf. S. Externbrink, *Le coeur du monde. Frankreich und die norditalienischen Staaten (Mantua, Parma, Savoyen) im Zeitalter Richelieus 1624–1635*, Münster, Lit, 1999.
34 See the letters in A. V. Hartmann (ed.), *Les Papiers de Richelieu. Section politique extérieure. Correspondance et Papiers d'Etat. Empire Allemand II (1630–1635)*, Paris, Pedone, 1997.
35 F. Dickmann, *Friedensrecht und Friedenssicherung: Studien zum Friedensproblem in der Geschichte*, Göttingen, Vandenhoeck & Ruprecht, 1971.
36 K. Repgen, 'Der päpstliche Protest gegen den Westfälischen Frieden und die Friedenspolitik Urbans VIII', *Historisches Jahrbuch*, 1956, vol. 75, pp. 94–122, repr. in his *Von der Reformation zur Gegenwart. Beiträge zu Grundfragen der neuzeitlichen Geschichte*, Paderborn, Schöningh, 1988, pp. 30–52.
37 Cf. Albrecht, *Maximilian I*, pp. 285–337.
38 D. Albrecht, 'Ferdinand II', in A. Schindling and W. Ziegler (eds), *Die Kaiser der Neuzeit 1519–1918*, Munich, Beck, 1990, pp. 125–41.
39 Hartmann, *Papiers de Richelieu*, p. 535.
40 H. Kissinger, *Diplomacy*, New York, Touchstone, 1994, p. 64.
41 Ibid., p. 62.
42 J. Wollenberg, *Richelieu. Staatsräson und Kircheninteresse. Zur Legitimation der Politik des Kardinalpremier*, Bielefeld, Pfeffersche Buchhandlung, 1977.
43 On the idea of tolerance in the Thirty Years' War see W. Schulze, *Pluralisierung als Bedrohung: Toleranz als Lösung*, in H. Duchhardt (ed.), *Westfälischer Friede*, pp. 115–40.

14 Interstate war and peace in Early Modern Europe

Heinz Duchhardt

This chapter deals with Europe in the Early Modern period and must be prefixed by two definitions. First, the term 'Europe' will be used for the geographic area that was loosely referred to under this term by contemporaries. This area is difficult to define with precision, and has always been subject to change. We will exclude south-east Europe from our considerations, which in the Early Modern period was not crystallized into politically distinct, state-like entities, and the Ottoman Empire which, according to its self-perception, belonged to another intellectual and mental sphere altogether. Second, the Early Modern period is taken as limited on the one hand by a new stage in state interactions at the end of the Middle Ages, and on the other by the extensive collapse of the old sociopolitical order on the Continent in the wake of the French Revolution.[1] In this context, the state wars of the late seventeenth and eighteenth centuries – for which the unfortunate term 'cabinet wars' has gained currency – will be the principal object of our reflections.

These wars were frequently dynastic: one line of succession became extinct, and a number of pretenders to the succession would present themselves, able to argue their own claims on the basis of varying interpretations of the close dynastic links among the European aristocratic families. Other causes of wars included the subjective impression of a geo-strategic problem, or considerations of commerce. What they all had in common was that the wars were waged by sovereigns, and no longer, as was often the case in earlier periods, by intermediary powers such as estates or city leagues; moreover, the wars of the Early Modern period were most commonly wars of state formation, in which entities tried to secure a favourable place in a competitive world.

Among the armed conflicts which are a distinguishing feature of the Early Modern period especially, and which have given historians grounds to emphasize its 'bellicosity',[2] these 'state wars' constitute only one form which exists alongside many others. The religious wars of the sixteenth and early seventeenth centuries, discussed in this volume by Aline Goosens (Chapter 12), arose from the breakup of western Christianity into various denominations, and were in many cases characterized by particularly great cruelty and mercilessness. This chapter will not consider social revolutionary uprisings which, from the point of view of the authorities, were highly dangerous to the system and therefore required rigorous military suppression. These intrastate disturbances could be caused by external crises (an example being the strains and increased taxes that went along with war), but could also lack a clear external cause: there may be clusters of reasons, such as the reduction of former privileges and local rights, the introduction of new legislation, increases in taxes and duties, or the introduction of new forms of military service. Finally, the late crusades – ideological wars conducted by Christian states against non-Christian (Muslim) polities – were likewise clearly distinct from 'normal' state wars and will not be dealt with here.[3]

As homogeneous as the (completely Christian) continent might have appeared to those outside at the end of the Middle Ages, it was hardly status quo-orientated but rife with competition between monarchs and polities. This state of affairs was caused both by the process of internal consolidation and concentration underway[4] – through bureaucratization of government and the strengthening of the estates (which, according to all political theory, were indispensable) – but also by the fixing, or rather shifting, of external borders. As there were no longer any areas in Europe which were not under rule, borders could in essence be changed only through war. This was problematic, as all Christian creeds and theologies defined killing as sinful and agonized over justifications for war. Western Christianity in its pre-Reformation form based its criteria for just wars on the criteria developed by Augustine, further summarized by Thomas Aquinas into the triad '*auctoritas principis*', '*intentio recta*' and '*causa justa*' (authority of the legitimate ruler, right intention and just cause), which alone justified an armed encounter.

Wars among Christian polities were thus only conceivable if they were founded in legal conflicts and feuds, assumed that a lawful state of affairs had been disturbed by one of the parties and aimed at the re-establishment of peace. As has been demonstrated in previous chapters, this also applied to the conduct of war in the Middle Ages, which only knew a minimum of violent acts, aiming merely to force one's opponent to acknowledge one's legal standpoint.[5] This is one reason why, towards the end of the Middle Ages and continuing into the sixteenth century, the most common form of inter-entity war was bipartite. Coalition wars remained exceptional, although many alliances may have been formed under the auspices of intensifying diplomacy. As a rule, a very small contingent of soldiers or knights was sufficient for such limited warfare.

The moment, however, when a single system of laws, a single 'Catholic' order in Europe, was no longer accepted by all participants, this construct of war as a legal conflict, which by the end of the Middle Ages was barely able to contain the dynamics of the emerging states, became obsolescent. The legal system underlying medieval concepts of just war was defined collectively by Roman law, the writings of the Church Fathers, glossators and papal statements. However, when whole polities such as England under Henry VIII, and not just a few sectarian groups like the Cathars or Hussites, turned their back on the legal system upheld authoritatively by the Roman Church, the whole foundation of the construct – the European peace order – crumbled. The great turbulence caused by inter-state religious wars in the sixteenth century can to a large extent be explained by the fundamental worry that religious disunity – whether one thinks of France or Spain/the Netherlands – would lead to the break-down of the unitary legal system. A new concept of the legitimacy of war had to be developed if the Catholic princes were to be persuaded to treat Protestants as legitimate fellow-rulers, rather than as heretics to be perse-cuted under Catholic just war theory.

This process was intensified by the fact that interstate relations had become considerably more complicated since the end of the fifteenth century, primarily because of the territorial expansion of states into less clearly controlled areas. Examples of this include the expansion of English power in Ireland, which was subjected to the English crown, the relatively rapid expansion of the Grand Principality of Moscow into non/semi-secularized areas, and the 'race for Italy', which brought the houses of Valois and Habsburg into secular opposition from 1494. This last example also illustrates the second factor: in this form a new, hitherto unknown syndrome among states and their rulers, whereby they believed themselves to be competing with another dynasty for space, power and riches. This syndrome initially developed in France, where the Valois royal dynasty saw themselves trapped or hemmed in by the *Casa d'Austria* (House of Austria), whom they regarded as a permanent threat. It became a real leitmotiv of state politics: the unpredictable hostile neighbouring state threatening one's own state's development and even existence. In this context, we see the first instance of the emergence of intra-European 'enemy images', or rather their creation through propaganda publications. However, they were not comparable in quality to the Christian world's much older perception of the external enemy, the Ottoman Empire; after its initial military advance to the outskirts of the imperial city of Vienna in 1529, 'the Turk' became *the* negative point of reference.

On the whole, the sixteenth century no doubt became the period in which such enemy images and stereotypes of considerable durability were developed, not least because of its many wars. In the Protestant parts of the German-speaking lands, the image of the Spaniard was extremely negative, as it was in the Low Countries, which were struggling for their emancipation from Spanish/Habsburg rule. Other antagonisms of the sort developed between Denmark and Sweden, and relations between England and Scotland went through very bad patches, notwithstanding the entan-glement of the ruling dynasties of both countries. The stereotypical concepts of the adversaries were only partially founded on religious denomination.

This applies to the seventeenth century also, when antagonisms between neighbours, most notably Poland and Russia, England and the Netherlands, or Spain and Portugal, developed and worsened. Other culture-specific stereotypes emerged, sometimes in a less antagonistic context: for example, the image of the Netherlands as the shopkeeper republic on the North Sea was envied by others because of its social cohesion and commercial success; although it was Europe's cultural trend-setter for decades, it was easy to look down upon as it lacked so much in terms of statehood (such as a ruler, court and well-developed bureaucracy).[6]

Religious and hence ideologically motivated conflicts in Europe subsided at the very latest with the advent of the Thirty Years' War, and were overtaken by a new generation of conflicts. They were no less emotionally justified, insofar as they were fought to satisfy the glory of the ruler, but were now legitimized by rational arguments – such as one's own state's security and legal claims – which were always easy to create against the backdrop of repeated intermarriage between ruling families. Subsequently, however, they were increasingly legitimized by the quest for the 'freedom' of Europe as against the 'universal–monarchical' tendencies of a single state, and by the need to restore the equilibrium or 'balance of power'.

As we can see from the importance of the 'glory of the prince' in this context, the main role in decisions regarding war and peace fell to the monarch in an (in theory) autocratically structured system. With the exception of some republican or estates-dominated entities such as the Netherlands, the *Confoederatio Helvetica* or Venice, pre-modern Europe had been a thoroughly regnal system, within which the monarchical states claimed and assumed clear precedence over non-monarchical entities. The cult of the ruler continued to grow throughout the Middle Ages and into the Early Modern period, climaxing with the cults of Philip II of Spain and Louis XIV of France. Only the Age of Enlightenment with its questioning of traditional structures and rationales in the late eighteenth century began to reduce the prince's position (culminating in Frederick II of Prussia's claim to be the first servant of his state). Before then, it was the omnipotent prince to whom alone it behoved to decide when to begin and to end a war. Of course he had to take material factors into consideration (the state's financial means, the state of the military and so forth), but his or her decisions were above all goal-orientated. Hence he or she contested warnings only too often or turned a deaf ear to them, as did Louis XIV in 1672[7] and Frederick II in 1740. Estates or parliaments were able to exert a certain amount of pressure in order to terminate a war if they felt defeat was inevitable, or if the state's finances could not sustain its further pursuit. But even then the ruler always had alternative forms and possibilities of financing the war at his disposal (such as the devaluation of coinage and subsidies from third powers). On the whole, even ministers were no more than accomplices of the ruler. Johannes Kunisch hit the nail on the head when he paraphrased Louis XIV in the title of

his seminal essay: '*La guerre – c'est moi*'.[8] This led some political philosophers of the time to conclude that the sole decision-making power of the
prince in matters military, his or her monopoly on the definition of what
could or could not be done in war, rendered monarchical states bellicose
in and of themselves. Several intellectuals of the Enlightenment therefore
argued that Europe could only attain a state of long-term peace once all
states had become republics.

In principle, the 'rationalization' of interstate relations after the end of
the age of confessional wars increased the chances of survival for polities,
as the annexation of a less powerful polity by one more powerful would
have provoked immediate reaction. This was due to the fact that a system
of balance which had always been precarious and unstable would have
been brought to the point of collapse. Hence attempts to absorb and annex
whole states were always doomed to failure (see, for example, the Netherlands in 1672) and were additionally alien to the status quo-orientated
thinking of the pre-modern age. Furthermore, such attempts had to face
the lofty hurdle of diplomatic interactions between states (in particular the
smaller ones), which had been intensified since the seventeenth century as
a means of falling back on a host of allies in case of need. Only thus can
the malaise be understood with which other European powers reacted
when the three largest among them truncated Poland at its first division.[9]
A state's right to existence was not normally questioned fundamentally,
regardless of whether it met the standards typical of the period or whether
it was able to protect itself. The 'world order', which was based on the
status quo, was not reliant on any one fundamental treaty document or
on any balance of terror, neither was it based on the inability to affect
change. Rather, it was based on the conviction that a state order – similar
to a social order – was, in the final analysis, something harmonious and
natural, and not to be jeopardized lightly. The powers might well jockey
for position on the Italian peninsula or in the Empire, but this would not
upset the European order as a whole. Thus the complete integration of
the Italian acquisitions – achieved by means of war or negotiation – into
Spain was not seriously considered in the 1720s and 1730s; instead, Italy
was left to a Habsburg Spanish branch *secundogeniture*. In the twin empire
of Poland–Lithuania, great care was taken to ensure that the independence of local law in the Lithuanian area of the empire remained
untouched. Under the *ancien régime*, states would not disappear because
they had been engulfed by more powerful ones, but rather because they
had been merged into another state through dynastic succession.
Theoretically, the sovereign state was considered to be an entity beyond
question, even if it had come into being as a result of a revolution, as was
the case for the Dutch Republic. Political differences may have existed
between the members of a state family, but never a system of chiefs and
underdogs, as in other periods or parts of the globe. This was an essential prerequisite for an immediate restoration of earlier political and

diplomatic relations at the end of the war. The recalling of diplomats was at any rate regarded as a necessary consequence of a declaration of war, while other relations (e.g. trade) were not brought to a complete stand-still. Even in war, one society was not entirely cut off from another. A certain internationality and intermixing resulted from the mere fact that armies could also include soldiers from opposing states and that highly specialized trades were not contained by state borders.

Armed conflicts between state units in the period of history under discus-sion were only ever 'limited' wars which were undertaken for the sake of very restricted aims, and were generally unthinkable without certain formal-ities – in particular the formal declaration of war. Such a declaration did not always say much about motive and cause, but tended to express how one belligerent party publicly legitimized an armed encounter as a just war.[10] The propaganda accompanying armed conflicts increased continu-ously over the course of the Early Modern period. Originally used in crusades and then in wars against the Ottomans to arouse emotion (and open purses), the art of war propaganda had been perfected since the age of Louis XIV: semi-official pamphlets, medals, printed material and symbolic presentations of the ruler as a war-hero and commander were all used. Wars – for which of course not only the solidarity, but also the financial resources of the subjects were needed – demanded a demon-stration of state unity: they were also periods during which criticism of the head of state could be most speedily articulated. The series of French internal rebellions during the endless wars of Louis XIV speaks for itself.

The public echo of wars should not be over-emphasized. Throughout the Early Modern period, wars never met with the approval of all or even the majority of social groups in most European states. Wars were the busi-ness of the elites, and as nobody knew when the next change of coalitions would take place, the expression of negative feelings about a current oppo-nent was inappropriate. Exceptions to this rule included the Dutch war of emancipation from Spanish rule, which produced wide hostility and strong emotions culminating in the *leyenda negra*, and the Franco–British wars of the mid-eighteenth century, which were perceived in terms of eternal enmity between the French and English peoples and their states.

Research has attempted to categorize the wars conducted in the Early Modern period, and this has produced no less than twelve types.[11] Without exception, they pursued limited aims (trade, reversal of legal and treaty infringements, etc.), even if combinations of such aims were conceivable and even if complexities of motives were the rule. There was not one war which could be reduced to a single reason. It was always an assortment of very individual motives which led key decision-makers to start wars: ambition and glory, commerce and the quest for safety, dynastic reasons and religious issues, to name but a few. It was always a mixture, and that was perhaps the reason also why one could conclude peace fairly easily without loss of face.

Even if the sovereigns proclaimed truly far-reaching war aims – such as the defence against the universalist aspirations of the Habsburgs as heirs of the Holy Roman Empire with its pan-European claims – they never placed the existence of the adversary's state structure in question. Even in those instances where historians believe they have found evidence to the contrary – for example, in the run-up to the Seven Years' War and the formation of the anti-Prussian alliance in 1756 – the crucial sources they cite are ambiguous.[12] The aims of war always remained limited; hence wars themselves were also limited, both in terms of duration, casualties and forces involved. It was no accident that in most of the interstate conflicts in the period considered, secret or open negotiations aiming to find a political settlement were started very quickly after the outbreak of hostilities. The extension of such preliminary and unofficial feelers often led to formal peace negotiations. As a rule, the conflicts were coalition wars, bringing with them all the benefits and difficulties of a co-ordinated military campaign.[13] It is a hallmark of early modern history that great successes – including that of Russia extending its power to the Baltic Sea – were achieved less on the battlefields and more at the conference table. Following the Westphalian peace negotiations, conference tables included increasing numbers of European states, allowing them to ensure that changes sought and obtained remained limited and did not upset the whole system.

The *anciens régimes* knew no 'absolute', let alone 'total', war. Military operations were conducted under the aegis of 'methodical' warfare, concentrating on the *rochade* designed to cut the enemy's supply lines (thereby gaining strategic or tactical advantages) and to push the enemy into unfavourable positions, forcing a retreat.[14] Decisive battles were extremely rare. Even during the Austrian War of Succession or the Seven Years' War hardly any battle was truly decisive. This also includes the fact that the civilian population was at best indirectly involved in the action through the provision of winter quarters, vitals and as hostages. The notoriously high human losses of the Thirty Years' War cannot be taken as typical for the entire period, and must be seen from the perspective of the suffering eyewitnesses. First, these death rates were very unevenly distributed throughout central Europe, to the point where regions with human losses of up to 50 per cent lay right next to regions which were hardly touched by the war; second, the deaths were due only in part to military action, and resulted mainly from famines, famine-related illnesses and epidemics – the indirect consequences of war. While Grimmelshausen's and Callot's depictions of the horrors of the Thirty Years' War are doubtlessly realistic, they must be seen in this larger context. Even the Thirty Years' War was not waged with genocidal intentions characteristic of 'total war'.[15]

There are other examples of a scorched earth policy, aimed at the systematic destruction of enemy territory, in wars of the *ancien régime* – as the Nine Years' War on the Upper Rhine demonstrated[16] – but this was not generally considered to be in accordance with the rules of war. The use of scatterbombs, which endangered the civilian population to a high degree, was deemed reprehensible. The civilian population was not the target of military action, but rather the enemy's military strong-point, and territorial changes were the aim, such as the attainment of a straighter or better defensible border. Frederick II once said that none of his wars had affected the Prussian peasants, who had continued to till their soil in spite of all the military efforts made by the state. There is a grain of truth in this claim: the *anciens régimes'* wars were more limited in their effects on the population in general than most wars both of the previous and subsequent eras.

After a war, peace was not necessarily or automatically concluded on the basis of territorial control at the time of the armistice. In most cases, the principle of a return to the status quo ante seems to have dominated peace negotiations. War was to be conducted between the armed forces of both sides (i.e. enlisted troops and those forced into the army by conscription). A military operation by a state, with the aim of destroying the whole population of another, was inconceivable under the *ancien régime*. What *was* conceivable, however, was the deployment of the military against refractory or non-conformist sections or groups of the population in order to force them back into what was perceived to be the old order, by means of threats or physical violence. Evidence suggests that such groups were rarely if ever identified according to ethnicity, whether one thinks of the French dragoons opposing the Huguenots or the suppression of other insurrections.

For the most part, warfare under the *ancien régime* still bore pre-modern characteristics. Opposing commanders might meet and hold banquets together, and high-ranking prisoners were often released upon giving their word of honour. Prisoners were exchanged on the basis of so-called cartels (bilateral agreements between the warring parties), in which case a predetermined sum was to be paid:[17] the human being as an 'instrument of war' was a precious commodity in short supply.

Exchanges of captives took place at the latest on the basis of the peace treaty, which was seen as indispensable for the working of the interstate system. In the seventeenth and early eighteenth centuries, peace treaties were usually concluded with, and later more frequently without, the help of mediators. As of the seventeenth century, treaties were always concluded for an indefinite period and contained a so-called 'oblivion' clause, i.e. a clause which enjoined all parties to forget, or in no way persecute, any previous act of belligerence.[18] The peace treaty could determine territorial losses or gains at home or overseas, and allow for military measures such as the razing of fortresses or territorial restitutions, and more rarely, for financial compensation (a remarkable counter-example to this is the Peace of Osnabrück of 1648). Protracted military occupation or control of the loser was never intended, a total or far-reaching demilitarization never decreed and the infrastructure of the inferior party never destroyed in its entirety. The loser was sufficiently punished by having to pay for the war and by territorial losses inflicted. After noteworthy attempts by Louis XIV to put smaller states such as Genoa or the Dutch Republic into a position of inferiority, defeated states were no longer subjected to acts which were regarded as dishonourable (such as the imposition of inspectors who assured compliance with treaty terms).

A correlation between the duration of the war and the duration of the ensuing peace is difficult to establish. The Thirty Years' War was followed by only a short peace, and in some regions it continued beyond 1648. The peace which followed the eight-year-long Austrian War of Succession barely lasted for the same length of time. Meanwhile, the peace after the Seven Years' War continued for over twenty-five years, notwithstanding the American War of Independence, the Turkish Wars and conflicts within the Holy Roman Empire.

The state system of the *ancien régime* was characterized by a large number of bi- and multilateral conflicts. Thus, there was barely a war-free year in the seventeenth century. On the one hand the dissolution of a particular hierarchical order triggered a jockeying for position of the powers; on the other, there was a tendency towards internal consolidation and centralization of polities. Almost all states found themselves in real or perceived periods of upswing during the seventeenth century, but could not yet consider themselves territorially satiated. Most of these states transferred their ambitions on to colonies, knowing full well that they could and would not be successful in competition with other leading powers. In the eighteenth century, a small number of great powers ('pentarchy'), operating as a form of 'cartel', determined and controlled changes in state structure, and increasingly became the driving forces in interstate dynamics. A formal institution (like the League of Nations or the United Nations) which would have enforced respect for political rules could not yet emerge under the *ancien régime*, in spite of the exhortations of the philosophers wishing for eternal peace.

Despite the fact that many seventeenth-century monarchs had their portraits painted in a warlike pose and battle armour, and that well into the eighteenth century it was thought that a ruler should be prepared to lead his army into battle himself – which Frederick II of Prussia, George II of Great Britain, Joseph II, Louis XIV and Louis XV actually did – one cannot speak of a specific cult of war under the European *ancien régime*. This did not detract from the bellicosity of that era: neither can a marked and pronounced culture of peace be identified. While the number of books written about peace and peaceful utopias rose markedly after the seventeenth century, the topic of peace did not become *the* leading theme in the philosophical, political and sociological works of the Enlightenment. On the whole, reflecting on peace may indeed have intensified in the eighteenth century, but not to the point of consigning war to the political or moral scrap heap.

The protagonists of the seventeenth and eighteenth centuries had a relatively clear concept of a conceptual, ideal world order. This was seldom the notion of 'Christendom' (western or universal), which, implying a particular hierarchy, had had its day. Instead, people now imagined a family of states based on the principle of the fundamental equality of individual members, but which was limited by the 'outer borders' of Europe. Across the oceans, other rules and political options prevailed, and the Ottoman Empire was to remain outside the order.[19] The Turkish Wars saw a completely different kind of warfare, one that the Sublime Porte could not change. This interstate system, which was increasingly referred to as 'Europe' following the transition from the seventeenth to the eighteenth century, was based on the same, or at least similar, points of reference: on a basic text common to all – the Bible – and on a common feeling of superiority with regard to foreign cultures (which was indeed the case in the military sphere). It was a closed system which was no longer subject to external threats and which therefore also developed its own quite specific rules of the game: the players were increasingly a limited number of great powers that took control and were active at the forefront of interstate politics. It is an irony of history that the system was eroded not from without, but rather from within.

Notes

1 J. Burkhardt, 'Frühe Neuzeit', in R. von Dülmen (ed.), *Das Fischer Lexikon Geschichte*, Frankfurt, Fischer Verlag, 1980, pp. 364–85.
2 J. Burkhardt, 'Die Friedlosigkeit der Frühen Neuyeit: Grundlegung einer Theorie der Bellizität Europas', *Zeitschrift für Historische Forschung*, 1997, vol. 24, pp. 509–74.
3 See the contribution in this volume by Jonathan Riley-Smith (Chapter 10).
4 P. Moraw, *Von offener Verfassung yu gestalteeter Verdichtung: das Reich im späten Mittelalter, 1250–1490*, Berlin, Propyläen, 1985.
5 P. Contamine, *La Guerre au Moyen Age*, Paris, Presses Universitaires de France, 1980.
6 H. Schilling, 'Die Republik der Vereinigten Niederlande – ein bewunderter und beargwönter Nachbar', in H. Duchhardt (ed.), *Europas Mitte: Deutschland und seine Nachbarn*, Bonn, Europa Union Verlag, 1988, pp. 20–8; H. Lademacher, *Die Niederlande: Politische Kultur zwischen Individualität und Anpassung*, Berlin, Propyläen Verlag, 1993.
7 P. Sonnino, *Louis XIV and the Origins of the Dutch War*, Cambridge, Cambridge University Press, 1988.
8 J. Kunisch, *Das Mirakel des Hauses Brandenburg: Studien yum Verhältnis von Kabinettspolitik und Kriegführung im Zeitalter des Siebenjährigen Krieges*, Munich, Oldenbourg, 1987, pp. 407–38.
9 T. Cegielski, *Das Alte Reich und die Erste Teilung Polens, 1768–1774*, Stuttgart, Steiner; Warszawa, PWN, 1988, pp. 1768–74.
10 Cf. K. Repgen, 'Kriegslegitimationen in Alteuropa: Entwurf einer historischen Typologie', in K. Repgen, *Von der Reformation zur Gegenwart: Beiträge zu Grundfragen der neuzeitlichen Geschichte*, Paderborn, Schöningh, 1988, pp. 67–83.
11 Repgen, 'Kriegslegitimationen'.
12 See Kunisch, *Das Mirakel*.

13 Ibid.
14 Several illustrative studies by Hans Schmidt are now readily available in his 1995 collection.
15 For Ludendorff's idea of total war, see the contribution by Robert Foley in this volume (Chapter 16). For different definitions of the concept, see B. Heuser, *The Bomb: Nuclear Weapons in their Historical, Strategic and Ethical Context*, London, Longman, 1999, ch. 3.
16 K. von Raumer, *Die Zerstörung der Pfalz von 1689 im Zusammenhang der französischen Rheinpolitik*, 1939, repr. Bad Neustadt an der Saale, Pfaehler, 1982.
17 Cf. H. Duchhardt, *Krieg und Frieden im Zeitalter Ludwigs XIV*, Düsseldorf, Schwann, 1987.
18 J. Fisch, *Krieg und Frieden im Friedensvertrag: eine universalgeschichtliche Studie über Grundlagen und Formelemente des Friedensschlusses*, Stuttgart, Klett-Cotta, 1979, section 5.
19 G. Parker, *The Military Revolution: Military Innovation and the Rise of the West, 1500–1800*, 2nd edn, Cambridge, Cambridge University Press, 1996.

Part IV

The era of ideological wars

Introduction

Beatrice Heuser

While the religious wars of the previous period and the English Civil War were also ideological wars, the era of interstate ideological conflict in a strict sense began with the French Revolution and its wars (1792–1802). The French Revolutionaries came into inevitable conflict with those states whose rulers sought to defend the old hierarchical order of their internal societies (which put those rulers on top) against the new internal order which was founded on the equality of all men. When the universalist revolutionary fervour was perverted into expansionist imperialistic nationalism under Napoleon (1802–15), France arrayed as enemies against herself the states which until 1806 formed the Holy Roman Empire (above all Austria and its possessions), Prussia, the United Kingdom of Great Britain and Ireland, and Spain. Together, they defeated Napoleon's France. In their determination to turn back the clock and to re-create the *ancien régime* (in which the monarchy, not the people, is sovereign) of France under Bourbon King Louis XVIII (1814–24), they soon readmitted France, its royalist credentials re-established, into their midst. France lost the Napoleonic conquests, but the peace imposed on her was not a humiliating one.

From 1815 (the Vienna Congress that devised this peace) until 1919, several systems existed which invariably consisted of great power domination of the world. The initial system assumed the co-operation of the great powers, but gave way to a series of military alliances which cataclysmically clashed in the First World War. The great powers – Austria, Russia, Britain, Prussia, France, and on the fringes of Europe, the Ottoman Empire – claimed not only the right to adjudicate on matters arising throughout Europe and in any area where they had colonies, but also a responsibility to intervene: either to protect the status quo against challenges, or in support of 'freedom' (mainly the bugbear of 'national' self-determination, somehow assumed to be liberal, democratic) against 'tyranny' (mainly defined as 'foreign' rule, assumed to be illiberal and oppressive).

Nationalism was one of the three most important ideologies of this era, together with democracy and socialism. For the French Revolutionaries, nationalism (the elevation of the nation to sovereignty as opposed to the king) originally went hand in hand with democracy and knew no ethnic boundaries. But simplifying somewhat, nationalism split to form twin concepts, only one of which, the French (and US American) version, remained linked to democracy and in principle universalist in application (any person, whatever his or her provenance, race, ethnicity, could become a French citizen under the French Revolution, as long as he or she subscribed to the ideals of the Revolution). The satanic twin that emerged was the ethnically oriented concept of nationalism. Friedrich Meinecke explained it as the German anti-model. This lent itself to an increasingly biological ('racist') interpretation (basically arguing that one's own nation was 'superior', as proved by – usually – its military exploits, in a Social Darwinist logic), and ultimately could become the justification of massacres in colonies and of the Holocaust.

There were many variations between these two extremes, as logical coherence is rarely found in practical politics. Britain and France, one incrementally, the other in rollercoaster succession of monarchies, republics, empires, and autocracy in the nineteenth and first half of the twentieth centuries moved towards democracy and nationalism of a generally more universalist variety, although not untarnished by notions of collective superiority. The Austro–Hungarian empire (succeeding the Holy Roman Empire that became defunct in 1806, but with a narrower territorial base) combined universalism (with elements of a meritocracy) with *ancien régime* inherited class hierarchy. Russia belatedly moved from its Middle Ages to an *ancien régime* of paternalistic class hierarchy. Prussia, which absorbed the rest of the non-Austrian-ruled Germanophone areas to form the Second Empire (which claimed the succession of the First or Holy Roman Empire, but was narrowly ethnically German), developed a form of social security while until 1918 clinging to the sovereignty of the Prussian king/German emperor, as opposed to the limited (some would say, make-believe) sovereignty of the adult male population, who had the right to elect a parliament, but not even indirect influence on the choice of the government. A plethora of little states, mostly constitutional monarchies, made up the rest of Europe. By the second half of the nineteenth century, all were enamoured to some greater or lesser extent with ethnic nationalism, which with inexorable logic turned them into all their neighbours' rivals. The worst manifestation of this rivalry arguably took the form of the Franco–Prussian War of 1870 to 1871 which, resulting in the defeat of France, contributed so decisively to German nationalist fervour among the subjects of the many Germanophone principalities that a majority enthusiastically supported the creation of the Second Empire, disempowering their local princes in its favour.

All these states were catapulted into a new world with the end of the First World War, when (communist) socialism first captured a state – of all states, backward Russia – and overnight became a force to be reckoned with. Like nationalism, the primary cell of socialism split into two, one becoming the socialism or social democracy or labour movement, which was content to operate within a democratic system and to respect other parties, and which insisted on a limited redistribution of wealth coupled with social security for the weaker members of society. The other was the Soviet-led socialism or communism which was founded on a revolutionary rejection of all monarchic or 'bourgeois democratic' forms of government, and in one form or another promoted the dominance of the workers' and peasants' class (the proletariat) over all others. But it did so without any democratically elected representation: in the Bolshevist (majority) form in which it was adopted in Russia and which became the model for (communist) socialism in the rest of eastern Europe, the proletariat was represented by the Communist Party which claimed to speak for it without having been elected in competition with other parties, i.e. without the second fundamental principle of democracy (besides that of the people's sovereignty). Confusingly, the states which operated under this system called themselves socialist democracies or people's democracies. Significantly, the mainstay of their ideology was that the interests of the individual were to be subordinated, where necessary, to the interests of the majority, while the liberal democracies that emerged in the West took the utmost care to guarantee rights of the individual even against the interests of a majority of others, limiting the state's control of its citizens. Differences between both types of ideologies could thus most clearly be demonstrated in attitudes to human rights (and indeed with regard to a different appreciation of the value of the life of the individual, reflected, in turn, in their military strategies).

A fourth political order emerged in the wake of the First World War, and proved to be applicable both to ethnic-racist nationalist and to (communist) socialist states. This was totalitarianism, in the form of a single political party's exclusive domination of the state and of most aspects of the population's life. Totalitarianism dominated Fascist Spain and Italy, National-Socialist Germany (which as the name suggests succeeded in fusing the social welfare aspects of socialism with the most rabid form of racism yet known) and (Communist) Socialist Russia. The expansionism of National-Socialist Germany and of Fascist Italy in the 1930s (as well as of imperial Japan in the Far East) threatened to upset the perceived order and balance of interests in Europe, to the point where Britain and France felt the need to stop the further expansion, triggering the Second World War. State control of the smallest detail of the lives of citizens came to an end in Germany and Italy with the defeat of Hitler and Mussolini, continued in a milder fashion in Portugal and Spain until 1974 and 1975 respectively, but stood strong in central and eastern Europe until the demise of communism in Europe in 1989/90.

Significantly, totalitarian regimes were able to instil their populations with the belief that any different regimes (the democracies, or totalitarian regimes of a different hue) were mortal enemies whose hostility could be eliminated only through a final defeat, either following an external war or an internal civil war (as communist socialism expected for its adversaries). This explains the prolonged tension between the Soviet Union and the states it dominated until 1989 on the one hand, and the western democracies on the other, which both sides defined as a struggle to the death of either system. That it did not turn into an all-out war in the way in which the democracies had struggled against National-Socialist Germany and Fascist Italy is thought to be linked with the fear both sides had of a nuclear war, and the closely knit alliance systems formed by both sides, one (the North Atlantic Treaty Organization) under American leadership, the other (the Warsaw Treaty Organization) under Soviet dominance, the latter of which became defunct with the disintegration of the Soviet empire in 1990.

In the wake of both world wars, which each resulted in the victory of Britain and the USA which now entered the European scene, actual international bodies were created with the purpose of resolving conflicts peacefully, aiming to bring all sovereign states into an assembly where such problems could be discussed. The first, the League of Nations, assumed voluntary membership and voluntary co-operation among the members, and foundered on this assumption. The second, the United Nations, reintroduced the nineteenth-century system of great power domination of the other powers by creating within the organization a Security Council which included those countries that happened to be great powers (mainly in a military sense, and victors of the Second World War) at the time of its foundation: the USA, the Soviet Union, China (first Nationalist China, then its successor Communist China), Britain and France. As in the nineteenth-century systems, no election by the other members legitimized this permanent position of these five great powers, and no mechanism exists even on the threshold of the twenty-first century to protect smaller states, or groups within the state of one of the great powers, against violence or other unacceptable behaviour at the hand of one of these 'Permanent Five' members of the UN Security Council.

Without communism, only militant ethnic nationalism (Serbia, Croatia) and Islam remain as serious rivals for liberal democracy, but in the final decade of the twentieth century flecks of ethnic nationalism tarnished the beauty even of liberal democracy's most shining examples. The primitive pride emanating from an assertion that one's own group (now almost universally defined as 'nation') is 'best' still brings out atavistic instincts and urges, even in Europeans.

Crucial for the emergence of the age of ideologies in Late Modern European, and largely, world history were a number of characteristics. The development of near-universal literacy and of the mass media are among them. They alone could rival and surpass the pulpit as vehicles to influence and indeed create mass opinion, which in turn was essential to the age of ideological wars. Totalitarianism could only have gripped societies in its close network of surveillance in an age of telephones, telegraph, train, radios, newspapers, and other means of modern communication and transport. It was also dependent on the full unfolding of strong state bureaucracies, which alone made it possible to *erfassen* (control and monitor) all citizens, introduce fully effective conscription and military service, mobilize otherwise unemployed citizens for war-related production and other services, put industries on a war footing, organize a comprehensive recycling of primary materials, and ration food and other raw materials. State-controlled, compulsory education allowed centralized indoctrination of the entire population resident within a state's boundaries, which in turn made it possible to create patriotic and nationalistic feelings, a sense of belonging to a state, its citizenry (nation in the Franco-American sense), of being part of a constructed national history creating a sense of collective identity. Public art (statues, memorials, murals in town halls or other public buildings) and public spectacles (such as commemorations of wars, inaugurations of public buildings or memorials, marches, national holidays, fund-raising for national causes, nationwide election campaigns) all forged national identity and depended on sophisticated administrative structures which were the essence of modern industrial states. The economic underpinnings – provided by mass production and profit in the industrial age – and the corresponding taxation system were essential to allow the full effectiveness of these states in contexts of war and peace. Even outside war, periodic sportive competitions or industrial trade fairs provided organized fora for national competition.

Other ideologies sought to some extent to emulate the states' comprehensive hold on their citizens' loyalties. Even out of power, Communism, National Socialism and Fascism used marches with torches, assemblies in the open air, flags and posters, collections and campaigns much in the way as did states. Among increasingly uprooted populations, who in the process of massive urbanization had lost their links with communities, families, religion, the sense of belonging was crucial and was generated anew by organizations campaigning for ideologies that provided new frameworks of references complementing spiritually what the organizations did socially: create a new home.

The larger the group that demanded loyalty and offered identity, the more rigorously it had to demand hatred of the counter-group, the *other* – whether this was the class enemy as in the French or Russian Revolutions or the Cold War, or the national enemy, or the racial enemy – and the crueller the treatment of the enemy in conflict or war. Concomitantly, enormous sacrifices were asked of one's own group, as witnessed by the wars of the French Revolution, of Napoleon, the Crimean War, the American Civil War, the wars of German unification, and finally the two world wars together with the Russian Revolution. Wars tended towards totality, although total war in its full horror as dreamt of by Ludendorff came only with Auschwitz.[1]

Moving towards the present, however, a positive development took place in Europe where a growing number of liberal democratic states ceased to regard war as a legitimate means of settling disputes among themselves, creating a European peace order within the confines of the gradually expanding European Community (now European Union (EU)). Its dilemma consists of the fact, as Robert Cooper has explained so persuasively,[2] that the EU area with its 'post-modern' attitude to war (post-modern in that its members have surrendered aspects of sovereignty) is still surrounded by states with a 'modern' attitude to war – where the sovereignty of statehood lies largely in its ability to conduct war, its monopoly on the use of force – and by pre-modern entities – entities that are still struggling to establish full statehood and a monopoly on the use of force. The EU members are thus still in danger of being drawn into wars elsewhere in the world (and not only in adjacent areas).

Notes

1 See Robert Foley's contribution in this book (Chapter 16), and Beatrice Heuser, *The Bomb: Nuclear Weapons in their Historical, Strategic and Ethical Context*, London, Longmans, 1999, ch. 3.
2 Robert Cooper, *The Postmodern State and the World Order*, London, Demos, 2000.

15 The revolutionary period, 1789–1802

Marc Belissa and Patrice Leclercq

The revolutionary period (1789–1802) has long been seen as the defining moment of the construction of the nation-state and its corollary, nationalism. For some historians of the nineteenth century who were both liberals and nationalists, it was the sole justification for revolutionary violence. Recent research has begun to change this perception. Françoise Brunel, for example, suggests that we should pay more attention to the differences between concepts of state, country and homeland (fatherland, *patrie*), and Jean-Yves Guiomar reminds us that the Revolution did not in fact create the association of state/nation, but rather the association state/homeland, which is different from the former in that it does not exclude a concept of universal citizenship. Finally, Florence Gauthier and Marc Belissa have shown that the constitution of what we today call the nation-state was not central to theories of natural rights which were the common language of patriots in many countries.[1]

War has a crucial influence on the revolutionary process. For Albert Soboul, war 'obliged the revolutionary bourgeoisie to turn to the people [for help] and to make concessions to them: this is how the social content of the nation became extended. [The nation] really dates back to the war, which was both national and revolutionary.'[2] This claim may be true in part, but it ignores relations between the French and the peoples surrounding them. The wars of the French Revolution were not merely national wars, but also wars of conquest – at least between September 1792 and March 1793, and afterwards under the Directoire. The Napoleonic wars were in certain ways a continuation, but were different in many respects, particularly where their more narrowly nationalist character is concerned, which is why we shall concentrate here on the period 1792 to 1802.

War was the major factor that shaped the entire revolutionary period. From 1792 to 1802, it was virtually continuous. From 1792 to 1795, France faced a coalition formed initially by Prussia and Austria (together with a few German princes), which was joined by Britain, Spain and the kingdom of Piedmont in 1793. In 1795, the Archduke of Tuscany launched the Bâle peace negotiations, leading Prussia to withdraw from the coalition, soon followed by Spain. From 1795 until the peace of Campo-Formio in 1798, Britain, Austria and the princes of the Holy Roman Empire remained at war with France. Britain did not sign the Peace of Amiens until 1802.

Continuity and rupture

The revolutionary wars were already perceived by contemporaries as something quite new. Twentieth-century historians have highlighted certain features they had in common with the wars of the *ancien régime*, yet novelty is their main feature. Some of the men, the structures and the equipment were the same as in previous wars, but the political aims with which they were used were fundamentally different. Thus, there was no equivalent of the *levée en masse* (the mass mobilization of 1793) under the *ancien régime*. The ideological aspects of the French revolutionary wars were new. While all wars contain an element of propaganda warfare (even during the *ancien régime*, attempts were made to justify the use of force ideologically, through propaganda), the revolutionary wars for the first time ever mobilized the masses ideologically around politically defined objectives (such as the defence of freedom and revolutionary rights, the liberation of enslaved peoples, the greatness of a regenerated France, and so on). Yet the revolutionary wars were not purely ideological wars for both sides. The war which was declared on 20 April 1792 was not exclusively the result of a rise of fanatical revolutionaries within the government; it was also the result of friction which existed before the Revolution.

The revolutionary period is distinctive in that war was waged on two fronts: the external war was waged against the coalition powers, and the internal war against their supposed accomplices within each society. These included suspected traitors and unenthusiastic supporters, but particularly rebels and especially those in the Vendée who rose against the Revolution. They waged a civil war for political, religious and economic motivations which were so different from those of the rest of the French that people talked about the inexplicable Vendée (Barère) which gave birth to a distinct regional entity. For this study we therefore have to keep an eye on both of these fronts and their influences on each other.

The protagonists

Right from the first revolutionary stirrings, the patriots feared intervention from 'foreign powers'. In 1789, rumours that British soldiers were being mobilized caused concern to the French National Assembly. The following year, the conflict between the British and the Spanish over Nootka Bay in North America seemed for many to be a prelude to a phoney war which France would fight on Spain's side and which would have allowed the French king to seize the political initiative once again. Although it is clear today that the European monarchies were in no hurry to intervene in France, the Reichenbach and then the Pillnitz conventions convinced the revolutionaries that there was a 'coalition of despots' against 'the land of freedom and human rights'. The fear of military intervention was by no means absurd: the Belgian and Liégeoise revolutions were crushed in November to December 1790 by the emperor's troops, acting with the benevolence of Prussia, the United Provinces and Britain.[3] This is why the French revolutionaries concluded that French *émigrés*, arming on the banks of the Rhine, were indicating that a full-scale invasion of France was being prepared. We know today that while the war unleashed in 1792 was desired and provoked by Louis XVI, the supporters of La Fayette and the Girondins (for different reasons, of course), the majority of the French were convinced that by declaring war on 20 April 1792, the *regenerated France* was merely defending against an imminent attack. The formerly royal army swiftly integrated volunteers, and, after the defeats of 1793 and their political repercussions, the nation-in-arms rose up against the despots, soon to be labelled 'enemies of humankind'. Indeed, in the French revolutionary rhetoric, the *tyrants* who resisted the universal application of human rights by threatening the freedom of the French, but also by 'putting the peoples in fetters', were described as 'slaves who oppose the sovereign of the world, namely humankind'. The true enemies of the patriot were thus not the soldiers on the other side – who were either cheated or enslaved – but the 'satellites of the despots', i.e. all those who consciously served the kings.[4]

In declarations made by the coalition of monarchs fighting against revolutionary France, the republicans were labelled 'disturbers of the European order'. In the British House of Commons, George III condemned them as 'anarchists' who wished to provoke disorder in foreign countries, without consideration for the rights of neutral countries, while pursuing objectives of conquest and aggrandisement.[5] For Lord Sheffield, the French leaders were a 'gang of thieves and cut-throats with whom no contact, nor deed, nor treaty must be maintained'.[6] To distinguish 'good Frenchmen' from 'blood-drinkers', the coalition of monarchs pointed to the Jacobins as those who terrorized the country and the Convention.

All those who lived through the revolutionary wars undoubtedly saw them as a contest between two political cultures: those of the *ancien régime* and of the new. Seen from this angle, one can say that it was about two competing worlds, but the contest was both internal and external. For Robespierre, for example, these wars pitched all the peoples of Europe against all enemies of liberty. The label 'enemy of humankind', used liberally by both sides, shows us that all of humankind was seen as the ultimate stake in this contest. The revolutionaries were convinced that they were working for the universal application of human rights, and not merely for the defence of the French people against the despots.

In western France, more specifically in the military Vendée area, republican *Bleus* faced the *Blancs* who defended the monarchy and the Catholic

Church. While the rebels called themselves Christians, the *Bleus* called them brigands, royalist fiends, fanatics, credulous Vendeans, or people of imbeciles.

Europe, states and national integration

Europe during the Enlightenment was an area throughout which there were networks of contacts. Some had existed well before 1789, but were then limited to social elites, merchants, craftsmen and intellectuals. Some of the great thinkers of the Enlightenment saw in these professional, cultural and diplomatic contacts reason for thinking that relations between peoples – as opposed to monarchs – were bound to be peaceful. The idea that Europe was one state made up of diverse provinces was commonplace for figures of the Enlightenment from Montesquieu, who rejoiced at it, to Rousseau, who lamented it.[7] For common people, direct contacts with foreigners were, of course, limited to certain groups: sailors, itinerant vendors, craftsmen and hirelings working in frontier areas. Yet knowledge of other countries grew with the gradual spread of literacy. The popularity of travel accounts soared.

For France, the wars were certainly a key moment in her national unification. They helped solder together the aggregate of disunited peoples of which Mirabeau spoke – with some exaggeration – in 1789. In reality, the process of unification had already been initiated by the *Fédération* movement in 1789 to 1790, but the decisive boost came from the wars.

Within the coalition camp, a distinction must be made between Prussia, Austria and Spain on the one hand, and the British Empire on the other. The first three still had states typical of the *ancien régime*. Their monarchs waged war, and if their subjects were fed anti-revolutionary propaganda, it was because they were not integrated into a national community with its own public political debate. By contrast, for Britain, it is clear – not least from the work of Linda Colley – that a process of British national conscience formation had begun.[8] Gallophobia and the fight against Bourbon France were key elements in this process. The British leaders made frequent reference to the 'perpetually troublesome power': France was the 'natural enemy' of England, whether she was ruled by Louis XIV or by the convention. In Britain, public opinion and a public political discourse existed: war was debated in Parliament, and the opposition both in and out of Parliament expressed support for the French Revolution. The press and politicized social networks relayed the debate to the population as a whole.

On a different level, two quite distinct communities which barely intermingled were in conflict in western France. The urban bourgeoisie that favoured the Revolution gained great advantages from the rising in the region and benefited significantly from the sale of nationalized property. The peasants, by contrast, often felt cheated by the reforms which seemed to make the differences between them and urban life greater. The strained relations between towns and country in the Vendée were one of the key causes of the civil war and were to outlive the conflict.

Limited or total war?

In the external wars of the French Revolution, the civilian populations were not direct targets of fighting (although they sometimes suffered its consequences), but were considered potential allies and helpers. Having decided that the new France could not wage war in the same way as the royal armies, deputies of the French National Assembly debated the appropriate conduct of French soldiers and officers on foreign soil. A variation on the revolutionaries' slogan 'war on the palaces, peace to the cottages' can be found on the medals submitted to an art competition in 1793: 'Peace to the people, war on the tyrants.' In 1792, the Belgian population, for instance, was encouraged by the French, but also by political exiles from Belgium and Liège (who had fled repression in their country in 1790), to help the troops who came to liberate them. General Dumouriez' proclamation upon entry into Brussels illustrates the way in which the revolutionaries intended to conduct relations with the civilian population: he promised that Belgian rights and sovereignty would be respected. In Mainz, Brussels and Chambéry, local patriots were encouraged to create their own political clubs and provisional administrations. The generals levied taxes, some of which were high, as in Cologne, or forced rich people to make them loans. Nevertheless, the situation deteriorated quickly, most notably in Belgium, from November 1792 onwards. Anti-religious acts such as the despoiling of churches for silver provoked violent reactions from local populations, who took revenge through night-time assassinations and even ambushes directed at the withdrawing French forces in March 1793.

In the Vendée, armed clashes continued in varied forms. From March to December 1793, republicans clashed with rebels who had merged with the Catholic and royal army. Until the La Jaunaye peace agreement of 17 February 1795, the rebels were no longer centrally organized; rather, they were a number of bands obeying chiefs who were unable to get along with one another. High-intensity fighting ceased in 1796 with the deaths of the last of these great chiefs, but political rebellion continued until 1815. The violence and savagery of the fighting that took place in the Vendée can be explained particularly by the inability of the republicans to distinguish between combatants and non-combatants among their adversaries. Women and children took part in uprisings or actively helped the rebels. For this reason the civilian population was targeted by the revolutionaries for acts of repression. The need to protect their own networks and hiding-places led the rebels not to take republicans prisoners: they were either freed or, more frequently, executed.

It is difficult to guess at the number of lives lost. All too often, historians add the casualties of the revolutionary wars to those lost during the Napoleonic wars. J. P. Bertaud thinks France lost 440,000 to 490,000 persons between 1792 and 1800, including deaths on the battlefield, in hospitals, and permanent or temporary emigration.[9] The total figure is even harder to estimate for the Vendée: it seems that nearly 250,000 died as a consequence of the conflict in that area, i.e. one third of the inhabitants.

In practice, the revolutionary wars were limited: extermination of the population as a whole was not the aim, arms of mass destruction did not exist, and generals avoided hounding enemy soldiers to death if they retreated from the battlefield, as this was considered hazardous for one's own forces. The Committee of Public Safety of Year II often complained about the generals' faint-heartedness. Some generals would be executed for their refusal to pursue the enemy to annihilation. However, if war was limited in practice, the defensive war of the revolutionaries was absolute in its political aims: everyone was mobilized (particularly with the *levée en masse*), no compromise with the enemies was acceptable as long as they had not withdrawn completely from French territory (under the motto of 'death or freedom'). Moreover there was a rhetoric of extermination of the enemy (reflected in the decree of 1 August 1793 ordering the destruction of the Vendée or the decree of 7 Prairial – the ninth month of the Republican calendar – of Year II that no English or Hanoverian prisoners should be taken).[10]

In the revolutionary battles, the individual mattered little; personal style gave way to collective action. Warfare was no longer seen as a pretext for making selfish courage shine. It was of little importance for the many if some individual, carried along by his valour, should distinguish himself in combat and overcome unimaginable perils, if the Republic as a whole, associated 'with this triumph, could not reap the material fruits of this bravado'.[11] The cult of child-heroes, the martyrs of freedom, was imbued with this spirit. The act of bravery of the young Agricol Viala who was killed by Marseilles federalists on 8 July 1793 was only seen as valuable because it stopped the federalists using the ferry of Bompas to advance against the revolutionary forces. 'The free man should be great enough to transfer his deeds to joint action, in such a way that all his movements – joined with those of an imposing force – contribute equally to a decisive success where firmness, heroism and the republican values of each person become merged.'[12]

A hierarchy of enemies

It is certain that this new type of revolutionary war, which was at once a war between political systems, between states, and for preponderance in Europe, made peace more difficult to establish, especially with Britain, whose future as a dominant European power was at stake.

Nevertheless, the Bâle peace agreement with Prussia lasted for about eleven months, while for many reasons that of Campo-Formio with Austria was broken a few months after it was signed. Prussia's objective was to conclude a peace with France so that it could concentrate on Poland which had just suffered a new division. The Prussian nobility did not unanimously support war against France, as they considered Austria to be their natural enemy, and saw the coalition with the empire as unnatural.

In the Vendée, the La Jaunaye agreements constituted but a short truce; none the less they showed a real willingness for peace on the side of the republicans, who treated the rebel Charrette as the representative of an actual state. Later, until 1800, successive French governments dealt rigorously with the chiefs of the Vendée but showed clemency towards the population.

The role of worldviews in the aims and means of war

Notwithstanding the ulterior strategic motives of those pushing for war in April 1792, the majority of the French, as we have noted, were convinced that the coalition powers were ready to take up arms against the French revolutionaries.[13] War was thus above all justified in France by the need to defend the Revolution. Reference was made to human rights, the freedom of choosing one's government, the social rights acquired under the Revolution, as well as the respect of people's rights against despots. The words of the second verse of 'The Marseillaise' are telling:

> Que veut cette horde d'esclaves
> De traîtres, de rois conjurés?
> Pour qui ces ignobles entraves,
> Ces fers dès longtemps préparés
> Français! Pour nous, ah! quel outrage!
> Quels transports il doit exciter!
> C'est nous qu'on ose méditer
> de rendre à l'antique esclavage![14]

Glory, honour and prestige were not invoked as values for the individual. Glory lay in the defence of the Revolution, honour belonged to the people who liberated foreign peoples, and prestige came with the promotion of human rights. Certain avowed patriots, however, rejected these terms as befuddling. A few weeks before the declaration of war, the newspaper *Les Révolutions de Paris* came out against the use of the term 'national honour' by the friends of Brissot and the Gironde.[15]

The opposing sides were perfectly aware of what was at stake in this conflict. On the side of the coalition, the defence of the European order, the public law of treaties, and the property and sovereignty of monarchs were the leitmotivs of the ideological legitimization of the war. But what European order? That of absolute princes proclaimed by Austria and Prussia, or that of the freedom of property and of peoples promoted by Britain? These fundamental differences came to the fore in October 1792 in the texts of Edmund Burke and Mercy d'Argenteau. The English intellectual believed that a political war should be waged in which the coalition should support an internal solution with the 'moderates' who opposed the Convention,[16] whereas the diplomat serving the Habsburg emperor believed that nothing could be expected from the 'moderates' and the emigrants, as they had no effective political power: the coalition, in his view, should therefore content itself to wage a classical war.[17]

The British counter-revolutionaries stressed the defence of European society against French ambition. It was the opening up of the River Scheldt and the conquest of Belgium by the forces of the Convention that drove a wedge between France and England. Pitt, the British prime minister, did not justify the war against them on the basis of the revolution of 10 August 1792 or the execution of Louis XVI, but on the basis of the invasion of Holland and the breach of the Treaty of Utrecht which the opening of the Scheldt constituted. He accused the French of disrespect for the principles of public law underpinning the European society of sovereign princes. For Burke and Pitt, the natural law of nations proclaimed by the convention was just a cover for invasion plans hedged by France. British alarmists pointed to the alleged link between the despotic policies of Louis XIV and the 'falsely humanitarian' ones of the Convention. Whether under Bourbon rule or under the rule of the 'so-called human rights', France to them remained a power that crushed freedom, a power that destroyed the European equilibrium, a state that sought to meddle with the affairs and the peace of other nations. Evidently, the line of argument revolved around much more than a simple defence of the existing order; it was their own particular notion of order and liberty that the British counter-revolutionaries sought to defend.[18]

Most patriots held that the French Revolution marked the reconquest of universal human rights, and was not just a strictly national movement. This is why it is seen as a milestone in the process of the civilization and pacification of the relationship between peoples. Once all peoples would be free, the normal causes of war (such as the ambitions of kings and treacherous alliances) would have disappeared; humanity would then be able to focus on developing its full potential. In 1790, the Constituent Assembly articulated this hope in its famous decree of 22 May by which France solemnly renounced all wars of conquest. The subsequent French declaration of war on the King of Hungary (as the Holy Roman emperor was dismissively called) did not cancel out the objective of perpetual peace, but defined it differently. By fighting against despots and for the peoples, the French revolutionaries were convinced that they were working for a future peace in Europe, and improving the prospects for a 'federation of free peoples'. This idea was widespread, and was written about abundantly in the press, in pamphlets and speeches. In this sense, one can speak of a culture of peace in revolutionary France.

The Revolution was seen as inaugurating a new, non-aggressive world order founded on peace, the rights of nations and universal trade. But what kind of peace, what rights for nations? From 1713 until 1795, addressing the question of how these relations between nations should be organized legally, Enlightenment thinkers outlined their different ideas on France's future foreign policy. A first model aimed to build a national power capable of defending its own interests in a political environment of independent nations, who held in common a positive right of peoples. A second model, characterized by Marc Belissa as an international polity of peoples' rights, aspired to construct a civic and federal society of nations that would guarantee the rights of peoples universally.[19] Thus a model of universal brotherhood was opposed to national power politics in the political debate of the eighteenth century, which during the French Revolution found its expression in a project emphasizing the reciprocity of the rights of peoples. This is of course a simplified sketch of these two principal models, as the actual positions of the leading revolutionary figures were constantly evolving and being reconstructed. The Girondists, for example, aimed to reconstruct the European and world orders around an Anglo–French axis, the leitmotiv of their external policy. The idea of some division of the world between the two free powers of Europe was found in certain political projects, entailing the dismemberment of the Spanish Empire. Other revolutionaries hoped to construct a federation of free peoples, together with Switzerland, Belgium and the United States of America.

Obviously, on all sides, these concepts of world order had implications for how war was fought. As we have noted, for the French, foreign peoples were not prima facie enemies, provided that they did not collaborate with their despots, but potential allies. Yet the actual encounter with them showed that they were often less enthusiastic about joining the French revolutionaries and imitating France than had been expected. In Belgium in 1793, and after 1795 in the 'sister republics' (including the Batavian, Swiss and Cisalpine republics), the *Grande Nation* absorbed other peoples; it was no longer a question of forming federations in which the respective rights of distinct nations would be guaranteed, but of constructing a French Europe in which the other minority peoples would prosper under the benevolent tutelage of the French Republic. Similarly, between 1792 and 1793, the Girondist hope for a Franco–British alliance led to secret diplomatic efforts alongside war efforts, accommodating London's wishes. This Girondist policy was in turn vigorously opposed by Robespierre.

These concepts of revolutionary war implied changes in the observance of the law of war (*ius in bello*) as it had been practised under the *ancien régime*, despite several points of continuity (exchanges of prisoners continued, the same definitions of combatants and non-combatants were applied to external wars, and war taxes both in money and in kind were collected as before 1789). These continuities are best explained by the technical requirements of war, and the fact that most officers had learned their skills in the wars of the *ancien régime*. None the less, new elements appeared: the Convention pledged to grant French citizenship to foreign deserters who joined the camp of freedom; patriotic refugees were organized into units; the abolition of privateering, a form of naval warfare, and the proclamation of a new law of war were discussed in the Assembly. Above all, the already alluded-to decree of the 7 Prairial of Year II, prohibiting the taking of English and Hanoverian prisoners, marks a departure from previous practice. The significance and extent of application of this decree remains the subject of much historical debate, but its very existence shows that revolutionary war was practised (and conceived) differently from the previous wars of the monarchs.

Although war was perceived by both camps as a struggle unto death between two value systems and two different concepts of world order, this did not necessarily mean that the two sides could never come to an arrangement. This is evident in the treaties of Bâle or Lunéville with Prussia and Austria. Meanwhile the fight against Britain was seen as different in nature. In most French discourses, England was described as a special enemy. Following the failure of the Girondist attempts to come to an agreement with Britain, London became the new Carthage that would have to be destroyed. From the British perspective, the fight against France became more of a national cause, influenced by an increasingly victorious France after 1795; even radical British supporters of the French Revolution saw themselves as obliged to support their government against the threat of invasion. Bonaparte's rise to power would reinforce the consensus in Britain on the fight against France.

Conclusion

For all belligerents, the revolutionary wars thus inherited certain characteristics of former conflicts. For each of them, the wars were about establishing or re-establishing the European order they wanted or at least one that would allow them to continue to exist. It was the new features of these wars, however, which made them a turning point in European history. For the French more than for their adversaries, the revolutionary wars were extremely complex and cannot be described summarily as mere interstate conflicts. A political and ideological struggle which took place on numerous fronts, with objectives varying, depending on the governments, these wars aimed to perpetuate the new regime and to establish an enduring peace in Europe.

Notes

1 F. Brunel, *Thermidor*, Brussels, Complexe, 1989; F. Gauthier, *Triomphe et mort du droit naturel en révolution*, Paris, PUF, 1992; J. Y. Guiomar, 'Le nationalisme face à la démocratie', in A. de Baecque (ed.), *Une histoire de la démocratie en Europe*, Paris, Le Monde, 1990; M. Belissa, *Fraternité Universelle et Intérêt national (1713–1795). Les cosmopolitiques du droit des gens*, Paris, Kimé, 1998.

2 A. Soboul, *Nation, patrie, nationalisme*, Actes du colloque de Moscou 1970, Paris, Société des Études robespierristes, 1975, p. 6.

3 Belissa, *Fraternité Universelle et Intérêt national*, p. 213, *passim*.

4 S. Wahnich, 'Anglais', in *Dictionnaire des usages socio-politiques, 1770–1815*, vol. 4, Paris, Klincksieck, 1989, pp. 35–63.

5 *Archives Parlementaires*, vol. 15, p. 177.

6 W. Cobbett, *Parliamentary History of England*, London, 1806–20, vol. 30, p. 81.

7 Belissa, *Fraternité Universelle et Intérêt national*, Part I.

8 L. Colley, *Britons. Forging the Nation 1707–1837*, New Haven, CT, Yale University Press, 1992; O. Dann and J. Dinwiddy (eds), *Nationalism in the Age of the French Revolution*, London, Ronceverte, 1988.

9 J.-P. Bertaud and D. Reichel, *Atlas de la Révolution française, vol. 3: l'armée et la guerre*, Paris, EHESS, 1989; J.-P. Bertaud, *Guerre et société en France de Louis XIV à Napoléon Ier*, Paris, A. Colin, 1998.

10 M. Belissa and S. Wahnich, 'Trahir le droit, les crimes des Anglais', *Annales historiques de la Révolution française*, 1995, no. 2, pp. 233–48.

11 'Discours sur les dangers de la patrie, avec les moyens de la sauver, de récupérer les frais de guerre, et de proclamer la liberté, la paix et la république universelle', *Bibliothèque nationale*, 8° Lb 41, no. 785.

12 Idem.

13 The speeches made in the popular societies and the administrative corps in the Assembly, the patriotic and royalist press, printed speeches, brochures and individual accounts converge to underpin this idea.

14 'What does this horde or slaves / of traitors, of perjured kings want? / For whom are these despicable shackles, / these irons, prepared long ago? / For us, Frenchmen! Oh what an outrage! / What outbursts of fury they should provoke! / It is us they are trying / to subject to ancient slavery!'

15 Belissa, *Fraternité Universelle et Intérêt national*, p. 288.

16 E. Burke, *Works*, London, 1854–55, vol. 3, pp. 395–409.

17 'Dépêche adressée au cabinet de Vienne par le comte Mercy-Argenteau', in *Correspondance du comte de Mirabeau et du comte de La Marck*, vol. 3, Paris, 1851, p. 348.

18 M. Belissa, 'Les stratégies de la contre-révolution: le débat sur la guerre au Parlement anglais', in *Actes du colloque de Cholet 1999* (forthcoming).

19 Belissa, *Fraternité Universelle et Intérêt national*, *passim*.

16 From *Volkskrieg* to *Vernichtungskrieg*
German concepts of warfare, 1871–1935

Robert T. Foley

Seventeen years after the German defeat in the First World War, Erich Ludendorff published a work of theory mapping out how Germany must fight the next war entitled *Der totale Krieg* [*Total War*].[1] In his book, a summation of the lessons of the First World War, Ludendorff rejected the teachings of Carl von Clausewitz, asserting that Clausewitz' magnum opus, *On War* 'belongs to a past development of history which has now been entirely superseded'. While he admitted that Clausewitz' teachings had served as a useful theoretical tool in the past, the ageing warrior believed that the nature of warfare had altered fundamentally during the First World War:

> The First World War was of a completely different character from the wars of the past 150 years. In this war, not only the armed forces of the participating states . . . but the peoples themselves were enlisted in the service of the war. The war was directed against the populations themselves, who thus became deeply involved . . . the struggle was carried out against the spirit [*Psyche*] and vital force of the enemy populations with the goal of dissolving and paralysing them. Thus, total war was born; war which is not only the concern of the armed forces but also directly touches upon the life and soul of every single member of the belligerent populations.[2]

To Ludendorff, with the First World War, war ceased to be one of army versus army; instead, it was one of nation versus nation.

As the nature of warfare had fundamentally changed, so too had the way in which wars were conducted. 'Total war' was war waged on all levels. Accordingly, the entire resources of the nation, both human and material, had to be exploited for war. Ludendorff advocated that the economy be adapted to supply the military efficiently. At the same time, the will of the people was to be shaped and harnessed through the use of propaganda. Ludendorff wrote that total war required a single leader, in his view a soldier, who could integrate effectively the various elements of total war – the armed forces, the economic resources and the propaganda effort – and who possessed the necessary strength of will to make the difficult decisions demanded in wartime. Importantly, Ludendorff wrote that the preparation for total war had to begin before the outbreak of hostilities. Conversely, while Germany's resources were being exploited to the fullest, the enemy's resources had to be diminished. Not only were the enemy's armed forces to be engaged in battle, but all his resources, both human and material, were to be attacked.

Moreover, as the methods of warfare changed, so too did the goals. While Clausewitz might have spoken primarily of annihilating the enemy's armed forces, Ludendorff now wrote of annihilating the enemy nation itself:

> In a total war, action follows action, battle follows battle, perhaps broken by shorter or longer pauses to reorganize strength; perhaps also the war degenerates again into trench warfare [*Stellungskrieg*] with long, extended fronts that cannot be moved and cannot be outflanked until finally the war reaches its end, in this case *not through the destruction of the enemy's armed forces, but rather through the collapse of the enemy's people.*[3]

It was only a small step from the ideas adumbrated by Ludendorff in his *Total War* to the '*Vernichtungskrieg*', or 'war of annihilation', waged so remorselessly by the Nazis in the Soviet Union in the Second World War,[4] and, indeed, many of Ludendorff's ideas appeared in the writings of fellow officers in the interwar period.[5] At the same time, however, Ludendorff's ideas were also firmly rooted in German military thought from the period before the First World War. Indeed, many of his ideas were restatements of those of fellow Wilhelmine officers. Ludendorff's concept of 'total war' and the 'war of annihilation' waged on the eastern front between 1941 and 1945 had their intellectual antecedents in the attempt by German officers before 1914 to interpret how the advent of '*Volkskrieg*', or 'people's war', would effect the conduct of war.

However, the First World War did not approach the level of intensity of the Second. Despite the important similarities between Ludendorff's ideas and the ideas of the pre-1914 period, there were equally important differences, both conceptual and practical, which meant that Germany could not wage a 'total war' in 1914 along the lines sketched by Ludendorff in 1935. The remainder of this chapter will examine some of the reasons why the *Kaiserheer* was not prepared to fight a 'war of annihilation' in 1914, while the *Wehrmacht* was in 1939, despite sharing many similar concepts of warfare.

*

While the military intellectuals of the Weimar Republic used the First World War as the basis for their discussions about warfare, naturally the military authors of the *Kaiserreich* made use of their most recent experience of war – the Franco–German War of 1870–71.[6] While this conflict is normally viewed even today as a model of a swift, decisive war, in fact it gave Germans an unpleasant taste of the difficulties inherent in defeating a 'nation' mobilized for war and committed to resistance. The two phases of the struggle offered German military intellectuals two separate models of war: the first, a war comprised of one or two campaigns resulting in the annihilation of the enemy's armed forces, followed by a dictated, if generally limited, peace. The second, a long, drawn-out conflict made up of perhaps several large but indecisive battles, but also of many small-scale engagements that drew upon and sapped the resources of the entire nation.

In the war's first phase, the German armies had been able to defeat spectacularly the armed forces of Napoleon III in the space of only six weeks. In two great battles, Sedan and Metz, the imperial army was anni-hilated and Napoleon taken prisoner.[7] It was upon this phase that most German intellectuals tended to focus, and the events thereof provided support for the concept of a short war that played such a role in pre-1914 German military thought.[8]

However, it was the war's second phase, which received far less atten-tion from German officers and historians, that was to prove far more indicative of the future. Further, it was this phase – the so-called *Volkskrieg* – that would serve as the basis for several German authors' concepts of warfare, concepts which would be echoed by Ludendorff sixty-five years later.

The *Volkskrieg* began with the formation of the Government of National Defence on 4 September 1870, which brought about the French Third Republic in the wake of Napoleon's surrender. This new government immediately determined to continue the war, responding to German peace conditions, which included the demand for the annexation of Alsace/Lorraine, with a call for a *guerre à outrance*. Recalling the ideals of the French Revolution, in October and November, the French government issued decrees designed to rebuild the crippled French army and to mobi-lize the French people for war. In an effort to create a 'nation-in-arms', the French government resorted to measures which would become familiar in the twentieth century. Bridges, railways and telegraphs were to be destroyed before being allowed to fall into enemy hands, and any portable material was to be evacuated from areas threatened by German occupa-tion. A *levée en masse* was declared on 2 November, obliging all able-bodied men between the ages of 21 and 40 for service. Under the direction of the particularly energetic Minister of the Interior, Léon Gambetta, the new republic was able to double the size of its armies in the field from around 500,000 men in September 1870 to over 950,000 by February 1871.[9] Further, the Government of National Defence encouraged parti-sans, the so-called *franc-tireurs*, to bring the 'war of the knife' to the German rear areas and supply columns.

Although they were unable to meet the professional German armies on equal terms, the inexperienced and ill-trained improvised armies of France none the less proved a troublesome foe to the Germans. While a large portion of the German field army was occupied with the investment of Paris, the remainder was forced to hunt down the newly raised French forces. Further, large numbers of soldiers (one for every four soldiers of the field army) were tied down guarding the German lines of communication from partisan attacks.[10] Although the Germans won a series of battles, the results proved indecisive; so long as Paris stood defiant, the French government refused to conclude peace.

French intransigence exacerbated Helmuth Graf von Moltke, the German Chief of the General Staff and *de facto* director of Germany's military effort. By December, the frustrated Moltke had begun making preparations for a long war, which would 'settle unilaterally a 100-year-old rivalry.'[11] Moltke was convinced that Germany would be forced to wage an '*Exterminationskrieg*', aimed at destroying the resources of the French nation, and hence its ability to resist.[12] Even after the fall of Paris, Moltke insisted that France had to be completely occupied. On 8 January, he declared to the Prussian Crown Prince: '[w]e must fight this nation of liars to the very end! Then we can dictate whatever peace we like.'[13]

Indeed, the bitterness felt by Moltke was also felt on the battlefield and was reflected in the way in which the war was prosecuted by both sides. Although the conflict might not have reached the intensity of the American Civil War, it was marked by acts of extreme violence committed by both belligerents.[14] A spiral of violence began with each side matching the other's actions. When *franc-tireurs* sniped at German columns passing a village or ambushed an isolated German force on orders from the German high command, the German soldiers took revenge.[15] This phase of the war created a deep animosity between the two countries that was felt even by German civilians,[16] and did much to reinforce for Germans images of the French that were maintained until the next Franco–German war over forty years later.

At all levels, the Germans felt justified in their actions. At the top, Moltke believed that the French government was behaving in a criminal manner by encouraging the French people to carry on what was obviously a lost cause.[17] In the field, the acts of the *franc-tireurs* caused the German officers to excuse the excesses of their men. After one bloody reprisal a young Bavarian officer, Friedrich Koch-Breuberg, recorded his thoughts in a passage that captures the feeling of outrage and bitterness felt by the Germans:

> The rage of the soldiers in Bazeille was such . . . that everything that happened there must be excused. Those who escaped honest battle with their lives were threatened with treacherous murder; those who fell wounded could expect that a hate filled woman or farmer would send them to kingdom come in a hideous way. The Bavarian soldiers were completely justified in seizing equally cruel counter-measures.[18]

Indeed, not only did the Germans feel justified in taking these counter-measures, but some saw them as a means by which the war could be brought more rapidly to an end. Thus, on 4 October, Alfred Graf von Waldersee, then aide-de-camp to Wilhelm I and later Chief of the General Staff, wrote in his diary:

> Our troops . . . have often to deal now with the armed peasants, the so-called *franc-tireurs*. . . . Severe measures are needed and are often applied. We have recourse to terrorising to nip this evil in the bud, or things can be made very uncomfortable for us. In regard to this point, I am in disagreement with otherwise very sensible people who keep advising mildness and who complain that the war is being conducted in too dreadful a manner. As war is essentially the most dreadful and ruthless thing imaginable, therefore one's object should be so to conduct it as to bring it to an end at the earliest possible moment, and to this end one should give the enemy a distaste for it as quickly as one can.[19]

The second phase of the German–French War was recognized by observers to have been different in its character from previous wars.[20] Moltke himself labelled this phase a '*Volkskrieg*', and wrote that a shift had taken place in warfare:

> The days are gone by when, for dynastical ends, small armies of professional soldiers went to war to conquer a city, or a province, and then sought winter quarters or made peace. The wars of the present day call whole nations to arms. . . . The entire financial resources of the State are appropriated to military purposes.[21]

Moltke feared this shift and was never quite able to reconcile this new type of warfare with his traditional approach. Thus, in his plans for war after 1871, 'two tendencies battled one another: the hope for a new Königgrätz and the fear of a new Loire campaign'.[22] By the end of his career, Moltke had become so concerned by the phenomenon that he warned that the next conflict might turn into another Thirty Years' War.[23]

Moltke's definition of 'people's war' was picked up and elaborated by a young member of his staff, Colmar Freiherr von der Goltz. Goltz began developing his ideas about *Volkskrieg* while working on the General Staff history of the war, and the research he undertook then served as the basis for a number of works, both historical and theoretical, which were designed to improve the German army's ability to fight a future *Volkskrieg*.[24]

The first of these works was *Leon Gambetta and His Armies*, originally serialized in the influential journal *Preußische Jahrbücher* in 1874.[25] While Goltz clearly recognized the limitations of the improvised armies of the French Republic, he was full of praise for the achievements of the Government of National Defence. To Goltz, the fact that France could reconstitute armies after suffering such a crushing defeat in the field showed the power of a modern nation under a determined and motivated leader. Moreover, Goltz believed the second phase of the German–French War had served as a warning of what a future war would be like. Germany ignored that warning at its peril.

In *Leon Gambetta and His Armies*, Goltz advocated a number of reforms that could improve Germany's ability to fight a future people's war, many of which would be repeated in 1935 by Ludendorff. First, Goltz wanted German reserve officers to receive better training and to be better integrated into German war planning. He believed that a more professional reserve officer corps meant that reserve formations would be able to fight more efficiently and in a wider range of roles. Aware of Germany's manpower shortages in 1870 to 1871, Goltz also believed that conscription should be applied more rigorously in the new Reich. To do this, he argued that Germany should reduce the time of active service demanded of new recruits from three to two years. In order to help ease the way for extended conscription, Goltz also proposed that young Germans be prepared for service by programmes run by schools and youth organizations. By preparing thoroughly in peacetime, Goltz hoped to avoid the improvised nature of Gambetta's armies, and hence make Germany capable of fighting a *Volkskrieg* more effectively than the French had in 1870 to 1871.

In a series of books published throughout his long career, Goltz ceaselessly advocated his ideas for preparing Germany for the next war. With *The Nation in Arms*, a book that has recently been called 'the most significant work of military theory from Wilhelmine Germany',[26] Goltz created a work of theory to support his historical writings,[27] and his ideas finally reached a broad audience. In this work, he looked back constantly to the *Volkskrieg* of 1870 to 1871 for his model for the future. Goltz believed that wars could no longer be won with a few great battles or a few campaigns and that a future war would pit nation against nation. This being so, Goltz believed that it might be necessary to 'flood a country with troops and to exert extreme pressure upon the population for years on end'.[28] In extreme cases, he felt a prolonged resistance might necessitate the 'occupation of the whole country and the cutting off of its communication with the outside world'.[29]

Both Moltke and Goltz equated the concept of 'people's war' with a 'nation-in-arms', i.e. they both saw the ability of France to mobilize the resources of the entire nation in 1870 to 1871 as a different form of warfare that had to be met in kind. Both felt that the next war would be fought between states employing the entire resources of the nation. Thus, the next war would not be one of France versus Germany, but rather one of the French versus the Germans, a war that might drag on for years and a war that would only end when one side had exhausted its resources.

Two aspects were prominent in Moltke's and Goltz' ideas about how a future 'people's war' was to be waged. First, the war was to be won by employing one's resources more efficiently. Second, the war was to be taken to the enemy's territory, thus denying him the resources of the occupied territory.

Moltke's pessimism and Goltz' ideas about how Germany had to prepare for future war were at first not widely accepted by their colleagues. In addition to providing for a model of a decisive war, the war of 1870 to 1871 allowed different interpretations of the French *Volkskrieg*, which helped prevent the *Kaiserheer* from being prepared to fight a 'total war' in 1914. While Moltke and Goltz defined *Volkskrieg* as the ability of a nation to mobilize its resources, to others the term was synonymous with the previously developed concept of '*Kleiner Krieg*', or 'small war'.[30] This interpretation rejected the idea that a change in the nature of warfare had occurred, and thus no special changes in approach to future warfare were necessary. This being so, most agreed that a future *Volkskrieg* could be countered by conventional means.

To these authors, the German difficulties in defeating the French Republic in 1870 to 1871 could be explained by German failures, rather than French successes. For example, Fritz Hoenig, a retired captain who had served through the Franco–German War, published a work on the *Volkskrieg* in which he argued that it could have been prevented had the German higher commands not underestimated the threat of the new French armies.[31] Another retired officer, Georg Cardinal von Widdern, held a similar view. The lesson he drew in his *The War on the Rearward Communications of the German Army and the Etappendienst* was that the German army did not react forcefully enough to the partisan threat when it first materialized. Had they reacted quickly and with great severity, Cardinal believed that the French would have realized how costly a long campaign would really be and would have given up quickly.[32]

Regardless of how the *Volkskrieg* was interpreted, the Franco–German War had convinced most German soldiers that France was Germany's implacable enemy and that another war was inevitable at some point in the future. To them, the end of the war had not solved the Franco–German rivalry; it had merely set the scene for the next conflict.[33] To these officers, France would have to be dealt with once and for all in order for Germany to gain her rightful status as continental Europe's pre-eminent power. Thus in 1909, Alfred von Schlieffen, who had served until 1906 as Chief of the General Staff, could write in his influential article, 'War today', that 'the Peace of Frankfurt brought about the end of the struggle between Germany and France in appearance only. If their arms remain laid down, a latent war still continues.'[34]

The interpretation that the second phase of the Franco–German War could have been avoided if proper measures had been taken in good time reinforced the idea common among German officers – the next conflict against France could be won quickly. While France alone was the enemy, most officers felt the German army could master the threat without having to fundamentally rethink their approach to war.

However, beginning in the 1890s Germany's strategic situation began to worsen, largely due to German diplomatic manoeuvring. In 1892, France and Russia signed an alliance pledging assistance in case of war. Germany now faced a two-front war, and the fear of being encircled by enemies gripped the German military. All observers could see that Germany now faced enemies overwhelmingly superior in numbers. Paradoxically, this fear of '*Einkreisung*' led to renewed calls for preventive war from the German military establishment, rather than for a lessening of international tensions.[35] The worldview of German soldiers continued to be influenced by ideas of Social Darwinism. To them, if Germany failed to expand her power, she would eventually be consumed by a stronger power. By 1910, German soldiers had become convinced that a war would have to be fought before Russia had completed her massive armament programme (believed to be scheduled for around 1917) or else Germany would have no chance of victory. Thus, they did everything in their power to engineer an appropriate *casus belli*.[36]

While earlier a smaller but highly trained army might have been all that was needed to defeat France alone, now that France was allied with Russia and most likely with Great Britain too, Germany clearly needed a larger army. This recognition caused a growing number within the German army to embrace the concept of a 'nation-in-arms'. However, two factors prevented this concept of 'nation-in-arms' being taken to its logical conclusion of 'total war'. The first of these was resistance to army expansion with its more rigorous application of conscription from conservative elements in the army and the government. While the pressure to enlarge the army came mainly from the body charged with war planning, the General Staff, resistance came from those in the army who held a somewhat different view of Germany's enemies from that of the General Staff. To many in the Wilhelmine army, most notably those in the Ministry of War, the threat to Germany came as much from elements within the Reich as from external enemies. They believed the army needed to be kept free of these elements, namely socialists and democrats, in order that the army could continue to support the current regime and current social make-up of Germany.[37] The universal conscription and short terms of service needed for the creation of a 'nation-in-arms' had long been the goals of the Left in Germany.[38] Thus, to many conservatives, the adoption of these steps would be a capitulation to democratic forces. Further, many believed that universal conscription would bring too many undesirable elements into the army, thus reducing its effectiveness and, more importantly, political reliability.[39]

The second factor stopping the concept of 'people's war' becoming 'total war' came from the beliefs of those now calling for army expansion. The

General Staff, with a young Erich Ludendorff at the head of its Operations Section, believed that Germany could not win a prolonged conflict against the entente.[40] Thus, the army increases they demanded fitted their plans for a short war.[41] The increases were designed to create the number of units necessary to carry out its plan to destroy the French army in a rapid campaign. In order to accomplish this they needed to put the largest number of men into the field at the war's outbreak as possible. Thus, although the General Staff were prepared to use the tool of a 'people's war' – a 'nation-in-arms' – they were not yet prepared to take the idea any further.

It took four years of bloody combat and a revolution for German soldiers to go from their idea of 'people's war' to Ludendorff's concept of 'total war'. As the war stretched on beyond its anticipated duration, German soldiers were surprised by the resilience not only of their enemies but their own nation. The German economy did not totally collapse and industrial workers and city dwellers had proved themselves to be reliable, effective soldiers. The war demonstrated to them that, contrary to pre-war prophecies, modern nations could adapt to fight a long war. For Germany, this adaptation meant a *de facto* change in government, as a military dictatorship under Hindenburg and Ludendorff increasingly took over Germany's war effort from the traditional elites from August 1916. This team attempted, as never before, to harness German resources, including an effort to conscript all able-bodied Germans for the army or war-related industries. However, with fewer resources than the entente, Germany was bound to lose what had become a war of attrition. To Ludendorff and many other Germans, the attempt to harness Germany's resources in the First World War had begun too late; by 1916, Germany had lost too many good men and had squandered too many resources inefficiently. Ludendorff's *Total War* must be seen as an attempt to prevent such an occurrence in a future war by preparing for the next war, that would surely be a 'total war', before it was too late and to teach how such a war should be fought. In 1930s' Germany, Ludendorff's ideas would find fertile ground in which to grow.

Notes

1 As head of the Operations Section of the *Grosser Generalstab* between 1908 and 1912, Erich Ludendorff had played a crucial role in German strategic planning before the First World War. During the war, he served as the intellectual component in the Hindenburg–Ludendorff team, which functioned as the command element on the northern section of the eastern front (*Oberbefehlshaber Ost*) from 1914 to 1916 and then as the directors of Germany's war effort as the Third *Oberste Heeresleitung* from 1916 to 1918. For a detailed biography, see F. Uhle-Wettler, *Erich Ludendorff in seiner Zeit*, Berg, Kurt Vornwinckel Verlag, 1995.
2 E. Ludendorff, *Der totale Krieg*, Munich, Ludendorff's Verlag, gmbh, 1935, pp. 4–5. Although Ludendorff claimed that he did not intend to write a 'theory of war' (p. 3), this book was clearly meant to serve as a guide from which

German officers should learn. *Der totale Krieg* must be seen as the culmination of ideas introduced in his *Kriegserinnerungen 1914–1918*, Berlin, Mittler, 1919, and *Kriegführung und Politik*, Berlin, Mittler, 1921.

3 Ludendorff, *Der totale Krieg*, p.100, emphasis added.

4 Cf. H. Speier, 'Ludendorff: the German concept of total war', in E. Mead Earle (ed.), *Makers of Modern Strategy: Military Thought from Machiavelli to Hitler*, Princeton, NJ, Princeton University Press, 1943, repr. 1971, pp. 306–21.

5 See W. Deist, 'Die Reichswehr und der Krieg der Zukunft', *Militärgeschichtliche Mitteilungen*, 1988, vol. 45, pp. 81–92.

6 I deliberately use the term 'Franco–German War' rather than the more common English, 'Franco–Prussian War', because this was the term used for the conflict in the new German Reich. To the new 'German' elite, this name symbolized the unifying nature of the war.

7 M. Howard, *The Franco–Prussian War: The German Invasion of France, 1870–1871*, London, Rupert Hart-Davis, 1961, pp. 167–223.

8 This fixation on a short war has received much attention. For an introduction, see J. Wallach, *The Dogma of the Battle of Annihilation: The Theories of Clausewitz and Schlieffen and Their Impact on the German Conduct of Two World Wars*, Westport, CT, Greenwood, 1986; and L. L. Farrar Jr., *The Short-War Illusion: German Policy and Domestic Affairs, August–December 1914*, Santa Barbara, CA, ABC-Clio, 1973.

9 W. Serman, 'French mobilization in 1870', in S. Förster and J. Nagler (eds), *On the Road to Total War: The American Civil War and the German Wars of Unification, 1861–1871*, Cambridge, Cambridge University Press, 1997, pp. 289–94; and Howard, *Franco–Prussian War*, pp. 233–56.

10 Over 100,000 troops were detailed to guard the lines of communication through which the supplies for Germany's 450,000-man field army came. G. Cardinal von Widdern, *Der Krieg an den rückwärtigen Verbindungen der deutschen Heer und der Etappendienst*, vol. 1, Berlin, Eisenschmidt, 1893, pp. iv–v.

11 R. Stadelmann, *Moltke und der Staat*, Krefeld, Scherpe, 1950, p. 280. On German mobilization and manpower problems, see P. Bronsart von Schellendorf, *Geheimes Kriegstagebuch, 1870–1871*, ed. P. Rassow, Bonn, Athenäum-Verlag, 1954; and G. Lehmann, *Die Mobilmachung von 1870/71*, Berlin, Mittler, 1905.

12 Kaiser Friedrich III, *Das Kriegstagebuch von 1870–1*, ed. H. O. Meissner, Berlin, Mittler, 1926, p. 325.

13 Recorded by Grand Duke Friedrich of Baden in his diary. H. Onken, *Grossherzog Friedrich I von Baden und die deutsche Politik von 1854–1871*, vol. 2, Stuttgart, Deutsche Verlags-Anstalt, 1927, p. 300f. Cf. Kaiser Friedrich, *Kriegstagebuch*, p. 253.

14 An American observer and veteran of the Civil War, General Philip Sheridan commented that 'the [French] people must be left with nothing but their eyes to weep with over the war'. Quoted in Howard, *Franco–Prussian War*, p. 380. Cf. A. Graf von Waldersee, *A Field-Marshal's Memoirs*, trans. F. Whyte, London, Hutchinson, 1924, p. 75.

15 Grosser Generalstab, *Der deutsch–französische Krieg, 1870–1*, vol. 2, Berlin, Mittler, 1875, App. CXII; Howard, *Franco–Prussian War*, p. 378f.

16 Even Bismarck's wife believed that the French should be 'shot and stabbed to death down to the little babies'. M. Busch, *Bismarck: Some Secret Pages from his History*, vol. 1, London, Macmillan, 1898, p. 273.

17 E. Kessel, *Moltke*, Stuttgart, K. F. Koehler, 1957, p. 575ff.

18 Quoted in M. Messerschmidt, 'The Prussian army from reform to war', in Förster and Nagler, *Total War*, p. 279.

19 Waldersee, *Memoirs*, p. 74f.

20 For the development of the concept of *Volkskrieg* in German military thought before 1914, see R. T. Foley, *Attrition: Its Theory and Application in German Strategy, 1880–1916*, University of London, Ph.D. thesis, 1999, pp. 14–34 and *passim*.

21   H. Graf von Moltke, *The Franco–Prussian War of 1870–71*, trans. A. Forbes, London, Harpers, 1907, p. 1.
22   Stadelmann, *Moltke*, p. 325. Cf. S. Förster, 'Facing people's war: Moltke the Elder and German military options after 1871', *Journal of Strategic Studies*, 1987, vol. 10, no. 2, pp. 209–30; G. Ritter, *The Sword and the Scepter*, vol. 1: *The Prussian Tradition, 1740–1890*, trans. H. Norden, Coral Gables, FL, University of Miami Press, 1969, pp. 230ff.
23   He gave this oft-quoted warning during his last speech to the Reichstag on 14 May 1890. Förster, 'Facing people's war', p. 223f.
24   On Goltz' long and varied career, see H. Teske, *Colmar Freiherr von der Goltz. Ein Kämpfer für den militärischen Fortschritt*, Göttingen, Musterschmidt, 1957.
25   C. von der Goltz, 'Leon Gambetta und die Loirearmée', *Preußische Jahrbücher* Bd 34, 1874. This work was later published as *Leon Gambetta und seine Armeen*, Berlin, F. Schneider, 1877.
26   G. Krumeich, 'The myth of Leon Gambetta and the "people's war" in France, 1871–1914', in Förster and Nagler, *Total War*, p. 646.
27   C. von der Goltz, *Das Volk in Waffen: Ein Buch über Heerwesen und Kriegführung unserer Zeit*, Berlin, R. von Decker's Verlag, 1883. In addition to going through five editions in Germany before the war and a sixth after, this book was widely translated.
28   C. von der Goltz, *The Nation in Arms*, trans. Ph. Ashworth, London, Hugh Rees, 1906, p. 465. This was based on the fifth German edition (1898).
29   Ibid., p. 486.
30   This concept covered actions outside of a general war, what would be called today 'low-intensity conflict'.
31   F. Hoenig, *Der Volkskrieg an der Loire im Herbst 1870*, 6 vols, Berlin, Mittler, 1893–99. On Hoenig's career and writings, see J. Hoffmann, 'Der Militärschriftsteller Fritz Hoenig', *Militärgeschichtliche Mitteilungen* 1970, 1/70, pp. 5–25.
32   See n. 10 above.
33   German sources from before 1914 are full of references to the forthcoming show-down. See A. J. Echevarria, 'On the brink of the abyss: the warrior identity and German military thought before the Great War', *War and Society*, 1995, vol. 13, no. 2, pp. 23–40.
34   A. Graf von Schlieffen, 'Der Krieg in der Gegenwart', *Cannae*, Berlin, Mittler, 1925, p. 273 (originally published in *Deutsche Revue*, January 1909). For an English translation see R. T. Foley (ed.), *Schlieffen's Military Writings*, London, Frank Cass & Co., 2001. Kaiser Wilhelm II ordered that copies of Schlieffen's article be distributed and read to all commands.
35   The idea of a preventive war had often been mooted by German soldiers between 1871 and 1914. Moltke the Elder first raised the issue shortly after the Franco–German War, once it became apparent that France was quickly regaining her military strength. M. Jähns, *Feldmarschall Moltke*, Berlin, Ernst Hoffmann, 1894, pp. 572ff. W. Kloster, *Der deutsche Generalstab und der Präventivkrieggedanke*, Stuttgart, Philanthropia, 1932.
36   See D. Stevenson, *The Armaments and the Coming of War: Europe, 1904–1914*, Oxford, Clarendon Press, 1996, pp. 149ff. A. Mombauer, 'Helmuth von Moltke and the German General Staff – military and political decision-making in imperial Germany, 1906–1916', MS D. Phil. thesis, University of Sussex, 1997.
37   See B. Schulte, *Die deutsche Armee, 1900–1914. Zwischen Beharren und Verändern*, Düsseldorf, Droste Vertag, 1977.
38   N. Stargardt, *The German Idea of Militarism: Radical and Socialist Critics 1866–1914*, Cambridge and New York, Cambridge University Press, 1994, p. 50ff.
39   On the question of army expansion and conservative opposition, see S. Förster,

Der Doppelte Militarismus: Die deutsche Heeresrüstungspolitik zwischen Status-quo-Sicherung und Aggression 1890–1913, Stuttgart, Franz Steiner, 1985.

40 The ideas expressed by Schlieffen in his 'Der Krieg in der Gegenwart' are representative of the General Staff's views before 1914.

41 Despite growing fears that the next conflict might indeed drag on, the General Staff did not alter its plans for a short war. See S. Förster, 'Der deutsche Generalstab und die Illusion des kurzen Krieges, 1871–1914', *Militärgeschichtliche Mitteilungen*, 1995, vol. 54, pp. 61–95.

17 Enemy image and identity in the Warsaw Pact

Michael Ploetz

Mentality

During the Cold War, the mercantile and generally rather peaceable societies of the West found themselves engaged in a protracted conflict with an adversary whose mentality was shaped by an entirely different set of values. Frequently, western decision-makers and political scientists found it quite difficult and even tedious to understand the strange mindset of their communist opponents. During the Vietnam War, for instance, the sophisticated inhabitants of Robert McNamara's Pentagon found it more worthwhile to listen to their own 'scientific' monologues than to analyse the strategy and mentality of the Vietnamese communists.[1] Similarly, the strategic concepts of the Warsaw Pact were often not analysed as an intellectual system in their own right but translated into the familiar and comforting terms of western strategic thought. In his plea for arms control, Hedley Bull did not treat the USSR as a distinct polity with a gruesome record of internal and external violence but rather as some sort of nineteenth-century European state not too dissimilar to the USA.[2]

During the heyday of *détente*, this kind of intellectual ethnocentricity dominated the political discourse in the West. The American Sovietologist Richard Pipes was certainly the most influential critic of this train of thought. Although it should have been self-evident that the terms war, peace and *détente* had distinct meaning in the minds of middle-class Americans from that held by people who owed the rapid ascent of their political careers to their participation in Stalin's crimes,[3] even today Pipes continues to be heavily criticized for his alleged role in unleashing the second Cold War. Yet typically, there seems to be more interest in the patterns of Pipe's discourse than in his findings, as checked against available evidence.[4] By 1981, the exiled Russian historians Mikhail Heller and Alexander Nekrich had already reached similar conclusions to Pipes about the expansionist tendencies of the Soviet system and the Soviet meaning of the word *détente*.[5] The opening of the East German archives in the wake of German reunification has again confirmed Heller's, Nekrich's and Pipe's assessment of Marxist–Leninist intentions. Since the archival evidence is not dramatically different to what the leaders of the Warsaw Pact publicly declared to be their aims, the formerly classified documents provide corroboration of all earlier research that was based on open sources. Furthermore, sophisticated theories were not needed to understand the mindset of the communist leaders: it was sufficient to learn their vocabulary and to take them at their word.

Marxism–Leninism and the continuation of war by other means

Their belief that they knew which course history would take was an important pillar of the self-esteem of the ruling Marxist–Leninists in Moscow and East Berlin. Their bellicose mentality derived from their faith in their historical mission. They saw themselves as an avant-garde destined to free mankind from war and exploitation by globally eradicating private property in the means of production. As late as 1976, East Germany's Communist Party (the SED) stated in an updated issue of its party programme:

> The change in the international correlation of forces in favour of Socialism, the increasing influence of the community of Socialist states on the historical development, the deepening general crisis of Capitalism, the increased class struggle against Imperialism, the national liberation movement, all this accelerates the revolutionary world process in the last quarter of our century. These events confirm our certainty that all countries on earth will inevitably reach Socialism and Communism.[6]

In order to establish the strictly egalitarian utopia of communist society, it was first necessary to defeat what the Communists used to call imperialism. Although imperialism was officially defined in quasi-sociological terms as the highest stage of bourgeois capitalism, the everyday usage of this term by Communist officials and leaders could hardly be called sociological. In November 1980, Erich Honecker, the leader of the SED, received a classified paper on foreign policy in which imperialism was called 'the main enemy of the human race'.[7] Confined in its circulation to the highest leadership level, this paper described 'war, military aggression, economic blackmail, and colonial plundering' as the distinctive and unalterable features of imperialism. Moreover, since imperialism was characteristically aggressive and warlike, it was only logical to conclude that *détente* and the East–West *rapprochement* of the 1970s had been forced on to this system by the growing military strength of the Warsaw Pact. Contrary to the 1930s, external constraints now prevented a crisis-ridden imperialism from taking recourse to fascism and war.[8] According to the conceptual framework of this paper, the two social systems could not simply co-exist as more or less disinterested neighbours. Instead, they were interlocked in a deadly zero-sum game in which the gains of the one side necessarily counted as losses for the other. Thus, strengthening socialism meant harming imperialism. In presupposing an unalterable enmity between the Warsaw Pact and the liberal democracies of the West, this policy paper only reiterated what Marxist–Leninists regarded as self-evident truth.[9] Peace between the two social systems could only be a truce in the form of non-aggression pacts.[10] Lenin himself had made it clear that a peaceful world could only be established by protracted class war:

> Only after we have thrown down, completely defeated and expropri-
> ated the bourgeoisie, not only in one country but throughout the world,
> will war become impossible. . . . The 'social' clerics and opportunists
> are eagerly anticipating a peaceful future world, but they distinguish
> themselves from revolutionary Social Democrats by the fact that they
> do not want to think about or attend to the bitter class struggles and
> class *wars* that are necessary to make such a bright future a reality.[11]

Ceasing the fight against imperialism was simply inconceivable for orthodox Marxist–Leninists. Moreover, the events of the 1970s strongly reinforced their belief in the eventual triumph of their cause. In January 1979, Boris Ponomarev, the head of the International Department of the CPSU, analysed the strategic situation:

> the Imperialist camp is neither on a global scale nor in the historical
> perspective on the offensive. Currently, a big campaign is launched
> against the Socialist community and the Communist parties precisely
> because the Socialist community has grown stronger. . . . While we
> are stronger, our foreign policies are more popular, the peoples know
> that we want peace, the Imperialist camp is being damaged.[12]

While seeking to free the human race of its 'main enemy', the Warsaw Pact pursued a grand strategy orchestrating military, political and propagandistic means. In the 1970s and early 1980s, the 'peace struggle' moved to the fore of this strategy. By inciting western grass-roots protests against nuclear armaments, the monolithic Warsaw Pact hoped to impose one-sided disarmament on an increasingly disunited NATO. Inevitably, the main target of the peace struggle were NATO's nuclear weapons. In December 1975, Erich Mielke, head of the East German Stasi, explained to his officers that in the long term 'military *détente*' was meant to prevent 'the Imperialists from being able to bring about a thermo-nuclear catastrophe. It is also about putting further constraints on Imperialism's freedom of action, on its aggressive impulse.'[13]

In this context, Mielke stressed that the revolutionary movements of the Third World could always rely on the unflinching support of the socialist states.[14] Mielke hoped that the growing military preponderance of the Warsaw Pact would eventually enable the Marxist–Leninists to forestall all interventions against communist takeovers on the part of imperialism, 'the mortal enemy of the working class'. In 1977, he stressed that the military emasculation of the West would usher in a revolutionary high tide culminating in global 'social progess'.[15] Commenting on the role of the armed forces in a socialist revolution, the Polish sociologist Jerzy Wiatr had already written in 1968: 'The building of the new state begins with the destruction of the military basis of the bourgeois system and with its replacement by the armed and organised proletariat.'[16]

In 1976, Heinz Hoffmann, a veteran of the Spanish Civil War and until his death in 1985 Defence Minister of the German Democratic Republic (GDR), voiced his conviction that 'hitherto history does not know of a single case in which a Socialist revolution has been led to victory without guns exercising their authority, or being at least cocked and loaded'.[17] Although Hoffmann maintained that even a 'missile and nuclear weapon war' would be a just war on the side of socialism,[18] bringing down imperialism by another world war was definitely not what he advocated. Instead, armed forces could be employed in various ways to achieve political ends. For Hoffmann, military strength could be translated into political leverage: 'Even those forms of the employment of the armed forces that Clausewitz described as "a mere threatening of the enemy and a supplement to negotiations" are essentially a continuation of politics.'[19]

Hoffmann did not completely exclude the possibility of a peaceful takeover of power, but he thought it more likely that the far-flung political aims of a socialist revolution dictated violent means:

> As the most fundamental social change in history, the Socialist revolution may only succeed in creating a new and humane order if it tears down the old class rule to its very foundations, and if it is always ready and able to suppress and to overcome the violent resistance of the deposed classes. . . . Counter-revolutionary violence can and must only be answered and eliminated by revolutionary violence. . . . Whoever disregards this fundamental lesson of class struggle, whoever brings about only half a Revolution, it is he who is putting it at hazard and, sooner or later, he will have to pay dearly for this with many casualties.[20]

Erich Mielke was in total agreement with such views. In 1976, he attacked the French and Italian 'Euro'-communists in one of his lectures because they no longer believed that the dictatorship of the proletariat was necessary 'to eliminate Capitalism' and to establish socialism in western Europe. On principle, Mielke rejected all criticism of the Warsaw Pact, since this would undermine the 'unity and unanimity of all revolutionary forces' and reduce the scope for 'socialist internationalism'.[21]

Given Mielke's openly stated aim of 'rolling back and eliminating the Capitalist system',[22] the unity of all revolutionary forces was indeed of crucial importance. His call for unity, however, was not only addressed to the Communist parties. Since the Communists were nowhere near strong enough to seize power on their own, a policy of wide-ranging coalitions had to be pursued. This strategy had already been recommended by Lenin, who further advised his supporters to eliminate their erstwhile allies as soon as the common enemy was defeated.[23] In order to gain as many allies as possible, the Communists preferred to initiate single-issue movements around a minimal consensus. Nevertheless, the Communist peace struggle was not only meant to disarm NATO, as a Soviet army textbook explained in 1977:

> It is one of the most important tasks of the Communist and workers' parties in the Capitalist countries to win over the majority of the working people and to create a broad front of anti-Imperialist forces. The struggle of the Communist and workers' parties for the realization of general democratic rallying cries and peace, contributes to the formation of a political mass army for the Socialist revolution. The general democratic struggle does not postpone the Socialist revolution, but brings it closer. The front of the anti-Imperialist struggle is indivisible; a defeat which Imperialism suffers in one sector, weakens its entire system.[24]

Since the unity of all progressive forces was necessary to defeat imperialism, the preservation of unity enjoyed top priority for the Communist peace fighters. To the Communists, however, unity with others always meant the latter's unconditional subordination to Communist leadership. People who refused to perform this act of intellectual abdication were automatically counted among the enemy. Since Marxist–Leninists had no conception of neutrality, they refused to recognize honourable motives in any of their pacifist or humanitarian critics. Instead, even Amnesty International was categorized by the East German secret police as an 'Imperialist propaganda institution' and 'an anti-Communist and neocolonialist instrument of diversion'. This was merely because it championed the cause of prisoners 'from Socialists, Capitalists and Third World Countries respectively', thus not sparing the socialist countries in view of their all-justifying cause.[25]

During the early 1980s, the Communist peace fighters were not merely trying to forestall the deployment of new American intermediate-range nuclear forces (INF) in Europe; they were also waging a relentless underground campaign against Western pacifists who were neither willing to ignore the Soviet arms buildup, nor ready to turn a blind eye to the violent oppression of pacifism in eastern Europe. Ironically, in East Germany the peace struggle had contributed to the formation of an independent peace movement that was soon to become a political opposition. According to Marxist–Leninist dialectics, however, the independent peace campaigners were nothing but enemies of peace:

> In the GDR, a large and unified peace movement operates in complete agreement with the foreign policies of the Socialist state. Any 'opposition' against it, would not only be disturbing but objectively hostile towards peace.[26]

Thus, the self-proclaimed Communist monopoly on peace transformed NATO into an embodiment of imperialist evil and all eastern European dissidents into traitors and *de facto* warmongers. To this conceptual framework of institutionalized paranoia, spying on one's own population became an obvious need and logical corollary. Simultaneously, the SED had to issue ever new defamations in order to justify the unwarranted arrests of independent peace campaigners:

> Spreading the lie that the Socialist countries suppress, arrest, or harass citizens for their commitment to peace is a particularly unbridled defamation of Socialism as a social system. . . . The conviction of some individuals who have committed crimes in the Socialist countries under the banner of peace is used . . . to turn the peace forces in the NATO-states against Socialism, and to denounce the peace and arms control policy of the Warsaw Treaty states as 'dubious' and 'hypocritical'.[27]

Since the Communists were unable to put their pacifist critics in the West behind prison bars, they themselves pursued them with open and covert campaigns of intimidation, sabotage and defamation. Their most feared and hated adversary was the 'Convention Movement' which had been initiated in 1982 by the campaign for European Nuclear Disarmament (END). This movement comprised organizations like the Italian Communist Party, the West German Greens, the Bertrand Russell Peace Foundation and the Dutch Interchurch Peace Council (IKV). Although people like E. P. Thompson, Petra Kelly, Mient Faber and Mary Kaldor were among the most outspoken and influential critics of NATO in the West, the Communists categorized them as imperialist agents. In 1985, for instance, Mielke told the head of the Soviet KGB that he strongly suspected Kelly of being an agent of the CIA.[28] Despite a complete lack of evidence, the Marxist–Leninists convinced themselves that people like Faber and Kaldor were nothing but 'paid agents of the enemy and professional troublemakers'.[29] The attempts of the 'Convention Movement' to forge a pan-European peace movement transcending both blocs were interpreted by the Communists as just another element in a massive conspiracy. They felt that its purpose was 'to distract the peace movement from the direction of the main thrust'. Of course, 'the human rights discussion' was only one of those means by which a huge array of 'hostile forces' was trying to sidetrack the peace movement so that it could no longer imperil NATO's alleged war preparations. The Marxist–Leninists thus saw the 'Convention Movement' as a fifth column in a 'general attack against the peace movement' – 'a complex, coordinated, and centrally controlled action of all available ideological-propagandistic, psychological, intelligence, and subversive means, methods and forces'.[30]

The communist 'peace struggle' against imperialism was indeed an all-out effort that respected neither neutrals nor apolitical subjects. For example, in East Germany workers were indoctrinated to look upon their workplace as their personal 'battlefield for peace'.[31] In Mielke's eyes, even sport was just another arena for class struggle where socialism had to establish its quasi natural supremacy by 'defending' itself against imperialist plots and counter-offensives.[32]

Given that imperialism was claimed to secretly long to start a new world war against socialism, employing elaborate conspiracies to blacken the image of the Warsaw Pact among the peace movements, and even trying to strip the socialist athletes of their gold medals, the Communists could see themselves as being confronted with utter evil. To hate this enemy was a measure of self-protection and therefore became a required civic duty. According to the dictionary of the East German secret police, hatred was 'estimable and sublime' when it was directed against the bourgeois class enemy. This kind of hatred did not content itself with 'repugnance and avoidance' but longed to 'annihilate or to harm' the enemy: 'Hatred is an essential and determining part of the Chekist feelings, a decisive foundation for the ardent and irreconcilable struggle against the enemy.'[33] Similarly, a Soviet army textbook posited: 'The training of a burning hatred for the class enemy is an indispensable element of the moral-political and psychological preparation of the Soviet soldier.'[34] This hatred, however, was not only directed against the sinister rulers of the imperialist camp; the textbook clearly stated that practically all Americans were hateworthy because

> From their early childhood onwards, the youth of the USA is educated in a militarist spirit, in a spirit of hostility and of mistrust towards the human being. School, church, educational facilities, clubs, and youth organisations – in the end everything is set up to prepare the young people to kill.[35]

Marxism–Leninism and its historical lineage

The 'International Relations theory' of Pharaonic Egypt depicted the world as being divided into two realms. One was the district of the sun-god Re, the Pharaonic empire, a realm of order, threatened and surrounded by the other realm which was dominated by chaos. Thus, the Egyptians never fought expansionist wars. Even when they attacked and repressed other peoples, they were merely defending the borders of Re's realm against the incursions of chaos.[36] Likewise, the Marxist–Leninists believed the world was divided into two camps: on the one hand, the Socialist realm of peace, order and human dignity; on the other hand, the imperialist realm of chaos, war and exploitation.

However, the Marxist–Leninists also believed in a secularized version of Judeo–Christian eschatology which depicted history as a teleological process that was headed towards a logical conclusion. According to Christian eschatology, the faithful would enter a new and heavenly Jerusalem after evil had been quelled in a final and cataclysmic battle. Thus, witches and heretics were burned, Jews marginalized and persecuted. The sectarian violence which befell Europe in the Later Middle Ages and the Early Modern period, along with approximately eighty million lives taken by Communists in this century, were the logical consequences of an almost identical perception of the world. By proclaiming their monopoly on goodness, both Christian sectarians and Communists defined all their real or perceived enemies as embodiments of evil.

While the ruling Communists were willing to employ all forms of violence to liquidate their enemies, they were much less eager to sacrifice their own lives. Thus, the possibility that the entire human race might perish in a nuclear war had already induced Khrushchëv to renounce the Leninist dogma of the inevitability of war.[37] Brezhnev's Politburo was particularly concerned with acquiring a global monopoly on the use of force, as he had hoped to bully the western societies into dismantling their nuclear defences through a process of intimidation and persuasion. While the Warsaw Pact was steadily building up its military and paramilitary forces during the 1970s,[38] Communist diplomacy was trying to lure NATO into signing rather one-sided arms control treaties by misrepresenting their own strength in central Europe.[39]

In 1939 and 1968, the militarily unopposed occupation of the Baltic states and Czechoslovakia had demonstrated the political utility of military preponderance. In the case of the Baltic states, however, the lacking resistance of their armies had not saved a considerable part of their population from deportation and liquidation in the ensuing process of Sovietization.[40] Furthermore, the people who had carried out 'the social cleansing' of the Stalin era played leading roles in Brezhnev's Politbüro. The highly influential Mikhail Suslov, for instance, had implemented the second Sovietization of Lithuania from 1944 onwards.[41] If their peace offensive would have succeeded in stripping western Europe of its nuclear defences, these people would have certainly not shied away from exporting 'permanent peace' to the western part of the continent. As in the case of the Soviet attack on Finland in 1939, the final onslaught on a defenceless western Europe might have been launched on the invitation of self-appointed Communist counter-governments. When the West German

'Bundestag' gave its final assent to the deployment of new American Intermediate Range Nuclear Forces in November 1983, a Communist-controlled self-styled 'Parliament of the Majority' was set up outside any government structures, disputing the constitutional, democratically elected Parliament's right to decide on this 'vital matter'.[42]

In view of the mindset of Communists and the long litany of Communist crimes against humanity,[43] the Cold War was neither an accident nor a tragic misunderstanding. The bipolar international system of the Cold War was contingent upon the dualistic concept of class enmity that stood at the centre of the Marxist–Leninist worldview. In its essence, the Cold War was a clash between liberal democracy and a modernized version of the two very old myths of a dualist world structure and an eschatological development towards the ultimate victory of one over the other. This conflict could only come to an end with the defeat, militarily or intellectually, of one side.

Notes

1 D. Pike, *PAVN: People's Army of Vietnam*, Novato, CA, Presidio, 1986, pp. 2–5, here p. 231.
2 H. Bull, 'Die Ziele der Rüstungskontrolle', in U. Nerlich (ed.), *Krieg und Frieden im industriellen Zeitalter: Beiträge der Sozialwissenschaften*. vol. 1, Gütersloh, C. Bertelsmann Verlag, 1966, pp. 257–78.
3 R. Pipes, 'Why the Soviet Union thinks it could fight and win a nuclear war', in R. Pipes, *US–Soviet Relations in the Era of Détente*, Boulder, CO, Westview Press, 1981, pp. 135–70.
4 S. Dalby, *Creating the Second Cold War: The Discourse of Politics*, London, Pinter, 1990, pp. 65–85.
5 M. Heller and A. Nekrich, 'Geschichte der Sowjetunion: Zweiter Band: 1940–1980', in M. Heller and A. Nekrich, *Geschichte der Sowjetunion: Sonderausgabe in einem Band*, Königsstein/Ts, Athenäum, 1981, pp. 312–87.
6 'Programm der Sozialistischen Einheitspartei Deutschlands vom 22. Mai 1976', in E. Liesner-Triebnigg (ed.), *DDR-Gesetze: Textausgabe mit Anmerkungen*, Cologne, Verlag für Wissenschaft und Politik, 1988, p. 7.
7 Stiftung Archiv der Parteien und Massenorganisationen der DDR im Bundesarchiv (henceforth SAPMO-BArch), DY30/vorl.SED 42440, 'Das internationale Kräfteverhältnis und die weltpolitische Entwicklung zu Beginn der 80er Jahre', p. 212.
8 Ibid., p. 48.
9 Ibid., p. 49.
10 For a comprehensive analysis of non-aggression pacts see R. Ahmann, *Nichtangriffspakte: Entwicklung und operative Nutzung in Europa 1922–1939: Mit einem Ausblick auf die Renaissance des Nichtangriffsvertrages nach dem Zweiten Weltkrieg*, Baden-Baden, Nomos, 1988.
11 W. I. Lenin, 'Das Militärprogramm der proletarischen Revolution', in *Krieg, Armee und Militärwissenschaft: Eine Auswahl aus Lenins Schriften in zwei Bänden: vol. 1*, Berlin, Verlag des Ministeriums für Nationale Verteidigung, 1958, pp. 628–38, here p. 630.
12 SAPMO-BArch, DY30/IV2/2.035/56 ('Information über die Gespräche zwischen Genossen B.N. Ponomarjow . . . und Genossen Hermann Axen . . . am 25. und 26. Januar 1979'), p. 298.

13 Der Bundesbeauftragte für die Unterlagen des Staatssicherheitsdienstes der ehemaligen Deutschen Demokratischen Republik (henceforth BStU), ZA, SdM 1296, 'Referat des Genossen Minister zur Militär- und Sicherheitspolitik der SED und der Entwicklung der internationalen Klassenauseinandersetzung zwischen Sozialismus und Imperialismus (Suhl – 17.12.1975)', p. 237.

14 Ibid., pp. 216–17.

15 BStU, ZA, SdM 1297, E. Mielke, 'Zur Militär- und Sicherheitspolitik der SED und der Entwicklung der internationalen Klassenauseinandersetzung zwischen Sozialismus und Imperialismus', 27 January 1977, pp. 197–8.

16 J. J. Wiatr, 'Sozio-politische Besonderheiten von Streitkräften in sozialistischen Ländern', in *Kölner Zeitschrift für Soziologie und Sozialpsychologie: Sonderheft 12/1968: Beiträge zur Militärsoziologie*, Cologne and Opladen, Westdeutscher Verlag, 1968, p. 110.

17 H. Hoffmann, 'Streitkräfte in unserer Zeit', *Einheit*, 1976, vol. 1, no. 3, pp. 354–63, here p. 359.

18 Ibid., p. 356.

19 Ibid.

20 Ibid., p. 359.

21 BStU, ZA, MfS ZAIG 8669, 'Ausführungen des Genossen Minister auf der zentralen Aktivtagung zur Auswertung des IX. Parteitages der SED (25. Juni 1976)', pp. 48–9.

22 Ibid., p. 49.

23 See W. I. Lenin, 'Der Linke Radikalismus', Die Kinderkrankheit im Kommunismus', in *W. I. Lenin: Ausgewählte Werke*, Moscow, Progress, 1987, pp. 515–91.

24 A. S. Milowidow *et al.*, *Krieg und Armee: Philosophisch-soziologischer Abriß*, Berlin, Militärverlag der DDR, 1979, p. 142. The Soviet edition was published in 1977.

25 BStU, ZA, MfS ZAIG 5161, 'Auskunftsbericht über *Amnesty International (AI) Stand*: Mai 1978', p. 123.

26 Bundesarchiv-Zwischenarchiv-Dahlwitz-Hoppegarten (henceforth BA-ZA-DH), DZ9.12.60., 'Betr.: Empfang einer Delegation des Bundesvorstandes der Deutschen Friedens-Union vom 29.11. bis 2.12.1982 in Berlin', p. 1.

27 BA-ZA-DH, DZ9.K.295.1578, Institut für Internationale Politik und Wirtschaft der DDR, 'Interne Studie zur Strategie und Taktik des Kampfes feindlicher Stützpunkte und spalterischer Kräfte gegen die Friedensbewegung', May 1985, p. 21.

28 BStU, ZA, MfS ZAIG 5385, 'Notiz über das Gespräch des Genossen Minister mit dem Vorsitzenden des KfS [KGB] der UdSSR, Genossen Armeegeneral V.M. Tschebrikow, am 1. und 2.4.1985 in Moskau', p. 37.

29 BA-ZA-DH, DZ9.55.273, 'Anlage: 3 zum Orginalprotokoll Nr.2/84, 16.01.1984', p. 5.

30 BA-ZA-DH, DZ9.K.295.1578, 'Interne Studie zur Strategie und Taktik des Kampfes feindlicher Stützpunkte und spalterischer Kräfte gegen die Friedensbewegung', May 1985, pp. 12–13, 20, 1.

31 See photograph of 'Backwarenkombinat Eisenhüttenstadt', in Kuhrt, Eberhard *et al.* (eds), *Am Ende des Sozialismus: Vol.2: Die wirtschaftliche und ökologische Situation der DDR in den achtziger Jahren*, Opladen, Leske & Buderich, 1996, p. 53.

32 BStU, ZA, MfS SdM 1307, 'Schlußwort des 1.Vorsitzenden auf der 8. Tagung der zentralen Leitung der SV Dynamo', pp. 256–7.

33 S. Suckut (ed.), *Das Wörterbuch der Staatssicherheit: Definitionen zur 'politisch-operativen Arbeit'* Berlin, Ch. Links, 1996, p. 168.

34 M. P. Korobejenikow *et al.*, *Soldat und Krieg: Probleme der moralisch-politischen und psychologischen Vorbereitung in der Sowjetarmee*, Berlin, Militärverlag der DDR, 1972, p. 133.

35 Ibid., p. 35.
36 R. Gundlach, ' "Ich habe den Abscheu Gottes entfernt"– Die religiöse Grundlage der pharaonischen Kriegsführung', in H. Wißman (ed.), *Krieg und Religion*, Würzburg, Königshausen & Neumann, 1994, pp. 11–24.
37 P. Kondylis, *Theorie des Krieges: Clausewitz – Marx – Engels – Lenin*, Stuttgart, Klett-Cotta, 1988, pp. 286–7; T. Dietrich, H. Ehlert and R. Wenzke, 'Die bewaffneten Organe der DDR im System von Partei, Staat und Landesverteidigung: Ein Überblick', in T. Diedrich *et al.* (eds), *Im Dienste der Partei: Handbuch der bewaffneten Organe der DDR*, Berlin, Ch. Links, 1998, pp. 4–5.
38 Diedrich, Ehlert and Wenzke, 'Die bewaffneten Organe', pp. 1–68.
39 G. Arbatow, *Das System: Ein Leben im Zentrum der Sowjetpolitik*, Frankfurt, S. Fischer, 1993, pp. 226–9.
40 S. Myllyniemi, 'Die Folgen des Hitler–Stalin–Paktes für die Baltischen Republiken und Finnland', in B. Wegner (ed.), *Zwei Wege nach Moskau: Vom Hitler–Stalin–Pakt zum 'Unternehmen Barbarossa'*, Munich, Piper, 1991, pp. 75–92.
41 H.-J. Torke (ed.), *Historisches Lexikon der Sowjetunion, 1917/22 bis 1991*, Munich, c.H. Beck, 1993, p. 328.
42 BA-ZA-DH, DZ9.502.2516. 'BRD: In Aktionen und Erklärungen der Friedenskräfte kam zum Ausdruck', 8 December 1983, pp. 1–3.
43 For the latter see S. Courtois *et al.* (eds.), *Le livre noir du communisme*, Paris, Edition Robert Laffont, 1997.

18 Conclusions

Beatrice Heuser and Anja V. Hartmann

Our review of almost three millennia of European history has yielded a number of conclusions, besides the most obvious one that each of the periods considered shows not only features distinguishing it from all others, but also a remarkable spectrum of variation within itself. Diversity is thus the hallmark, rather than uniformity or immutability, and we can clearly dismiss all theories of International Relations (IR) built on the assumption of a 'striking sameness in the quality of international life through the millennia' (Kenneth Waltz quoted in Andreas Osiander, Chapter 2, this volume).

A preliminary warning: *faux amis*

While diversity of cultures is often very obvious, its analysis is sometimes encumbered with the existence of *faux amis*, i.e. words or concepts with different meanings in different periods and different cultures. The tradition or periodic rediscovery of older words, concepts or myths, which in each tradition and rediscovery undergo some changes, is in itself a tradition throughout European history. This tradition has even given birth to a special branch of history, dealing exclusively with the history of concepts and ideas (*Ideengeschichte, Begriffsgeschichte*). Although our main focus is not on words or concepts, some of the central terms we have been dealing with underwent fundamental transformations in the course of history. First of all, it must be stressed that a crucial term like the Latin *natio* has been employed since Classical Antiquity, but with changing connotations. It was widely used in the Middle Ages (designating a number of different groups – from clerical delegations from a particular area to students speaking the same language or the collectivity of the inhabitants of one kingdom or even city), but this is not evidence that the concept was used in the programmatic way in which it was redefined by the French Revolution: one nation as source of all sovereignty, one state. The latter made 'nationalism' more than the simple expression of group pride, variations of which existed throughout the ages, and which until this day can easily be married with other loyalties – to 'Queen and Country', to an oligarchic system of government, to a one-party state. Its mere use throughout the centuries is thus not proof that all the political connotations attached to the term today were in people's minds earlier. This point is of course central to the question of the perenniality of patterns of behaviour in inter-'national' relations, as we have seen. Equally, when a Roman of the period of Augustus uses the word *Res publica* or when a Venetian of the Renaissance uses it for the *Serenissima*, or when it is used for France during the French Revolution, or for Turkey since the First World War (including the periods of dictatorship), the term is by no means used to denote the identical idea or thing. The Greek *timê*, or honour, meant different things in different cultures: Greeks and medieval knights were often ready to die for it, while in our day the concept is profoundly devalued throughout most of Europe, and hugely overshadowed by mercantile calculations of 'interest'. The same word can also been used with different senses during one and the same period by different cultures. Famously, the peoples' democracies behind the iron curtain had a different view of the meaning of *democracy* than did the western liberal democracies during the Cold War. The first pitfall we highlight here is thus to think that a word, used by people in different ages and different cultures, actually carries the identical meaning.

A related trap consists of *concepts* which seem familiar, but are in fact distinctive. Terms denoting rule (for example, of the domination of several entities or groups by one) differ through the ages, and what we, retrospectively and anachronistically, call the Athenian empire is less structured and bureaucratized than the *Imperium Romanum* that coined the expression, and different yet again from each of the Holy Roman, French, British or Habsburg empires. While all of these put themselves in the tradition or even succession of the Roman Empire, each had its distinctive (and sometimes ahistorical) interpretation both of the precedent and what it aimed to be itself. Similarly, Pre-Christian Roman concerns for a just cause for a war do not translate automatically into Christian just war theory, which generally defined the war aim with the restoration of the *status quo ante bellum*, i.e. as the narrow redressing of wrongs committed by the other side. A modern example of a reinvention of the tradition of the Christian just war thinking is the United Nations' Security Council definition of the coalition's war aims in the Gulf War against Iraq of 1990 to 1991, consisting of the liberation of the invaded Kuwait and the destruction of Iraq's nuclear weapons industry on the basis of Iraq's membership of the Non-Proliferation Treaty it had breached with this construction programme. As the example of the Punic Wars shows, the Romans in comparable circumstances would have taken the invasion of an allied country as a *casus belli* (indeed as a *casus foederis*, a case in which the alliance could be invoked), but would probably not have stopped short of sacking Baghdad. Just war thinking thus does not equal just war thinking, even if the same terms are used and the concept seems familiar superficially.

Diversity of communities

The communities we have studied have ranged from tribes (the *gentes* of Bernhard Zeller, Chapter 8) to very sophisticated states. What all had in common was leaders or leading elites who in most cases commanded some kind of troops as a basic instrument to wage war against others. At the same time, the leaders governed a mass more or less following in their pursuit of war if not peace. While for many periods we have no or little evidence to go on when it comes to the establishment of what mass opinion was, we can show that leaders succeeded in persuading men of fighting age to follow them into war. Still, for a long time, leading elites, troops and masses formed distinct groups with partially different cultures and partially different collective identities. In earlier centuries, leaders', troops' and masses' reasons for engaging in war often overlapped rather than being identical, as Anja V. Hartmann shows in her chapter. For more modern examples we can say that leaders, troops and masses often shared beliefs crucial to war and peace, even if there was a band of variation. The very idea of a mobilization of masses in wartime was only born with the *levée en masse* of the French Revolution, trying to abolish any distinction between soldiers and citizens.

Parties to conflicts were rarely equipped with identical mental dispositions, although there are examples of close proximity of culture for the enemies in a war. While Athens and Sparta are famous for their different cultures, the collective mentalities of the Carthaginian and Roman elites during the Punic Wars may have been similar, but the Romans more than anybody else were set on unlimited conquest. Romans and barbarians converged only when barbarian leaders tried to assimilate Roman customs, but it is clear that the barbarians, tutored by Christianity, created cultures in war and peace very distinct from what the Roman Empire had known. The crusaders confronted very different cultures while intracultural clashes characterize other medieval wars, from the barons' wars to the Hundred Years' War, and, in direct succession to the latter, the dynastic wars of the *ancien régime*. The religious wars, however, found different worldviews on each side, Catholics continuing to dream of a unitary world united by one church and one emperor, the Protestants having espoused a much more fragmented view of the interstate and indeed intercommunity order. Extreme differences existed between the French Revolutionaries and their adversaries. The First World War saw a rare convergence of attitudes and views on all sides; what Robert Foley shows for Germany largely holds for military leaders and strategic thinkers on all sides by the time the lights went out in Europe. The Second World War has often been interpreted as the culmination of an ideological civil war in Europe, which notwithstanding its intracultural aspect reflected Europe's profound division into three important subcultures: the democratic, the communist and the Fascist-racist. The elimination of the third (until a variant of it resurfaced in Yugoslavia at the end of the Cold War) left a contest of two unequal worldviews with their significant, different prognoses of the future of the world. Adversaries were thus more often than not of a different mental disposition and saw the world, themselves, their adversaries, war and peace in different terms. Nevertheless, differences in culture did not necessarily count among the reasons for war; they could just as well be a consequence of a war engaged upon because of other causes, as parties to war obviously tend to emphasize their differences rather than their commonalities.

Within the communities, we find confirmed the notion of the layered (or multiple) identity, stemming from anthropology and research on identity: an Athenian thought of himself as an Athenian as well as a Hellene, as a member of his family or clan, as well as distinct in relation to others within his community (women, children, hoplites, slaves) and any enemy without, whether a rivalling Greek *polis* or alliance, or barbarians. Again, the picture is so complex as to make modelling all but impossible: identities shift, identities are constructed. This leads us to the recognition of the existence of different subcultures within all the cultures we have considered, of hawks and doves, of different political or ideological views, side by side, in close proximity or close succession. The European states of the late nineteenth century were haunted not only by Social Darwinist, nationalist warmongers, but each had pacifist societies pressing for the creation of enduring international regimes designed to contain or even ban wars.

Indeed, one can identify layers of culture and inheritance: not one culture that we have encountered is completely free from the contradictions of different elements within it, often the heritage of preceding periods and a merger of cultures. Since the Dark Ages, medieval European culture mixed pagan warrior cults with the Judaeo-Christian heritage, producing amazing amalgams, as Jonathan Riley-Smith shows (Chapter 10): in crusading appeals God and Christ are described as feudal lords who had lost their inheritance and had to be defended by their vassals. Mixing older dynastic thinking with ideas of the Enlightenment, Frederick the Great of Prussia could think of himself puritanically as first servant of the state, and yet claim it was the prince's first obligation to enlarge his family's territorial possessions. The second half of the nineteenth century produced both internationalist socialism (and pacifism) and fierce nationalism throughout Europe. The century ranging from the Franco–Prussian War of 1870 to 1871 to the convention on air warfare of 1977 has seen, side by side, total disregard for the distinction between combatants and noncombatants (particularly in the context of aerial bombardment), and increasingly codified humanitarian restraints on warfare. It is thus clearly not enough to speak of the *Zeitgeist*, the mentality of an era, as our evidence suggests that one era, one culture, contain several contradictory subcultures, with differing attitudes to war and peace. Instead, one can find logically incompatible or contradictory beliefs and concepts side by side in one community; indeed, even within one individual's mind.

Finally, a self-perception of identity may be surpassed in importance by the perception of others: casting the Persians in the role of the Greeks' former enemies the Parthians, or calling the Palestinians Philistines, or describing the United States as behaving towards its allies like the Holy Roman Empire towards the other states of Europe influences one's own collective attitude towards them. When the Byzantine Empire was under attack from the Turks, it was largely irrelevant how the Byzantines viewed them or their relationship, given that the Turks were uncompromisingly set on conquest. Or, to give an extreme case, it was irrelevant how German citizens with Jewish ancestors thought of themselves if the National-Socialist regime defined them as *Untermenschen* whom they wanted to exterminate.

Four patterns of identity

Notwithstanding the diversities between communities and the possible variations of culture and identity within each community, certain patterns of identity can be singled out as being particularly crucial for the identification of friend and foe. Four such patterns seem to be more influential than others throughout the centuries, although with changing importance.

The first pattern of identity often applied as criterion of solidarity or enmity concerns the individual's or group's regional provenance. (This is true even for late medieval and modern Europe despite the fact that virtually all of Europe's populations were the mongrel descendants of successive strata of migrant settlements between the fourth and eleventh centuries in particular. It testifies to the great degree of ultimately peaceful assimilation and the successful construction of new collective identities in the subsequent centuries.) In the armies of the Middle Ages and the Modern period, the grouping of soldiers according to their regional origin was popular in mercenary troops – for example, for the Croats in the Thirty Years' War – but subsisted well into the national wars of the twentieth century. Nevertheless, regional identification could also work the other way round: during the Dutch Revolt, mercenaries from all countries fighting for Philip II of Spain were classified as Spanish by both francophone and Dutch-speaking rebels, and during the Thirty Years' War, anybody fighting for the Swedish king was classified as Swedish. Military as well as political leaders often chose their entourage according to regional principles, hoping that common regional roots would ascertain loyalty and faith. Similarly, the medieval use of the term *natio* carried a component of (often very vague) regional affinity. In later centuries, the invention of a 'German' or a 'British' identity owes much to the Roman geographical term for a region, applied again later by classically educated intellectuals to an ethnic collectivity which previously would have used other terms to designate themselves. These older terms were either particular (Chatti, Suabians, Angles, Saxons, Normans, Scots) or collective (Franks,

Allemanni, English), but not coterminous with those which in the Late Modern era came to stick as official names of recognized states. The convergence of regional identity and state formation is strikingly obvious in the concept of 'natural' boundaries, easy to define in the case of Britain and much disputed between France and Germany in the nineteenth century. It is worth reminding ourselves here that Britain and France developed larger collective identities exceptionally early, while the great majority of European 'national' identities came to be attached to territories and states only in the nineteenth and twentieth centuries.

The second pattern of identity – language – is closely related to regional identity, though not completely interchangeable with it. Language seems to have been of varying importance in different cultures. Ancient Hebrews used the term 'shibboleth' to identify enemies (who could not pronounce it properly). For the Ancient Greeks, the ability to understand each other's dialect was seen as a uniting factor, notwithstanding the remaining differences provoking mistakes or mockery. Likewise, people throughout the former Yugoslavia from the 1920s to the 1990s convinced themselves that Serb and Croat was close enough to constitute *one* language, Serbo-Croatian, while since the fissure of Yugoslavia in the early 1990s just as significant a number have convinced themselves that there are several different languages in Bosnia-Hercegovina alone; tiny regional variations are now invested with an importance for which Serbs, Croats and Bosniacs became prepared to kill and rape if not to die. But language was not always used as an identifying or dividing criterion in war and peace. Easily equally great linguistic differences existed (and continue to exist) between *Plattdeutsch* (low German), Frisian and Dutch on the one hand and standard German on the other; yet for a variety of other historic reasons of the nineteenth century, Low German speakers were integrated into Germany, Frisians into both contemporary Germany and the Netherlands, and Dutch speakers with their different dialects into both the Netherlands and Belgium. Linguistic differences within each of these three countries continue to matter, but have so far not caused their fissure. Language – and not dialect – was used as the differentiating factor by the English in the Hundred Years' War, when English began to win out over Norman French which had been the language of court and government since the Norman Conquest. Language was hyped up as the criterion for 'Germanness' in the early nineteenth century, which originally resulted in the view that *all* German speakers (including Austrians and Swiss) should be integrated into a German ethnically defined nation-state yet to be created. The state that was eventually created in 1871, however, excluded both Austria and Switzerland, and many other regions inhabited by germanophones to the south, north and above all east of the German Empire. Hitler's dream of incorporating all of them into his empire logically meant the occupation of all of eastern Europe to the Volga, and, given the heterogeneity of communities and language groups throughout this area, this invariably meant bringing non-germanophones into the Reich along with German speakers.

A third pattern of identity – again related to regional and linguistical identity without overlapping completely – is common descent. Common descent could be founded on kinship resulting from a shared mythical ancestry, as in Greek and Roman tradition where Homer's epics continually influenced the forming of alliances and the justification of war and peace. Colonization and the concept of the mother country had roots in the relations between Greek city-states and bred the idea of a family of communities or states. This idea was transformed in early modern concepts of dynasty and dynastic rights highlighting parental ties between the European monarchies. Common descent could also be derived from ethnic similarities, as Bernhard Zeller shows for the emergence of the early medieval *gens*. For a long time, the concept of common descent was flexible and could be infringed, weakened or contradicted by competing myths, by marriage and by migration. Bernhard Zeller has also shown how tribes assimilated the cultural heritage of the Roman Empire, and other examples of the adoption of another people's mystical ancestry exist, to mention merely the famous 'our ancestors, the Gauls' taught to the autochthonous populations in the schools of the French Empire. Only the twentieth century saw the most horrifying hypertrophies of the idea of ethnic identity, when common descent was used not only as a positive criterion for identification but as a negative criterion for 'selection' and annihilation of those supposedly excluded from the inherited bonds of blood.

While common descent is concerned with the past, the fourth pattern of identification regards the future on earth and beyond and comprises religious as well as ideological identity. The fear of divine punishment heavily influenced the extent of warfare between the Greek city-states, and the Crusades as well as many religious wars in Early Modern Europe were to a considerable extent waged for the sake of saving the individual souls of the combatants. An oracle's prophecy could have crucial effects on the course of war in Ancient Greece, the results of the inspection of animals' entrails or birds' flights were taken into account by Roman politicians and military leaders, the singing of *Ave Marias* encouraged medieval knights and early modern mercenaries, and monarchs asked their confessors for advice in matters of war and peace. Likewise, differences in religion often provoked war, from the persecution of Christians in ancient Rome to the pogroms against Jews in medieval Europe, from the oppression of the Cathars to the Hussite Wars, from the Crusades to the Thirty Years' war, from the burning of witches to the extermination of millions of Jews in Nazi Germany. Religious identity often fostered ideological orientations, but the development of ideology in contrast to religion only started with the French Revolution. Like religion, ideology served not only as a justification for wars, but it could even make war against those of other religious or ideological persuasion a 'holy' duty, executed in order to liberate or illuminate others who could not yet enjoy the benefits of freedom, equality, brotherhood, communism, Fascism, capitalism and so on. Instead of the *Ave Maria*, the *Marseillaise* or the *Internationale* strengthened the courage of the fighting troops, the priests were replaced by ideologues or experts, and the gods were dethroned in favour of *Weltanschauung*. Nevertheless, there are wars – like the 'cabinet' wars of Early Modern Europe – lacking the religious or ideological component so dominant in other conflicts.

All patterns of identity could be – and were in the course of European history – drawn upon in the formation of political entities, be it city-states, empires or larger territorial states. After the demise of the western Roman Empire and before 1789, shared faith and/or loyalty to a prince or a town played an important role in the self-perception of many communities. Language was rarely important (France, where a common language was imposed with the Edict of Villers-Cotterêts of 1539, was *the* exception), as the language of government almost invariably differed from the vernacular, and was thus the language of an elite. When state structures began to form, state officials explored ways in which they could activate and control the loyalties of their states' populations. The peasants of late nineteenth-century France who were turned into Frenchmen by the onset of the First World War were 'nationalized' through the objectively existing French state bureaucracy. Given all modern states' desire to control or at least influence the education of their citizens, collective memories are largely influenced by the school curriculum in any given state. In this way state-wide traditions were created by building on regional ties and a common language. This process of 'nation-building' thus included the creation of a citizen body within a pre-existing state, with loyalties, myths and other points of reference shared between them. The importance and the power of states in creating national identity has been researched extensively, but many functional elements of this process of building large group identity can be traced into previous centuries, previous cultures. The bureaucrats and military of imperial Rome did as much to keep the empire together as did those of the Habsburgs or the officials who created the first Indonesian 'national' identity. Civil servants of England and later of the British Empire had received their training as clerks and later as students of 'Greats' in Oxford and Cambridge, which must have produced just as much of a uniform system of reference in the Middle Ages and eighteenth to nineteenth centuries as 'national' school curricula or the common provenance of French officials from the École Normale d'Administration do today. The conditioning effect on a young officer of passing through the Prussian military academy under Scharnhorst and Gneisenau can hardly have been less than that of passing through Westpoint or Saint Cyr today, even though the latter are imbued with republican values.

The integration of the idea of a common descent as well as of religion and ideology in the process of state formation was largely promoted through festivities and celebrations. While it is true that 'national' celebrations of Bastille Day or Armistice Day have been instrumentalized very consciously for nation-building in the late nineteenth and twentieth centuries respectively, Christian feasts formed universal points of reference previously, and loyalties to dynasties were periodically regenerated by the pageantry of coronations, funerals, royal weddings, and the princes' perambulations in their realm. One can even note an overlap with modern 'nation-building' and the regeneration of national solidarity with royalism in events such as the death of the Princess of Wales in a car crash in 1997, and public reactions to it. Focusing more specifically on war and peace, it is difficult to dismiss the notion that the English king's victory at Agincourt in 1415 had effects comparable in many respects to the British victory in the Second World War, the commemoration of which even fifty years later still produced a heightened feeling of national solidarity. Ecclesiastical foundations designed to express thanks for the divine grace of a victory in battle, and to pray for the war dead, can be traced back at least to Battle Abbey for the victory of William the Conqueror at Hastings in 1066, the Abbey of Bouvines founded by Philip Augustus for his victory of 1214, and All Souls College in Oxford, commemorating the dead of the Hundred Years' War. Parallels with war grave foundations of the twentieth century are striking, even if the latter are emphatically *national* foundations, rather than *royal* or religious ones.

These and other mechanisms of group identity-building have clearly reached new dimensions with the growth of extensive mechanisms of state control, with literacy and widely distributed newspapers, and in our century with radio and television. But comparable mechanisms have existed throughout history, and the common experience of war, or of triumph and victory, have played solidarity-building roles since the Trojan War. It is fascinating to note that appeals to group solidarity could on occasion have an effect well beyond the audience targeted, as Jonathan Riley-Smith has shown regarding the crusading movement, which, much to the despair of successive popes, mobilized the poor and women when they had intended to mobilize only knights.

While we have attempted to categorize types of identity, in reality there were infinite variations on these themes, and no two wars were characterized by the same perceptions of the identities of friends and foes. The importance of these various notions of identity for our purposes lies in the fact that they determined notions of friend and foe throughout history. They were thus a crucial variable in the equation of war and peace, idiosyncratic to each culture and era. Perceptions of collective identity are thus one crucial variable, this changed over time and from culture to culture, countering any notion of the permanence and immutability of patterns of war and peace.

Diversity in war and peace

One clear conclusion of our comparative study is that it is wrong to reduce the causes of any war, or indeed the causes of any peace, to a single factor. Throughout we see the confluence of a number of motives, individual agendas, factors from different spheres of life, from economic constraints or needs to personal ambition, from anything that 'Realists' would term the quest for power to the quest for the salvation of one's soul. Indeed, one must take issue with Thucydides who spoke of the 'truest' reason for the Peloponnesian War. All reasons he gives are true in the sense of plausible (we have to acknowledge a limit to our understanding of what another ever thinks or has thought), but one or several may be more *important* than others.

It is thus not useful, it seems from our studies, to reduce the cause of any war exclusively to one level of interpretation, such as the systemic (or what was thought of as the 'order' of the contemporary world or universe) patterns of behaviour in relations between governments, personalities and ambitions of individuals, economic pressures and incentives, geostrategy or culture. Instead, all these aspects should be looked at jointly: it would be untenable to substitute one monocausal interpretation (that international relations are determined both by the quest and balance of power) for another (that personal ambition in and of itself can be the sole necessary and sufficient cause for a war, or that culture can play such a role). The multiplicity of causes involved in going to war bears crucial consequences for the conditions of peaceful co-existence between different communities. If the causes for war can never be reduced to one factor only, peace arrangements relying on one solution and one reason or cause only are naturally prone to failure. Neither economic well-being, nor religious tolerance nor territorial exchanges alone can guarantee a prolonged peace, if other aspects are left aside and continue to produce points of disagreement and consequently new causes for war.

The intensity of war also differed along a very wide spectrum and could range from complete annihilation of the enemy's population (or their enslavement) to very restricted battlefield victories. All wars, even the 'cabinet wars' of Louis XIV, could quickly develop a tendency towards escalation to greater cruelty affecting non-combatants – more about which below. There is in turn no clear correlation between the lasting nature of peace settlements and the duration of the wars preceding them, with some notable exceptions such as the Thirty Years' War and the relative durability of the Westphalian Peace; other periods saw clashes of great intensity give way to ephemeral peace settlements, as the first half of the twentieth century illustrates. The same peace could be seen both as a turning point, reflecting a change in attitude towards violence in some, and as a mere respite by others. Not surprisingly, societies in which a culture of war prevailed tended towards the latter, if they did not disdain peace altogether.

Did this affect the form that wars took? Only as a function of the actual ideas, shared or not shared, that the belligerents had. If the monarchs of the *ancien régime* agreed that wars had to be limited, then so was war; if all the combatant parties of the Great War were determined to wage annihilation battles that would decide the war for them, then hecatombs of casualties would result. It mattered little if the islanders of Melos wanted to reason with their Athenian enemies if the latter were set on slaughter; the view of the party wishing for a more limited form of war rarely mattered if an opponent sought to impose unlimited war, as any form of terrorism or guerrilla warfare shows even for situations where the latter is the weaker party.

What of the correlation between perceptions of identity, of the world order, and of peace settlements? The more irreconcilable (religious or ideological, including racialist) the differences between friend and foe were perceived to be, the less likely peace. The *anciens régimes,* respecting each other as equal princes in one common world order, concluded peace as easily as they engaged in their limited wars. Religious foes and ideological enemies, however, tended to conceive of peace solely in terms of the collapse of one side or the other, the elimination of one religion or ideology (or race, ideologically perceived) or the other. (The absolute defeat of Napoleonic France and of Hitler's Germany are two examples, as is the Roman attitude towards Carthage in the absence of any clear religious or ideological antagonism, but in the context of a predominant worldview in Rome which saw order only in terms of the total defeat of one side or the other.) The only alternative lay in the occurrence of a profound paradigm shift about the inevitability of the conflict and towards forms of peaceful co-existence (examples include Augsburg, Westphalia, the stand-off of the Cold War through shared fear of nuclear war). Only peace founded on the perception on both sides that war was intolerable could last.

Oddly, both militaristic and pacific societies went to great lengths to fulfil rituals of going to war. With the exception of barbarian incursions into the Roman Empire, and later of banditry, of which Jan Willem Honig tells us the Middle Ages were full, wars were usually formally and elaborately declared; if proxy wars and all mischief short of war carried out during the Cold War stand out as an exception, it is none the less clear that this was a declared conflict of ideologies, about the seriousness and scale of which few harboured any illusions, even if eastern rhetoric went beyond even that of US President Ronald Reagan, as Michael Ploetz has shown.

World orders and violence

Our survey suggests that a wide range of different views of a larger order existed over the centuries, and that it did indeed have much to do with thinking about war and peace. If one believed in gods or a God, who would punish terrestrial transgressions of rules and laws established by them/Him, great efforts were made to explain the justice of a cause in relation to such rules. Instances of persecutions of those defined as God's enemies, of those who refused to sacrifice to the gods, show a tendency towards greater cruelty, greater violence, an abandonment of distinctions between combatants and non-combatants where these would normally have been upheld. By contrast, wars fought between princes and cultures who saw each other very much as brothers with only minor legal quarrels to settle through the judgement imposed by the fortunes of battle, tended, it seems, to treat war in a more sportsmanlike fashion. They saw themselves and their adversaries as equal parts of a common world order which all had a vested interest in preserving, plus or minus a certain redistribution of power and wealth. Classical examples are some of the wars among the Greek city-states (in others we find examples of genocidal slaughter!), medieval and modern wars among the princes for territory and dynastic rights. Revolutionary wars, in other words wars based on an ideology which aimed to bring down the internal social order as much as the world order more generally, concomitantly tended to produce larger numbers of casualties. The most classical example is that of the French Revolution and the Russian revolutionary wars, but the religious wars, starting with the Hussites and ending, if not with the Augsburg convention on religious tolerance of 1555, with the Westphalian Peace of 1648, very much fit this picture; perhaps the wars of Alexander the Great can be included in this category.

The perception of another group but also of one's own society does seem to have much to do with the extremes of violence to which one can go in warfare with them. If the enemy was defined as intrinsically, irreconcilably evil, the notion of sparing him and his unnecessary pain, destruction and killing was absurd. Societies that valued life little, that practised slavery and relished the spectacle of killing men and beasts for public pleasure, concomitantly developed few inhibitions about the treatment of defeated enemies. Cruelty well in excess of what one would have inflicted on members of one's own society was practised if one could define the enemy as subhuman, as did the conquering Spaniards in central and southern America, as did the Germans with the east Europeans they subdued in the Second World War (significantly, they dealt quite differently with the occupied French, whom they regarded as of higher standing, much as the Romans treated the Greeks better than the barbarian tribes they encountered to the north and west of Italy). For reasons of space, our survey sadly lacks a chapter on colonialism, a subject which would offer up many valuable insights.

Closely linked to the view of the world and of its order, and to the perception of the enemy, are notions of what is and what is not permissible in warfare. Rules limiting the effects of warfare seem to have existed, again, throughout European history. It is striking, however, that there are horrifying examples in all periods of such rules having been violated, ignored, circumvented. The pogroms of Jews that were unleashed in the context of crusades, bringing them close to Total War in the Ludendorffian sense in some areas, were contrary to the intentions of the popes who proclaimed the crusades, as was the sack of Constantinople by the crusaders in 1204. The armies fighting for Louis XIV of France and Frederick the Great of Prussia were commanded on pain of death not to loot and pillage, yet there is much evidence of these orders being broken, and indeed Louis XIV ordered a burnt earth policy for parts of his adversaries' territory; by the time of the First World War, conventions on the treatment of prisoners of war were internationally recognized, yet there is ample evidence of individual shootings of prisoners on both sides. The paradox of warfare as politically controlled violence cannot always be retained in reality, and Clausewitz was doubtless right when he commented that all wars have an inherent tendency towards boundless violence. Not all soldiers could or can resist the temptation of 'going berserk' like the old Norse warriors when violence is unleashed; on the whole well-trained, professional soldiers seem best able to cope with the contradiction of controlled violence, as the limited wars of the *condottieri* in the Italian Renaissance and the 'cabinet wars' of the seventeenth and eighteenth centuries suggest.

Yet in all periods, the fact that otherwise recognized rules in warfare were from time to time broken cannot be seen as evidence of lawlessness, of a lack of all limitations. The very horror with which contemporary commentators would talk about instances when rules were broken confirms the existence in their minds of such restraints. Indeed, chroniclers or historiographers often used such instances to explain the subsequent fall of a people or a ruler, his punishment by some higher power of justice. It is also clear, however, that rules were established implicitly or explicitly from case to case, and could be interpreted very widely. More rules did not necessarily mean less violence, as the Third Reich demonstrated so horrifyingly. Rules can indeed serve as an excuse for more violence, rather than exclusively as a means to limit violence, as they are usually understood today.

The absence of any strictly linear development (say, from brutal warfare to increasingly humane conduct, or from limited war – sparing of civilians – to increasingly total war – deliberately targeting civilians) is equally striking. General Erich Ludendorff would have recognized Alexander's genocide in captured towns and Roman war aims in the Third Punic War as 'total' in his sense; the Gallo-Roman cities burnt down by Atilla and his Huns, the depopulation of Le Havre by the English in the Hundred Years' War, the sack of Magdeburg in the Thirty Years' War, have much in common with the burning of Oradour or Lidice, or the bombing of Dresden and Tokyo in the Second World War. Religious groups were persecuted to total extermination of communities periodically throughout history, whether these were Christians generally, Cathars, Jews, Hussites or Huguenots. Late medieval wars were 'limited' in that they were sparing of soldiers, yet, in the form of the *chevauchée*, they were particularly wasteful of civilian lives and property.

Nevertheless, there seems to be an *acquis* in the European ('western') macroculture which has steadily built on and gradually enhanced previous limitations of war. This development can be seen as linear, starting with the Greek revulsion against the deliberate killing of children, strongly enhanced by Christian qualms about killing in any form, elaborated by chivalric ideas of sparing women, clergy and children, and finally codified in the Hague and Geneva conventions. In each of the periods we have considered, such limitations were brutally ignored on many occasions: one need only point to the many instances of deliberate air bombardment of civilians since the advent of air power, which go so clearly against the postulate of distinguishing between combatants and non-combatants. Yet the ideals have lived on, even if at times they were minority opinion.

Thinking war, peace and world orders

We thus find that there is a correlation between the way people have viewed war and violence, and peace and a larger 'world' order, although it is a very complex one, with as many subtle variations as there were different cultures and eras in history.

Throughout the case studies in this volume, wars and peace depended on the view of one's own group's identity and the identity of the enemy, and of the picture of the world in people's minds. If the world was seen as divided between irreconcilable foes, if war was pre-programmed, then peace was unlikely to be achieved unless one side or the other was totally defeated. The exception to this rule was the occurrence of a paradigm shift on all sides in favour of peace and co-existence with what had previously been seen as irreconcilable enemies. If the world was seen as divided between competing but essentially similar entities, wars could be limited and peace easily established, but was not necessarily of long duration.

For simplicity, we have identified four main patterns of identity affecting people's attitudes towards war and peace throughout European history, namely regional origin, language, common descent or kinship, and religion and ideology. All four patterns of identity could be adopted by political or military leaders as well as by fighting troops and by the ordinary people or the mass, without necessarily overlapping completely. The identification of an individual with a certain community brought about through one of the four patterns could easily be contrasted with or overridden by another association produced through another of the four patterns or even through different aspects of one and the same scheme of identity. Apparently, only the nation-state that first appeared with the French Revolution has been particularly effective in integrating them all and in connecting them exclusively to the state level. But this has not led to a pattern whereby only the nation-state – however defined – has commanded the loyalties of people in the interest of its *raison d'état*. Wars continue to be fought to defend regional or linguistic identity, notions of common kinship (real or constructed), religion and ideology.

As we enter the twenty-first century – be it the age of the 'post-national nation-state', a 'post-modern' world order at least for Europe or something quite different – the patterns of identity naturally tend to loosen their ties with the nation-state. While the processes of individualization and globalization undermine the authority of states from within and without, collective identities are again set free from the symbiotic connection with the state. A pessimistic perspective could thus lead to the conclusion that the dangers of war threaten to multiply as regional origin, language, common descent or kinship, and religion and ideology reclaim their rights in the relations between communities on the sub-state as well as on the supra-state level.

Taking into account these obvious risks, our results can nevertheless lend themselves to a more optimistic outlook, namely that the decline of the nation-state does not necessarily favour the rise of a total anarchy in world order. More inclusive forms of identity – although often heavily disputed between conflicting communities – can also be invoked as guiding principles in intercommunity relations and actually have successfully been put to a peaceful use under different circumstances. One needs only to think of Mikhael Gorbachëv's famous speech before the UN in 1988 in which he appealed to people's sense of living in one world, confronted by the same problems and needs, and his famous metaphor of the common European house. Although in the long run war might not be inevitable in every case, history suggests that sometimes there is a cultural predisposition for peace. What predominates – bellicosity or peacefulness – depends on mentality and culture, just as much as on economic factors, fiscal cost–benefit calculations and all the other materialistic factors that are usually recited. Neither mentality nor culture are immutable or God-given but are ever-changing and constructed in complex ways. Therefore one can seek to influence them and thus humankind's propensity for war or peace.

Select bibliography

Classical Antiquity

Adcock, F.E. and Mosley, D.J., *Diplomacy in Ancient Greece*, New York/London, Thames & Hudson, 1975.

Albert, S., *Bellum iustum. Die Theorie des 'gerechten Krieges' und ihre praktische Bedeutung für die auswärtigen Auseinandersetzungen Roms in republikanischer Zeit*, Kallmünz, Lassleben, 1980.

Ameling, W., *Kartago, Studien zu Militär, Staat und Gesellschaft*, Munich, Beck, 1993.

Austin, M.M., *The Hellenistic World*, Cambridge, Cambridge University Press, 1983.

Badian, E. (ed.), *Ancient Society and Institutions: Studies Presented to Victor Ehrenberg*, Oxford, Blackwell, 1967.

Badian, E., *Publicans and Sinners: Private Enterprise in the Service of the Roman Republic*, Oxford, Blackwell, 1972.

Badian, E., *Roman Imperialism in the Late Republic*, Oxford, Blackwell, 1968.

Barceló, P., *Hannibal*, Munich, Beck, 1998.

Barceló, P., *Karthago und die Iberische Halbinsel vor den Barkiden*, Bonn, Rudolf Habelt, 1988.

Bauslaugh, R.A., *The Concept of Neutrality in Classical Greece*, Berkeley, University of California Press, 1991.

Bosworth, A.B., *Conquest and Empire*, Cambridge, Cambridge University Press, 1988.

Brunt, P.A., *Italian Manpower 225 BC–AD 14*, Oxford, Clarendon Press, 1971, reissued 1987.

Clavadetscher-Thürlemann, S., *Polemos Dikaios und Bellum Iustum: Versuch einer Ideengeschichte*, Zürich, Juris Druck, 1985.

Cornell, T. and Matthews, J., *Atlas of the Roman World*, Oxford, Phaidon Press, 1982.

Crane, G., *Thucydides and the Ancient Simplicity. The Limits of Political Realism*, Berkeley, University of California Press, 1998.

Ducrey, P., *Le traitement des prisonniers de guerre dans la Grèce antique*, Paris, Boccard, 1968.

Dyson, S.L., *The Creation of the Roman Frontier*, Princeton, NJ, Princeton University Press, 1985.

Eckstein, A.M., *Senate and General: Individual Decision-making and Roman Foreign Relations, 264–194 BC*, Berkeley/Los Angeles/London, University of California Press, 1987.

Erdkamp, P., *Hunger and the Sword: Warfare and Food Supply in Roman Republican Wars (264–30 BC)*, Amsterdam, J. C. Gieben, 1998.

Errington, R.M., *The Dawn of Empire: Rome's Rise to World Power*, London, Hamish Hamilton, 1971.

Finley, M.I., *Ancient History: Evidence and Models*, London, Chatto & Windus, 1985.

Fisher, N.R.E., *Hybris. A Study in the Values of Honour and Shame in Ancient Greece*, Warminster, Aris & Phillips, 1992.

Frank, T., *Roman Imperialism*, New York, Macmillan, 1914.

Garnsey, P. and Whittaker, C.R. (eds), *Imperialism in the Ancient World*, Cambridge, Cambridge University Press, 1976.

Green, P., *The Greco–Persian Wars*, Berkeley, University of California Press, 1996.

Gruen, E.S., *Culture and National Identity in Republican Rome*, Ithaca, NY, Cornell University Press, 1992.

Gruen, E.S., *Studies in Greek Culture and Roman Policy*, Leiden, Brill, 1990.

Gruen, E.S., *The Hellenistic World and the Coming of Rome*, Berkeley/Los Angeles/London, University of California Press, 1984.

Hall, E., *Inventing the Barbarian*, Oxford, Oxford University Press, 1989.

Hall, J.M., *Ethnic Identity in Greek Antiquity*, Cambridge, Cambridge University Press, 1997.

Hanson, V.D., *Warfare and Agriculture in Classical Greece*, Pisa, Giordini, 1983; 2nd edn, Berkeley, University of California Press, 1998.

Hantos, T., *Das römische Bundesgenossensystem in Italien*, Munich, Beck, 1983.

Harris, W.V., *War and Imperialism in the Roman Republic 327–70 BC*, Oxford, Clarendon Press, 1979.

Hopkins, K., *Conquerors and Slaves*, Cambridge, Cambridge University Press, 1978.

Hornblower, S. (ed.), *Greek Historiography*, Oxford, Oxford University Press, 1994.

Hornblower, S., *The Greek World 479–323 BC*, 2nd edn, London, Routledge, 1991.

Hornblower, S. and Spawforth, A. (eds), *Oxford Classical Dictionary*, Oxford, Oxford University Press, 1996.

Hoyos, B.D., *Unplanned Wars: The Origins of the First and Second Punic Wars*, Berlin/New York, Walter de Gruyter, 1998.

Jones, C.P., *Kinship Diplomacy in Greco-Roman Antiquity*, Cambridge, MA, Harvard University Press, 1999.

Jones, C.P., *Kinship Diplomacy in the Ancient World*, Cambridge, MA/London, Harvard University Press, 1999.

Kagan, D., *On the Origins of War and the Preservation of Peace*, New York/London/Toronto/Sydney/Auckland, Doubleday, 1995.

Karavites, P., *Capitulations and Greek Interstate Relations*, Göttingen, Vandenhoek & Ruprecht, 1982.

Keppie, L., *The Making of the Roman Army*, London, Batsford, 1984; repr. London, Routledge, 1998.

Kostial, M., *Kriegerisches Rom? Zur Frage von Unvermeidbarkeit und Normalität militärischer Konflikte in der römischen Politik*, Stuttgart, Steiner, 1995.

Lancel, S., *Carthage*, Oxford/Cambridge, Blackwell, 1995.

Lazenby, J.F., *The Defence of Greece*, Warminster, Aris & Phillips, 1993.

Lazenby, J.F., *Hannibal's War: A Military History of the Second Punic War*, Warminster, Aris & Phillips, 1978.

Lazenby, J.F., *The First Punic War: A Military History*, London, University College London Press, 1996.

Lewis, D.M., *Sparta and Persia*, Leiden, Brill, 1977.

Mantovani, M., *Bellum Iustum: Die Idee des gerechten Krieges in der römischen Kaiserzeit*, Bern, Peter Lang, 1990.

Mitchell, L.G., *Greeks Bearing Gifts*, Cambridge, Cambridge University Press, 1997.

Momigliano, A., *Some Observations on the Causes of War in Ancient Historiography*, Studies in Historiography, London, Weidenfeld & Nicolson, 1966.

Palmer, R.E.A., *Rome and Carthage at Peace*, Stuttgart, Steiner, 1997.

Pritchett, W.K., *The Greek State at War*, 5 vols, Berkeley, University of California Press, 1971–1990.

Rice, E.E., *The Grand Procession of Ptolemy Philadelphus*, Oxford, Oxford University Press, 1983.

Rich, J.W., *Declaring War in the Roman Republic in the Period of Transmarine Expansion*, Brussels, Latomus, 1976.

Rich, J.W. and Shipley, G. (eds), *War and Society in the Greek World*, London/New York, Routledge, 1993.

Rich, J.W. and Shipley, G. (eds), *War and Society in the Roman World*, London/New York, Routledge, 1993.

Richardson, J.S., *Hispaniae: Spain and the Development of Roman Imperialism 218–82 BC*, Cambridge, Cambridge University Press, 1986.

Richardson, J.S., *The Romans in Spain*, Oxford, Blackwell, 1996.

Rüpke, J., *Domi Militiae: Die religiöse Konstruktion des Krieges in Rom*, Stuttgart, Steiner, 1990.

Ryder, T.T.B., *Koine Eirene. General Peace and Local Independence in Ancient Greece*, Oxford, Oxford University Press, 1965.

Sage, M.M., *Warfare in Ancient Greece: A Sourcebook*, London/New York, Routledge, 1996.

Said, E., *Orientalism: Western Conceptions of the Orient*, Harmondsworth, Penguin, 1979.

Ste Croix, G.E.M. de, *The Origins of the Peloponnesian War*, London, Duckworth, 1972.

van Wees, H., *Status Warriors. War, Violence, and Society in Homer and History*, Amsterdam, Gieben, 1992.

van Wees, H. (ed.), *War and Violence in Ancient Greece*, London, 2000.

Versnel, H.S., *Triumphus. An Inquiry into the Origin, Development and Meaning of the Roman Triumph*, Leiden, Brill, 1970.

Warmington, B.H., *Carthage*, New York, Frederick A. Praeger, 1960.

Watson, A., *International Law in Archaic Rome*, Baltimore, MD/London, Johns Hopkins University Press, 1993.

Christianity and the Middle Ages

Allmand, C.T., *The Hundred Years War*, Cambridge, Cambridge University Press, 1988.

Barnie, J., *War in Medieval Society*, London, Barnes & Noble, 1974.

Bull, M., *Knightly Piety and Lay Response to the First Crusade: The Limousin and Gascony, c.97– c.1130*, Oxford, Clarendon Press, 1993.

Burne, A.H., *The Crecy War: A Military History of the Hundred Years War from 1337 to the Peace of Bretigny, 1360*, London, Greenhill, 1991; originally published 1955.

Chazan, R., *European Jewry and the First Crusade*, Berkeley, University of California Press, 1987.

Cole, P.J., *The Preaching of the Crusades to the Holy Land 1095–1270*, Cambridge, MA, The Medieval Academy of America, 1991.

Contamine, P., *Guerre, état et société à la fin du moyen âge. Etudes sur les armées des rois de France, 1337–1494*, Paris/The Hague, Mouton, 1972.

Contamine, P., *War in the Middle Ages*, trans. M.C.E. Jones, Oxford, Blackwell, 1984.

Cram, K.-G., *Iudicium Belli: Zum Rechtscharakter des Krieges im deutschen Mittelalter*, Münster/Cologne, Böhlau, 1955.

Curry, A., *The Hundred Years War*, London, Macmillan, 1993.

Downing, B.M., *The Military Revolution and Political Change: Origins of Democracy and Autocracy in Early Modern Europe*, Princeton, NJ, Princeton University Press, 1992.

Duby, G., *Le dimanche de Bouvines, 27 juillet 1214*, Paris, Gallimard, 1973.

Duncan, A.A.M., *The Nation of Scots and the Declaration of Arbroath, 1320*, London, Historical Association, 1970.

France, J., *Victory in the East: A Military History of the First Crusade*, Cambridge, Cambridge University Press, 1994.

Hillenbrand, C., *The Crusades: Islamic Perspectives*, Edinburgh, Edinburgh University Press, 1999.

Holt, P.M., *Early Mamluk Diplomacy (1260–1290). Treaties of Baybars and Qalawun with Christian Rulers*, Leiden, Brill, 1995.

Housley, N., *The Later Crusades*, Oxford, Oxford University Press, 1992.

Howard, M.E., *War in European History*, Oxford/London, Oxford University Press, 1976.

Howard, M., Andreopoulos, G.J. and Shulman, M.R. (eds), *The Laws of War. Constraints on Warfare in the Western World*, New Haven/London, Yale University Press, 1994.

Joinville, *Vie de Saint Louis*, ed. J. Monfrin, Paris, Classiques Garnier, 1995.

Jones, A., *The Art of War in the Western World*, New York, Oxford University Press, 1987.

Jones, W.R., 'The English church and royal propaganda during the Hundred Years War', *Journal of British Studies*, 19 (1979), pp. 18–130.

Kaeuper, R.W. and Kennedy, E. (eds), *The Book of Chivalry of Geoffroi de Charny*, Philadelphia, University of Pennsylvania Press, 1996.

Kedar, B.Z., *Crusade and Mission. European Approaches Toward the Muslims*, Princeton, NJ, Princeton University Press, 1984.

Keen, M.H., *Chivalry*, New Haven/London, Yale University Press, 1984.

Keen, M.H., *The Laws of War*, London, Routledge, 1965.

Köhler, M.A., *Allianzen und Verträge zwischen fränkischen und islamischen Herrschern in Vorderen Orient*, Berlin/New York, Walter de Gruyter, 1991.

Lloyd, S., *English Society and the Crusade*, Oxford, Clarendon Press, 1988.

Maier, C.T., *Preaching the Crusades. Mendicant Friars and the Cross in the Thirteenth Century*, Cambridge, Cambridge University Press, 1994.

Oman, Sir C., *A History of the Art of War in the Middle Ages*, London, Methuen, 1978; originally published 1924.

Pelikan, J., *The Christian Tradition. A History of the Development of the Doctrine. 3: The Growth of Medieval Theology (600–1300)*, Chicago, IL, The University of Chicago Press, 1978.

Powell, J.M., *Anatomy of a Crusade*, Philadelphia, Pennsylvania University Press, 1986.

Prestwich, M., *Armies and Warfare in the Middle Ages. The English Experience*, New Haven, CT/London, Yale University Press, 1996.

Riley-Smith, J.S.C. (ed.), *The Atlas of the Crusades*, London, Times Books, 1991.

Riley-Smith, J.S.C., *The Crusades. A Short History*, London, Athlone, 1987.

Riley-Smith, J.S.C., *The First Crusade and the Idea of Crusading*, London, Athlone, 1986.

Riley-Smith, J.S.C., *The First Crusaders*, Cambridge, Cambridge University Press, 1997.

Riley-Smith, J.S.C., *The Oxford Illustrated History of the Crusades*, Oxford, Oxford University Press, 1995.

Riley-Smith, J.S.C., *What Were the Crusades?*, 2nd edn, London, Macmillan, 1992.

Rogers, C.J. (ed.), *The Military Revolution Debate: Readings on the Military Transformation of Early Modern Europe*, Boulder, CO, Westview Press, 1995, pp. 55–93.

Siberry, E., *Criticism of Crusading*, Oxford, Clarendon Press, 1985.

Strickland, M., *War and Chivalry: The Conduct and Perception of War in England and Normandy, 1066–1217*, Cambridge, Cambridge University Press, 1996.

Sumption, J., *The Hundred Years War, Vol. I: Trial by Battle*, London, Faber, 1990.

Tyreman, C., *England and the Crusades 1095–1588*, Chicago, IL/London, University of Chicago Press, 1988.

Verbruggen, J.F., *The Art of Warfare in Western Europe during the Middle Ages*, trans. S. Willard and S.C.M. Southern, Amsterdam, North Holland, 1977.

Wolfram, H., *History of the Goths*, trans. T.J. Dunlap, Berkeley/Los Angeles/London, University of California Press, 1987.

Wolfram, H., *The Roman Empire and Its Germanic Peoples*, trans. T.J. Dunlap, Berkeley/Los Angeles/London, University of California Press, 1997.

Wright, N., *Knights and Peasants. The Hundred Years War in the French Countryside*, Woodbridge, Suffolk, The Boydell Press, 1998.

Early Modern history

Anderson, M.S., *The Rise of Modern Diplomacy*, London/New York, Longman, 1993.

Asch, R.G., *The Thirty Years' War. The Holy Roman Empire and Europe 1618–1648*, Basingstoke, Macmillan, 1997.

Barudio, G., *Der Teutsche Krieg 1618–1648*, Frankfurt, Fischer Taschenbuch Verlag, 1988.

Benedict, Ph., Marnef, G., Van Nierop, H. and Venard, M. (eds), *Reformation, Revolt and Civil War in France and the Netherlands, 1555–1585*, Amsterdam, 1999.

Bosbach, F. (ed.), *Feindbilder. Die Darstellung des Gegners in der politischen Publizistik des Mittelalters und der Neuzeit*, Cologne, Böhlau, 1992.

Bosbach, F., *Monarchia universalis: ein politischer Leitbegriff der frühen Neuzeit*, Göttingen, Vandenhoeck & Ruprecht, 1988.

Burckhardt, J., 'Die Friedlosigkeit der Frühen Neuzeit. Grundlegung einer Theorie der Bellizität Europas', *Zeitschrift für Historische Forschung*, 24 (1997), pp. 509–74.

Duchhardt, H., *Balance of Power und Pentarchie. Internationale Beziehungen 1700–1785*, Paderborn, Schöningh, 1997.

Duchhardt, H. (ed.), *Bibliographie zum Westfälischen Frieden*, Münster, Aschendorff, 1996.

Duchhardt, H., *Krieg und Frieden im Zeitalter Ludwigs XIV*, Düsseldorf, Schwann, 1987.

Englund, P., *Die Verwüstung Deutschlands: eine Geschichte des Dreißigjährigen Krieges*, Stuttgart, Klett-Cotta, 1998.

Fisch, J., *Krieg und Frieden im Friedensvertrag: eine universalgeschichtliche Studie über Grundlagen und Formelemente des Friedensschlusses*, Stuttgart, Klett-Cotta, 1979.

Fischbach, C.R., *Krieg und Frieden in der französischen Aufklärung*, Münster/New York, Waxmann, 1989.

Goosens, A., *Les Inquisitions modernes dans les anciens Pays-bas à la Renaissance, 1520–1633*, 2 vols, Brussels, Editions de l'Université de Bruxelles, 1998–99.

Greengrass, M., *The French Reformation*, Oxford, Blackwell, 1987.

Hale, J.R., *War and Society in Renaissance Europe, 1450–1620*, London, Fontana Paperbacks, 1985.

Hartmann, A.V., 'Der Gedanke kollektiver Sicherheit im Dreißigjährigen Krieg. Drei Beispiele', in Malettke, K. (ed.), *Frankreich und Hessen-Kassel zur Zeit des Dreißigjährigen Krieges und des Westfälischen Friedens*, Marburg, N.G. Elwert, 1999, pp. 79–90.

Hartmann, A.V. (ed.), *Les Papiers de Richelieu*. Section politique extérieure. Correspondance et Papiers d'Etat. Empire Allemand II (1630–1635), Paris, Pedone, 1997.

Hartmann, A.V., *Rêveurs de Paix? Friedenspläne bei Crucé, Richelieu und Sully*, Hamburg, Krämer, 1995.

Hartmann, A.V., *Von Regensburg nach Hamburg. Die diplomatischen Beziehungen zwischen dem französischen König und dem Kaiser vom Regensburger Vertrag (13. Oktober 1630) bis zum Hamburger Präliminarfrieden (25. Dezember 1641)*, Münster, Aschendorff, 1998.

Heller, H., *Iron and Blood: Civil Wars in Sixteenth-Century France*, Montreal/London, McGill–Queen's University Press, 1991.

Holt, M.P., *The French Wars of Religion, 1562–1629*, Cambridge, Cambridge University Press, 1995.

Lloyd, H., *The Rouen Campaign, 1590–1592: Politics, Warfare and the Early Modern State*, Oxford, Clarendon Press, 1973.

Lot, F., *Recherches sur les effectifs des armées françaises des Guerres d'Italie aux Guerres de Religion, 1494–1562*, Paris, SEVPEN, 1962.

Parker, G., *The Military Revolution: Military Innovation and the Rise of the West, 1500–1800*, Cambridge, Cambridge University Press, 1988.

Parker, G., *The Thirty Years' War*, London, Routledge & Kegan Paul, 1984.

Parrow, K.A., *From Defense to Resistance: Justification of Violence During the French Wars of Religion*, Philadelphia, PA, American Philosophical Society, 1993.

Potter, D., *War and Government in the French Provinces: Picardy, 1470–1560*, Cambridge, Cambridge University Press, 1993.

Redlich, F., *De Praeda Militari, Looting and Booty, 1500–1815*, Wiesbaden, Steiner, 1956.

Redlich, F., *The German Military Enterpriser and His Workforce, 13th to 17th Century*, Wiesbaden, Steiner, 2 vols, 1964–65.

Salmon, J.H.M., *The French Religious Wars in English Political Thought*, Oxford, Clarendon Press, 1959.

Sonnino, P., *Louis XIV and the Origins of the Dutch War*, Cambridge, Cambridge University Press, 1988.

Thompson, I.A.A., *War and Government in Habsburg Spain, 1560–1620*, London, Athlone, 1976.

Wood, J., *The King's Army: Warfare, Soldiers and Society During the Wars of Religion in France, 1562–1576*, Cambridge, Cambridge University Press, 1996.

Yardeni, M., *La conscience nationale en France pendant les guerres de religion, 1559–1598*, Paris, Beatrice-Nauwelaerts, 1971.

Zemon Davis, N., *Society and Culture in Early Modern France*, Stanford, CA, Stanford University Press, 1975.

Modern history

Belissa, M., *Fraternité Universelle et Intérêt national (1713–1795). Les cosmopolitiques du droit des gens*, Paris, Kimé, 1998.

Belissa, M., *Les stratégies de la contre-révolution: le débat sur la guerre au Parlement anglais dans Actes du colloque de Cholet 1999* (forthcoming).

Bertaud, J.-P., *Guerre et société en France de Louis XIV à Napoléon Ier*, Paris, A. Colin, 1998.

Bertaud, J.-P. and Reichel, D., *Atlas de la Révolution française, vol. 3: l'armée et la guerre*, Paris, EHESS, 1989.

Brunel, F., *Thermidor*, Brussels, Complexe, 1989.

Colley, L., *Britons. Forging the Nation 1707–1837*, New Haven, CT, Yale University Press, 1992.

Dalby, S., *Creating the Second Cold War: The Discourse of Politics*, London, Pinter Publishers, 1990.

Dann, O. and Dinwiddy, J. (ed.), *Nationalism in the Age of the French Revolution*, London, Ronceverte, 1988.

Farrar Jr., L.L., *The Short-War Illusion: German Policy and Domestic Affairs, August–December 1914*, Oxford, ABC-clio Inc, 1973.

Foley, R.T., *Attrition: Its Theory and Application in German Strategy, 1880–1916*, University of London, Ph.D. Thesis, 1999.

Förster, S., *Der Doppelte Militarismus: Die deutsche Heeresrüstungspolitik zwischen Status-quo-Sicherung und Aggression 1890–1913*, Stuttgart, Steiner, 1985.

Förster, S., 'Facing people's war: Moltke the Elder and German military options after 1871', *Journal of Strategic Studies*, Vol.10, no.2 (1987), pp. 209–30.

Howard, M., *The Franco–Prussian War: The German Invasion of France, 1870–1871*, London, Routledge, 1988.

Kondylis, P., *Theorie des Krieges: Clausewitz – Marx – Engels – Lenin*, Stuttgart, Klett-Cotta, 1988.

Ludendorff, General E., *The Nation at War*, trans. A.S. Rapoport, London, Hutchinson, 1936.

Mombauer, A., *Helmuth von Moltke and the Origins of the First World War*, Cambridge, Cambridge University Pres, 2001.

Ritter, G., *The Sword and the Scepter Vol.1: The Prussian Tradition, 1740–1890*, trans. H. Norden, Coral Gables, FL, University of Miami Press, 1969.

Stargardt, N., *The German Idea of Militarism: Radical and Socialist Critics 1866–1914*, Cambridge, Cambridge University Press, 1994.

Stevenson, D., *The Armaments and the Coming of War: Europe, 1904–1914*, Oxford, Clarendon Press, 1996.

von Moltke, H.G., *The Franco–Prussian War of 1870–71*, trans. A. Forbes, London, Harper & Bros, 1907.

Wallach, J., *The Dogma of the Battle of Annihilation: The Theories of Clausewitz and Schlieffen and Their Impact on the German Conduct of Two World Wars*, Westport, CT, Greenwood, 1986.

Index

Aachen (Aix-la-Chapelle) 118
Achaeans 34
Achaemenids 58
Achilles 56
Adrianople, battle of (AD 378) 107
Aegina, Aeginans 39
Aeolians 34
Agincourt, battle of (1415) 144, 147, 245
Alamanni 103, 105–7, 111
Alans 103
Alba, Duke of 168, 171
Albigensian Crusade (1209–29) 89
Alboin 103
Alexander the Great of Macedon 8, 27, 48–58, 63, 76–78
Alexius I Comnenus, Byzantine Emperor 95
Alsace 90, 216
Ambracia 35
American Civil War (1861–65) 202, 217
American War of Independence 193
Amiens, peace of (1802) 204
Amphictyonic League 36
Angell, Norman 14, 21
Anjou 90, 141
Antiochus III 29, 64, 69
Antwerp, sack of (1579) 168
Appian 62
Aquitaine 141
Arabs 88f., 90, 93f., 96f., 99, 116
Aragon 90, 150, 161, 170
Argives 35, 43, 50f.
Ariarich 107
Ariovistus 104
Aristophanes 39
Aristotle 38
Arkadians 27, 41

Arrian 49
Artemisium, battle of (480 BC) 53
Athalaric 110
Athanarich 107
Athanasius, Saint 92
Athens, Athenian Empire (Delian League) 19, 26, 48–58, 239; see also Greeks
Atilla 249
Augsburg, agreement of (1555) 247f.
Augustine of Hippo, Saint 68, 135, 186
Augustus 30f., 55, 62, 66, 238
Aurelian, Roman Emperor 106
Austria, Austrians 156, 197, 203, 206, 209f., 212, 242; Austro-Hungarian Empire 198; see also Habsburgs, Holy Roman Empire
Austrian Succession, Wars of the (1740–48) 156f., 191, 193
Avars 116, 118
Ayala, Balthazar 170

Babelon, Jean-Pierre 163
Baghdad 99
Bâle, peace of 209, 212
Balts, Baltic states 128, 130, 135, 189, 233
Barcids 64, 68f.; see also Hannibal, Hasdrubal
Basil I, Byzantine Emperor 94, 96
Basil II, Byzantine Emperor 98
Basil, Saint 92
Bavaria 88, 176f.
Beckhouse, Marcel 169
Belgium 205, 207, 210f., 242
Bernard of Clairvaux 133–5
Bertaud, J.P. 208
Black, Jeremy 160

Bloch, Marc 14
Bodin, Jean 171
Boeotians 27
Bohemia 85, 87, 90, 156, 177
Bosnia-Hercegovina 242
Bourbons 156
Bourdieu, Pierre 8
Bouvines, battle of (1214) 245
Brabant 114f., 144, 170
Breitenfeld, battle of (1632) 177
Bretigny 151
Brezhnev 233
Brissot 209
Brittany 150
Bruegel, Jan van (the Elder) 168
Brunel, Françoise 203
Brussels 207
Bulgaria, 88, 98
Bull, Hedley 4, 226
Burgundy, Burgundians 90, 111, 143, 145, 150, 161, 166, 177
Burke, Edmund 210
Burkhardt, Johannes 156, 175
Burton, Montague 17
Byzantine Empire 85–90, 91–100, 108–10, 241

Caen 148
Caesar 30, 62, 68, 104
Calais 142
Calvin, Jean 155
Cambrai, peace of (1529) 156
Cambrésis 114
Camerlynck, Jan 169
Campo Formio, peace of (1798) 204, 209
Capelle, La 115f.
Capua 78
Cardinal von Widdern, Georg 220
Carnegie, Andrew 17
Carr, Edward Hallet 17
Carthage 27–30, 32, 62–9, 72–80, 212, 239, 247
Cassiodorus 110
Castile 150, 161, 170
Cateau-Cambresis (1559) 156
Cathars 89, 187, 243, 249
Catherine de Medici 163, 165, 167
Cato the Elder 78f.
Caucasus 92
Chaeronea, battle of (388 BC) 27
Chalcis 25
Chambéry 207
Charlemagne 86f., 116, 118, 135, 162

Charles I, King of England and Scotland 171
Charles IX, King of France 165
Charles the Bold, Duke of Burgundy 161, 166
Charles V, Holy Roman Emperor 155, 161f., 166, 169
Charles VI, King of France 118, 142, 145–7
Chastellain 161
China 6, 8, 200
Chremonidean War 55
Christianity 7f, 31, 85–90, 91–4, 111, 118, 121f., 127–38, 146, 155, 161, 163, 185f., 233, 238f., 249f.; Catholicism 110, 127–38, 161, 162, 164f, 167, 175–7, 181f., 187, 205, 239; Orthodox (Greek, Russian) 127f., 161; Protestantism 156f., 162–7, 176f., 180–2, 187, 239; *see also* Huguenots, Hussites
Church, *see* Christianity
Cicero 68
Cimbri 30, 65
Claudius I, Roman Emperor 31
Claudius II, Roman Emperor 106, 109
Clausewitz, Carl von 10, 214, 229, 249
Clouet, Jean 161
Clovis I, Frankish King 89, 110f.
Cniva 106
Cold War xii, 1f., 201, 226–34, 247
Coligny, Admiral of 168
Colley, Linda 206
Cologne 207
Columbus, Christopher 155
communism, *see* Marxism-Leninism
Comte, Auguste 16
Constant, Benjamin 16
Constantine I (the Great), Roman Emperor 85, 97, 107, 109
Constantine VII Porphyrogenitus, Byzantine Emperor 95, 99
Constantinople 88, 108–10, 249; *see also* Byzantine Empire
Cooper, Robert 202
Copernicus, Nicholas 155
Corcyra, Corcyreans 41, 44
Cordova, Khalif of 99
Corinth 35, 44
Corinthian War (395 BC) 26, 40; Corinthian League 27
Covadonga, battle of (722) 89

Cranach, Lucas (the Elder, the Younger) 168
Crassus 30
Crécy, battle of (1346) 142, 144
Crépy, peace of (1544) 156
Crete, Émir of 100
Crimean War (1853–1856) 202
Croats, Croatia 177, 200, 241f.
Croesus 52
Crusades xiii, 89, 113, 127–38, 243
Cynoscephalae, battle of (197 BC) 29
Cyrus the Great 52
Czechoslovakia 233; *see also* Bohemia

Dacia 106, 108
Dalmatians 29, 177
d'Argenteau, Mercy 210
Darius I 52, 54, 57
Darwin, Charles, and Darwinism, Social Darwinism 1, 4, 17, 198, 221, 240
Davies, David 17
Dawkins, Richard 1
Delbrück, Hans 113f.
Delos 56; Delian League, *see* Athens
Denmark 87, 187
Dhondt, Jan 118
Diodorus 49, 62
Dioscorides 99
Dominicans 133
Dorians 34f.
Dresden 249
Duby, Georges 117
Dumouriez, General 207
Dürer, Albrecht 168
Dutch Revolt, *see* Eighty Years' War

Ebro Treaty 76
Edda 31
Edward I, King of England 146
Edward III, King of England 114–16, 118, 141f., 149f.
Edward VII of the United Kingdom 89
Egmont, Count 164
Egypt 26f., 53, 122, 134, 231
Eighty Years' War (1559–1648) 159, 160, 162–5, 170, 241
Einhard 116f.
Elis 38, 44
Elizabeth I, Queen of England 163
empires 238; *see also* Roman Empire, Holy Roman Empire, Great Britain, France

England 89, 114–22, 141–51, 187f., 190; *see also* Great Britain
English Civil War (1641–9) 197
Epirots 29
Erechtheus 39
Eretrians 25, 52
Eudes of Châteauroux 132, 134
Eumathios Philokales 98
European Union (EU) 1, 6, 202
Eurymedon, battle of (early 460s) 53
Eusebius 90, 97

Faber, Mient 231
Fabius Pictor, Q. 77
Farnese, Alessandro 164
Fascism 199, 201
Fastolf, Sir John (Shakespeare's Falstaff) 143f.
Ferdinand I, Holy Roman Emperor 161
Ferdinand II, Holy Roman Emperor 181f.
Finland, Finns 176, 233
Finley, Moses 56
Fischer, Joschka 1
Flanders 120, 122, 146f., 150, 170
France 114–22, 133f., 141–51, 156, 158–71, 177f., 187f., 190, 192, 197, 199, 206, 217, 221, 238, 242, 244, 247; French Revolution 5, 8, 197, 201f., 203–12, 216, 237–9, 243, 248; French Empire 243
Francis I, King of France 161f., 165
Francis II, King of France 165
Franciscans 133
Franco-Prussian War (1870–71) 198, 215, 218–20, 240
Franks 104–11
Fredegar 111
Frederick II (the Great), King of Prussia 157, 188, 192f., 240, 249
Frederick II, Holy Roman Emperor 88
Frederick, King of Bohemia (the Winter King) 179
Freud, Sigmund 1
Frisians 242
Fritigern 107f.

Gambetta, Léon 216, 218f.
Gascony 141
Gattinara 162
Gaudalete, battle of (711) 88

Gaugamela, battle of (331 BC) 54, 58
Gauthier, Florance 203
Gennobaudes 106
Genoa 193
gens 80, 102–11, 131, 239, 243
Geoffroi de Charny 119
George II, King of the United
    Kingdom 193
George III, King of the United
    Kingdom 205
George V, King of the United
    Kingdom 89
Gepids 103f.
Germans, Germany 147, 177, 180,
    200, 202, 214–22, 241f., 247, 249;
    (Second) German Empire
    (1871–1918) 198; Third *Reich*
    (Empire, 1933–45) 249; German
    Democratic Republic (GDR) 227,
    229–31; Federal Republic of
    Germany 233; *see also* Holy Roman
    Empire
Geti 110
Ghent 169
Gilpin, Robert 18
Girondins 205, 209, 211f.
Gloucester, Duke of 117
Gneisenau, General A. Neithardt von
    244
gods 31, 54f., 67, 76, 80, 247; God
    87, 90, 92f., 118, 121, 127–38, 147,
    155, 162, 240, 247f., 251
Golden Fleece, Burgundian Order of
    the 143f.
Goltz, Colmar Freiherr von der
    218–20
Gorbachëv, Mikhail 251
Goths 88, 94, 103–11
Granada, fall of (1492) 89
Grandson, battle of (1476) 90
Granicus, battle of (334 BC) 54
Great Britain 193, 197, 199, 203–5,
    210, 212, 221, 241f.; British Empire
    206, 244
Greeks, ancient 3, 6f., 9, 11, 18,
    25–32, 46, 48–58, 63f., 67f., 72, 75,
    78, 91, 240–3, 248, 250; *see also*
    Byzantine Empire
Greeks, modern 177
Grimmelshausen, Johann (Hans)
    Jakob Christoffel von 191
Grotius, Hugo 171
Gryphius, Andreas 174
Guiomar, Jean-Yves 203

Gulf War, Second (1990–1) 238
Gustavus Adolphus 176, 179–81

Habsburgs 87, 90, 150, 156, 160f.,
    165, 168, 177, 179f., 187, 189, 191,
    210
Hainault 114f., 119, 143
Halbwachs, Maurice 7
Hannibal 8, 28, 69, 76–8, 80
Hanover, Kingdom of 208, 212
Harold, King of England 122
Hasdrubal 76
Hastings, battle of (1066) 122, 245
Hellenes, *see* Greeks
Heller, Mikhail 226
Henry IV, King of England, 147
Henry IV, King of France (Henry of
    Navarre) 163
Henry V, King of England 118, 142,
    144f., 147
Henry VI, King of England 118, 142
Henry VIII, King of England 187
Henry of Marcy 133
Henry the Proud, Duke of Bavaria 88
Hercules 31, 76, 161
Herodotus 34–6, 39–41, 43, 49–52,
    57f.
Heruls 103
Heule, Jack of 169
Hieronymus of Syracuse 69
Hindenburg, Field Marshal von
    Beneckendorf und von 222
Hitler, Adolf 3, 199, 242, 247
Hobbes, Thomas, and Hobbesianism
    5, 18–20, 118
Hoffmann, Heinz 229
Hohenstauffens 90
Holland 170; *see also* Netherlands, The
Holsti, Ole 3
Holy League 137
Holy Roman Empire 87, 161, 180,
    191, 193, 197f., 204, 210, 241
Holy War, *see* just war theory
Homer 35f., 49f., 54, 57f., 243
Honecker, Erich 227
honour 41, 43f., 119f., 146, 209, 238
Horace 55
Horn, Count 164
Howard, Michael 142
Huguenots 181, 192, 249
Humbert of Romans 130, 135
Hundred Years' War 85, 88f., 114,
    116, 118, 141–51, 239, 242, 245,
    249

Hungary, Hungarians 87f., 137, 177, 210
Huns 88, 94, 104, 107
Hussites 85, 90, 187, 233, 248f.; *see also* Christianity, Protestants

Iliad 39, 49
Ilyrians 28
India 27, 54f.
industrialization 14–17, 201
Innocent III, Pope 130, 132, 135
international relations, theories of xiif., 1–7, 9, 11, 14–23, 33, 41f., 45f., 55–7, 237
Ionia 52, 56; Ionian Revolt 52, 56f.
Ireland, Irish 177, 187
Iriye, Akira 7
Isabella Valois, consort of Edward II 141
Isidorus of Seville 104
Islam 130–3, 200
Isocrates 56
Issus, battle of (333 BC) 54
Italy, Italians 177, 187, 189, 199f.

Jacobins 205
Jacqueline of Bavaria, Countess of Holland, Zeeland and Hainault 119–21
James VI of Scotland and I of England 89
Janis, Irving L. 4
Japan 199
Jean Froissart 117, 143
Jean Le Fèvre 144
Jeanne III (d'Albret), Queen of Navarre 163
Jerusalem 130f., 133, 135, 161
Jews, Judaism 7, 67, 90, 127, 131, 136, 233, 240, 241, 243, 249
jihad, see just war theory
Joan of Arc, Saint 145
Johann Georg I of Saxony 181
John II, King of France 142
John of Capistrano 132
John, King of England, 118, 141
Jordanes 103, 110
Joseph II, Holy Roman Emperor 193
just war theory 68, 73, 86–8, 92, 121, 130, 145, 186, 190, 238
Justinian I 86, 91f., 94

Kaldor, Mary 231
Kallias, peace of (450 BC) 53f.

Kant, Immanuel xii, 1
Kelly, Petra 231
Kennedy, John F. 3
Khrushchëv, Nikita 233
Kinship, 35, 37, 51f., 56, 58, 243
Kissinger, Henry 181f.
Koch-Breuberg, Friedrich 217
Königgrätz, battle of (1866) 218
Kunisch, Johannes 188

L'Hospital, Michel de 162
La Jaunaye, peace of (1795) 207
Lafayette 205
Languet, Hubert 162
Le Havre 249
League of Nations 193, 200
Lelantine War 25
Lenin, Vladimir Ilich 230
Leo the Mathematician 99
Leo VI, Byzantine Emperor 93f.
Léonis 161
Lepanto, battle of (1571) 137
Leukas 35
Leuktra 27
Levant
Leyden 164
Leyenda negra 176, 190
Lidice 249
Liège 205, 207
Linklater, Andrew 20
Livy 62, 76f.
Locris 40, 68
Lombardy 97, 103, 116
London 169
Lorraine, Lotharingians 90, 134, 177, 216
Louis IX (Saint), King of France 122, 134, 149
Louis XI, King of France 167
Louis XIII, King of France 180, 181
Louis XIV, King of France 89, 156, 178, 188, 190, 193, 206, 210, 246, 249
Louis XV, King of France 193
Louis XVI, King of France 171, 205, 210
Louis XVIII, King of France 197
Low Countries, *see* Netherlands
Lucan 30
Ludendorff, General Erich 202, 214–16, 222, 249
Lunéville, Treaty of 212
Lutatius Treaty (241 BC) 75
Luther, Martin 155

Ma'arrat, sack of (1098) 136
Macedon, Macdeonia 30, 32, 48, 64f.,
    69, 77; Macedonian Wars 29
Machiavelli, Niccolo 18, 20
McNamara, Robert 226
Macrianus 107
Magdeburg, sack of (1631) 175, 249
Magnesia, battle of (189) 29
Maine 141
Mainz (Mayence) 107, 207
Mallobaudes 107
Mamertines 75, 79
Mamun, Khalif of 99
Mantua, Duke of 180
Mantzikert, battle of (1071) 96
Marathon 52, 55
Maria Theresia, Queen of Austria
    157
Marnix 164
Marseilles 208
Marxism-Leninism 199–201, 226–34
Masinissa 29, 78, 80
Maurice, Byzantine Emperor 97
Maximian, Roman Emperor 106
Maximilian I of Bavaria 181
Mazarin, Jules Cardinal 178
Meinecke, Friedrich 198
Melos 42, 247
mercenaries 176f.
Messana 65, 68
Messenia 42, 75; Messenian War 25
Metz, battle of (1870), 216
Michael Psellus 98
Mielke, Erich 228–32
Milan 134
Miletus 34, 36
Miltiades 52
Mirabeau 206
Mithridates VI of Pontus 30
Moesia II, Roman province 108
Moltke, Helmuth Graf von (the Elder)
    217–20
Mongols 88, 128, 130
Monroe, Robert 177
Mons 163
Monstrelet, Enguerran 143
Morgarten, battle of (1315) 90
Morgenthau, Hans 17f.
Münster, peace of; *see* Westphalian
    peace treaties
Murten, battle of (1476) 90
Muslims 131–3, 136
Mussolini, Benito 199
Mytilene 41, 45

Nancy, battle of (1477) 90
Napoleon (I) Bonaparte 3, 197, 202,
    212, 247; Napoleonic Wars 203
Napoleon III, Emperor of France 216
national identities 242
National Socialism 199–201, 215, 243
nationalism 198
Nedao, battle of (454) 104
Nekrich, Alexander 226
Netherlands, The 114f., 156, 159,
    160–71, 176, 179, 187f., 189, 193,
    205, 242
Nicaea 96
Nicephoros Phocas, Byzantine
    Emperor 92, 97
Nicholas I Mystikos, Patriarch 95, 97,
    100
Nietzsche, Friedrich 17
Nijmwegen, peace of (1679) 157
Nine Years' War 191
Nördlingen, battle of (1634) 177
Normans 88–90, 149
North Atlantic Treaty Organization
    (NATO) 6, 200, 230, 232f.
North, John 66
Norwich 169

Octavian, *see* Augustus
Odovakar, Gothic King 108–10
Olivares, Count 166
Olivier de la Marche 161
Olympic Games 37f., 44
Olynthians 41f.
Oman, Sir Charles 113f.
Oradour 249
Orange-Nassau 163f.
Organization of Petrol-Exporting
    Countries (OPEC)
Osnabrück, peace of; *see* Westphalian
    peace treaties
Otto I (the Great), Roman Emperor
    87
Otto III, Roman Emperor 87
Ottoman Empire 137, 157, 185, 187,
    194, 197

Palatinate, the 175
Palestinians 241
Papacy 86f., 89, 128–38, 150, 157,
    181; *see also* under individual popes
Pappenheim 177
Paris, siege of (1870–71) 217; Treaty
    of (1259) 141
Parthia, Parthians 30f., 48, 55, 241

Patay, battle of (1429) 143
Pausanias 53
Pechenegs 88, 92, 95
Peloponnesian Wars (434–431 BC) 3, 19, 26, 33, 37, 39f., 56, 2246; Peloponnesian League 26, 37
Perdikkas 57
Pere IV of Aragon 150
Pericles 9, 39
Péronne 115
Persepolis 49
Perseus 29, 34, 51
Persians, Persian Empire 26f., 34f., 38f., 48–58, 88, 93f., 241
Peters, Jan 177
Philip Augustus 245
Philip I of Macedon 54, 56
Philip II of Macedon 27
Philip II, King of Spain 161–4, 166f., 171, 188, 241
Philip IV, King of France 146f.
Philip IV, King of Spain 166
Philip V of Macedon 28f., 64, 69, 77
Philip VI, King of France 115f., 150
Philip the Good, Duke of Burgundy 119–21, 161
Philistines 241
Phokis, Phokians 40, 50
Photios 100
Phrygia 54
Piedmont 203
Pipes, Richard 226
Plataia 26, 52, 55, 57f.; battle of Plataia (479 BC) 53
Plato 38
Plutarch 39, 49
Poitiers, battle of (1356) 118, 133, 142, 144
Poitou 141
Poland, Poles 87, 157, 177, 189, 209
Polybius 9, 29–31, 39, 54, 56, 62f., 65, 68, 74
Pompey 30, 62
Ponomarev, Boris 228
Portugal 147, 188, 200
Prague, peace of (1635) 182
Probus, Roman Emperor 106
Procopius 94, 107
Prussia 156–8, 192f., 197, 203, 205f., 209f., 212, 244
Ptolemy I of Egypt 49
Ptolemy II of Egypt 55
Punic Wars 28, 64f., 68f., 72–80,

238f., 249; *see also* Carthage, Roman Empire
Puy, Le 133
Pydna, battle of (168) 29, 64
Pyrenees, treaty of the (1659) 156
Pyrrhus of Epirus 74

Quintus Curtius 49

Ranke, Leopold von 7
Reagan, Ronald 247
'realist' international relations theory *see* international relations
Reformation, the 85, 155, 160, 165, 186
Reims 142
Reinhard, Wolfgang 8
Religion 54, 56, 67, 76, 85f., 99f., 145f., 155–7; Religious Wars 85, 160–71, 185–6; *see also* Judaism, Christianity, Islam
Respublica Christiana 131, 155, 157, 186, 194 *see also* universal monarchy
Rhegians 750
Richard II, King of England, 118, 147
Richelieu, Cardinal 180–2
Rijswijk, peace of (1697) 157
Robert of Artois 134, 150
Robespierre 205, 211
Roman Empire, xiii, 3, 6f., 27, 31f., 48, 51, 62–9, 72–80, 85, 90, 103–7, 116f., 160, 238f., 243f., 247f.; *see also* Byzantine Empire, Holy Roman Empire,
Romans, *see also* Roman Empire
Rome, sack of (1529) 168
Romulus Augustulus, Roman Emperor 109
Rugians 103
Russell, Bertrand 231
Russia, Russians 128, 156–8, 187, 191, 197, 199, 221; Russian Revolution 201f., 248; *see also* Soviet Union

Sachsen-Weimar, Bernhard von 178
Saguntum 28, 68, 76f., 80
Saint Bartholomew's Day Massacre (1572) 163, 168
Salamis, battle of (480 BC) 26, 34, 53
Samians 36
Samnites 27
Sandwich 169

Saracens 145
Sardinia 28, 73, 75
Sarmatians 103
Savoy 177
Saxony, Saxons 88f., 104, 116, 175,
    181
Scharnhorst, General Gerhard Johann
    David 244
Schlieffen, Alfred von 220
Schmalkaldic League 165
Schmitt, Carl 17
Scipio Aemilianus 28, 30
Sciri 103
Scots, Scotland 146–8, 177, 187
Sedan, battle of (1870) 216
Seleucids 69
Sempach, battle of (1386) 90
Serbia, Serbs 200, 242
Seven Years' War (1756–63) 191,
    193
Shakespeare, William 144
Sheffield, Lord 205
Sicily 26, 28, 33, 35, 56f., 63, 74f.,
    77, 88, 90
Silesian Wars (1740–42 and 1744–45)
    157
Simonides of Keos 50, 57
Simonides, New 56
Slavs 88
Slovenians 177
Soboul, Albert 203
Socialism 229; *see also* Marxism-
    Leninism
Soviet Union 1f., 17, 200, 215, 226,
    230–2
Spa 163
Spain 28, 131, 144, 147, 159,
    160–71, 176f., 179, 187f., 189, 197,
    199f., 203f., 206; *see also* Aragon,
    Castile; Spanish Civil War 229;
    Spanish Succession, Wars of the
    (1701–14) 156
Sparta 19, 25–32, 48–58, 239; *see also*
    Greeks
Spencer, Herbert 16
Stuart, Elizabeth, consort of King
    Frederick of Bohemia (the Winter
    Queen) 177
Suebi 108
Suevi 103
Suffolk, Duke of 144
Sulla 30
Sullivan, Robert 20
Suslov, Mikhail 233

Sweden, Swedes 156, 176–82, 187,
    241
Switzerland, Swiss 90, 156, 188, 211,
    242
Sybaris, Sybarites 36
Symeon of Bulgaria 94f., 98
Syracuse 77

Tarentum 77
Teutons 30
Thebes 40, 50
Theoderic the Great, Gothic King
    103, 108f.
Theophilos, Byzantine Emperor 97,
    99
Thessalians 27, 50
Thirty Years' War (1618–48) 156,
    159, 163, 174–82, 188, 191, 193,
    241, 243, 246, 249
Thomas Aquinas, Saint 145
Thompson, E. P. 231
Thrace 107f.
Thucydides 8f., 18, 19f., 31, 33, 35–7,
    39–46, 49, 53, 56f., 246
Thuringia 103, 175
Tokyo 249
Tongres 105
total war 214f., 222, 249; *see also*
    Ludendorff, World War II
Totalitarianism 17, 199, 201; *see also*
    National Socialism, Marxism-
    Leninism
Touraine 141
Trajan 31
Trier (Trève) 105
Troy, Trojan War 49–51, 56, 58,
    111, 245
Troyes 149, 151
Tunisia 161
Turkey, Turks 26, 88, 93f., 137,
    161f., 165, 177, 187, 190, 238, 241;
    Turkish Wars 193f.; *see also*
    Ottoman Empire
Tuscany, Archduke of 203

Union of the Soviet Socialist
    Republics (USSR), *see* Soviet Union
United Nations (UN) 1, 3, 6, 193,
    200, 238, 251
United States of America 2, 200, 211,
    226, 230–4, 241
universal monarchy 131, 146, 155f.,
    161f., 179, 180, 182, 186, 188, 194;
    see also Europe

Urban, Pope 133
Utrecht and Rastatt, peace of (1714) 157

Valens, Roman Emperor 107
Valentinian, Roman Emperor 107
Valois 149f., 156, 160, 187
Vandals 103, 108, 116
Vendée, 204f., 207–9
Venice 177, 188, 238
Verbruggen, Jan-Frans 114
Verdun, treaty of (843) 87
Vergil 68, 111
Vervins, treaty of (1598) 163
Viala, Agricol 208
Vienna Congress (1815) 197
Vietnam War 226
Vikings 88
Visigoths 108, 111

Waldersee, Alfred Graf von 218
Wales 146
Walker, R.B.J. 20
Wallenstein, Duke of Friedland 178
Walloons 170; *see also* Belgium
Waltz, Kenneth xii, 18, 237
Warsaw Treaty Organization 200, 227, 229, 231, 233
Wasas 156
Watiq, Khalif 99
Wemding 176
Wenskus, Reinhard 102

Western European Union (WEU) 6
Westphalian peace treaties (1648) xiii, 156f, 159, 174, 178, 181f., 191f., 246–8
Wiatr, Jerzy
Widukind of Corvey 104
Wilhelm I, German Emperor 218
William I (the Conqueror), King of England and Duke of Normandy 149, 245
William, Duke of Orange 163, 168, 170
Williams, Roger 167
Wilson, Woodrow 3, 17
Wolfram, Herwig 109f.
Woods, James B. 165
World War I 21, 89, 197, 199, 214f., 238f., 244, 249
World War II 4, 199, 215, 239, 245, 248f.
Württemberg 175

Xanthippos 75
Xenophon 27, 36, 38–42, 44, 49, 58
Xerxes 26, 52, 54

York 133
Yugoslavia 1, 214, 242; *see also* Bosnia-Hercegovina, Croatia, Serbia

Zeno, Byzantine Emperor 108
Zwingli, Huldrich 155